Every
TEACHING
OF JESUS
in the Bible

LARRY RICHARDS

Illustrated by
Dan Pegoda
and
Paul Gross

THOMAS NELSON PUBLISHERS
Nashville

Library of Congress Cataloging-in-Publication Data

Richards, Larry, 1931-
    Every teaching of Jesus in the Bible / Larry Richards ; illustrated by Dan Pegoda and Paul Gross.
        p.   cm.
    ISBN 0-7852-0703-1 (pbk.)
    1. Jesus Christ--Teachings. I. Title.
    BS2415 .R52 2001
    232.9'54—dc21
                                        2001034285
                                        CIP

Printed in the United States of America

            1 2 3 4 5 6 7 8—06 05 04 03 02 01

CONTENTS

See Expository and Scripture Indexes for Complete Topical and Scripture Listings

INTRODUCTION

E very teaching of Jesus is of compelling interest to Christians. In part this is because we recognize Jesus as the fullest, the most complete, and the final revelation of God. As God come among us as a human being, Jesus was uniquely able to explain the Old Testament and to reveal new truths about God the Father and God's plans and purposes.

When we read the Gospels and compare the teachings there with the teachings of first-century rabbis, we begin to understand how vital it was that Christ appear. Long before, Moses had promised that God would send a prophet like himself to His people, who would explain the true meaning of the older revelation. It is increasingly clear as we see how Jesus' teachings diverged from those of the rabbis that by the first century His coming was urgent indeed.

It is also interesting that among the first questions asked by those who heard Jesus teach was, "Is this The Prophet?" (John 6:14). Israel, too, was looking for an authoritative interpreter of God's will. Christ answered that question in His Sermon on the Mount, in which Jesus announced that He had come to "fulfill" the Law—an idiom which meant that He was about to give a full and complete explanation of the true meaning of the Torah, God's Old Testament revelation. This is particularly important, as we're reminded that to truly understand the Old Testament, we must read it through the lens provided by the coming, the teachings, the death, and the resurrection of Jesus Christ.

The teachings of Jesus are important for another reason too. Not only did Christ provide the keys by which we might rightly interpret the Old Testament, Christ also introduced truths which are to shape our personal relationship with God and with others today. Christ's teachings are vitally relevant to our daily life. His words are to shape our values, determine our priorities, and—as we live by them—transform our character.

The teachings of Jesus are not always easy for us to understand. This is in part because they were spoken in a particular time and place, in a culture that is strange to us. It is also in part because the way of life that Jesus marks out for us, and the values He calls us to adopt, are foreign to human nature. Jesus calls us to exchange success for servanthood, to abandon pride for humility, and to reject materialism for spiritual values that the people of this world view as foolishness. Such teachings go against the grain of our humanity, and rather than take Christ at His word we may be tempted to reinterpret or explain away His more challenging teachings.

Yet the teachings of Jesus introduce us to a life that Christ promised would be marked by power, by joy, and by fulfillment. As Christ's disciples once remarked when asked by the Lord if they would abandon Him as others had, "Where shall we go? You have the words of eternal life" (John 6:68).

It's difficult to organize a book on every teaching of Jesus. One reason is that, like any itinerant preacher, Jesus repeated the same sermons again and again. Each Gospel writer chose his material carefully to appeal to a distinct audience, and frequently the same illustrations or stories are placed in different contexts, in order to make different points. It's important when we look at parallel passages in the Gospels to remember that Matthew may place a teaching in one situation, and Mark in another, and that in each context Christ may use the same saying to make a different point.

The fact that the Gospels are organized to reach different first-century peoples also makes it difficult to attempt a chronological organization of Jesus' teachings. For instance, a major section of Luke's account has no parallel in Matthew or Mark, and John is not organized chronologically at all.

It seemed far more reasonable to me to group Jesus' teachings by topic. For this reason you find chapters in this book that look at what Jesus taught about God's kingdom and about prayer. You'll find chapters that deal with what Jesus said to the crowds, and what Jesus taught His disciples privately. You'll also find chapters on Jesus' parables and on His prophecies, and chapters on what Jesus said when He interacted with His opponents, the religious elite of His time. You'll also find chapters on the post-resurrection teachings of Jesus, and on the recorded words the glorified Christ spoke after His return to heaven.

Our goal in each of these chapters is to seek to understand what Jesus taught in the given context, and to discover how those words spoken milleniums ago touch our lives today.

There's another feature of this book that you'll find helpful. Throughout it we pause to look at the "hard sayings of Jesus"—those words which trouble and puzzle us, and make us wonder "What did Jesus mean by *that*?" In fact those hard sayings often are especially important. They challenge us to reevaluate our assumptions about faith and life and renew our commitment to our Lord.

It has been a rich privilege to study afresh every teaching of Jesus recorded in the New Testament. May you be richly blessed as you consider afresh what Jesus has to say to you.

Larry Richards
April 2001

LISTEN TO HIM

Some 1,500 years before Jesus of Nazareth burst onto history's stage, a man named Moses—through whom God had given Israel the greatest revelation of Himself known to man—had written about a coming Prophet. Warning Israel against reliance on any occult source of information, Moses promised, "The LORD your God will raise up for you a Prophet like me" (Deut. 18:15). Moses promised that this ultimate prophet would be "from your midst, from your brethren," and commanded: "Him you shall hear." Today we would phrase these last words a little differently. Moses was simply saying, "When He appears, listen to Him."

There are so many aspects to Jesus of Nazareth, so many ways to view Him. Jesus is God the Son, existing eternally with the Father. Jesus is the ultimate revelation of the Father, God come to be with us in the flesh. Jesus is the suffering Savior, who gave His life on Calvary in the Great Exchange, taking our sins on Himself and giving His own righteousness to all who trust in Him.

In this book, however, we are going to look at Jesus as the ultimate Teacher, the Prophet promised by Moses and who was to be "like" this great lawgiver in one critical revolutionary way.

THE PROPHET LIKE MOSES

MOSES' PREDICTIONS (DEUTERONOMY 18:9–22)

Moses' prophecy of a coming Prophet is recorded in Deuteronomy, a book that records Moses' sermons given to the Israelites just before his death and just before their conquest of the Promised Land.

The need for prophets. In the ancient world as today, people hungered for some glimpse of the future—some source of guidance that would help them avoid hidden pitfalls and set them on a safe path. While today individuals read their horoscopes in the daily paper or call the Psychic Hotline as advertised on TV, in the ancient

Other cultures looked to the occult. God sent prophets to guide His people.

world military strategy and national policy, as well as the decisions of individuals, were typically determined after consulting some occult source.

As Moses spoke to the Israelites just before the conquest of Canaan, he made it very clear that God's people were never to look to any occult source for guidance:

When you come into the land which the LORD your God is giving you, you shall not learn to follow the abominations of those nations. There shall not be found among you anyone who makes his son or his daughter pass through the fire, or one who practices witchcraft, or a soothsayer, or one who interprets omens, or a sorcerer, or one who conjures spells, or a medium, or a spiritist, or one who calls

up the dead. For all who do these things are an abomination to the LORD, and because of these abominations the LORD your God drives them out from before you. You shall be blameless before the LORD your God. For these nations which you will dispossess listened to soothsayers and diviners; but as for you, the LORD your God has not appointed such for you (vv. 9–14).

Rather than look to the occult for guidance, God's people were to look to Him only. God promised that He would provide all the direction His people might need. For Israel guidance was available from three sources. The first was the written word. The second was the Urim and Thummim, objects symbolizing "yes" and "no" which were carried in the high priest's vestments and which could be consulted when necessary (Ex. 28:30; Num. 27:21; Ezra 2:63). The third source of guidance from God was the prophet, a spokesman for God who communicated God's will to His people.

The promise of prophets. It is this third source of supernatural guidance that Moses goes on to describe in Deuteronomy 18:17–22.

And the LORD said to me: . . . "I will raise up for them a Prophet like you from among their brethren, and will put My words in His mouth, and He shall speak to them all that I command Him. And it shall be that whoever will not hear My words, which He speaks in My name, I will require it of him. But the prophet who presumes to speak a word in My name, which I have not commanded him to speak, or who speaks in the name of other gods, that prophet shall die." And if you say in your heart, "How shall we know the word which the LORD has not spoken?"— when a prophet speaks in the name of the LORD, if the thing does not happen or come to pass, that is the thing which the LORD has not spoken; the prophet has spoken it presumptuously; you shall not be afraid of him.

These words of Moses, in common with many prophecies, have a dual fulfillment. On the one hand verses 18 and 19 refer to a specific individual: a person whose role in sacred history will be like that of Moses. On the other hand, verses 20–22 refer to a movement: the appearance in Israel of a number of spokespersons, men and women, whom God would commission as His messengers to speak His word to leader and commoner alike.

Recognition of true prophets. Moses specified three tests that were to be applied when any person appeared and claimed to speak for God.

1. A prophet must be a Jew, "from among your brethren."
2. A prophet must speak in the name of the Lord, and not represent any other deity.

3. A prophet must be authenticated by the fulfillment of his prophecy. What the prophet says must "happen or come to pass."

Deuteronomy 13 gives us another test of the true prophet. Even should a person claiming to be a prophet appear, actually perform signs or wonders (miracles), and then encourage the people to "go after other gods" and serve them, "you shall not listen to the words of that prophet" (Deut. 13:1–3). Rather God's people are to remain committed to His written revelation, and so "walk after the LORD your God and fear Him, and keep His commandments" (Deut. 13:4).

Only a Jew, who speaks in the name of the Lord, whose words come true, and whose words are in complete harmony with God's written revelation, could be honored as a prophet. All others and their teachings must be rejected by God's people.

An implied test for "the" Prophet. One other test is implied for the "Prophet like me" of whom Moses spoke. Moses had been commissioned by God to set a totally new course for God's people. God used Moses to break the bonds of their slavery in Egypt and to give the Israelites a Law to live by, a Law which revealed how a people of faith might live in intimate relationship with God. As prophet, Moses gave Israel a revelation that was stunning in its scope, a revelation that literally recast humankind's understanding of God.

Yet Moses foresaw a day when God would send another Prophet—a Prophet like Moses, whose revelation would be just as stunning, just as far-reaching, as that of Moses himself. The Prophet like Moses would also be the source of a revelation so stunning in its scope, so unexpected in its nature, that this Prophet too would recast humankind's understanding of God.

Throughout Old Testament history God's people looked ahead, waited, and wondered. When would the Prophet like Moses appear? What stunning revelation would He bring? And how could their very understanding of God and His purposes, their understanding of how to live in an intimate relationship with God, be transformed without violating Moses' teachings?

We see that wonder in the pages of the Gospels, as eager listeners ask John the Baptist, the forerunner of Jesus, "Are you the Prophet?" (John 1:21). John answered, "No." But within a few days the One who *was* "the Prophet" did appear. As the ministry of Moses transformed the experience of the people of Israel, so the ministry of Jesus Christ has transformed the lives of people everywhere.

JESUS' FULFILLMENT OF MOSES' PREDICTION

It is clear to anyone who knows the gospel story that Jesus' impact on the history of faith was even more revolutionary than that of Moses. Moses set the course of sacred history for a single people; Jesus set the course of history and eternity for all humankind. But did Jesus meet the other tests established in Deuteronomy by which the Prophet was to be recognized?

Clearly Jesus was a Jew, born in the Holy Land of a Jewish mother whose genealogy could be traced through King David to Abraham (Matt. 1:1–17), and even to Adam himself (Luke 3:23–38).

Just as clearly Jesus spoke in the name of the Lord God of Israel, whom He claimed as His Father. Although later in Jesus' ministry His enemies charged that Jesus' miracles were energized by Satan rather than God, no one claimed that Jesus Himself spoke in the name of anyone other than the Lord.

The test of harmony with Scripture. Jesus' pronouncements were also challenged as to their harmony with Old Testament revelation. Jesus answered His accusers early in His public ministry, as He taught a great crowd in what we call the Sermon on the Mount (Matt. 5–7).

> Do not think that I came to destroy the Law or the Prophets. I did not come to destroy but to fulfill. For assuredly, I say to you, till heaven and earth pass away, one jot or one tittle will by no means pass from the law till all is fulfilled
> (Matthew 5:17, 18).

These words have often been misunderstood, as commentators have supposed that Jesus meant that in His life and death the prophecies of the Old Testament were fulfilled, or that in Jesus the requirements of God's Law were met. In fact Jesus' reference to "fulfilling" the Law and the Prophets" [a phrase that encompassed the entire Old Testament] was an expression commonly used by rabbis. For Israel's rabbis were deeply concerned not only with the words of the Old Testament writings but also with their meaning. To "fulfill" a law was to grasp its truest meaning, and to explain it to others.

Jesus was simply stating that He had not come to destroy—to diminish or to render inoperative—God's Old Testament revelation. Instead, in His teaching Jesus would reveal the true meaning of all that had been taught before! As utterly revolutionary and shocking as what Jesus had to say might seem, His new revelation was in complete harmony with all that had been recorded in God's Word.

And as for Jesus' view of the authority of that Old Testament revelation, Scripture was so sure and certainly the Word of God that not even the tiniest flaring marks on a Hebrew letter (the "jot" and the "tittle") could fail to come to pass. Jesus' teachings might conflict with a first-century rabbi's understanding of God's Word, but everything that Jesus said was in complete harmony with Old

As "the prophet like Moses" holding a Scripture-scroll, Jesus revealed the true meaning of the Old Testament.

Testament revelation and in fact would reveal the true meaning that generations of scholars had failed to perceive.

The test of words come true. Moses had written that unless a person claiming to be prophet was authenticated by the fulfillment of his words, that person's teaching was to be disregarded. There is no question that Jesus met this test. When Jesus spoke to a paralyzed man and told him to stand, pick up his bed, and walk, that person walked (Matt. 9:5–7)! When Jesus commanded an evil spirit to leave the individual it had plagued, the evil spirit was forced to leave (Mark 1:23–26). Even members of the Jewish Sanhedrin, the supreme religious court of the Jews, could

not deny that Jesus of Nazareth met the test of a true prophet. One of their members, a man named Nicodemus, who came to examine Jesus one night, confessed, "Rabbi, we know that You are a teacher come from God, for no on can do these signs that You do unless God is with him" (John 3:2).

Yet being *a* prophet was not in itself proof that Jesus was *the* Prophet spoken of by Moses. But even that was proven by the kinds of signs that Jesus' ministry produced.

The ultimate miracle-working test. Jesus confused his first-century contemporaries. They had been expecting not only the Prophet like Moses but also the Messiah, a person prominent in Old Testament prophecy. This individual was anointed (chosen, empowered) by God to deliver God's people and establish God's kingdom on earth, with its capital in Jerusalem. Many had eagerly assumed that Jesus was the Messiah, at least the promised Prophet, or perhaps both. Yet as Jesus continued to teach and to heal throughout Galilee and in Judea, He made no attempt to establish the promised kingdom of God on earth. Even Jesus' most ardent supporters began to have doubts. Among the doubters was John the Baptist, who had been imprisoned by Herod. Puzzled by Jesus' actions, John sent some of his followers to ask Jesus, "Are you the Coming One, or do we look for another" (Matt. 11:3).

Rather than answer their question directly, Jesus simply told the delegation to return and to "tell John the things which you hear and see: The blind see and the lame walk; the lepers are cleansed and the deaf hear; the dead are raised up and the poor have the gospel preached to them. And blessed is he who is not offended because of Me" (Matt. 11:4–6).

Nearly all that Jesus said to John's friends was taken from a prophecy in Isaiah 35. That great prophetic chapter depicts the blessings of a day when God Himself "will come and save you" (v. 4). The prophet goes on to say, "Then the eyes of the blind shall be opened, and the ears of the deaf shall be unstopped. Then the lame shall leap like a deer, and the tongue of the dumb sing" (vv. 5, 6).

In all the centuries during which God had spoken to His people through prophets, in all the years He had authenticated His spokesmen through signs and wonders, never had these particular miracles been performed! These wonders were reserved for the Prophet like Moses; for the Messiah who would appear to save God's people; for that moment in time when God Himself would come to His people as a human being!

And these were the signs John's followers witnessed that day they spent with Jesus. The unique signs which were to mark the One who fulfilled Old Testament prophecy were performed by Jesus of Nazareth. He was not simply a prophet. He was the Prophet like Moses, whose coming marked a radical transformation in God's way of dealing with lost humankind.

And so we fully understand the significance of God's words to ancient Israel through Moses.

> I will raise up for them a Prophet like you from among their brethren, and will put My words in His mouth, and He shall speak to them all that I command Him. And it shall be that whoever will not hear My words, which He speaks in My name, I will require it of him (Deut. 18:18–19).

Thus we understand the importance of Jesus' ministry as a teacher and the importance of exploring every teaching of Jesus that is recorded in God's Word.

SOURCES FOR THE TEACHINGS OF JESUS

There are four reliable sources we can consult to find the teachings of Jesus. These are the four Gospels that launch the New Testament. While there are other early documents from the second century A.D. which claim to contain sayings of Jesus, and while there are other religious writings that claim to be "gospels," only the four Gospels that are found in the New Testament were accepted as Scripture in the early church.

AUTHENTICITY OF THE FOUR GOSPELS

There is no question that the four Gospels of the New Testament were known and accepted in the early church. Testimony to the authenticity of Mark is provided by Papias (c. A.D. 60–130), who is quoted in the ecclesiastical history written by Eusebius (A.D. 265–339). The relevant quote states:

Mark, having become the interpreter of Peter, wrote down accurately, though not indeed in order, whatever he remembered of the things said or done by Christ. For he neither heard the Lord nor accompanied him, but afterward, as I said, he was in company with Peter, who used to offer teaching as necessity demanded, but with no intention of giving a connected account of the Lord's discourses. So Mark committed no error in thus writing some single points as he remembered them. For upon one thing he fixed his attention: to leave out nothing of what he had heard and to make no false statements in them (Eusebius, CH 3.39).

Irenaeus, who ministered around A.D. 200, recorded the conviction of the church about the Gospels.

Now Matthew published also a book of the Gospel among the Hebrews in their own dialect, while Peter and Paul were preaching the Gospel in Rome and founding the Church. After their death Mark, the disciple and interpreter of Peter, he too handed down to us in writing the things preached by Peter. Luke also, the follower of Paul, put down in a book the Gospel preached by that one. Afterwards John, the disciple of the Lord, who also leaned upon his breast, he too published a Gospel while residing in Ephesus [in] Asia. (as quoted in *Evidence of Tradition*, Daniel J. Theron, Baker Books, Grand Rapids, 1957)

While quotes from early Christian writers could be multiplied, these two establish a number of important points.

- All four Gospels were recognized as authentic in the early church.
- All four Gospels were written in the first century A.D.
- The Gospel authors either relied on their own personal experience with Jesus (Matthew, John), on the testimony of an eye-witness (Mark), or on investigative reporting and interviewing of those who had seen and heard Jesus personally (Luke, 1:1, 2).

- The first-written Gospel was Matthew, with Mark and Luke following shortly after the deaths of Peter and Paul, around A.D. 68. John's Gospel was written last, most believe in the late first century.
- The goal of the Gospel writers, as reflected in Mark, was not to "give a connected account" of events or to record them "in [chronological] order," but rather to accurately report Jesus' teachings and actions.

In fact, each of the Gospels is written to a specific cultural audience, and the intended audience affected each writer's choice of what to include, and how to shape his accounts to best communicate Jesus to his audience. Thus, while there are differences in the accounts of events and teachings provided in the four Gospels, each author "committed no error in thus writing some single points as he remembered them."

INTENT OF THE FOUR GOSPELS

Each of the four authentic Gospels gives us an accurate account of what Jesus did and what He taught. Given that this is true, it is reasonable to ask, "Why then four Gospels?" The answer is that each writer was shaping his portrait of Jesus to fit a different cultural audience.

Matthew: the Gospel for the Jews. Eusebius stated that Matthew "published also a book of the Gospel among the Hebrews in their own dialect." Whether the Gospel of Matthew was first written in Hebrew or Greek is debated; however, there is no doubt that Matthew wrote his Gospel for the Jewish people. Matthew frequently quotes or alludes to the Old Testament, selecting passages that demonstrate that Jesus is the Messiah promised there.

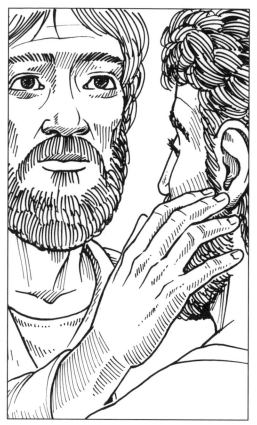

Jesus' miracles provided proof that He was the promised prophet like Moses.

———————————— ❖ ————————————

Matthew's Gospel is also shaped to answer questions that would naturally be raised by a people saturated in Old Testament lore. The Jews had longed for the appearance of God's promised Messiah as well as the kingdom the prophets predicted He would rule. The path that Jesus took, to the cross rather than to the throne, disturbed and puzzled those Jews who trusted Jesus and yet were unable to resolve the questions that His death and resurrection raised. So Matthew goes to great pains to demonstrate that Jesus is the promised king, to show that a previously unrevealed form of God's kingdom had been established by Jesus, and to explain that the delay in establishing the kingdom as foreseen by the prophets is only that—a delay.

While the account of Jesus' life is similar in the Synoptics (Matthew, Mark, and Luke—the three Gospels which are organized within a roughly chronological framework), many differences can be accounted for by Papias' statement that the writers did not intend to give their accounts "in order." They intended to be accurate, but they would fit and sort events in ways that best communicated Jesus to the audience for which they wrote.

Mark: the Gospel for the Romans. The theological issues that were of primary importance to the Jews had no appeal to the practical Romans. The Romans were men of action who admired strong, decisive individuals who were task oriented and whose lives were marked by accomplishment. While Mark records the memories of Peter concerning what Jesus did and said, Mark shaped his account to appeal to the Roman mind. In Mark we see Jesus as a man of action. One of the key words in Mark's account is "immediately." Mark often tells of something Jesus did, and then reports that Christ "immediately" set out on another task, which in every case He successfully accomplished. Neither the forces of nature nor any other power, natural or supernatural, could stand in Jesus' way. Mark's bold, brief portrait of Jesus had great appeal to those whose attitudes were shaped by the culture of Rome.

Luke: the Gospel for the Greeks. Luke's account of Jesus' life has been called the most beautiful of all literary works in Greek. Not only did Luke's writing style appeal to those who were culturally Greek, Luke's portrait of Jesus appealed to the Greek mind as well.

The Greeks were captivated by the concept of *aretae,* "excellence" or "perfection." To the Greeks' way of thinking nothing was more important than excelling, athletically and in every other way. Yet in Greek thought the perfect man was essentially selfish: his

Each Gospel was written to present Christ to a different cultural group.

energies were rightly devoted to perfecting *himself.* In his Gospel, Luke presents Jesus as the ideal human being, the person who has achieved excellence. But Jesus shows us that perfect manhood is not selfish but selfless. In his Gospel Luke gives us a portrait of a Jesus who is especially sensitive to the poor and oppressed, and who places great value on women—a shocking departure in Jewish, Greek, and Roman cultures alike. Yet Luke's portrait is utterly convincing. No one can read his Gospel without becoming aware that in Jesus we see a man who represents what every human being ought and yearns to be. And thus Luke's portrait of Jesus both rebukes and draws the individual whose cultural orientation is Greek, rather than Jewish or Roman.

John: the universal Gospel. The Gospel written by John is distinctly different from the three Synoptics. John does not work within even a loose chronological framework. He does not shape his account to communicate Jesus to any cultural group. Rather, John reports seven miracles of Jesus and seven associated and lengthy discourses. While in Matthew Jesus is presented as the Messiah, in Mark as the practical man of action, and in Luke as the perfect man, John focuses our attention on Jesus as the Son of God. Yes, Jesus was a true human being who lived among us; but Jesus was also God the Son! And while this truth is established in each of the other Gospels, it is written in great, bold strokes and underlined in John.

Together the four Gospels give us a balanced portrait of Jesus Christ, a Person so unique and so complex that no single account could begin to capture Him.

It is these four authentic Gospels that serve as the source for our study of the teachings of Jesus.

CONFLICT IN THE GOSPEL ACCOUNTS

It is popular these days for scholars to debate which of the sayings of Jesus recorded in the Gospels are "authentic." That is, which words did Jesus actually speak, and which were put in his mouth by the writers and the supposed redactors of the books of Matthew, Mark, Luke, and John. One group of so-called biblical scholars, participants in the "Jesus Seminar," gather regularly to vote verse by verse on whether or not Jesus spoke the words attributed to Him!

Other scholars have charged the Gospels with inaccuracies and errors because of supposed discrepancies in their accounts. It is helpful to sample some of these "errors," and see how we might respond to them.

Sequence errors. Matthew and Luke each give an account of the temptation of Jesus (Matt. 4; Luke 4). But Matthew describes Satan's offer of all the kingdoms of the world as the third temptation, while Luke describes Satan's challenge to Jesus to throw Himself from the pinnacle of the Temple as the third.

If the gospel writers intended to a maintain strict chronological order in their accounts, this would constitute an "error." But from the earliest times the church understood, with Papias, that the Gospel accounts were written "down accurately, though not indeed in order." The writers organized their material to fit their readership. To the Jew, the offer of all the kingdoms of the world would be the culminating temptation to One born to be a King. But to the Greek, the temptation to prove that God was with Jesus in His time of deep distress seemed far more significant. The difference is not an error, but rather an indication of how carefully the writers, under the inspiration of God's Spirit, shaped their accounts to fit their intended audiences.

Account conflicts. Matthew 8:28–34, Mark 5:1–19, and Luke 8:26–39 each tell a story about a demon-possessed man or men whom Jesus frees by casting legions of demons out into a herd of pigs.

While the similarities between the events are so great as to lead us to believe that each account is of the same incident, there are enough differences to trouble the reader. In Mark and Luke there is a single demoniac, in Matthew there are two. In Matthew the event occurs in "the country of the Gergesenes"; in the other two "the country of the Gadarenes." It would seem that there must be error here, for while Mark and Luke agree on the details, Matthew's account differs.

Yet the conclusion that the only explanation here is that there is error in the Gospel accounts seems much too hasty.

Suppose that a friend and I both witness an accident. I hurry home and tell my wife that I've seen an accident, and that two ambulances pulled up beside a Mercedes that seemed to be a total wreck. My friend also sees the accident, and tells his family that the accident involved a car and an overturned pick-up truck, and that a medivac helicopter landed in the Wynn Dixie parking lot. Do we conclude from this that one of us must be in error—just because our accounts differ? Hardly! We simply and rightly conclude that while I emphasized the make of the total wreck and told about the ambulances, my friend added detail about the pick-up truck and the helicopter. Neither of us was in error: the discrepancy is due to the simple fact that each of us selected what seemed important to us to report.

Does the fact that Matthew mentions two demoniacs while Mark and Luke focus on one mean that one account or the other must be in error? No more than the fact that

EVIDENCE FOR EARLY ACCEPTANCE OF THE GOSPELS

Approximate Dates	Sources	Gospels received
A.D. 100–140	Quotes in Apostolic Fathers	Matthew Mark Luke John
140–220	Quotes in Church Fathers	Matthew Mark
(c. A.D. 180)	Muratorian Canon	Luke John
220–400	Origen Eusebius Atheanasius Synod of Rome (A.D. 367) Synod of Carthage (A.D. 397)	Matthew Mark Luke John

my friend and I selected different things to emphasize in our description of the accident means that one of us was wrong.

But what about the differences in locale? The event must have happened in the country of the Gadarenes or in the country of the Gergesenes. Both accounts can't be right! Or can they?

Again, let's suppose I'm telling a friend of mine that I've just moved to Florida. I tell another friend I've moved to Pasco County, and then tell a third friend that I've settled in Hudson. Why did I lie to two of the three friends? Obviously, I didn't! I moved to the city of Hudson in the county of Pasco in the state of Florida. Each designation for the place where I've moved is absolutely correct!

There is no reason why something similar can't explain the "error" in the accounts of Matthew, Mark, and Luke—and in fact there is some evidence that just this kind of multiple administrative levels explains the discrepancy in the biblical accounts.

We need to be extremely careful before we conclude that apparent conflict in the Gospel accounts marks an error in God's Word.

Omissions, additions, and other differences. When we come to direct quotes of Jesus in the four Gospels, we sometimes find omissions, additions, and other differences in the writers' records of the teachings of Jesus. While this troubles some, we ought to be aware that of all so-called discrepancies in the Gospels this is the easiest to explain.

Often Jesus' teachings reported in Matthew 5–7 are compared with His teaching in Luke 6. The first passage is called Jesus' Sermon on the Mount, and the second His Sermon on the Plain, as details of locale given in each Gospel make it clear two different sermons are being reported. While the teaching in the two sermons is very similar and on the same topics, the words recorded are not exactly the same.

Two comments need to be made here. First, Jesus preached and taught in Galilee and Judea for some *three years*. During that time he taught hundreds of times, and essentially shared the same teachings again and again. Why would anyone expect that even a verbatim record of two or three such teaching times would match word for word? Second, remember that while each Gospel writer provides an accurate account, each also shaped what he wrote to fit his intended readership. The mere fact that there are differences, and that some passages on a particular theme omit or include material not found in another Gospel's account of teaching on that theme, in no way suggest error or even discrepancy.

What we must conclude is simple. In the four Gospels in our New Testament we have the authentic words of Jesus, the teachings of that Prophet like Moses of whom God said, "Him you shall hear" (Deut. 18:15). Of Him God also said, "It shall be that whoever will not hear My words, which He speaks in My name, I will require it of him" (Deut. 18:19).

We are to listen to Jesus' teachings.

And we are to heed what He says.

Every early Christian source indicates that the Gospels were accepted as Scripture by Christians from the very beginning of the church.

THE PROPHET'S PREPARATION

God's people had been waiting eagerly for two towering Old Testament figures. One was the Messiah, destined to deliver Israel and rule as King. The other was the Prophet like Moses, destined to unlock the secrets of the older revelation. No one quite realized that these two were one, or that a single individual would blend in His own Person the three institutions that marked Israel as God's own: the institutions of prophet, priest, and king.

Yet this was God's plan, as was the fact that God Himself intended to take on that tripartite role. Then in the fullness of time, God broke into space and time, entering the flow of human history as an infant, as Jesus Christ, growing up among us until it

was time to step forward and take on the predicted roles.

Jesus would initiate each of His three roles in turn. His first role was that of Prophet, sent to teach and to reveal God through all He said and did. The bulk of the Gospels describes Jesus' public and private teachings, and thus is devoted to the fulfillment of Jesus' prophetic role.

Jesus did not begin to function as Priest until He died and offered up His blood to God in satisfaction for our sins. As the Book of Hebrews emphasizes, Jesus continues to function as our High Priest during this present age.

While Jesus is the Old Testament's messianic King, Christ will appear in this role as King of kings and Lord of lords only at history's end (see Revelation 19:16), although today He rules His church and in our hearts.

So it is clearly appropriate to focus our attention on the teachings of Jesus as recorded in the Gospels. In His earthly ministry Jesus functioned primarily as Teacher, that Prophet like Moses whose revelations would set sacred history on a totally new course.

A TEACHER COME FROM GOD

John's Gospel begins with an introduction of Jesus as the eternal Word.

In the beginning was the Word, and the Word was with God, and the Word was God. He was in the beginning with God. All things were made through Him, and without Him nothing was made that was made. (John 1:1–3).

This famous passage establishes a number of important things. The one called the Word is God, yet at the same time is distinct from God. The Word has been God from before the beginning; the Word is the creator of the material and spiritual universe.

The Greek word translated "word" here is *logos*, a significant and complex Greek term. On one level *logos* was simply speech,

Even Jesus' enemies knew he was a teacher sent by God.

talk, or even a treatise on some subject. In Greek philosophy the *logos* was the organizing principle of the universe, which gave existence itself shape and meaning. Theologically *logos* was a powerful term that is linked with revelation but is also a term which expressed the active presence of God when He involved Himself with His people. And now John tells us that the Word, who is the focus of God's self-revelation and involvement with His own, "became flesh and dwelt among us" (John 1:14).

The Prophet like Moses was far greater than Moses, for He was the very Word of God. The Word who had spoken to Israel through Moses had appeared in Person as a human being, to speak for Himself and to give the world the ultimate revelation.

Nicodemus had said, "We know you are a teacher come from God" (John 3:2), but Nicodemus was wrong. Jesus was God, come to teach!

JESUS' CHILDHOOD

The Scriptures are largely silent about Jesus' childhood. Matthew and Luke give us the birth stories (Matt. 1:18–2:23; Luke 2:1–40). Luke adds a few details about the year the boy Jesus became a man (2:41-52).

That was the year Jesus turned twelve, and like other Jewish boys He became *bar mitzvah*, a "son of the law," responsible to live by the Law Moses gave to Israel. That Law laid an obligation on all responsible adult males to come to the temple to worship during Israel's major religious festivals. And so that year Jesus went with His parents when they traveled from Galilee to Jerusalem for the Feast of the Passover.

When the family returned, Jesus stayed behind but was not missed until nightfall. The next day the anxious parents returned to Jerusalem and finally found Jesus in the temple, "sitting in the midst of the teachers, both listening to them and asking them questions," and amazing bystanders by "His understanding and answers" (vv. 46, 47). Mary herself was surprised, but burst out, "Why have you done this to us?" The next verse contains an authentic account of the first recorded words that Jesus spoke: "Why did you seek Me? Did you not know that I must be about My Father's business?" (v. 49).

The Son of God had come to earth on a mission for His Father and would fully commit Himself to the task.

But the time had not yet come. And so Jesus returned to Nazareth, and Luke tells us He "was subject to" His parents, as any dutiful Jewish son. (v. 51)

While the Scripture is silent on the youth and young adulthood of Jesus, we know from the words of His Nazareth neighbors that Jesus took up the trade of carpenter, trained by His step-father Joseph (Matt. 13:55; Mark 6:3). And so for another eighteen years after the incident at the temple, Jesus lived an obscure life. It was not until He was about thirty (Luke 3:23) that Jesus stepped into the public spotlight and began to teach.

JESUS' BAPTISM

We next meet Jesus by the side of the river Jordan, speaking with His cousin John the Baptist. John had appeared suddenly from the wilderness and had begun preaching. Stridently John warned Israel that the time had come to get right with God, and he offered baptism as a sign of repentance—a willingness to put away sins and begin living a holy life.

When Jesus presented Himself for baptism, John objected, not because he knew Jesus was God's Son (John 1:33), but because John had known Jesus all his life and was aware that Jesus lived an exemplary life. Surely Jesus had no need to repent. He was already living the kind of life that John was calling for. But Jesus insisted, and Matthew is the one who recorded what He said: "Permit it to be so now, for thus it is fitting for us to fulfill all righteousness" (3:15).

While the meaning of Jesus' words has been debated, the best interpretation of what He said is the simplest. Jesus wished to be baptized simply because it was the right thing to do. Jesus would publicly identify with John and his message. John was God's messenger, and Jesus would take His stand publicly with His cousin.

In a sense these first words of the adult Jesus, although addressed to John, instruct us. It's not enough to stand on the sideline while others speak out for what is right. To "fulfill all righteousness" you and I need to take a public stand beside them, however others might misunderstand our actions.

JESUS' TEMPTATION
(MATTHEW 4:1–11; LUKE 4:1–13)

There was one more thing that Jesus had to do before He could begin His public ministry. Matthew and Luke both tell us that Jesus was led by the Spirit into the wilderness. There He was "tempted for forty days by the devil" (Luke 4:1, 2).

Again, in the Gospel account Jesus does not teach us directly. His dialog was with Satan. Yet Jesus' actions are instructive. Clearly, Jesus is teaching *by example*. As we look at each temptation we see just how powerfully Christ's example does teach.

The nature of temptations. The Greek word for temptation is *peirasmos*, a word also translated by "test" or "trial." The *International Encyclopedia of Bible Words* (p. 593) notes that "a temptation is a difficult situation, a pressure that brings a reaction through which the character or commitment of the believer is demonstrated."

The temptation to turn stones to bread (Matt. 4:1–4; Luke 4:1–4). Both Matthew and Luke describe this temptation first. Jesus had gone without food for forty days, and the text tells us that when those days had ended, "He was hungry" (Matt. 4:2). This detail is fascinating. Studies on fasting indicate that after two or three days without food hunger goes away. Only after all the body's stored resources have been exhausted does hunger return. Jesus had exhausted all His physical resources when the tempter suggested, "If You are the Son of God, command that these stones become bread" (v. 3).

The "if" here is a first-class conditional, a Greek construction in which the condition is assumed to have been fulfilled. What Satan said was, "Since you are the Son of God . . ." Since you have power to turn these stones to bread, use that power to satisfy your body's hunger.

Jesus responded by quoting from Deuteronomy 8:3: "Man shall not live by bread alone, but by every word that proceeds from the mouth of God."

Man. Although Jesus was the Son of God, in the Incarnation He voluntarily set aside the prerogatives of deity. He had become a true human being, vulnerable to all those forces to which we His brothers are susceptible. Jesus would not meet Satan's tests in the strength of His essential Deity, but rather He would meet Satan's tests in the weakness of His humanity.

Only because Jesus made this choice can we learn from His example. When we are tempted as Jesus was, we can respond as Jesus did—and we can share His victory!

By bread alone. In Scripture, as it did in the ancient world, bread symbolizes maintaining our life in this world. Jesus was hungry; He felt a tremendous need for bread to sustain life itself. Yet for human beings created in the image of God, there is more to reality than our physical needs and desires. In the last analysis human beings are spiritual rather than material beings. And we are not to let the material dominate.

By every word of God. While everything in Jesus' body cried out for bread, He knew that the Father had not yet completed His test. Jesus had heard no word from God directing Him to eat, and so He would not surrender to His hunger. Because Jesus refused to surrender to His hunger, but rather looked to God for direction, Christ avoided Satan's snare.

This is how we are to meet this kind of temptation in our own lives. Our bodies are the source of so many of the hungers that drive us. Yet we are essentially spiritual beings, and we are to look to the Word of God to guide us, not to our desires or even our needs.

The temptation to prove God's presence (Matt. 4:5–7; Luke 4:9–12). Now Satan takes Jesus to the pinnacle of the Jerusalem temple, probably the high point overlooking the inner courtyard, and suggested that Jesus throw Himself down. Surely angels would catch Him, for Psalm 91 records God's promise to His Messiah that angels would guard Him "lest you dash your foot against a stone" (v. 12).

The Spirit had led Jesus into the wilderness. There Jesus had been alone. He had no food to eat, and was under constant attack by Satan. The attack intensified when Jesus had exhausted all His physical resources and His hunger returned. The nature of this temptation is revealed in Satan's challenge and in Jesus' response.

If you are the Son of God (Matt. 4:6; Luke 4:9). There is a subtle change here. Earlier Satan had used a first class conditional when

This location of one of Jesus' temptations is thought to be the corner overlooking the temple court.

he suggested "If [since] you are the Son of God." Now Satan uses a mixed grammatical construction where the "if" expresses doubt. "If by some chance you really are the Son of God . . . and it doesn't seem too likely!"

How easy it would be for Jesus to prove to Himself and to all that despite the last forty days God had not deserted Him. Jesus could step out into space, and before He reached the ground angels would appear to catch Him! How tempting that must have been to Jesus who in His humanity was in a weakened, vulnerable state.

Jesus' reply. This time Jesus quoted Deuteronomy 6:16: "You shall not tempt the LORD your God." Here *peirasmos* is unmistakably used in the sense of "test." This Deuteronomy verse refers back to a time when the Israelites were in the Sinai

desert after their release from slavery in Egypt (Exod. 17:1–7). When the water ran out the people angrily confronted Moses, almost ready to stone him. God did provide water, but marked the incident as Moses recorded the fact that "the people tempted [tested] the LORD, saying, 'Is God among us or not?'"

The warning in Deuteronomy 6:16 is clear. We are not to put God to the test, asking Him to prove that He is with us. However difficult our circumstances, however powerfully the situation may seem to suggest that we have been abandoned by God, we are not to demand that God prove His presence with us.

Jesus stepped back from the pinnacle of the temple, choosing to live by faith rather than by sight. Christ knew God was with Jesus whether His human nature could sense that presence or not.

Even so, God is with us—even when we feel most alone.

The temptation to choose the good (Matt. 4:8–10; Luke 4:5–8). Satan took Jesus to a high mountain and, in a moment of time, displayed all the kingdoms of the world. Satan promised them all to Jesus if He would only worship him.

This is perhaps the most subtle temptation of all. While the worship of Satan held no attraction for Jesus, it must have been tempting to consider having immediate control over all the world's kingdoms.

To understand this we must recall Old Testament prophecies that portray the world under Messiah's rule. When Jesus rules, there will be no more injustice, no more crime, no more suffering. If Jesus had at that moment accepted Satan's offer, the last two thousand years of human history would have been far different. There would have been no wars, no inquisition, no holocaust. Generation upon generation would have lived and died in peace. And surely this was appealing to Jesus, who cares for all supremely.

But they would have lived . . . and died. And there's the rub.

For if Jesus had accepted the crown before the cross, eternity would have been a disaster for us all.

So Jesus responded, "Away with you, Satan! For it is written, 'You shall worship the LORD your God, and Him only you shall serve'" (Matt. 4:10). This quote also is drawn from Deuteronomy, from chapter 10 and verse 20. It reminds us that however "good" any course of action might seem to us, it is God who determines what is truly good. And we are to bow down to Him, to acknowledge His sovereignty, and in every situation to choose His will, even when an alternative choice seems good to you and me.

Jesus' use of Scripture. Jesus' responses to Satan's temptations also involve teaching by example.

When urged to satisfy any physical need or craving, we can resist as we remember that we are essentially spiritual beings, to be guided by God's Word.

When feeling alone and abandoned because of circumstances, we can remember that like Jesus we are called to walk by faith, not by sight.

When confronted by the option of choosing that which seems and may even be a good thing, or hewing to what we know to be the will of God, we are to worship God by serving His will.

Yet perhaps the most important lesson Jesus teaches us in this incident is that imbedded in God's Word are truths that we can and are to live by. And surely, as Jesus relied on God's Word transmitted by Moses, you and I are to rely on the teachings of Jesus Christ, that Prophet like Moses who came not only to save but also to teach.

WHO DO MEN SAY
THAT I AM?

It is popular with some to portray Jesus as a simple Jewish rabbi whose teachings were firmly rooted in the mainstream of Judaism. It was the disciples or the apostle Paul, they say, who imposed on Jesus a deity He never claimed, and who "invented" Christian faith. In their search for the "historical Jesus" such persons discard many of the sayings and teachings of Jesus, regarding as authentic only those which fit their picture of a misunderstood prophet. But what happens when we treat the Gospel narratives as authentic and let Jesus tell us about Himself? We discover a Jesus very different from the one men say that He is.

From the very first Jesus' ministry was marked by miracles. Mark describes a time early in Jesus' ministry when Jesus astonished His listeners. Christ was in Capernaum, teaching in the synagogue. He amazed His hearers, for "He taught them as one having authority, and not as the scribes" (Mark 1:22). The scribes, who were considered experts in Scripture, quoted the opinions of previous rabbis as authority for their views;

Jesus spoke as one who was Himself an authority.

During that same meeting Jesus demonstrated His authority. He cast out a demon! Again Mark tells us that all were amazed, whispering to each other, "What is this? A new teaching—and with authority! He even gives orders to evil spirits and they obey him." (Mark 1:27 NIV). That same evening Jesus, who was staying at Simon Peter's house, "healed many who were sick with various diseases, and cast out many demons" (Mark 1:34).

There was no confusion in the minds of those first-century eyewitnesses. Something new and wonderful was taking place. A teacher had appeared who could speak with authority, and whose "new" teachings were authenticated by the miracles and wonders that the Old Testament promised would be performed by the coming "Prophet like Moses."

It's important then to ask what this Person who amazed His contemporaries had to say about Himself. As we look into the Gospels we find no confusion in Jesus' teaching about Himself. Jesus knew who He was. And He announced His identity in both private conversation and public sermon.

JESUS, THE PROMISED MESSIAH

The Old Testament prophets had made it clear. One day God would send Israel a deliverer, a descendant of King David who would bring God's Old Testament people back to the Lord and to greatness. This chosen individual was known as the Messiah, literally "the Anointed One." One of the earliest claims that Jesus made about Himself was that He was the promised Messiah.

THE ANNOUNCEMENT AT NAZARETH (LUKE 4:14–30).

When Jesus visited His hometown of Nazareth He was already a celebrity. He had been teaching and healing in Galilee, and was being praised everywhere.

On the Sabbath Jesus attended the synagogue and was invited to read from the Scriptures. It was customary in first-century synagogues to offer visitors the opportunity to read and to make comments, and everyone must have been eager to hear what their suddenly famous neighbor would say.

That Sabbath morning Jesus read a messianic prophecy from the Book of Isaiah:

The Spirit of the LORD is upon Me,
Because He has anointed Me
To preach the gospel to the poor;
He has sent Me to heal the broken-
    hearted,
To proclaim liberty to the captives
And recovery of sight to the blind,
To set at liberty those who are oppressed;
To proclaim the acceptable year of the
    LORD (Luke 4:18, 19).

Jesus then rolled up the scroll and, with all eyes fixed on Him, told His friends and neighbors, "Today this Scripture is fulfilled in your hearing" (v. 21).

There was no mistaking Jesus' meaning. Christ was publicly presenting Himself as the promised Messiah!

The significant silence (Isa. 61:2). When we go back to the original text in Isaiah we note that Jesus stopped quoting in the middle of a thought. The Isaiah text reads, "To proclaim the acceptable year of the LORD, a and the day of vengeance of our God."

Jesus announced that He had come to preach good tidings, to heal the broken-hearted, and to proclaim the acceptable year of the LORD. But Jesus was not yet ready to announce "the day of vengeance of our God."

This silence about the day of vengeance is significant, for there are two strains of teaching about the Messiah in the Old Testament. One emphasizes His mission of restoration and healing. The other emphasizes His role in judging the nations and Israel, and so purging the world of sin. Jesus' significant silence that Sabbath morning was a clear indication that His present mission was to bring salvation and wholeness. Later it would become clear. The promised "day of vengeance of our God" would await a second coming of our Lord (2 Thess. 1:6–10).

The neighbors' reaction (Luke 4:22). Jesus' announcement of God's grace (His "gracious words") was met with amazement. The Greek word translated "marveled" is neutral, and indicates neither positive nor negative emotions. But soon the crowd turned antagonistic. "Isn't this Joseph's son?" they began to mutter.

Jesus had grown up in Nazareth, the supposed son of Joseph. He had lived among them, very possibly walking each day to the nearby city of Sephoris to work as a carpenter. Jesus was undoubtedly known as a good neighbor, but He had taken no advanced theological training. Jesus was just one of them—an ordinary Jew of Galilee, a province whose people were looked down upon by the elite of Judea as less committed to God and His Laws than they should be.

And now Jesus claimed to be the Messiah! To his neighbors Jesus must have seemed to be putting on airs, despite the reputation He was gaining beyond their little town.

Jesus' claim rejected (Luke 4:23–27). The hostility of the crowd must have been palpable. Jesus responded to the growing hostility by pointing out a historical fact: "no prophet is accepted in his own country" (v. 24). The history of the Jews was filled with stories of prophets like Jeremiah, Amos, and Ezekiel, whose contemporaries refused to accept them or their message. The response of the Nazarenes to Jesus fit a long-established pattern, for God's people had long been stiff-necked and rebellious (Acts 7:51, 52).

Jesus then pointed to two incidents in Israel's history. The prophet Elijah had been sent to a widow in pagan Sidon, although there were plenty of widows in Israel. And Elisha had healed the Syrian general Naaman of leprosy although there were many lepers in his homeland. The implication was clear. If God's own people would not welcome their Messiah and His message of God's grace, the Messiah would offer His gifts to Gentiles. And Gentiles would experience the healing that Israel refused to accept!

Jesus attacked (Luke 4:28–30). Jesus' neighbors clearly understood His warning. The text says they "were filled with wrath" (v. 28). That Jesus would claim to be the Messiah was bad enough. That He would suggest that Israel's Messiah might turn to the hated Gentiles, who had oppressed God's people for centuries, seemed like blasphemy! The men in the synagogue grabbed Jesus and dragged Him to the brow of a cliff, intending to throw Him over to His death.

The incident foreshadows the future of Jesus. John tells us that Christ "came to His own, and His own did not receive Him" (John 1:11). Jesus' messianic claims were rejected, and in the end He was nailed to a cross, judged a blasphemer by the religious leaders. Yet after His resurrection the messianic message of salvation and healing was indeed shared with the whole world, and the hated Gentiles did respond. Jesus came to save all, and "as many as received Him, to them He gave the right to become children of God, to those who believe in His name" (John 1:12).

THE WOMAN AT THE WELL (JOHN 4)

In view of Luke 4, it is fascinating to look at Jesus' conversation with a Samaritan woman. The first thing we notice is that the conversation took place with a Samaritan, and a Samaritan woman at that.

The Samaritans. The district of Samaria lay between Judea and Galilee. Its inhabitants were a mixed race descended from pagan peoples imported by the Assyrians after their conquest of Israel in 722 B.C. The annals of Sargon, the Assyrian conqueror, claim that he carried away 27,790 Jews from Israel's capital city, Samaria, and state that "the city I rebuilt—I made it greater than it was before. People of lands which I had conquered I settled therein."

The new inhabitants worshiped their own gods, but when the sparsely populated areas became infested with wild beasts, they appealed to the king of Assyria to send them Israelite priests to teach them how to worship the God of their new land. The result was a religion in which elements of the biblical faith were mixed with pagan elements. In the words of 2 Kings 17:33, "they feared the LORD, yet served their own gods—according to the rituals of the nations from among whom they were carried away."

When the Jews returned from captivity, these mixed peoples wanted to help them rebuild the Jerusalem temple. The offer was decisively rejected: these "Samaritans" were not descendants of Abraham, Isaac, and Jacob, and had no covenant relationship with the Lord. From that time on the hostility between the two peoples grew. By the first century, most pious Jews traveling from Galilee to Judea would take the long route, crossing the Jordan and traveling through Perea to avoid passing through the lands of the hated Samaritans. To the Jews Samaritans were corrupters of the true faith delivered by Moses, and as the shocked Samaritan woman blurted out when Jesus asked her for a drink, "How is it that You, being a Jew, ask a drink from me, a Samaritan woman?" And John explains, "For the Jews have no dealings with Samaritans" (John 4:9).

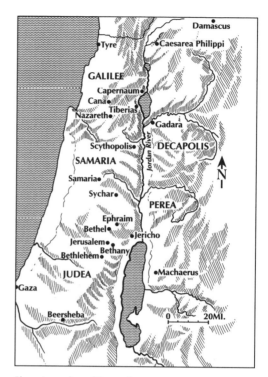

Pious Jews viewed Samaritans as pagans.

The rabbis' view of women. First-century Jewish rabbis considered women a snare and source of temptation. As my wife and I develop in the companion book in this series *Every Woman in the Bible*, no Jewish teacher would ever be alone with a woman, and most would refuse even to look directly at a woman, much less speak with one.

On two counts, then, Jesus' conversation with the woman at the well crossed boundaries established in first-century Judaism, and illustrate Christ's commitment to include outsiders in His messianic ministry of salvation and healing.

The conversation (John 4:7–26). Many have commented on the skill with which Jesus led the Samaritan woman to belief in him, and have presented this passage as a model for contemporary personal evangelism. For our purposes, however, we need

to focus on claims Jesus made, culminating in His announcement that He Himself is the Messiah whom the Samaritans as well as the Jews expected to appear.

Jesus, the source of living water (4:7–14). Gradually Jesus moved the conversation from the water one might draw from Jacob's well to a spiritual water "springing up into everlasting life."

In the idiom of the day "living water" was water that flows, as in a stream, in contrast to water that is still, as in a pond or jar. In Jewish theology, purifying rites required the use of living water, so first-century mikvahs (ritual baths) were constructed so that water flowed into them from streams or after rains. Jesus' reference to living water would have been understood as a reference to purification from sin and to a cleansing that would put one right with God.

Jesus taught that God seeks worshipers from among all peoples.

Jesus not only claimed to be the source of living water, but also to be able to cause living water to "become in [whoever drinks] a fountain of water springing up into everlasting life" (v. 14). Rather than be forced to visit the ritual bath again and again, Jesus would provide a continual cleansing that would result in everlasting life.

Jesus, the Prophet like Moses (John 4:15–24). The Samaritan woman had not understood what Jesus was saying (v. 15), so Jesus took another tack. He told her to find her "husband," and then demonstrated an intimate and clearly supernatural knowledge of her personal life: "You have had five husbands, and the one whom you now have is not your husband" (v. 18). This the woman clearly understood. Jesus must be a prophet (v. 19)! The woman immediately asked a theological question, for who could better settle a burning debate

between the Jews and Samaritans than a prophet?

The Jews had maintained that God must be worshiped at Mount Zion. The Samaritans argued for Mount Gerazim. Who was right?

Christ answered that the Jews were the ones who knew what they were doing. But, he went on, "the hour is coming when you will neither on this mountain, nor in Jerusalem, worship the Father" (v. 21). In making this statement Jesus was truly taking the role of the Prophet like Moses, for His words would set sacred history on a new course. "The hour is coming, and now is, when the true worshipers will worship the Father in spirit and truth; for the Father is seeking such to worship Him" (v. 23).

The Old Testament way of worship, with its carefully crafted rules and rituals, were about to be replaced with a worship that was in greater harmony with spiritual realities.

Jesus, the Messiah (John 4:25–26). At this "the woman said to Him, 'I know that Messiah is coming' (who is called Christ). 'When He comes, He will tell us all things.' Jesus said to her, 'I who speak to you am He.'"

This claim was made clearly and simply. "I who speak to you am He." There could be no confusion or mistake. Jesus claimed to be the Messiah. He was not just one of many first-century Bible teachers. Jesus was the Messiah sent from God, destined to bring salvation and healing to the lost.

It's fascinating to look at the two responses to Jesus' presentation of Himself as the Messiah. His neighbors in Nazareth angrily rejected His claim. But an outcast, a woman of Samaria with no covenant claim on God's mercy, believed. And many in her village were drawn to Jesus, stating, "Now we believe, not because of what you said, for we ourselves have heard Him and we know that this is indeed the Christ, the Savior of the world" (John 4:42).

JESUS, SON OF GOD, SAVIOR OF THE WORLD

According to the Gospels, Jesus claimed to be the promised Messiah—and more! Jesus made it clear that He was the Son of God, the Savior of the world. This too was stated both in private conversation and public address.

JESUS AND NICODEMUS (JOHN 3)

Nicodemus was a member of the Sanhedrin, the supreme religious and civil court of the Jews. John reports that one night Nicodemus visited Jesus, undoubtedly to learn just what the suddenly popular teacher had in mind. Nicodemus began by acknowledging the fact that the religious leaders knew that Jesus spoke with divine authority.

"Rabbi, we know that You are a teacher come from God; for no one can do these signs that You do unless God is with him" (John 3:2).

This is a stunning confession, for the very same religious leaders who *knew* that Jesus spoke with God's authority were to become His most bitter enemies. Yet the course of the conversation that Nicodemus had with Jesus must have seemed even more stunning. For Jesus stated truths that, while reflected in the Old Testament, had been lost sight of by most in first-century Judaism.

You must be born again (John 3:3–12). Jesus immediately challenged Nicodemus' understanding of relationship with God by announcing that a person must be "born again." Jesus was referring to an inner transformation, the infusion of new life by the very Spirit of God.

Judaism based its claim to God's favor on physical descent from Abraham and on careful observance of the revealed laws and regulations that governed a Jew's life in this world. Christ's words constituted a rejection of these foundational beliefs of Judaism. No descendant of Abraham, Jesus announced, can even catch a glimpse of God's kingdom without being born again, and this work of the Spirit is as invisible as the wind which rustles in the trees.

When Nicodemus expressed shock, Jesus rebuked him. How could Nicodemus be "the teacher of Israel, and . . . not know these things" (John 3:10)? The prophet Ezekiel had promised in God's name, "I will give them one heart, and I will put a new spirit within them, and take the stony heart out of their flesh, and give them a heart of flesh, that they may walk in My statues and keep My judgments and do them" (Ezek. 11:19, 20). Through Jeremiah, Ezekiel's contemporary, God committed Himself to make a new covenant with the house of Israel. At that time God would "put My law in their have been even more shaken by Jesus' next claims. Jesus understood these things because He "came down from heaven" (v. 13). Jesus said that He was in fact God's "only begotten Son," given by the Father to provide everlasting life to whoever would believe in Him.

The term "only begotten" (*monogenes*) is better translated "one and only," for it indicates a unique and eternal relationship between Jesus and God the Father. Only God the Son could possibly deal with mankind's sin and provide eternal life. So the Father had sent His Son into the world, not to condemn the world, but that through the Son the world might be saved.

BIBLE BACKGROUND:
THE SERPENT IN THE WILDERNESS

Jesus told Nicodemus He must be "lifted up" as Moses had lifted up "the serpent in the wilderness." The allusion is to a story told in Numbers 21. The camp of the Israelites was infested with poisonous serpents, and many people died from their venomous bites. God told Moses to fashion a metal serpent and attach it to the top of a pole. The pole was then to be erected in the center of the camp, and the people were told that anyone who had been bitten could come, look at the serpent, and be healed.

The remedy seemed ridiculous. What medical value could there be in simply looking at a metal serpent? Yet it worked! When a person came, as God had commanded, to view that serpent, he or she was healed. The image had no value in itself, yet it served to focus faith on the God who promised healing.

Jesus spoke of a time when, as Moses lifted up the serpent to serve as a focus for ancient Israel's faith, Christ Himself would become the focus of all humankind's faith. God's promise of salvation and healing would be mediated through Him, and His cross would

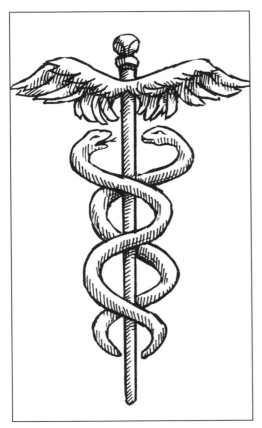

Some assume this symbol of healing is rooted in the story of Moses lifting up a bronze serpent in the wilderness.

minds, and write it on their hearts" (Jer. 31:33).

Clearly God had always intended that His people be born again, and that their new lives in the Spirit should be marked by responsiveness to an internal rather than an external law!

Speaking as the Prophet like Moses, Jesus was about to unlock the secrets of the Old testament and to set sacred history on a course that was new, yet in fullest harmony with God's recorded Word.

God's only begotten Son (John 3:13–17). If Nicodemus was stunned by the announcement that he must be born again, he must become the agency through which sins were forgiven and new life given to all who believe.

A matter of life and death (John 3:18–21). There is some debate as to whether this passage records the words of Jesus or represents John's commentary on what has gone before.

In any case, these verses state truly vital truths.

He who believes in Him is not condemned; but he who does not believe is condemned already, because he has not believed in the name of the only begotten Son of God. And this is the condemnation, that the light has come into the world, and men loved darkness rather than light, because their deeds were evil. For everyone practicing evil hates the light and does not come to the light, lest his deeds should be exposed. But he who does the truth comes to the light, that his deeds may be clearly seen, that they have been done in God.

Later Paul explained that, as all have sinned, all stand guilty before God (Rom. 3:19, 20). The Law offers no salvation option: it simply condemns. All humankind is already condemned, however an individual may strive to please God. But now the Son of God has entered the world, and there is a salvation option open to all! One can trust in the Savior and avoid condemnation. Or one can refuse to believe and continue already condemned.

Why would anyone then reject God's offer of salvation? People reject because in Christ light has come into the world—and sinful men prefer darkness. To come to the light means acknowledging the fact that we are sinners and without hope, and this was something that all too few in Israel were willing to do.

Yet some would respond, as some had responded to John the Baptist's call to repentance. Those who came to Jesus,

acknowledging that as sinners they desperately needed God's salvation, would live by the truth. These alone would find the forgiveness and the healing they sought.

BIBLE BACKGROUND:

HARD SAYINGS OF JESUS

"He who does the truth comes to the light" (John 3:21).

Jesus is not speaking of an unregenerate man who finds himself drawn to the light. Here Jesus is speaking of those first-century hearers who, like John the Baptist, already had a faith relationship with God (see also Abraham, Gen. 15:6). As Jesus points out, "Everyone practicing evil hates the light and does not come to the light" (John 3:20).

Jesus' words to Nicodemus were clear and plain. He presented Himself as the Son of God and as the Savior of the world. Jesus also functioned as the Prophet like Moses. No longer would faith be expressed through externals—through temple ritual and careful attention to the details of Old Testament law. From now on faith would be expressed through, and only through, an individual's personal response to Jesus Christ as God's Son and Savior.

Jesus, and Jesus alone, would become the door through which all who hoped to have a personal relationship with God must enter.

JESUS AND "THE JEWS" (JOHN 5)

Jesus did not hesitate to identify Himself as God's Son and Savior in public as well as in private conversation. John 5 tells of an incident that took place at one of the annual religious festivals held in Jerusalem and attended by all adult Jewish men able to come. At the festival Jesus healed a man who had been paralyzed for thirty-eight years. The healing took place on a Sabbath, and this incensed the religious leaders.

In reading this and other passages in John's Gospel, it's important to know that when John mentions "the Jews," he does not mean "the Jewish people." Instead this is John's way of referring to the religious elite—the Pharisees, the Sadducees, the experts in Old Testament Law—who became Jesus' most vicious enemies. As we will see later in our study, the fact that Jesus healed on the Sabbath became one of their primary complaints against Him. The intensity of the hostility that the Sabbath healings aroused is seen in John's comment, "for this reason the Jews persecuted Jesus, and sought to kill Him, because He had done these things on the Sabbath" (John 5:16).

In this case the healing led to a loud and public debate between Jesus and the religious leaders.

Jesus' claim of deity (John 5:17–23). Christ's initial response to the Jews' criticism of His Sabbath healing seems innocent enough. Jesus simply said, "My Father has been working until now, and I have been working" (v. 17). There was however far more to this statement than first meets the eye. Jesus did more than claim that God the Father was involved in the healing, and thus it was justified. In speaking of God as "My Father" in this context, Jesus was making a claim to deity! John comments, "Therefore the Jews sought all the more to kill Him, because He not only broke the Sabbath, but also said that God was His Father, *making Himself equal with God*" (v. 18; italics mine).

Ignoring His opponents' outrage, Jesus went on to further define the relationship between Himself and the Father. Jesus was

indeed the Son of God. His every action was in complete harmony with God's will, for God the Father was at work through Him (v. 19). The miracles Jesus performed proved that the Father loved the Son and was revealing Himself in the Son (v. 20). Jesus in fact exercised key prerogatives of the Father: He gave spiritual life to whomever He chose (v. 21), and the right to judge humanity had been committed by the Father to the Son (v. 22).

It follows that the Son is to be honored as God, just as the Father is honored as God. Even more, it should be clear that "he who does not honor the Son does not honor the Father who sent Him" (v. 23).

There could hardly be a clearer public statement. Whatever men might say about Jesus Christ, He Himself claimed to be God!

Jesus' presentation of Himself as Savior (John 5:24–30). Not only is Jesus the Son of God. He is the Savior, the source of everlasting life. "Most assuredly," Jesus stated, "he who hears My word and believes in Him who sent Me has everlastingly life, and shall not come into judgment, but has passed from death into life" (v. 24). In these words Jesus states in another form what He told Nicodemus: "God so loved the world that He gave His only begotten Son, that whoever believes in Him should not perish but have everlasting life" (John 3:16).

Again Jesus emphasized the fact that everything hinges on a person's response to Him and His message. Jesus announced that the hour had come, and the issue was joined. "The dead will hear the voice of the Son of God, and those who hear will live" (5:25). Jesus was not speaking of the resurrection here, but rather of the fact that all human beings are, in the words of the apostle Paul, "dead in trespasses and sins" (Eph. 2:1). Those who are spiritually dead will be given spiritual life, but only if they "hear [respond to] the voice of the Son of God" (John 5:25).

The title "son of man" emphasizes Jesus' true humanity as well as His messiahship.

BIBLE BACKGROUND:

JESUS, THE SON OF MAN

Frequently in the Gospels Jesus refers to Himself as the Son of Man. In this passage He states that the Father has given Him authority to execute judgment "because He is the Son of Man" (John 5:27). What is the significance of this title of the Savior? The *New International Encyclopedia of Bible Words,* p. 573, states:

First, it emphasizes Jesus' humanity. In the OT, "son of man" is often used in addressing Ezekiel. In the context of that book it is clear that the title simply means "man" and carries there a special emphasis on the distinction between humanity and God. The NT makes it clear that Jesus took on true human nature, and one implication of the title is to affirm his humanity.

Second, it is used in place of "I." There are a number of passages in which it seems best to take the phrase in this way (e.g. Mt. 12:8; 17:22; 19:28; 20:18, 28).

Third, it identifies Jesus as the focus of OT eschatological prophecy. . . .

Fourth, it identifies Jesus with humanity in his suffering for us. Often this phrase was chosen by Jesus when he spoke of his coming suffering and death (e.g., Mt. 12:40). Jesus the Son of Man did come from heaven (Jn 3:13), but he had to be lifted up in crucifixion, suffering for all so that all who believe in him may have eternal life (Jn 3:14).

In John 5:27, then, Jesus emphasizes the fact that it is His true humanity that qualifies Him to pass judgment on humankind. Jesus has shared our every experience and has demonstrated in His own life that perfection of which we all fall short.

Jesus' claims authenticated (John 5:31–47). Jesus has made truly stunning claims. He is God the Son, the equal of the Father. And He is the source of everlasting life, the only hope of human beings who are spiritually dead and condemned. But how can these claims be supported?

"If I bear witness of Myself" (John 5:31). The New King James Version translates Jesus' words, "If I bear witness of Myself, My witness is not true." A better translation is "My witness is not *valid*." Old Testament rules of evidence established the legal principle that to substantiate anything in a court of law there must be testimony from two or three witnesses. The testimony of one person could not be accepted. So what Jesus said of Himself might be rejected as invalid.

John the Baptist (vv. 32–35). Jesus might point to John the Baptist as a witness—but says that He will not. Mere human testimony would not compel belief.

"The works which the Father has given Me to finish" (v. 36). Jesus' claims, like His teaching, have been supernaturally authenticated! God has performed miracles through Him. And, according to Nicodemus, this evidence was compelling. "We know," Nicodemus said, speaking for the religious leaders, "that You are a teacher come from God; for no one can do these signs that You do unless God is with him" (3:2).

The healings and the exorcisms Jesus performed were the first witness Christ called to validate His claims. Even those hostile to Jesus had grudgingly acknowledged that their testimony was compelling!

The Scriptures (5:38–41). Jesus next calls the Word of God as a witness. The religious leaders searched the Scriptures "for in them you think you have eternal life" (v. 39). Yet it was the very Scriptures they searched which "testify of Me."

Here the great error of first-century Judaism is exposed. Judaism saw God's law itself as the way to eternal life, and so studied it intently in order to learn what they must do to gain merit with God. Yet in their careful listing of dos and don'ts they missed the Old Testament's clear testimony to Jesus.

Isaiah explains this apparent blindness. Having missed the grace of God,

> The word of the LORD was to them,
> "Precept upon precept, precept upon
>   precept,
> Line upon line, line upon line,
> Here a little, there a little,"
> That they might go and fall backward,
>   and be broken
> And snared and caught.
>   (Isa. 28:13)

Because the true message of Scripture was lost through Israel's attention to the details, when the Savior of whom the Scriptures spoke appeared, He was rejected out of hand.

"One who accuses you–Moses" (John 5:45). Jesus sums up. Jesus has presented Himself to His people as the Son of God, the promised Savior. His claims have been validated by the miracles He has performed and by the testimony of Scripture itself. Moses, whom all Jews acknowledged was God's authoritative spokesman, had written about Jesus—and the religious leaders simply had not believed Moses' testimony.

There was no need for Jesus to accuse these men who so viciously attacked Him. The very one to whom they, Moses, would be their accuser.

Whoever men may say Jesus is, we see again that there is no doubt who Jesus claimed to be. Jesus is the Messiah of Old Testament prophecy. Jesus is God the Son. Jesus is the Savior of the world, the giver of everlasting life to all who trust in Him.

JESUS, BREAD OF LIFE (JOHN 6)

When Jesus performed a great miracle, feeding thousands with just five barley loaves and two small fish, many in the crowd were convinced. Jesus truly was "the Prophet who is coming into the world" (v. 14). Hadn't Moses fed the Israelites with manna (Ex. 16)? And hadn't Jesus just fed the multitudes? The parallel was too obvious for anyone to miss.

After the miracle, Jesus and His disciples retreated across the Sea of Galilee. The excited crowds eagerly followed. Would Christ feed them continually as Moses had fed their forefathers for forty years?

Jesus understood their motive perfectly. "You seek Me, not because you saw the signs, but because you ate of the loaves and were filled" (John 6:26). Jesus then warned his listeners not to labor "for the food which perishes, but for the food which endures to everlasting life" (v. 27).

BIBLE BACKGROUND:

HARD SAYINGS OF JESUS

"Labor . . . for the food which endures to
everlasting life" (John 6:27)

Does this saying conflict with the gospel offer of salvation to all who simply believe? Is Jesus introducing works ("labor") into the salvation equation? The answer is in the context. Jesus' questioners were intent on obtaining an endless supply of bread. Jesus urged that instead they focus their attention on that which can provide eternal life. It's not the bread that perishes but that which sustains everlasting life with which we're to occupy ourselves.

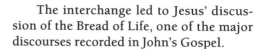

The interchange led to Jesus' discussion of the Bread of Life, one of the major discourses recorded in John's Gospel.

The significance of bread. Bread was the staple food of the common people in Judea and Galilee, and as such was a symbol of life itself. But bread also had a spiritual significance. The Jews saw in Moses' provision of "bread from heaven" hidden significance. As bread sustained biological life, so the "manna" of the Law, contained in the first five Old Testament books, was thought to sustain spiritual life. Thus it is not unusual to find references to the Torah [here the five books containing the Law of Moses] in Jewish writings presenting Torah as the bread of God. Philo comments on Exodus 15:

You see of what sort the soul's food is. It is a word of God, continuous, resembling dew, embracing all the soul. . . . This bread is the food which God hath given to the soul for it to feed on, His own utterance and His own word, for this bread, which He hath given us to eat, is "this word." [Philo, *Leg. Alleg.* 3:59, 60]

Jesus rejects the common view (John 6:28–35). Jesus had urged the crowd to focus not on literal but spiritual bread, and their next question related back to Moses' Law. What should they do to "work the works of God?" There was nothing. All anyone could do was to "believe in Him whom He [God] sent" (v. 29).

Despite the fact that just the day before the crowds had seen and participated in Jesus' miracle of the loaves and fishes, spokesmen from the crowd challenged Christ. What miraculous sign would Jesus do to establish Himself as on a par with Moses, who "gave them bread from heaven"? (v.31). It was at this point that Jesus abruptly confronted the common understanding of the symbolic significance of bread.

"Moses did not give you the bread from heaven" (v. 32). This emphatic declaration decisively rejects the notion that Moses' Law was the bread of God and thus was capable of sustaining spiritual life. This is as important for us to understand as it was for Jesus' hearers. So many receive eternal life as a gift of grace—and then turn to the Law as though it could nourish our new life. In His confrontation of the crowd Jesus made it absolutely clear that there is no life-sustaining power in the Law.

No, the one who sustains as well as gives eternal life is none other than Jesus Himself: "He who comes down from heaven and gives life to the world" (v. 33).

The mystery of faith (John 6:35–40). The crowd to whom Jesus spoke had seen Him and His miracles, yet they did not believe. Who then would believe? Jesus states that "all that the Father gives Me will come to Me" (v. 37). There is an initiating work of grace performed by God in the hearts of those who believe. The evidence that this initiating work of grace has taken place is that those so touched by God "will come to Me."

Jesus indeed had come down from heaven to do God's will, and He would receive as the Father's gift all those who believe in Him. When the judgment of the Last Day comes, every one of those who "see the Son and believe in Him" will be raised to eternal life.

The mystery of the Incarnation (John 6:41–51). Jesus' claim to have "come down from heaven" was met with disbelief. Wasn't Jesus an ordinary man, whose parentage was well known? How then could He claim to have "come down from heaven" (v. 42)? But Jesus was more than a man, as He himself had publicly proclaimed. Jesus was the Son of God. Yet Jesus would only be recognized by those who were responsive to God.

Again Jesus announced that "no one can come to Me unless the Father who sent Me draws him" (v. 44). Jesus supported this statement with a quote from the Old Testament: "And they shall all be taught by God" (Isa. 54:13). Those who had "heard and learned from the Father" would surely come to Jesus (John 6:45), and those who had not "heard and learned from the Father" would never see beyond Christ's humanity.

And so in Jesus' statement "I am the living bread which came down from heaven" (v. 51), we have Christ's own statement about His incarnation. Although born a man, His origin is from heaven itself.

The mystery of participation in Jesus' death (John 6:51–59). Verse 51 marks a transition. Jesus had spoken of His incarnation. As the living bread Jesus came down from heaven, a sustaining Word from God. Now Jesus began to speak of His death. To live forever, a person "eats of this bread . . . and the bread that I shall give is My flesh, which I shall give for the life of the world."

The crowds, which had been quick to see a parallel with Moses in Jesus' provision of the bread they'd eaten the day before, were now unable to get beyond the literal meaning of His words. "The Jews" (for now the religious elite were involved in the debate) "quarreled among themselves, saying, 'How can this Man give us His flesh to eat?'" (v. 52).

Jesus continued, insisting that only one who "eats My flesh and drinks My blood has eternal life" (v. 54). It is a by-faith participation in Christ's death that saves, and this participation alone.

❖

BIBLE BACKGROUND:

HARD SAYINGS OF JESUS

"He who eats My flesh and drinks My blood abides in Me, and I in Him" (John 6:56).

J. F. Strombeck explains. "This is figurative language illustrating spiritual truth. To eat and drink is to partake of that which sustains life. By the vital process of digestion and assimilation that which one eats and drinks becomes a part of his physical self. To eat His flesh and drink His blood is to partake of Him so that He becomes as vital and inseparable a part of one's spiritual self as the food becomes a part of the body." [Bsac-96:381-Jan 39-112]

We partake of Jesus by faith, and as we do He becomes a part of us and we of Him.

The response of the crowds (John 6:60–71). The text tells us that "many of His disciples, when they heard this . . . went back and walked with Him no more" (vv. 60, 66). It's important to note that the term "disciple" is used in more than one way in the New Testament. The twelve men we typically call "the Disciples" were individuals Jesus chose and trained for leadership in the church. Here however "disciple" is used in the general sense of a follower or adherent of a school of thought. As Jesus began His ministry, He initially attracted many adherents or followers. But as Jesus' teachings became more and more difficult, and as Jesus spoke more and more clearly about His identity, many fell away.

Even the Twelve complained about the difficulty in understanding (and accepting?) Jesus' presentation of Himself as the Bread of life (v. 61). Even they missed the life-giving power of the analogy. But when asked if they too would go away, Peter spoke up for them all. "Lord, to whom shall we go? You have the words of eternal life. Also we have come to believe and know that You are the Christ, the Son of the living God" (vv. 68, 69).

It's good to remember these words when we're troubled by teachings we can't quite understand. All too many are ready to stand in judgment on God's Word, and to reject what they do not fully understand. Yet when doubts arise, the appropriate question remains, "To whom will we go if we turn away from Jesus? Where else can we hope to find truth? There is no one, no place at all, for Jesus, the Christ, the Son of the Living God, has the words of eternal life."

JESUS, THE LIGHT OF THE WORLD (JOHN 8)

Jesus' public claim to be "the Light of the world" sparked yet another angry debate with the religious leaders. His words were,"I am the light of the world. He who follows Me shall not walk in darkness, but have the light of life" (John 8:12).

In a discussion of symbolism in John's Gospel, Merrill C. Tenny writes,

The figures of light and darkness define the plot of the Gospel, for they represent the opposing powers of righteousness and evil, and the contrasting results of belief and unbelief. In the introductory words of the Prologue the light of life is the life that was manifest in Christ. Through Him the divine radiance was focused on the world as a searchlight plays on a dark landscape (1:4–5). . . . Sin and its consequent estrangement may have produced a twilight in which the way of life had become obscure, but Christ provided the illumination necessary to lead men back to God. [Bsac V121 #481 Jan 64-15]

Jesus' presentation of Himself as the Light of the world was a powerful affirmation that only those who follow Him might truly understand the issues of life. All who failed to follow Jesus would stumble about in the dark; only those who whose eyes were opened by Him would walk in the light.

Jesus' claim caused an immediate and hostile reaction from the Pharisees, who were sure that they themselves were God's gift to the blind!

The Pharisees first objected to Jesus' claim on legal grounds. Any claim supported by only one witness was not valid in a Jewish court, and Jesus was bearing witness to Himself (John 8:13). Jesus responded to this charge as He had responded earlier (see the discussion of John 5:31–39, on page 28). God the Father joined Jesus in presenting Him as the Light of the world.

It was Jesus' reference to God the Father that brought the debate into fresh, significant focus.

"You know neither Me nor My Father" (8:19–24). Jesus' statement that His Father bore witness to the truth of His claim was met with a sarcastic retort: "Where is Your Father?" (v. 19). Since the Father was not available to appear in court, the Jews implied, whatever Jesus said should be disregarded.

The truth, Jesus responded, was that the religious leaders did not know Jesus—although they supposed they did. If they had known Him they would also have known the Father.

These were fighting words, for Jesus' claim of a special relationship with God was always regarded as blasphemous (see, for example, John 5:18). Yet despite the fact that Jesus had spoken publicly, "no one laid hands on Him" (8:20).

BIBLE BACKGROUND:

GOD AS FATHER IN JUDAISM

The Old Testament contains references to God's father-like love for Israel. Psalm 103:13 reminds Israel, "As a Father pities his children, so the LORD pities those who fear Him." But it is not until the first and second centuries that rabbinic writings speak of God as Israel's Father. Thus Rabbi Eleaar ben Azariah argued that one should never say he chooses what is right because he has no desire to do wrong. Commenting on Leviticus 20:26, Azariah wrote, "He should say, I have the desire, but

what shall I do, since my Father in heaven has laid a prohibition on me."

But if first-century rabbis spoke of God as a Father in heaven, why the reaction when Jesus claimed God as His Father? The answer seems to lie in the fact that imbedded in the Old Testament concept of "Father" is the notion of source or origin. "Father Abraham" bore the title because he was the founder of the Jewish people. Yet God too was the One who brought Israel into being. As long as God was viewed as Father in this sense, as the creator of the nation, there seems to have been no problem in speaking of Him as Father, or even "our Father."

But Jesus' claims went beyond this. Jesus claimed a unique relationship with God, and His references to God as His Father were understood as a claim of equality with God (John 5:18). In John 8, as we will see, the Jews' assumptions about God and their relationship with Him are open to further challenge!

Intensifying the conflict, Jesus announced that the religious leaders of Israel would die in their sins if they did not believe that He was indeed the Light of the World.

"Who are you?" (John 8:25–30). Jesus did not bother to answer the question the Jews then asked. Christ had presented Himself to Israel as the Messiah and as God's Son "from the beginning." But Jesus did add one thing. When they had lifted up (crucified) the Son of Man they would know that Jesus was who He claimed to be. As Paul writes in the opening verses of Romans, the cross and the empty tomb served as God's unmistakable stamp of approval on all that Jesus claimed about Himself. For Jesus, who was "born of the seed of David according to the flesh" was later "declared to be the Son of God with power according to the Spirit of holiness, by the resurrection from the dead" (Rom. 1:3, 4).

"You shall know the truth" (John 8:30–32). This time Jesus' words had convinced many in the crowd, and they believed on Him. The words in John 8:31, 32 then are addressed to those who believe, and not to the lost. Christ said, "If you abide in My word, you are My disciples indeed. And you shall know the truth, and the truth shall make you free."

These verses are not a warning but a promise. Jesus is not suggesting that those who believe might fail to abide and be lost. Jesus is talking about discipleship. Those who take Jesus' words to heart, who live by them daily, are His true disciples. Such persons will know the truth, for they will experience it; and those who live in the realm of God's truth are set free. The rest of humankind will stumble about in darkness, never able to discern the path that leads to health and wholeness. Jesus' disciples, walking in His light, will be free indeed.

Slaves of sin (John 8:33–36). These words about freedom further aroused the ire of the Jews. Why, to be made free implied that they were slaves! "We are Abraham's descendants, and have never been in bondage to anyone" (v. 33).

The objection was foolish on its face. Never in bondage? What about the Roman soldiers stationed in the Fortress Antonia, standing beside the Jerusalem temple itself? For centuries Jews lived as a subject people ruled by pagans. Never in bondage to anyone? Patently untrue!

But Jesus was speaking of spiritual rather than political bondage, and responded, "Whoever commits sin is a slave of sin" (v. 34). There is an interesting feature of Roman law that speaks to Jesus' comment. In Roman law a person might become a slave by being born to a slave, by being sold into slavery by parents, or by capture in war. However, a free man who chose to submit to another as master, and

thus to act *as if he were a slave,* might actually become a slave.

What then about those Jews who claimed to be free men? Whatever claim they might make of piety, every one had committed sins. And by so doing, they had become slaves of sin.

Only the Son of God, come in the flesh, could set free those who had become slaves of sin. And unless they—and we also—turn to Him, "you will die in your sins" (v. 24).

Two families of mankind (John 8:37–47). This further infuriated the Jews, but before they could speak out, Christ continued.

Biological and spiritual descent (vv. 37–39). "I know that you are Abraham's descendants, but you seek to kill Me. . . . I speak what I have seen with My Father, and you do what you have seen with your father." The Jews might be biological descendants of Abraham, but spiritually they bore no resemblance to him at all.

This line of argument was devastating, for as noted earlier, the individual Jews assumed that they had standing with God because of their descent from Abraham. They were sure that the merit Abraham had gained with God was sufficient to cover the shortcomings of the millions of Jews who sprang from him. There was no question in the religious leaders' minds that a descendant of Abraham who made an honest effort to keep Moses' Law would *have to be* accepted by God.

But now Jesus was making a distinction between biological descent from Abraham and spiritual descent. It is no wonder the Jews immediately objected: "Abraham is our father" (v. 39). They would permit no distinction between biological and spiritual descent from the patriarch.

The test of family resemblance (8:39-43). But the proof of Jesus' distinction was implicit in the way the Jews responded to

Spiritually the test of family membership is relationship with Jesus, not biological descent.

❖

the truth. When Abraham heard God's Word, Abraham believed and accepted it wholeheartedly. When Jesus came—the Prophet like Moses—and told Israel the truth, the Jews tried to kill Him! "Abraham did not do this" (v. 40).

The conclusion Jesus drew followed directly. If the Jews' response to revelation was to reject it and seek to kill the Messenger, there was no way that they could be Abraham's offspring. Their response showed that they must belong to a totally different family.

Again the Jews protested. "We have one Father—God" (v. 41). And again Jesus applied the test. If God were their Father they would have loved Jesus, for Jesus had been sent by God (v. 42). The Jews' reaction to Jesus showed conclusively that they were not related to Abraham or to Abraham's God.

Your father the devil (John 8:44–47). Since reaction to revelation is the test of family membership, who do the Jewish leaders most resemble? Whose action set the pattern for their rejection of Jesus? The answer is clear from Scripture. Satan had set the pattern of rebellion against God and of refusal to submit to Him. In rejecting Jesus, the Jews were acting just as Satan had behaved in rejecting submission to God! And when the Jews tried to kill Jesus, they provided proof positive that Satan was their spiritual father.

You are of your father the devil, and the desires of your father you want to do. He was a murderer from the beginning, and does not stand in the truth, because there is no truth in him. When he speaks a lie, he speaks from his own resources, for he is a liar and the father of it (v. 44).

Summing up, Jesus explained, "He who is of God hears God's words; therefore you do not hear, because you are not of God" (v. 47).

❖

BIBLE BACKGROUND:
HARD SAYINGS OF JESUS

"You are of your father the devil" (John 8:44)

It's popular to speak of the "universal fatherhood of God" and claim that all human beings are God's children. It is true that in one sense, as Paul says in Acts 17:28, "we are also His offspring." God is the source of the human race, and each individual can trace his or her very existence back to the creative act of God. He is our Father, in the sense of our Creator, and in that sense we are His offspring But when we use Father in the sense of head of His family, the situation is very different. God is the Father of some, not all. He is the Father of those who have received Jesus as Savior, and have thus been given the right to become the sons of God (John 1:12).

It is this distinction that Jesus focuses on in John 8. The person who is God's child in that family sense loves Jesus and responds to God's words (John 8:42, 47). The person who does not love Jesus or respond to the words of God is a member of another family entirely. And the spiritual head of that family is Satan himself.

There are two and only two families of mankind—those who are Christians, and those who are not. And however angry it may make those who are not Christians to hear it, however moral or upright their lives may seem to be, their rejection of Jesus undoubtedly means that they are Satan's own.

"Before Abraham was, I AM" (John 8:48–57). Jesus' analysis was utterly devastating. Unable to argue with Jesus, the Jews tried to discredit Him. They claimed that Jesus must be a Samaritan, pretending to be a Jew. And what's more, He must be demon-possessed (v. 48)!

Jesus simply repeated His claims, adding "if anyone keeps My word he shall never see death" (v. 51).

The leaders jumped on this statement. Abraham was dead. The prophets were dead. Was Jesus making Himself out to be greater than these dead heroes of the faith?

Jesus answered that Abraham had rejoiced to see His day and was glad. The Jews quickly pointed to this statement as an obviously false note in Jesus' teaching. Jesus wasn't even fifty years old. How could Abraham, who had died nearly 2,000 years before Jesus was born, have seen Jesus' day?

Christ's answer was simple, decisive, and totally consistent with everything He had been saying. "Most assuredly, I say to you, before Abraham was, I AM" (v. 58). Those capitalized letters tell us exactly what Christ was saying. The Old Testament's personal name of God, Yahweh, was constructed on the Hebrew verb for "to be," and is often translated "I AM." How could Abraham have seen Jesus'

day? Yes, Abraham had died long before Jesus was born. But Jesus existed long before Abraham lived! For Jesus was the great I AM, Yahweh Himself, the God the Jews assumed they worshiped, come in the flesh to live among them.

And rather than worship Him, the Jews picked up stones intending to kill Him.

There was no mistake. Jesus presented Himself to His own people as God the Son. And their reaction to the Savior revealed that this generation had no place in the family of God.

JESUS, THE GOOD SHEPHERD (JOHN 10)

From the time of Abraham the people of Israel had raised sheep and cattle. Understanding of the relationship between sheep and shepherds was deeply imbedded in the culture and in the Old Testament. It was natural that the term *shepherd* should be used to represent a spiritual overseer who would care for his congregation as a shepherd cared for his sheep. Thus there are frequent allusions in both Testaments to this spiritual relationship (Ps. 23:1; 80:1; Isa. 40:11; 63:14; Jer. 31:10; Eph. 4:11; 1 Peter 5:1–4). Even political leaders are at times called shepherds (Isa. 44:28; 63:11).

Biblical images of Christ as Shepherd are linked with three time periods. As the Good Shepherd, Christ gives His life for His sheep (Ps. 22; John 10:11, 15). As the Great Shepherd, Christ cares for His sheep today (Heb. 13:20; John 10). And Jesus will come again as the Chief Shepherd, to establish God's rule on earth (1 Peter 5:4). In Jesus' discussion of Himself as the fulfillment of the shepherd image, Christ once again publicly asserted His claim to be the Son of God and the Savior of His people.

The Good Shepherd discourse again is set in Jerusalem. And again it was stimulated by a challenge from Pharisees. Jesus had given sight to a man who had been born blind, and despite the careful examination of

Jesus' analogy of Himself as the shepherd of God's sheep communicated many spiritual realities.

the man and witnesses, the religious elite refused to acknowledge the miracle as evidence authenticating Jesus as God's messenger. Their adamant refusal to believe led Jesus to present His claims again, using the analogy of shepherd and sheep.

BIBLE BACKGROUND:
HARD SAYINGS OF JESUS

"If you were blind, you would have no sin; but now you say 'We see.' Therefore your sin remains." (John 9:41).

Jesus had just healed a blind man, a motif prominent in the prophets (Isa. 42:16–19; Jer. 5:21). Yet the Pharisees refused to accept the evidence of Jesus' healing, all the time

claiming spiritual insight. Only if they were willing to acknowledge their previous and continuing blindness could their eyes be opened. Deliberate rejection of the light makes forgiveness of sin impossible.

THE SHEPHERD ANALOGY (JOHN 10:1–5)

Jesus' illustration contrasts Himself and the Pharisees and the other religious elite of Judea.

Jesus entered by the door (John 10:1–2). During winter sheep were kept in walled pens. There was a single door through which the shepherd entered the pen. Anyone trying to gain access by climbing over the wall was "a thief and a robber." Jesus had come as the Old Testament had predicted, authenticated by miraculous signs. Clearly, having entered by the door, He must be the true Shepherd of the sheep.

Jesus is recognized by doorkeeper and sheep (John 10:3–5). During winter several flocks were typically kept in one pen. A shepherd whose flock was in that pen would be known to the doorkeeper. The true shepherd then "calls his own sheep by name and leads them out" (v. 3).

The relationship between a shepherd and his sheep was a personal one. Shepherds knew each sheep and named them, and sheep recognized the voice of their shepherd. They would follow the familiar voice, but would not follow the voice of a stranger.

When Jesus appeared, those who were truly His recognized His voice and followed Him. They did not need the attesting miracles. Tuned to the Shepherd's voice, God's sheep recognized Jesus as the Messiah and responded to Him. The failure of the Pharisees and other religious leaders to respond to Jesus' voice showed that they were not God's sheep at all.

THE ANALOGY EXPLAINED (JOHN 10:6–18)

The analogy puzzled Jesus' hearers, so He went on to specifically identify several elements.

Jesus as the door (John 10:7–10). When in the fields, shepherds sheltered their sheep in a rough pen, often made of thorn bushes. At night the shepherd slept in the doorway, the single point of access to the sheep, to protect them from marauding animals. His own body served as the door of the sheep

and guaranteed their security. All those who had come before Jesus claiming to be deliverers were actually "thieves and robbers," eager to exploit the sheep rather than guard them. But the true sheep did not respond to their voice.

Jesus' motives are far different than those of the false deliverers. Jesus came determined to save the sheep rather than exploit them. Those who recognize His voice and pass through the door will be saved. This is the greatest difference between Jesus and all others: "I have come that they may have life, and that they may have it more abundantly" (v. 10).

Jesus as the Good Shepherd (John 10:11–18). Now Jesus reveals what is implied in His coming as the Good Shepherd. In the process Jesus contrasts Himself and the religious leaders of His day, who were mere hirelings.

- The Good Shepherd gives His life for the sheep (vv. 11, 15).
- The hireling doesn't care about the sheep but will abandon them when danger threatens (vv. 12, 13).
- The Good Shepherd knows His sheep and is recognized by them (v. 14).
- The Good Shepherd is loved by the Father because He lays down His life for the sheep (v. 17).
- The Good Shepherd sacrifices Himself voluntarily; His life is not taken from Him (v. 18).
- The Good Shepherd lays down His life in response to the command received from the Father (v. 18).

In the process of developing the stated and implicit contrasts between Himself and the religious leaders, Jesus again spoke of God as "My Father." He claimed both to be known by the Father and to know Him (vv. 14, 15).

BIBLE BACKGROUND:
HARD SAYINGS OF JESUS

"Other sheep I have which are not of this fold" (John 10:16).

Some have taken the "other sheep" to which Jesus refers as followers of other religions. In biblical and historic context, "this fold" clearly refers to the Jews who recognized Jesus' voice and followed Him. The "other sheep" were Gentiles who later responded to the gospel message. As the context clearly establishes Jesus as the door, and emphasizes recognition of *His voice* as the test by which His sheep are distinguished, the notion that the "other sheep" are followers of other religions is clearly specious.

JESUS AS GOD THE SON
(JOHN 10:25–38)

The miracle of healing the man born blind and Jesus' Good Shepherd analogy reached a number of His listeners, and the debate intensified. Jesus was then followed by a number of "the Jews" [the religious leaders] who demanded, "If You are the Christ, tell us plainly" (v. 24).

Jesus and the Father (John 10:25–30). Jesus carefully explained again what He had been teaching. Jesus' works (miracles) had already authenticated His claims. The reason that the Jews didn't believe Jesus was the Messiah was that they were not "My sheep." As for His sheep, Jesus will give them eternal life. He can do this because Jesus' sheep were given to Him by the Father. Jesus concluded, "I and My Father are one" (v. 30).

The Jews try to stone Jesus again (John 10:31–34). Rather than accept Jesus' words, the Jews accuse Him of blasphemy, "because You, being a Man, make Yourself God" (v. 33).

BIBLE BACKGROUND:
HARD SAYINGS OF JESUS

"He called them gods, to whom the word of God came" (John 10:35)

The Jews had condemned Jesus for calling Himself the Son of God. Jesus now confounded them by pointing to a reference in Psalm 82, in which the psalmist condemns unjust judges. These were men who should have administered justice according to God's Law, thus representing His will to the people. From the psalm Jesus pointed out that even sinful human beings who had been commissioned by God were given the courtesy title of "gods" (82:6). If such persons, who failed to do the will of God, could bear the divine title, how could the Jews condemn Jesus for claiming to be the unique Son of God, when His works (miracles) demonstrated conclusively that God was with Him?

Clearly Jesus' contemporaries understood Him to claim deity. Again, whatever men today might say about Jesus, there is no doubt that He identified Himself as God the Son, one with God the Father.

Summing up, we see from the Gospels that Jesus, the Prophet like Moses who came to set sacred history on a new direction,

- Claimed to be the promised Messiah (Luke 4:14–30; John 4).
- Claimed to be the Son of God, the Savior of the world (John 3; John 5).
- Claimed to be the Bread of Life, come from heaven to provide eternal life (John 6).

- Claimed to be the Light of the world, the "I AM" [Yahweh] of the Old Testament (John 8)
- Claimed to be the Good Shepherd, one with God the Father, come to die for His sheep (John 10).

As we continue on in this study, we do so in the firm conviction that Jesus' teachings truly are authoritative, for the words of Jesus are the words of God Himself.

JESUS' KINGDOM CHALLENGE

Matthew describes the beginning of Jesus' public ministry with the comment, "From that time Jesus began to preach and to say, 'Repent, for the kingdom of heaven is at hand'" (4:17). Mark adds his testimony. "After John was put in prison, Jesus came to Galilee preaching the gospel of the kingdom of God, and saying, 'The time is fulfilled, and the kingdom of God is at hand. Repent, and believe in the gospel'" (1:14, 15).

Clearly much of Jesus' early ministry focused on this phenomenon called the "kingdom of God"—and just as clearly it was gospel, good news, that Jesus announced. But what was this kingdom of which Jesus spoke? In what sense was it "at hand"? And in what sense was it Good News?

The Gospels mention the kingdom of God or the kingdom of heaven eighty-five times. All but two of these are found in direct or indirect quotes from Jesus. Clearly the kingdom had a significant role in Jesus' teaching. Some have tried to distinguish the kingdom of heaven, an expression found thirty-two times in Matthew's Gospel, from the kingdom of God, the term used in the other Gospels. However, Matthew was writing to the Jews. And the Jews showed great reverence for God's name, frequently substituting "heaven" for the name of the deity out of respect. For these reasons, and because the arguments in favor of a distinction are so weak, it's best for us to understand Matthew, Mark, and Luke to be dealing with the same concept when speaking of the kingdom of heaven and the kingdom of God. Therefore, the many references to this kingdom make it important to determine what it is that Jesus means when He uses the phrase "kingdom of God."

THE KINGDOM OF GOD IN THE OLD TESTAMENT

The concept of the kingdom of God, central in Jesus' teachings, is well established in the Old Testament, even though the phrase itself is never found there. What we do find in the Old Testament is a distinctive concept of "kingdom," the conviction that the kingdom of God is an eternal, universal, and yet present reality, and the belief that the full establishment of the kingdom of God on earth lies ahead in the future.

THE CONCEPT OF "KINGDOM"

Today we're used to thinking of a kingdom, like a nation, as a geographical entity. It is an identifiable territory with its own government, laws, language, and customs.

An important difference, however, is basic to the biblical concept. The *New International Encyclopedia of Bible Words* (Zondervan, p. 377) points out that "in the Old Testament, 'kingdom' is best expressed by the idea of reign or sovereignty. One's kingdom is the people or things over which he or she has authority or control." We see this concept in Psalm 103:19: "The LORD has established His throne in heaven, and His kingdom rules over all." There may be no distinct territory. There may be no recognized body of laws, no common customs, no unified language, and those who live within the kingdom may not even acknowledge its existence. But because God reigns, and because ultimately all is under His control, it is appropriate to speak of the universe itself as His kingdom.

GOD'S ETERNAL, UNIVERSAL, AND PRESENT KINGDOM

The Old Testament contains many expressions honoring God as ruler of all. Such verses portray the Lord as exercising sovereignty over a kingdom that is eternal, universal, and yet present.

Note these three themes in the following Old Testament verses.

The kingdom imagery in the Bible emphasizes God's rule in the lives of His people.

All Your works shall praise you, O LORD,
And Your saints shall bless You.
They shall speak of the glory of Your
  kingdom,
And talk of Your power,
To make known to the sons of men His
  mighty acts,
And the glorious majesty of His kingdom.
Your kingdom is an everlasting kingdom,
And Your dominion endures throughout
  all generations
  (Ps. 145:10–13).

How great are His signs, and how mighty
  His wonders!
His kingdom is an everlasting kingdom,
And His dominion is from generation to
  generation.
Daniel 4:3

Additional testimony is found in Exodus 15:18—"The LORD shall reign forever and ever"—and especially in the coronation psalms that celebrate God's enthronement.

> Sing praises to God, sing praises!
> Sing praises to our King, sing praises!
> For God is the King of all the earth;
> Sing praises with understanding.
> God reigns over the nations;
> God sits on His holy throne.
>   Psalm 47:6–8

> The LORD reigns, He is clothed with
>   majesty;
> The LORD is clothed,
> He has girded Himself with strength.
> Surely the world is established, so that it
>   cannot be moved.
> Your throne is established from of old;
> You are from everlasting.
>   Psalm 93:1, 2

The nations may not acknowledge God's rule or submit to Him, and yet God *is* in control, and the entire universe is His everlasting kingdom.

THE KINGDOM'S FUTURE

While the Old Testament celebrates the hidden rule of God over all things, Old Testament prophets portray a time when the Lord's rule will be visible and acknowledged by all. This future expression of the kingdom of God is tightly linked to the appearance of God's anointed, the Messiah. While in one sense God rules now and always, Zechariah looks forward to a day when "the LORD shall be King over all the earth. In that day it shall be— "The LORD is one," and His name is one" (14:9).

The association of this future kingdom with the Messiah is found in multiplied passages. For instance, Isaiah 9:6, 7 predicts,

> For unto us a Child is born,
> Unto us a Son is given;

> And the government will be upon His
>   shoulder.
> And His name will be called Wonderful,
>   Counselor,
> Mighty God, Everlasting Father, Prince
>   of Peace.
> Of the increase of His government and
>   peace
> There will be no end.
> Upon the throne of David and over His
>   kingdom,
> To order it and establish it with judg-
>   ment and justice
> From that time forward, even forever.
>   Isaiah 9:6, 7

Daniel, in interpreting a dream of King Nebuchadnezzar, also envisioned the day when God's kingdom rule would take on visible form. Daniel told the Babylonian ruler of a future day when "the God of heaven will set up a kingdom which shall never be destroyed; and the kingdom shall not be left to other people; it shall break in pieces and consume all these kingdoms, and it shall stand forever" (Dan. 2:44).

To show how pervasive is the theme a future earthly expression of the kingdom of God, here is a partial list of prophetic passages that deal with it: Is. 2:1–4; 4:2–6; 11:1–13; 24:1–23; 32:1–5; 33:17–24; 35:1–10; 52:7–10; 60:1–61:6; 66:15–23; Jer. 31:27–34; 33:14–26; Ezek. 20:33–42; 34:20–31; Dan. 2:31–45; 7:1–28; 9:20–27; Hosea 3:4, 5; Joel 2:28–3:2; 3:9–21; Amos 9:9–15; Obad. 15–21; Micah 4:1–5; Zech. 2:1–13; 14:1–21; Mal. 3:1–5; 4:1–6.

It's clear that the concept of the kingdom of God and two of its expressions are established in the Old Testament. The first and foundational expression of the kingdom of God is found in affirmations that God is King over all the earth, in the sense of being in sovereign control of all. His kingdom may be hidden to all except those who view it through the eyes of faith, but it is real nevertheless.

The second expression of the kingdom of God found in the Old Testament is imbedded in prophecy. Those men who spoke God's word looked forward to a future time when God's kingdom would take on visible expression. The day was coming when God, in the person of His Messiah, would establish the rule of God on earth and command the obedience of all.

A powerful messianic psalm envisions the day when God will "set My king on My holy hill of Zion." The psalmist continues,

> "I will declare the decree;
> The LORD has said to Me,
> 'You are My Son,
> Today I have begotten You.
> Ask of Me, and I will give You
> The nations for Your inheritance,
> And the ends of the earth for
>   Your possession.
> You shall break them with a rod of iron;
> You shall dash them to pieces
>   like a potter's vessel.'"
> Now therefore, be wise, O kings;
> Be instructed, you judges of the earth.
> Serve the LORD with fear,
> And rejoice with trembling.
>   (Ps. 2:7–11)

God's rule may be hidden throughout most of human history. But God will break into history to establish His kingdom here on earth. In view of that coming day of God's iron rule, this world's kings and judges would be wise to serve the Lord with fear!

JESUS AND THE KINGDOM OF GOD

As noted above, the kingdom of God was a prominent theme in Jesus' teaching. Some see it as the dominant theme. Jesus is quoted referring to the kingdom of heaven or the kingdom of God eighty-two of the eighty-five times "kingdom" is mentioned

in the Gospels. These phrases are uniquely His.

The questions that we need to answer are, "What did this phrase mean to Jesus?" and, "How did He use it?" There's little question that when Jesus spoke of the kingdom of God or the kingdom of heaven, His hearers, steeped in Old Testament lore, imagined that Jesus was speaking of the earthly kingdom foretold by the prophets. Even after His resurrection, Jesus' disciples asked if He was about to "restore the kingdom to Israel," an unmistakable reference to the prophet's vision (Acts 1:6). Jesus' response is significant. He did not suggest that the Old Testament vision had been in error or was now set aside. Instead Jesus simply commented that the *time* of fulfillment was in the Father's hands. Rather than being concerned about the promised earthly kingdom, Jesus told His disciples to wait in Jerusalem for the coming of the Holy Spirit, after which their focus would be giving witness to Him throughout the world (Acts 1:7, 8).

Something fascinating had taken place. Jesus had come announcing that the kingdom of God was at hand. And yet the kingdom of which He spoke seems to fit neither of the Old Testament expressions of that kingdom!

At this point we need to return to a point made earlier. Jesus clearly fulfilled Moses' promise of a prophet like himself whom God would send, and to whom God's people were to listen. As we noted, that prophet would set sacred history on a new and unexpected course. And it seems clear that in speaking of the kingdom of heaven, or the kingdom of God, Jesus introduced *a new and unexpected form of God's kingdom here on earth.*

It also will become clear that much of Jesus' public teaching concerned the new expression of the kingdom of God that Jesus initiated. This is especially true as we explore Jesus' Sermon on the Mount and Sermon on the Plain, and Jesus' parables, as

Jesus' Sermon on the Mount established the principles on which His kingdom is based.

well as a number of Jesus' kingdom sayings. So in this chapter we'll focus on what I've called Jesus' kingdom challenge—a challenge presented in Christ's most famous public sermon.

TWO SERMONS, NOT ONE

Matthew 5–7 is known as Jesus' "Sermon on the Mount." The reason is simple. Matthew 5 begins, "And seeing the multitudes, He went up on a mountain, and when He was seated His disciples came to Him" (5:1). It's important to note here that "disciples" is used in the general sense of "followers" or "adherents," rather than in the specific sense of

"the Twelve." We know this from Matthew 7:28, which tells us that when Jesus had finished, "the people were astonished at His teaching." The Sermon on the Mount, then, was public teaching, not private instruction given to the twelve men He was training for leadership.

Two blocks of teaching which parallel the content of the Sermon on the Mount are found in Luke's Gospel. One of these is contained in Luke 6, and the other in Luke 12. Luke 6 so closely parallels Matthew 6 that some have suggested it is Luke's report of the same event.

However, this assumption is both unlikely and unnecessary. It is unlikely because Luke 6:17 describes the setting clearly: "He came down with them and stood on a level place with a crowd of His disciples." The settings of the Sermon on the Mount and what some call the Sermon on the Plain are clearly distinct. The notion that these are two different reports of the same event is also unnecessary. Jesus lived and taught in Galilee and Judea for at least three years. Anyone who has ever had an itinerant ministry knows that when traveling a basic message will be repeated over and over again, usually with some variation. It is beyond question that the basic themes emphasized by Jesus in His teaching were repeated time after time. Jesus undoubtedly preached the same sermons again and again during the early months of. His ministry, and just as undoubtedly He did not repeat Himself word for word.

This last point helps us when we place passages side by side and note differences. Rather than trouble us as so-called discrepancies, the differences can help! For instance, Matthew 7:11 quotes Jesus as saying "If you then, being evil, know how to give good gifts to your children, how much more will your Father who is in heaven give good things to those who ask Him?" The parallel passage in Luke 11:13 reads, "If you then, being evil, know how to give good gifts to your children, how much more will your heavenly Father give the Holy Spirit to those who ask Him?" Does the difference here between "give good gifts" and "give the Holy Spirit" mean that one of the two gospel writers has misquoted Jesus? Or is it more likely that Jesus made this point a number of times, and that the saying in Luke can be used to help us interpret the "good gifts" Jesus had in mind when uttering what Matthew records?

For anyone with a high view of Scripture, the notion that such differences represent errors in Scripture is unacceptable. For anyone who has spoken often and in different settings, the variation is easily explained. And for anyone who understands that we are to use Scripture to inter-

pret Scripture, the variations become keys to help us better understand Jesus' message.

With this in mind, we need to look closely at the Sermon on the Mount, the most complete and coherent record of Jesus' early teaching.

THE KINGDOM EMPHASIS

The Sermon on the Mount is intimately related to what Jesus had to say about the kingdom of heaven. There are several indications that this is the case.

The Beatitudes are about the kingdom (Matt. 5:3–10). The sermon begins with a presentation of what is known as the Beatitudes. The first and the last Beatitude each state "for theirs is the kingdom of heaven." The fact that both the first and the last in this series contain the same phrase is the mark of a literary device known as "inclusio," and indicates that the kingdom is the subject of each item in the series. Thus each beatitude is making some statement about life in the kingdom of heaven.

The commandments are about the kingdom (Matt. 5:19, 20). In the Sermon on the Mount Jesus sets out to establish the true meaning of the commandments imbedded in the earlier revelation, the Old Testament. He warns that even those who are most righteous according to the present understanding of the commandments "will by no means enter the kingdom of heaven."

Jesus' listeners are to seek first the kingdom of heaven (Matthew 6:33). Rather than give priority even to the necessities that support life in this world, Christ's listeners are to concentrate on seeking the kingdom of heaven.

Entry into the kingdom of heaven depends on doing the will of Jesus' Father in heaven (Matthew 7:21). It is not what people say about Jesus, even calling Him "Lord, Lord" that counts. Participation in the kingdom of heaven calls for us to do the will of God.

While these references do not in themselves tell us what Jesus means by "kingdom of heaven," they do tell us that the Sermon on the Mount is about this kingdom that Jesus proclaims, and about life in that kingdom.

It's helpful here to note that some have tried to force Jesus' teaching in the Sermon on the Mount into the Old Testament framework and argue that these teachings relate to the Messianic kingdom the Old Testament indicates is to come. Others have seen the Sermon on the Mount as a new Law, setting higher standards of living for Christians. Neither of these views does justice to Jesus' teaching about the kingdom of God, nor should the kingdom be identified with the Church. As we will see, Jesus' kingdom teachings have universal application for those of any era who seek to live in harmony with the will of God. Yet they also have special application to you and me, for we are called today to live as citizens of that new expression of God's kingdom which was inaugurated when Jesus came.

THE SERMON ON THE MOUNT

For an introduction to the kingdom of God in Jesus' teaching we need to carefully work our way through Jesus' Sermon on the Mount.

The Beatitudes (Matt. 5:3–10). The Greek word Jesus used to characterize the individuals He describes is *makarios*, which means "blessed." There is a clear distinction between being blessed and being happy, a distinction lost in the title of a recent book on this passage entitled *The Be Happy Attitudes*. In Matthew the believer is blessed by God, in the sense of being approved by God. He is also blessed in the sense of being rewarded by Him. But there is no promise here of "happiness."

At the same time, it's true that the beatitudes do describe the attitudes, or the values and commitments, of the person who is blessed. In the Beatitudes we have a description of the inner man, not a list of the things the blessed (approved) individual does or does not do. Thus at the very beginning of the Sermon on the Mount Jesus challenges his listeners to look inward for marks of the kingdom of God, rather than to look at externals.

What then are the attitudes or values of which God approves, and which convey their own blessings?

Blessed are the poor in spirit, for theirs is the kingdom of God (v. 3). Isaiah 66:2 helps us understand this verse. God says through the prophet, "On this one will I look: on him who is poor and of a contrite spirit, and who trembles at My word." The poor in spirit are deeply aware of their spiritual poverty and conscious of their utter dependence on God. Theirs is the kingdom of God, for utter and complete dependence on God is the key to living in His kingdom.

Blessed are those who mourn, for they shall be comforted (v. 4). In Jesus' day it was customary to hire professional mourners to accompany a funeral procession. We can imagine many who, while busily wailing and shrieking, inwardly rejoiced as they counted their earnings. But here Jesus speaks of those who are deeply moved by the condition of society and the plight of others. It is also true that it is the person who truly cares about others who will be comforted. Not only do they look forward to God's ultimate setting right of all things, they are the ones who reach out to others to offer help. In being others-centered rather than self-centered we discover the blessing of God.

Blessed are the meek, for they shall inherit the earth (v. 5). Meekness is a trait

It's hard for us to grasp that mourning is a source of blessing.

celebrated in Scripture (2 Cor. 10:1; Gal. 5:22, 23; Col. 3:12; James 1:19–21). Far from weakness, meekness speaks of a way of relating to God and others that abandons the drive for success at the expense of others in favor of concern for the benefit of others. While the blessing, "they shall inherit the earth," will be fulfilled literally in the future, there's a sense in which it is fulfilled in our daily lives now. The meek person is not driven by materialistic desires, and thus the meek can find contentment in whatever God has given them to enjoy.

"Blessed are those who hunger and thirst for righteousness, for they shall be filled" (v. 6). The blessed person feels intensely that he can't get along without righteousness. He hungers and thirsts to know and to do God's will. It is this kind of person who will be filled, and find fulfillment. Only in doing God's will can the deepest longings of the human heart be satisfied.

"Blessed are the merciful, for they shall obtain mercy" (v. 7). Mercy in Scripture is a loving response motivated by another's need and helplessness. Those who are merciful are sensitive to the deepest needs of others, for they recognize that they too are needy. It is the awareness of their own needs that lead the merciful to look to God, who is "rich in mercy, because of His great love with which He loved us" (Eph. 2:4).

BIBLE BACKGROUND:

THE BEATITUDES: MATTHEW 5:3–10

Nelson's *Illustrated Bible Handbook* suggests another way of looking at the Beatitudes, seeing them as kingdom values versus the cultural values which dominate in all human societies. Here are the contrasting value systems, suggested on page 472 of that book.

Jesus' values	Cultural Values
Blessed are those who . . .	*Blessed are those who are. . .*
(v. 3) are poor in spirit	self-confident
	competent
	self-reliant
(v. 4) mourn	pleasure-seeking
	hedonistic
	"the beautiful people"
(v. 5) are meek	proud
	powerful
	important
(v. 6) hunger for righteousness	satisfied
	"well-adjusted"
	practical
(v. 7) are merciful	self-righteous
	able to take care of
	themselves
(v. 8) are pure in heart	"adult"
	sophisticated
	broadminded
(v. 9) are peacemakers	competitive
	aggressive
(v. 10) are persecuted because	adaptable
of righteousness	popular
	"don't rock the boat"

Blessed are the pure in heart, for they shall see God (v. 8). Jesus warned his listeners on another occasion that "out of the heart proceed evil thoughts, murders, adulteries, fornications, thefts, false witness, blasphemies." (Matt. 15:19). Again we see God's approval is not granted to those who follow rules, but to those who conform to His character. Only the pure in heart can see God and His ways clearly, as well as walk in fellowship with Him (see also 1 John 3:2, 3).

"Blessed are the peacemakers, for they shall be called sons of God" (v. 9). In Scripture "peace" speaks of health and wholeness. The most significant peace is that which we have with God through Jesus, as He restores us to a wholeness which reestablishes relationship with God. Gospel peacemaking may be partly in view here. Yet the peacemaker's task includes restoring broken relationships and broken people as well.

In Jewish idiom, to be called a "son of" something suggests identity or likeness. A "son of a carpenter" is a carpenter, and here a "son of God" is one who bears likeness to God Himself.

"Blessed are those who are persecuted for righteousness' sake, for theirs in the kingdom of heaven" (v. 10). Those who live according to the will of God will find themselves at odds with the world around them. Jesus put it this way in speaking with His disciples:

If the world hates you, you know that it hated Me before it hated you. If you were of the world, the world would love its own. Yet because you are not of the world, but I chose you out of the world, therefore the world hates you (John 15:18, 19).

Those whose priorities and values are described in the beatitudes are approved by God but not by their fellow men. Many have suggested that this final beatitude provides a litmus test that identifies those who are living out the other beatitudes. A person who is truly poor in spirit, who mourns and is meek, who hungers for righteousness, and who is merciful, pure in heart, and a peacemaker, will unintentionally so expose the flaws of those around him that he will be persecuted by them.

Verses 11 and 12, which are often taken as another Beatitude, are in fact commentary on verse 10. The persecution that can be expected includes being reviled and all sorts of accusations of evil. And the persecution is said to be "because of Me" rather than "for righteousness sake." Those who are so persecuted are to "rejoice and be exceeding glad, for great is your reward in heaven, for so they persecuted the prophets who were before you" (v. 12).

It's important to note that the reward for the persecuted awaits heaven, while the other rewards are experienced as we live here and now in the "kingdom of heaven." Heaven waits. But blessedness is available now for those who chose to live in the kingdom Jesus came to introduce.

The impact of a life of which God approves (Matt. 5:13–16). Jesus has described what life is to be like for those living in His kingdom. He has emphasized the personal rewards of this lifestyle, rewards which grow out of the kind of person the kingdom citizen is. In these next verses Jesus speaks of the mission of the kingdom citizen in his or her society. The kingdom citizen is to be salt and light.

You are the salt of the earth (Matt. 5:13; Mark 9:49–50; Luke 14:34). In biblical times salt was used as a preservative. There was no refrigeration, so perishables like the fish caught from the Sea of Galilee would be salted and then transported to Jerusalem and other cities for sale. While some salt was obtained by evaporation of the waters of the Dead Sea, which are seven times saltier than normal sea water, much of Palestine's salt was mined from a great ledge of rock salt that ran through a valley near that sea.

While sea salt could not "lose its flavor," the rock salt mined from the ledge could and often did lose its saltiness. It was leached out by water and humidity, or it might be so contaminated by sand and gravel that it was useless as a preservative.

Jesus makes it plain to His listeners that if they are to function as a preservative in society, delaying its decay, they *must* live by the priorities and values established in the Beatitudes.

His meaning is illustrated by the history of Christianity in many lands. In England and the United States it was the grief of Christians over the plight of slaves that led to the abolishment of slavery. And it was the passion of the merciful that led to the establishment of schools, hospitals, and orphanages. Today it is the concern of Christians for the unborn that drives establishment of homes for unwed mothers, the opening up of avenues for adoption, and the effort to serve as the conscience of a society which condones the killing of millions of infants before they even see the light of day.

You are the light of the world (Matt. 5:14–16; Mark 4:21; Luke 11:33). In this

Christian character can no more be hidden than a city reflecting the noon-time sun.

analogy Jesus identifies two sources of light: a city set on a hill and a lamp set on a lampstand.

Jesus begins by stating that a "city that is set on a hill cannot be hidden" (Matt. 5:14). In the Middle East today, as in Jesus' time, homes are often made of mud bricks covered with a light layer of mud or whitewash. The sun shining on the city made it glow with reflected light; it could not be hidden, because it did not blend in with the hillside.

The believer today is to reflect God's light so that he or she too cannot be hidden. A citizen of the kingdom Jesus describes simply would not blend in with his surroundings.

In biblical times, too, a lamp was always kept burning in a home. These lamps were simple clay cups filled with olive oil into which a bit of flax was dropped to serve as a wick. These lamps were not designed to drive the darkness away. Instead the lamps provided a point of light which oriented the individual enough so that he could find his way.

As a lamp, the citizen of Jesus' kingdom is to stand out against the darkness, a point of light that orients others in the house to find their way. The lamp is never hidden, nor put under a basket, for that would defeat its reason for being.

In the same way, kingdom citizens are to "let your light so shine before men, that they may see your good works and glorify your Father in heaven" (v. 16). We may feel that the light we shed is puny indeed compared to the darkness all around. But we are to stand up and let our light shine. The good works that flow from a life lived with Beatitude values will glorify God.

Jesus' relationship to the Old Testament revelation (Matt. 5:17–20). In this very significant paragraph Jesus makes it clear that the kingdom lifestyle about which He teaches is different from and yet in harmony with the Old Testament revelation. Jesus was fully aware that His teaching would be misconstrued, and that some would charge that He intended to "destroy" the "Law and the Prophets," as the Old Testament was referred to. The Greek word here is *kataluso*, which means to abolish or undo. Jesus had not come to set aside the older revelation at all. Instead Christ announced that He intended to "fulfill" the Old Testament.

This saying has been seriously misunderstood by commentators, who have supposed that Jesus "fulfilled" the Old Testament in the sense of being the One to whom it pointed, or the One who would keep all the prophets' promises. But Christ's first listeners understood exactly what Jesus was saying. Christ intended to "fulfill" the Scriptures in the sense that every Jewish rabbi yearned to do—by giving a full and accurate account of its true meaning! Jesus would now explain what God had always intended His people to understand from Scripture, and Jesus' interpretation would be the true one.

Because Jesus' interpretation would be so at odds with that of contemporary rabbis, He underlined His commitment to the Scriptures. Not the tiniest mark used in forming Hebrew letters (one jot or one tittle) was irrelevant (Matt. 5:18). But Jesus then made a stunning statement. To even enter the kingdom of heaven a person's righteousness must exceed that of the "scribes and Pharisees" (v. 20). The phrase refers to one group rather than two: those scribes who are Pharisees. The Pharisees were a relatively small group of men who had dedicated themselves to keep every detail of Mosaic law as interpreted by the rabbis. Scribes were experts in the Law, who had dedicated their lives to studying and teaching it. A scribe who was a Pharisee was the elite of the elite in Judaism. And Jesus said that unless His listeners' righteousness exceeds the righteousness of men known for their dedication to keeping and teaching God's commandments, that listener would "by no means enter the kingdom of heaven."

Whatever the true meaning of the Old Testament which Jesus would reveal, that true meaning had not been grasped by Judaism's elite, who were striving to please God in vain.

BIBLE BACKGROUND:
HARD SAYINGS OF JESUS

"Whoever therefore breaks one of the least of these commandments, and teaches men so, shall be called least in the kingdom of heaven; but whoever does and teaches them, he shall be called great in the kingdom of heaven" (Matthew 5:19).

Jesus has just affirmed the authority of the Old Testament, but promised to fulfill it (explain its true meaning). The "doing and teaching" referred to here are doing and teaching in harmony with Christ's explanation of the commandments, not with the legalistic interpretations of the scribes and Pharisees.

Lessons on the true meaning of the commandments (Matt. 5:21–48). Jesus now gives a series of illustrations that unveil the error of the scribes and Pharisees, and lay the foundation for His reinterpretation of God's commands. Each of the illustrations begins with the phrase, "You have heard that it was said to those of old. . . ." Note that Jesus does not begin by stating what the Old Testament actually says but by stating what His listeners *had heard* that the Old Testament said. Jesus had no quarrel with Scripture. But He did have a quarrel with what the rabbis taught about the Scripture.

In each of the five illustrations Jesus moves from an *action* or *behavior* which the scribes understood the Law to be about, to focus on an *inner attitude* or *motivation*. Note the contrasts.

"You shall not murder" (vv. 21–26). The Scribes warned, "whoever murders will be in danger of the judgment." But Jesus warned, "whoever is angry with his brother shall be in danger of the judgment."

"You shall not commit adultery (vv. 27–30). Jesus again shifted the focus to inner attitude: "But I say to you that whoever looks at a woman to lust for her has already committed adultery with her in his heart."

BIBLE BACKGROUND:
HARD SAYINGS OF JESUS

"If your right eye causes you to sin, pluck it out and cast it from you; for it is more profitable for you that one of your members perish, than for your whole body to be cast into hell" (Matthew 5:29).

Jesus' statement emphasizes the futility of seeking an external remedy for an internal problem. First-century rabbis blamed the eye for causing lust. As a result they would gaze downward when meeting any woman, refusing to look at her. Jesus suggests that this is hardly enough. If the eye is really at fault, rip it out! We need to remember in this context that Jesus said plainly that the real problem was not the eye, but the heart, for "out of the heart proceed evil thoughts, murders, adulteries" (Matt. 15:19).

"Whoever divorces his wife, let him give her a certificate of divorce" (vv. 31–32). Old Testament law permitted divorce but did not specify grounds (Deut. 24:1). Jesus looks at the motive for divorce and again shows that motive counts: "except for sexual immorality."

"You shall not swear falsely, but shall perform your oaths to the Lord" (vv. 33–37). The rabbis distinguished between binding and non-binding oaths, building their argument on whether an oath was really "to the Lord" or not. Jesus taught "let your 'Yes' be 'Yes' and your 'No' 'No.'" There is no room for deceit or lies, whether one is under oath or not!

"An eye for an eye and a tooth for a tooth" (vv. 38–42). This principle in Old Testament law was intended to prevent feuds by limiting the action an injured person might take against another. Normally a price for the lost eye or tooth was negotiated, and the case resolved by monetary payment. But the rabbis saw in this principle found in Exodus 21:24 justification for doing harm to those who harm you. Jesus rejected this view and taught, "Whoever slaps you on your right cheek, turn the other to him also."

"You shall love your neighbor and hate your enemy" (vv. 43–48). Only the first phrase, "you shall love your neighbor" is found in Scripture (Lev. 19:18). The rabbis deduced the obverse, "and hate your enemies." Jesus however taught, "love your enemies, bless those who curse you, do good to those who hate you, and pray for those who spitefully use you and persecute you."

There are several things to note about this series of illustrations. They cover various types of Old Testament content and illustrate how the rabbis interpreted each. The references to murder and adultery show how the rabbis treated the prohibitions in Old Testament law. The reference to divorce illustrates how they treated the permissive statements in Old Testament law. The reference to taking oaths showed how they drew deductions from a passage dealing with one's duty to God (compare Lev. 19:12) and applied it to human relationships. The reference to the "eye for an eye" showed how the rabbis took a legal principle imbedded in the Old Testament justice system and used it to justify personal revenge.

In each instance the rabbis approached the Old Testament as if its purpose was to regulate behavior.

In contrast, Jesus approached the Old Testament as if its regulations and principles were intended to reveal God's moral character and to call men to be like Him. The message of the Law as Jesus interpreted it was that "you shall be perfect, just as your Father in heaven is perfect" (Matt. 5:48).

Thus the issue in the older revelation was not so much murder as the anger that led to it. The issue was not so much adultery as the lust that led men to treat women as objects rather than persons. The issue in divorce was not when it was lawful, but one of loyalty and commitment to the marriage covenant. The issue in the laws governing oaths was not when an oath might be broken but the essential integrity and reliability of the individual's words. The issue in the "eye for an eye" principle was not what repayment for injury one has a right to demand, but the inappropriateness of revenge where forgiveness is called for. And the issue in the call to love one's neighbor was not distinguishing whom one might lawfully hate, but was rather being like God and seeking to love even one's enemies.

The scribes and Pharisees, focused on the details of their dos and don'ts, had distorted the message of the Old Testament and its commandments. They emphasized the letter of the law and eagerly went about trying to establish their righteousness, never realizing that, rightly understood, the Law called for an inner transformation which only God could work.

No wonder Jesus warned that the righteousness of those who would enter the kingdom of heaven must exceed the righteousness of the scribes and Pharisees! The righteousness that the law called for was of a very different nature than the righteousness the elite of Judaism strove to achieve.

Marks of the kingdom: an in-secret relationship with God as Father (Matt. 6:1–18). Jesus has established that the kingdom of heaven has to do with the heart, not with external dos and don'ts. Now Jesus goes on to show that the kingdom of heaven involves an in-secret relationship with God as Father.

A matter of motives (vv. 1–18). Jesus' illustrations of alms-giving and fasting focus on two religious duties that the Pharisees associated with piety. Without rejecting the practices, Jesus again calls for an examination of motives. Jesus warns against doing charitable deeds "to be seen by" men (v. 1), and against praying in public to "be seen by men" (v. 5). Those who seek to establish a reputation for piety have their reward: they are thought by others to be pious.

In contrast, those who live in the kingdom of heaven will act "in secret" and out of a desire to please God, with whom they have a Father-child relationship. The fact of relationship with Him assures the kingdom citizen that God, who "sees in secret" surely "will Himself reward you openly" (v. 6).

A matter of dependence (vv. 7–13). The one who lives in the kingdom of heaven does not depend on human beings but depends on the Father, who "knows the things you have need of before you ask him" (v. 8). This dependence is expressed in the simplest of prayers, which stands in contrast with the prayers of the heathen who assume that answers to prayer depend on "their many words" rather than the loving attention the Father gives His children (v. 7). (For a discussion of the Lord's Prayer [Matt. 6:9–13], see chapter 11.)

BIBLE BACKGROUND:
HARD SAYINGS OF JESUS

"For if you forgive men their trespasses, your heavenly Father will also forgive you. But if you do not forgive men their trespasses, neither will your Father forgive your trespasses" (Matthew 6:14, 15; compare 18:23–35; Mark 11:25, 26)

Jesus is not changing the conditions of salvation, but expressing a reality. Forgiveness is much like a coin. It has a "heads" (forgiven) and a "tails" (forgiving). A coin with only one side is counterfeit, and just so is the notion that a person who is unforgiving can experience forgiveness. Only the person who has experienced God's grace will be able to be gracious to others.

An expression of faith (Matt. 6:16–18). Jesus now comments on a third external of which the Pharisees were proud. Most Pharisees fasted (went without food from sunrise to sunset) on Tuesdays and Thursdays. To make sure that everyone knew they were fasting, these men rubbed ashes on their faces and adopted a mournful expression. Even though such fasting is not called for in the Old Testament (while generosity and prayer are), fasting was thought to be a distinctive mark of piety.

Again Jesus focuses on motives and on the in-secret nature of an individual's relationship with God as Father. Rather than disfigure oneself, a person who is fasting should take pains to look normal, so that his fast may be a personal and private matter between him and God alone.

Marks of the kingdom: a new focus in life (Matt. 6:19–34). Jesus has emphasized the importance of the in-secret relationship with God as Father that characterizes citizenship in the kingdom of heaven. He now points out that this relationship will radically change our focus in life.

No more earthly treasures (vv. 19–23). Rather than lay up corruptible treasures on earth, the citizen of the kingdom of heaven will "lay up for yourselves treasures in heaven" (v. 20).

BIBLE BACKGROUND:
HARD SAYINGS OF JESUS

"The lamp of the body is the eye. If therefore your eye is good, your whole body will be full of light. But if your eye is bad, your whole body will be full of darkness. If therefore the light that is in you is darkness, how great is that darkness" (Matthew 6:22, 23; compare Luke 11:34–36).

The eye lets in light that enables a person to make moral choices. A "bad" (Greek *poneros*, "evil") eye distorts the light and thus one's moral choices are made without a clear grasp of right or wrong. This metaphor probably goes with verse 24, and reminds us that a person who divides his attention between God and material possessions will develop moral and spiritual blindness.

No more worries (Matt. 6:25–34). A relationship with God as Father guarantees that He will meet our every need. We no longer need to be anxious, even about necessities (v. 25), for "your heavenly Father knows that you need all these things" (v. 32).

Freed from the burden of worry about our material needs, we are to "seek first" the kingdom of God and His righteousness. To "seek first" means to desire God's kingdom above everything, and to actively pursue the lifestyle of righteousness that marks its citizens.

Marks of the kingdom: transforming power (Matt. 7:1–6). Jesus' words, "judge not, that you be not judged," have often been misunderstood as a warning that if we judge others, God will judge us. But this passage focuses on interpersonal relationships, not one's relationship with God.

Jesus' point is that a "norm of reciprocity" operates in human society. We tend to treat others as they treat us. If we are judgmental toward others, they will be judgmental toward us. For "the measure you use, it will be measured back to you" (v. 2).

What then if we treat others with the love and concern that Jesus has urged in this sermon? Then the citizen of the kingdom of

Casting pearls before swine was an image Jesus used to present a vital spiritual reality.

heaven can have a positive impact on others! But no impact can be had by offering to remove the specks in others' eyes. It is love and not law that will reach others.

BIBLE BACKGROUND:
HARD SAYINGS OF JESUS

"Do not give what is holy to the dogs; nor cast your pearls before swine, lest they trample them under their feet, and turn and tear you in pieces" (Matt. 7:6).

Baffling Bible Questions Answered (Baker) offers this explanation on page 234:

In 7:6 he [Jesus] warns them not to seek to impose high moral standards on unbelievers. The point of the analogy is that "dogs" are incapable of recognizing the sacred, and that

"pigs" care nothing for pearls. Why then should we expect those without any relationship with God to accept the moral standards of believers? Rather than respond to efforts at moral uplift, the corrupt are more likely to turn "and tear you to pieces" (Matt. 7:6).

Marks of the kingdom: Answered prayer (Matt. 7:7–12). The citizen of the kingdom of heaven is in a unique position to ask, knock, and seek. The answer is guaranteed not because of anything in us but because our heavenly Father will "give good things to those [children of His] who ask Him" (v. 11).

The call for decision (Matt. 7:13–27). Jesus' teaching on the Mount directly confronted the accepted understanding of the Scriptures, and required a decision.

Would His hearers commit themselves to Jesus and His teachings, or continue to follow the teachings of the scribes and Pharisees?

To underline the necessity for a choice Jesus used a series of illustrations, each of which presents two, and only two, options.

Two pathways (vv. 13–14). There are two paths Jesus' listeners may follow. One seems easy—the gate is wide and the path broad—but it leads to destruction. The other is narrow and the path difficult, but it leads to life.

Two trees (vv. 15–20). Jesus warns of false prophets and indicates how to recognize them. The image of grapes from thorn bushes and figs from thistles is drawn from daily life. The berries on the buckthorn and the flowers on some thistles might seem from a distance to be grapes or figs. But up close the difference is clear. In the same way it is not first impressions but the totality of a person's life that counts. And no one can fake a kingdom lifestyle for long.

Two claims (vv. 21–23). Some will claim to know and follow Jesus, calling Him "Lord, Lord." But words and even spectacular deeds are not evidence of personal relationship with the Father. What is evidence is commitment to and practice of the will of God. Saying and doing are different things indeed.

Two builders (vv. 24–27). Jesus concludes with the story of two men, one who built his house on a rock and the other who built on sand. His conclusion sums up the kingdom challenge presented in the Sermon on the Mount.

Therefore, whoever hears these sayings of Mine, and does them, I will liken him to a wise man who built his house on the rock; and the rain descended, the floods came, and the winds blew and beat on that house; and it did not fall, for it was founded on the rock.

But everyone who hears these sayings of Mine, and does not do them, will be like a foolish man who built his house on the sand; and the rain descended, the floods came, and the winds blew and beat on that house; and it fell. And great was its fall.

The response of Jesus' listeners to His sermon was astonishment, "for He taught them as one having authority, and not as the scribes" (7:29).

THE SIGNIFICANCE OF THE SERMON ON THE MOUNT

The Sermon on the Mount is perhaps the most significant of Jesus' public teachings. It constituted a direct challenge to the religious leaders of His time. The Sermon on the Mount also demonstrated that Jesus was willing to accept the role of the Prophet like Moses, and set a new direction for sacred history.

The radical content of the Sermon. Jesus' teaching was truly radical. He insisted that the rabbis of His day had misunderstood and misapplied the Scriptures. Rightly understood, the commandments spoke about the human heart and established man's need for an inner transformation. Rightly understood, the Scriptures were not a demand for behavioral conformity to a set of rules, but an invitation to enter a Father-child relationship with God. That relationship alone would work an inward transformation and would affect all of life. The Father-child relationship would transform motives, change priorities, free from anxiety, and even have an impact on the sinful society in which one lived.

But with Jesus' explanation of the true meaning of the Old Testament came responsibility. Jesus' listeners must choose between the rabbi's legalistic approach to God's Word and Jesus' relational interpretation. And only one who was ready to commit his or her life to do Jesus' words would be able to stand when the storm came at history's end to sweep all of mankind's works away.

The contributions of the Sermon to under-standing of the "kingdom of heaven. We noted that the Old Testament suggests two aspects of the "kingdom of heaven" or the "kingdom of God." One form of that kingdom is eternal, invisible, universal, and ever-present, expressed in God's ultimate control of all events.

The other form of the kingdom depicted in the Old Testament is visible, earthly, worldwide, and associated with the rule of the promised Messiah. When the Messiah comes to rule, all humankind will be subject to Him.

But Jesus is introducing a new form of the kingdom, a mystery form that was not unveiled in the Old Testament. In some way the kingdom of heaven is to be established in men's hearts and is to be marked by a personal, relationship with God as Father. The kingdom will take form on earth, but because it is an "in-secret" kind of thing, the kingdom of heaven will be hidden from those who are not citizens.

There is more to learn about this kingdom that was the focus of so much of Jesus' public teaching. We'll discover more, especially as we move on in the next chapter to explore the parables and stories that Jesus told about the kingdom.

PARALLEL PASSAGES IN LUKE'S GOSPEL

As I noted earlier in this chapter, material that parallels Jesus' teachings in the Sermon on the Mount is found in Luke's Gospel. Two major blocks of text in Luke need to be considered.

As pointed out earlier, Luke is not giving us another version of Jesus' sermon. Rather Luke is reporting what Jesus said about the familiar themes on different occasions. Thus we do not expect word-for-word correspondence between Luke's account and that of Matthew.

PARALLELS IN LUKE 6

Luke 6 contains what is called the Sermon on the Plain (6:17). It is the largest block of teaching in the Gospels which covers themes found in the Sermon on the Mount.

The Beatitudes (Luke 6:20–23; compare Matt. 5:3–10). Matthew lists eight beatitudes; Luke reports only four. But Luke adds "woes." In both testaments "woe" is an interjection, an exclamation of grief or denouncement. Jesus not only condemns but grieves when He pronounces a woe.

As expected, each "woe" is associated with a person's commitment to the values and priorities of human society in contrast to the values and priorities of the kingdom. The rich are to be mourned over because they have received all they will ever get (Luke 6:24). Those who are full are to be mourned over for they will hunger (v. 25). Those who laugh now are to be mourned over for they will weep. And those whom all admire are to be grieved for, for the fathers approved of false prophets in their day (v. 26). While the blessed are out of harmony with this world and its ways, those to whom Jesus announces woe are totally settled into this world and look for satisfaction here.

The call to love enemies (6:27–36; compare Matt. 5:39–48). While presented in a slightly different sequence the two passages contain the same teaching and make the same point. We are to "be merciful, just as your Father also is merciful." We are to look to God as our example and to live as children of His, in all we do displaying the family resemblance.

The warning against judging (6:37–42; compare Matthew 7:1–5). Again the content is the same, except that here Jesus adds two brief illustrations.

Our actions reveal our heart as fruit identifies a tree.

❖

Jesus warns that the blind cannot lead the blind, for both will fall in a ditch (Luke 6:39). Jesus has shown that the Pharisees were blind to the real meaning of the Scriptures. All who follow them will fall in the same ditch as their blind teacher.

Jesus comments that a disciple when fully trained will be like his teacher (v. 40). In the first century theological training was accomplished through a discipleship program. A learner attached himself to an established rabbi, eager not only to learn all that the teacher knew but also eager to adopt his teachers' way of life. Likeness, not information, was the goal. Yet the best a disciple can hope for is to become like his teacher.

If we connect the two sayings, Jesus is pointing out that only by choosing to be His disciple will a person be able to break out of the pattern of misinterpretation that has trapped the Pharisees and their disciples.

The test of good fruit (Luke 6:43–45; compare Matt. 7:15–20). In Matthew Jesus applied the analogy to the recognition of false prophets. Here he applies the analogy more broadly. There is a consistency between root and fruit. Man's inner nature is the source of his actions, and actions are the test of whether the individual is good or evil.

The necessity of choice (Luke 6:46–49; compare Matt. 7:21–27). In each of these passages Jesus emphasizes the necessity of committing oneself to hearing His sayings and doing them.

This is not a new legalism, and Jesus' teachings do not constitute a new or even an expanded law. Jesus' point is that His listeners must decide whether to commit themselves to Him and His interpretation of God's Law, or to follow the lead of the scribes and Pharisees. They cannot remain undecided. They must choose and act.

PARALLELS IN LUKE 11 AND 12

Other topics found in the Sermon on the Mount occur in Luke 11 and 12 but in distinctive contexts.

On prayer (Luke 11:1–4, 9–13; compare Matt. 6:9–13 and 7:7–11). The Lord's Prayer is recorded in these verses, with minor variations from the prayer in Matthew 6, and in company with an illustration also found in Matthew 7. Clearly Jesus wove together common elements in His teaching in such a way that they served different purposes in different settings. In Matthew the Lord's Prayer is an integral element in Jesus' teaching about an "in-secret" relationship with God as Father. In Luke it is an element in a sequence of stories and illustrations designed to encourage confidence in prayer.

On anxiety (Luke 12:22–31, 33–34; compare Matt. 6:19–34). In each Gospel the story is intended to encourage trust in God the Father's care, and to release the listener to "seek the kingdom of God." An interesting difference is that in Matthew the encouragement is directed to the crowds who hear Jesus speak, while in Luke the words may have been directed to the Twelve.

One thing, however, is sure. Only one who has committed himself or herself to Jesus can experience the release from anxiety that Christ promises here. The peace that frees us to give priority to the kingdom is a peace that only God can provide.

KINGDOM PARABLES AND SAYINGS

Some of Jesus' public teaching was particularly hard for His first-century hearers to understand. In fact, some of it Christ didn't want His hearers to understand at all! This is particularly the case when Jesus told parables describing the kingdom of heaven.

Many of Jesus' other references to the kingdom seem obscure even to us today. Yet the kingdom parables and Jesus' kingdom sayings are both critical if we are to grasp the new direction Christ was setting for the immediate future.

The Gospels record some forty-two stories told by Jesus to illustrate some truth. There are an additional thirty-three brief sayings and metaphors. Some con-

sider all of these to be parables. But Jesus identified certain of His stories with the kingdom, and the gospels identify these as parables. It is just those stories identified as kingdom parables or specifically linked by Jesus with the kingdom that we are concerned with in this chapter.

KINGDOM PARABLES

The kingdom parables that Jesus told fall into two categories. Seven of these parables contrast features of the unexpected kingdom that Jesus inaugurated, with features of the earthly kingdom expected by the Jews. All seven of these

The Parable	Matthew	Mark	Luke
The sower	13:3–9,18–23	4:3–8, 14–20	8:5–15
Wheat/tares	13:24–30, 37–43		
Mustard seed	13:31–32	4:30–32	13:18, 19
Leaven	13:33		13:20, 21
Hidden treasure	13:44		
Priceless pearl	13:45, 46		
Dragnet	13:47–50		

parables are reported in Matthew 13. Two of the seven are also found in Mark's Gospel, and three of the seven are reported by Luke.

Five additional kingdom parables are found only in Matthew's Gospel. Rather than contrast the expected and unexpected form of the kingdom, these five parables illuminate principles on which the unexpected kingdom operates.

The five are:

- The parable of the unforgiving servant (18:23–35)
- The parable of the generous landowner (20:1–16)
- The parable of the marriage feast (22:2–14)
- The parable of the ten virgins (25:1–13)
- The parable of the talents (25:14–30; Luke 19:11–27)

CONTRASTING KINGDOMS (MATTHEW 13)

The most obvious thing we note about the first set of parables, found in Matthew 13, Mark 4, and Luke 8 and 13, is that the disciples were surprised that Jesus had begun to speak in parables.

Why parables? When Jesus started telling the parables recorded in Matthew 13, His disciples asked "Why" He spoke to the crowds in parables. Jesus answered:

Because it has been given to you to know the mysteries of the kingdom of heaven, but to them it has not been given. For whoever has, to him more will be given, and he will have abundance; but whoever does not have, even what he has will be taken away from him. Therefore I speak to them in parables, because seeing they do not see, and hearing they do not hear, nor do they understand. And in

them the prophecy of Isaiah is fulfilled, which says:
"Hearing you will hear and shall
 not understand,
 And seeing you will see and
 not perceive;
For the hearts of this people
 have grown dull,
 Their ears are hard of hearing;
 And their eyes are closed,
Lest they should see with their
 eyes and hear with their ears,
Lest they should understand
 with their hearts and turn,
So that I should heal them."
(Matt. 13:13–15)

Later Matthew adds,

All these things Jesus spoke to the multitude in parables; and without a parable He did not speak to them, that it might be fulfilled which was spoken by the prophet, saying:

"I will open My mouth in parables;
I will utter things kept secret
 from the foundation of the world"
(Matt. 13:34, 35)

Mark's report gives a briefer account of these remarks where he relates two of the seven parables. He tells us that when the Twelve privately asked Jesus why He now spoke in parables, Jesus said,

To you it has been given to know the mystery of the kingdom of God; but to those who are outside, all things come in parables, so that
"Seeing they may see and not perceive,
And hearing they may hear and
 not understand;
Lest they should turn,
And their sins be forgiven them."
(Mark 4:11, 12)

Many of Jesus' parables unveil hidden truths about His kingdom.

Luke also reports the disciples' question and Jesus' answer.

> To you it has been given to know the mysteries of the kingdom of God, but to the rest it is given in parables, that
> "Seeing they may not see,
> And hearing they may not understand."
> (Luke 8:10)

The fact that all three gospel writers report Jesus' answer to the question, "Why parables now?" serves to emphasize the importance of Jesus' answer and to highlight the uniqueness of these seven kingdom parables. What then do we learn from Jesus' responses?

The parables are about the kingdom. Each report makes it clear that these parables concern the kingdom of heaven (Matt. 13:11) or the kingdom of God (Mark 4:11; Luke 8:10). There is no doubt about the subject of these parables.

The parables unveil "mysteries." Each writer tells us that the parables concern kingdom mysteries (Matt. 13:11; Mark 4:11; Luke 8:10).

In the New Testament "mystery" is a technical theological term. A "mystery" is some element of God's plan which was not revealed in the Old Testament, but which is revealed in the New. Its significance is clearly seen in Ephesians 3, where Paul writes,

He made known to me the mystery . . . which in other ages was not made known to the sons of men, as it has now been revealed by the Spirit to His holy apostles and prophets: that the Gentiles should be fellow heirs, of the same body, and partakers of His promise in Christ through the gospel (vv. 3–6).

It came as no surprise that Gentiles would be saved, for of this the Old Testament prophets spoke (see Is. 11:10). What was a surprise when it was now made known was that Gentiles should be "fellow heirs, of the same body" with Jewish believers! This indeed was a mystery "in other ages not made known" but now revealed, and it shocked many early Jewish Christians.

It is the same with the kingdom of which Jesus spoke. The Old Testament made it clear that God ruled in heaven and would rule on earth. But the form of the kingdom which Jesus preached was "in other ages not made known."

This very point is made in Matthew 13:35, when Matthew quotes Psalm 78:2: "I will open My mouth in parables; I will utter things kept secret from the foundation of the world."

The *subject* of these parables was the kingdom Jesus' coming inaugurated, and the *content* of these parables was previously unrevealed information.

Jesus did not intend the crowds to understand. This is something that many commentators have found hard to acknowledge. Yet both Mark and Luke focus on the significant theme in the extended quote from Isaiah we find in Matthew 13. Mark reports that Jesus spoke "to those who are outside" in parables, so that "Seeing they may see and not perceive, and hearing they may hear and not understand; lest they should turn, and their sins be forgiven them" (4:12).

And Luke gives even sharper focus. These kingdom parables are for His disciples, and as for "the rest," Jesus speaks in parables that "Seeing they may not see, and hearing they may not understand" (Luke 8:10).

The question that naturally springs to mind is, "Why?"

The Gospels tell us that Jesus came preaching the kingdom of heaven. Matthew reports His Sermon on the Mount, in which Jesus presented His listeners with a clear and necessary choice. God's people must now acknowledge Jesus' authority and adopt His revelation of the true meaning of the Old Testament, or they might continue to follow the mistaken pathway marked out by the scribes and Pharisees. During this same early period Jesus performed a variety of miraculous healings and exorcisms. The miracles demonstrated Jesus' authority over nature, over sickness, over demons, and even over death itself. These miracles were the visible stamp authenticating Jesus as one who spoke with divine authority. As we've seen earlier, Jesus also publicly claimed Himself to be the promised Messiah and the Son of God.

And yet the people hesitated! His listeners were impressed, but they wavered. They saw His healings, yet they would not commit themselves to Him.

It is in this context that Jesus began to speak in parables. His contemporaries had not responded to his plain talk about the kingdom. Now it was time to speak in parables so that "outsiders" and "the rest" would not be able to understand.

There are two possible explanations for Jesus' decision to turn to parables. The first explanation is a gracious one. We are responsible for the truth we know. As the majority in Judea and Galilee had failed to respond to Jesus' plainest teachings, He would now utter words they could not understand so that they would not be judged for their failure to respond to what He taught.

The other explanation is the more likely. According to Mark's gospel Jesus explained that He spoke in parables that "Seeing they may see and not perceive, and hearing they may hear and not understand; lest they should turn, and their sin be forgiven them" (4:12).

This quote, a paraphrase of Isaiah 6:9, 10, suggests Jesus' decision to speak in parables was judicial rather than gracious.

This is clearly the context of Isaiah 6. Isaiah is commissioned by God to speak to Israel but is told that those to whom he preaches will not listen. Their refusal to hear is God's judgment on this people who have sinned consciously and persistently, and they are doomed to go on in the way they have chosen "until the cities are laid waste and without inhabitant" and "the land is utterly desolate" (Is. 6:11).

Judicial hardening is not coercive, and it does not turn anyone toward sin. God only exercises judicial hardening when a person has both freely chosen and persisted in sin beyond all hope of change. And this seems to be the case in Jesus' ministry. Christ has presented himself to God's people as their promised King. And while His contemporaries are willing to grant that He is special, and almost certainly a prophet (see Matt. 16:13–16), they do not acknowledge Him for who He is. Jesus began to speak in parables only when it was too late for that first-century generation to turn and to find forgiveness and healing at Jesus' hands. Too late, because of their choice.

The mystery parables of the kingdom explained. We've noted that the subject of this first group of kingdom parables is the kingdom, and that their content is previously unrevealed truth about the mystery form of God's kingdom that Jesus has come to initiate. Before we look at each parable it's helpful to summarize their message in chart form. For each parable reveals an aspect of Jesus' kingdom that stands in sharp contrast with the messianic kingdom portrayed in the Old Testament; that kingdom which the Jews expected their Messiah to establish as soon as He appeared.

The parable of the sower (Matt. 13:3–9; Mark 4:3–8). The parable is a familiar one, drawn from daily life. In the first century, sowing was done by hand. The sower took a handful of seed and with a sweeping motion scattered it over the ground. Even though the ground had been prepared by the farmer, not all the seed would survive and grow. Some would be eaten by birds, some would land on stony land and though it germinated would soon wither. Other seeds would fall among weeds and be choked out. But some would fall on good ground, and produce a crop.

Jesus explained the point of this parable to His disciples (Matt. 13:18–23; Mark 4:14–20). The "seed" in the parable was "the word of the kingdom." Not all would respond to the teaching of Jesus or, later, to the preaching of His disciples. Jesus went on to identify some of the reasons for the failure to respond. In some, the "wicked one comes and snatches away what was sown in his heart" (Matt. 13:19) (seed sown by the wayside). Others seem to respond, but when persecution comes because of the word, they turn back (the seed fallen on stony places). Still others are so intent on the cares of this life and so set on riches that the word is choked out (the seed among thorns). But others are like good ground, and when they hear the word, it takes root in their lives and produces a rich harvest.

Yet the essential point of the parable is that unlike the kingdom predicted by the prophets that is national in scope and character, the kingdom Jesus now inaugurates is essentially an individual kind of thing, entered by those individuals who welcome God's Word and in whom that Word grows and produces crops.

The parable of the wheat and tares (Matt. 13:24–30). In this parable Jesus provides another image of the kingdom of heaven. It is like a man who sowed his field with good seed, but whose enemy came at night and seeded the field with "tares," probably a weed known as "bearded Darnel" which looks like wheat until the

PARABLES OF THE KINGDOM

The Parable	Expected Form	Unexpected Form
1. The Sower 13:3–9, 18–23	Messiah turns Israel and all nations to Himself.	Individuals respond differently to the Word's invitation.
2. Wheat/Tares vv. 24–30, 37–43	The kingdom's righteous citizens rule over the world with the King.	The kingdom's citizens are among the men of the world, growing together until God's harvest time.
3. Mustard Seed vv. 31–32	Kingdom begins in majestic glory.	Kingdom begins in insignificance; its greatness comes as a surprise.
4. Leaven v. 33	Only righteousness enters the kingdom; other "raw material" is excluded.	The kingdom is implanted in a different "raw material" and grows to fill the whole personality with righteousness.
5. Hidden Treasure v. 44	Kingdom is public and for all.	Kingdom is hidden for individual "purchase."
6. Priceless Pearl vv. 45, 46	Kingdom brings all valued things to men.	Kingdom demands abandonment of all values.
7. The Dragnet vv. 47–50	Kingdom begins with initial separation of righteous and unrighteous.	Kingdom ends with final separation of the unrighteous from righteous.

Adapted from Nelson's *Illustrated Bible Handbook*, p. 481.

heads appear. Both kinds of seed germinated and grew, and when heads appeared on wheat the landowner's servants were puzzled. The landowner explained this must have been done by an enemy. The servants then asked whether they should go through the field and pull up the false wheat. The landowners response was, "Let both grow together until the harvest, and at the time of harvest I will say to the reapers, 'First gather together the tares and bind them in bundles and burn them, but gather the wheat into my barn'" (v. 30).

This parable too Jesus privately explained to the Twelve (Matt. 13:37–43). In the parable Jesus Himself is the one who sows the good seed. The field is the world, and the good seeds are "the sons of the kingdom." The enemy is the devil, and the tares are "the sons of the wicked one." The reapers are God's angels, and the harvest takes place at the end of the age.

At the "end of this age" Jesus will send His angels to isolate those who "practice lawlessness," and then the righteous will "shine forth as the sun in the kingdom of their Father."

Again the main point of the parable is to contrast the unexpected and the expected forms of the kingdom. The prophets envisioned a day when the righteous would be established in the Messiah's earthly kingdom and the wicked would be punished. The separation of the evil from the good would take place at the launching of the earthly kingdom. But in Jesus parable His kingdom is marked by the righteous and the wicked mixed together in the world. And the separation of the evil from the good takes place not at the beginning of this kingdom's age, but at its end! And, at the end of this expression of God's kingdom, Jesus seems to suggests, the righteous will then enter "the kingdom of their Father," which like that of prophecy is launched with a separation of the wicked from the righteous.

It is fascinating to compare the image of angels separating out the evil from the good with Paul's vision of events at Jesus' return. Paul graphically describes the end of this age in 2 Thessalonians 1:6–10 in a way that clearly seems to parallel the end of the secret kingdom.

It is a righteous thing with God to repay with tribulation those who trouble you, and to give you who are troubled rest with us when the Lord Jesus is revealed from heaven with His mighty angels, in flaming fire taking vengeance on those who do not know God, and on those who do not obey the gospel of our Lord Jesus Christ. These shall be punished with everlasting destruction from the presence of the Lord and from the glory of His power, when He comes, in that Day, to be glorified in His saints and to be admired among all those who believe.

In many a sermon, the parable of the tares has rightly been preached as teaching that we are not to try to "purify" the church by calling for "believers only," and expelling those who do not meet our test. The reason is as Jesus said. There is a danger that in seeking to get rid of tares we might "also uproot the wheat with them." Rather than seek to create a pure church, we are called to fashion an accepting, welcoming church. We know that some among us will be tares. But we also know that some who are immature and fruitless now will one day prove to be wheat and produce a wonderful crop to the glory of our God.

The parable of the mustard seed (Matt. 13:31–32; Mark 4:30–32; Luke 13:18, 19). This parable is found in each of the synoptic gospels, marking it as particularly significant. The kingdom is like a mustard seed, tiny when planted but growing into a bush that outstrips the other garden plants, becoming a refuge for the birds of the air.

The great Hebrew Christian scholar Alfred Edersheim, in his *Life and Times of Jesus the Messiah* (p. 594) notes that:

The expression, "small as a mustard seed," had become proverbial, and was used, not only by our Lord, but frequently by the Rabbis, to indicate the smallest amount, which as the least drop of blood, the least defilement, or the smallest remnant of sun-glow in the sky. Such growth of the mustard seed was also a fact and well known at the time, and, indeed still observed in the text.

Edersheim also explains that birds finding refuge was a figure representing a mighty kingdom that gave shelter to all nations (compare Dan. 4:12 and Ezek. 31:6).

The messianic kingdom predicted in the Old Testament was to begin in great power and glory. The kingdom Jesus inaugurates begins in insignificance but grows great and provides rest and shade to all nations.

The parable of the leaven (Matt. 13:33; Luke 13:20, 21). In this parable Jesus pictures a woman making bread. She takes three measures of flour, the typical amount housewives used to prepare a family meal, and adds a bit of leaven (yeast). The leaven silently and steadily permeates and transforms the mixture from within. Edersheim suggests that "the Kingdom of God, when received within, would seem like leaven hid, but would gradually pervade, assimilate, and transform the whole of our common life."

Again a sharp contrast is drawn between the earthly kingdom described by the prophets and the expression of the eternal kingdom of God which Jesus initiated. On the basis of Old Testament prophecy the Jews expected the Messiah to allow only the righteous into His kingdom. But in Jesus' mystery kingdom sinners would become righteous through an inner transformation of those Christ welcomed.

The parable of the hidden treasure (Matt. 13:44). Jesus portrays a man who finds a treasure hidden in a field. He quickly sells all he has and buys the field. The emphasis in this parable is on the hidden treasure that the man discovers. Clearly its presence was not common knowledge. But the kingdom predicted in the Old Testament could not be missed by any, for the Messiah would rule the world.

So the mystery kingdom Jesus inaugurated would be hidden from most, yet holds such value when recognized for its treasure that an individual will gladly give all he or she has for it.

The parable of the priceless pearl (Matt. 13:45, 46). In this brief parable Jesus again tells of a person who sells all to possess a treasure. The treasure is a priceless pearl, and the person a pearl merchant.

The emphasis in the previous parable was on the fact the treasure was hidden and discovered by accident. In this parable the pearl merchant is searching. Yet the emphasis lies on the merchant's willingness to give all he has in order to possess the pearl.

One reason first-century Jews, oppressed by the Romans and the Herods alike, yearned for the messianic kingdom was their conviction that the appearance of the Messiah would bring not only freedom for Israel but power, wealth, and glory for them. In contrast, the kingdom Jesus portrayed would cost its citizens all those things that human beings tend to value, as Christ made clear in the Beatitudes (Matt. 5:3–10).

The parable of the dragnet (Matt. 13:47–50). In this parable Jesus pictures fisherman dragging a net behind their boats. Only when the nets have been pulled in can the trash fish be separated from the valuable. Jesus explains the parable by saying that "at the end of the age" God's angels will separate the wicked from the just, and cast the wicked into "the furnace of fire."

This parable reemphasizes a theme expressed earlier in the parable of the wheat and tares. The messianic kingdom of prophecy was to begin with the separation of the wicked from the righteous. Only the righteous would enter the kingdom. But the mystery kingdom Jesus inaugurates ends with the separation of the wicked and the just.

Jesus made clear in His Sermon on the Mount and in these parables that He truly had come to set sacred history on an unexpected and previously unrevealed course. The Old Testament affirmed God's rule over all, and also predicted a future expression of God's rule in a messianic kingdom. Jesus introduced yet another way God intends to express His rule—a form of the kingdom not known in the Old Testament. Jesus taught about the new expression here on earth of God's eternal rule by contrasting it with the messianic kingdom his hearers expected.

The parable of the dragnet reminds us that God will separate the righteous and sinners at the "end of the age."

The messianic kingdom of prophecy is marked by the visible and majestic glory with which it begins and the utter power and worldwide authority of its King. The messianic kingdom is a kingdom of the righteous, for the wicked are judged at its beginning, and in that kingdom the righteous are blessed with all good things.

The mystery kingdom, however, is a hidden kingdom that begins in insignificance, whose true nature as the ultimate treasure is hidden. Its citizens are sinners becoming saints, who live unacknowledged in every human society. And the citizens of Jesus' kingdom are called on to surrender the good things of this life in favor of the kingdom only they can perceive.

PRINCIPLES FOR KINGDOM LIVING

The second group of kingdom parables is found in Matthew's Gospel. Each is an extended story, to be distinguished from other stories Jesus told by Christ's specific identification of the story with His kingdom teaching. It's significant that all of these stories are found in Matthew's Gospel, with only the last repeated by Luke. Matthew, whose gospel account is shaped to prove that Jesus is the Old Testament's promised Messiah, must deal more thoroughly with the kingdom issue. Matthew must not only convince the Jews that Jesus is the one of whom the Old Testament speaks; Matthew must explain the nature of the unexpected form of God's kingdom that Jesus inaugurated, and also show how His kingdom relates to the kingdom envisioned by the prophets.

The five kingdom story-parables are:

- The parable of the unforgiving servant (18:23–35).
- The parable of the generous landowner (20:1–16).

- The parable of the marriage feast (22:2–14).
- The parable of the ten virgins (25:1–13)
- The parable of the talents (25:14–30).

The parable of the unforgiving servant (Matt. 18:23–35). The story is a familiar one. A certain king wanted to settle accounts with his servants. One man owed him ten thousand talents (seventy-five thousand pounds of precious metal!), the equivalent of many millions of dollars. The servant could not pay, and begged for more time. Moved by compassion the king unexpectedly forgave the entire debt!

But when the forgiven servant ran across a fellow servant who owed him 100 denarii, a very small amount, he demanded payment. The fellow servant begged for time, but the first servant had him thrown in prison "till he should pay the debt."

Later, when the king was informed, he called the servant before him and demanded, "Should you not also have had compassion on your fellow servant, just as I had pity on you?" (v. 33). The king then demanded payment in full.

Jesus concluded with a warning: "So My heavenly Father also will do to you if each of you, from his heart, does not forgive his brother his trespasses" (v. 35).

Several features of the parable must be noted in order to relate Jesus' teaching to the kingdom.

The servant's debt was unpayable. The story is about forgiveness, and the analogy is especially appropriate, for the word used for forgiveness here is the same that's used for canceling a debt. And the servant's debt had to be forgiven; he had no other hope.

In first-century Palestine a denarius represented a day's wages. From this a workman provided food, clothing, and shelter for himself and his family. Ten thousand talents was so great a sum that if a person lived 2,500 lifetimes he could not earn enough to repay the debt. In contrast, the 100 denarii owed the servant was a relatively paltry sum, and could have been repaid if the debtor were given time.

The servant asked for time. When called before the ruler the servant begged for time to repay the debt. But there was no way the debt could be repaid even if the servant had thousands of lifetimes to earn what was owed. The king's spontaneous decision to forgive the debt was truly stunning, and clearly far more than the servant had dreamed of, much less expected.

The servant's response to forgiveness. Just after the debt was forgiven the servant accosted a fellow servant and demanded payment of a relatively insignificant amount. He was unwilling to treat others as he had been treated by the king.

The king's anger. The king then recalled the first servant and demanded he repay everything after all. Jesus warned that God was serious about forgiveness, and that His disciples must forgive their brothers "from the heart."

BIBLE BACKGROUND:
HARD SAYINGS OF JESUS

"His master was angry, and delivered him to the torturers until he should pay all that was due to him.

So My heavenly Father also will do to you if each of you, from his heart, does not forgive his brother his trespasses" (Matt. 18:34, 35).

Does Jesus mean that God will not forgive a person who fails to forgive others? If so, doesn't salvation depend on what we do rather than on what Jesus did for us?

Jesus' story isn't intended to teach God's way of salvation, but is told in response to Peter's question about how many times he should forgive (18:21). Jesus indicates that it is unthinkable that we who have been forgiven so much should fail to forgive anyone anything! Jesus' warning emphasizes the fact that an unforgiving attitude is a serious matter. A person who is unwilling to forgive has not really understood grace or appropriated God's forgiveness.

This extended parable makes two things clear about Jesus' kingdom. First, God relates to those who live in this kingdom through grace expressed in forgiveness. We can never pay God what we owe. The Pharisees who assumed that one could win acceptance by striving to keep the Law were wrong. Second, those who have experienced God's forgiveness are to be forgiving, showing the same grace to others that they have received from God.

The kingdom Jesus inaugurates is not a kingdom of the righteous, but a kingdom of sinners who must relate to all by accepting and extending forgiveness.

The parable of the generous landowner (Matt. 20:1–16). Jesus had just astonished His disciples by telling them "it is hard for a rich man to enter the kingdom of heaven." This shocked the disciples because in first-century Judaism the rich were thought to have two advantages. First, the fact that they were rich was taken to indicate they were already favored by God (see Deut. 7:13; 8:18). And second, their wealth enabled the rich to give generously to the poor and thus gain merit with God. No wonder the disciples blurted out, "Who then can be saved?" (Matt. 19:25).

After some additional remarks, Jesus observed "many who are first will be last, and the last first," and went on to relate this kingdom parable.

The story-parable. Jesus stated that the kingdom of heaven is like a landowner who went to the town square to hire day laborers. They agreed for a denarius, the normal

pay for a full day's work. Several more times that day the landowner went out and hired more workers, each time saying only, "I will give you what is right." The landowner even hired workers at the eleventh hour, which was just before the end of the working day.

Deuteronomy 24:15 required employers to pay day laborers each evening. So when evening came, the workers lined up to receive their pay. The landowner paid those who had worked only an hour a full day's pay! In fact, he paid everyone a full day's pay. So those who had agreed early in the morning to work for a denarius complained. It wasn't fair that they should receive the same wages as men who not worked nearly as long.

The landowner answered, "Is it not lawful for me to do what I wish with my own things? Or is your eye evil because I am good?" And Jesus concluded, "So the last will be first, and the first last. For many are called, but few chosen" (20:15, 16).

Applying the story-parable. Here again we see a stunning kingdom principle introduced. In Jesus' kingdom, grace rules. And God is free to be as generous as He pleases with human beings. Those who saw their relationship with God rooted in merit (their long, hard work) were wrong. And so it is that many who are first, and thus in their own eyes deserve more, will be last; while those who depend on grace alone will be first.

How true it is that while many are called to know the grace of God, few respond to it.

The parable of the marriage feast (Matt. 22:2–14). When Jesus told this parable-story, his conflict with the chief priests and Pharisees was open and intense. This parable is specifically directed toward them.

The parable can be viewed as a drama in three acts. Each scene in the drama builds on customs that were well known to Jesus' listeners.

Weddings were important events. To reject an invitation was an insult.

The invitation rejected (vv. 1–7). It was customary to send two invitations to an important feast, one some time ahead of the event so the guests would be able to clear their calendars, and a second when the feast was ready, that the guests might arrive on time. In Jesus parable when this second invitation was delivered, the invited guests who were the king's first choice "made light of it." They not only ignored the king's invitation but injured and even killed his messengers. When the king heard, he sent his army to destroy the murderers and raze their city.

The invitation expanded (vv. 8–10). The invited guests had scorned their invitations, but the feast had been prepared. So the king sent his servants out into the highways to "gather together all whom they found, both bad and good," to fill the wedding hall.

The man without a wedding garment (vv. 12–14). The problem was not that the man the king singled out was dressed inappropriately. It was customary on very special occasions for a host to provide garments for his guests. The person singled out in the parable had only his own clothing, not the clothing provided by the king, and was "cast into outer darkness."

Interpreting the parable. In this parable the Jews were the intended guests, chosen by God Himself and first invited long before the feast was ready. But when Jesus came announcing that the feast (the kingdom) was ready, they either ignored His summons or became hostile and abusive. This treatment had doomed their generation.

So since the intended guests would not come to the feast which God had prepared, He would look elsewhere. God would send His servants out into the world and invite as many as they could contact to the wedding feast. That invitation would be extended to the bad and the good alike.

But those who came to the feast must wear a garment that the king provided. Those who tried to attend wearing their own garments would be taken away and cast into outer darkness. Isaiah had said it long ago: "We are all like an unclean thing, and all our righteousnesses are like filthy rags" (Is. 64:6). Only a person clothed in the righteousness that God provides is welcome at the feast.

This story also adds to our understanding of the kingdom Jesus inaugurated. It is not, like the messianic kingdom of the Old Testament, for Israel, but for everyone, whether they are bad or good. God clothes those who respond to His invitation to the wedding of His Son with His own righteousness. And no one without that righteousness can stand in His presence.

The parable of the ten virgins (Matt. 25:1–13). First-century Jewish weddings were major social events. When the time for the wedding banquet approached, the guests would gather to await the presentation of the groom with his bride. The ten virgins in the story were invited guests. But five of the virgins were foolish. While they brought lamps, to use in case the coming of the bridegroom were delayed, they brought no oil for their lamps (v. 3). The other five brought both lamps and oil. When the groom was delayed all fell asleep, and were awakened at midnight by the cry, "the bridegroom is coming" (v. 6). The five virgins who had oil for the lamps joined the wedding party. The five who were foolish scurried about trying to find oil. They pounded on the door, but the door remained shut, and the groom responded to their appeals by saying, "I do not know you."

Jesus applied the story saying, "Watch therefore, for you know neither the day or the hour in which the Son of Man is coming" (v. 13).

This story is clearly linked with the appearance of Christ at the end of the kingdom era. The five foolish virgins had made no preparation while the bridegroom delayed His coming. The wise had prepared by providing a stock of oil for their lamps.

Some have suggested that oil here is a symbol for the Holy Spirit, whom the five wise virgins possessed while the foolish did not. But the point of the parable does not depend on the symbolic significance of the oil. The parable story simply teaches that it's vital during the era of the hidden kingdom to prepare for the reappearance of Christ, the bridegroom. When all hear the shout, "the bridegroom is coming," it will be too late for those who have not prepared themselves to greet Him.

The parable of the talents (Matt. 25:14–30; Luke 19:12–27). In this parable Jesus spoke of an absent king who committed resources to his servants while he was away. Each of the three servants in the story had a different number of talents (monetary units, as are the minas in Luke's account) to invest. Two of the servants invested wisely and were able to offer the king a profit when he returned. Despite the different amounts earned, each of the two was commended and given the same promise: "Well done, good and faithful servant; you were faithful over a few things, I will make you ruler over many things. Enter into the joy of your lord" (Matt. 25:21, 23). In Luke the reward is authority over a number of cities (19:17, 19).

The third servant however hid his talent, and could only return to the king what he had originally been given. The king took his talent and gave it to the one who had ten.

Luke introduces another element into the story. In his telling of the parable Jesus notes that the ruler's citizens hated him and after he was gone sent a delegation to say, "We will not have this man to reign over us."

In Matthew's story the third servant is harshly judged, and in Luke's the citizens who refused to accept the absent king's authority were slain.

BIBLE BACKGROUND:
HARD SAYINGS OF JESUS

"For to everyone who has, more will be given, and he will have abundance; but from him who does not have, even what he has will be taken away" (Matt. 25:29; compare Matt. 13:12; Mark 4:24, 25; Luke 8:18).

The same saying is repeated in Luke 19:26, also in the story of the talents (minas). On the one hand this is a principle expressed in our commonplace proverb, "Use it or lose it." Any gift or ability a person fails to use is diminished if not lost. But in context, this saying describes a spiritual reality. God's revelation of Himself and His purposes is a gift that calls for a faith-response. Any failure to respond to known truth will result in losing sight even of the truth we once knew. On the other hand, the person who responds to God's Word will be given greater and greater understanding and insight.

Luke 19:11 gives us the key to interpreting this kingdom parable. Luke states that Jesus spoke this parable "because they thought the kingdom of God would appear immediately." Instead, the mystery kingdom established by Jesus would continue in His absence. During that undetermined period of time before Jesus' return, His servants are charged with the stewardship of His resources. When Jesus returns, those who used their resources wisely and for our Lord's benefit will be rewarded, and those who refused to acknowledge the authority of the absent king will be slain.

What then do these parables add to our grasp of the mystery form of the kingdom that Jesus introduced? It is a kingdom whose citizens are the forgiven and forgiving. It is a kingdom marked by God's grace and generosity, a principle which will cause those who had been first to be last and those who had been last to be first. It is a kingdom into which the evil and the good of all peoples will be invited, because those who had been chosen refused to heed the King's call. It is also a kingdom that will come to an end when Jesus returns. Thus those living during the mystery kingdom era must make personal preparations for Jesus' unexpected return. During this time citizens must be in willing submission to its absent king, and actively serve Him with all the resources He provides.

KINGDOM SAYINGS

In addition to the parables of the kingdom found in Matthew 13, and several extended parable-stories, the gospels report a variety of sayings of Jesus about the kingdom. Some of these are enigmatic. But each adds to our understanding of this important theme in Jesus' teaching.

Matthew 11:11; Luke 7:28. The saying is found in passages where Jesus eulogizes John the Baptist. In each passage Jesus identifies John as a figure promised in the Old Testament, God's messenger, who comes to prepare the way for the promised Messiah (see Mal. 3:1). This role meant that John's prophetic ministry was especially significant. "Assuredly, I say to you," Jesus announced, "among those born of women there has not risen one greater than John the Baptist."

What surprises us is what Jesus went on to say. "But he who is least in the kingdom of heaven is greater than he." In what sense is one who is least in the kingdom of heaven greater than John?

Jesus identified John the Baptist as the greatest prophet of the Old Testament era.

❖

John was the greatest of the prophets in that he had the privilege of announcing the imminent appearance of the Messiah. The other prophets who spoke of Him were distant in time. But those who actually enter the kingdom are greater than John in the sense of having an even higher privilege. John was killed by Herod before the death and resurrection of Jesus and thus died before the initiation of the church age and the establishment of the mystery form of God's kingdom.

John had been born of women. Those who were to enter the kingdom of Jesus would, as Jesus told Nicodemus, be "born again" (John 3:3). In both these senses the least in God's mystery kingdom are greater than John.

Matthew 11:12; Luke 16:16. In speaking of John's ministry Jesus made a peculiar remark. Similar remarks are reported by both Matthew and Luke. Matthew tells us that Jesus said, "From the days of John the Baptist until now the kingdom of heaven suffers violence, and the violent take it by force." Luke reports Jesus also said, "The law and the prophets were until John. Since that time the kingdom of God has been preached, and everyone is pressing into it."

The context of each verse indicates that Jesus identified the appearance of John the Baptist as one of history's turning points. John was Jesus' forerunner, and it was Jesus who, as the Prophet like Moses, would set sacred history on its new course.

In Matthew Jesus' point is that since John appeared to signal the beginning of the new age opposition has become more and more violent. The kingdom has advanced, as demonstrated in Jesus' miracles and through Jesus' teaching. But rather than sweep all opposition away before it, advancement of the kingdom has been marked by intense struggle with demonic and human opponents.

In the Luke quote Jesus observes that since John concern with the kingdom has intensified. Jesus had just condemned the Pharisees for being among those who "justify yourselves before men" (v. 15). Despite the hostility of such leaders, there were many who did respond to the preaching of the kingdom and eagerly sought to enter it.

Matthew 12:28; Luke 11:20. Jesus' opponents can't deny the fact of His many public miracles. The crowds have begun to wonder aloud if Jesus might not be the "Son of David," a title of the Messiah. Desperately the Pharisees accused Jesus of being in league with Satan. "This fellow does not cast out demons except by Beelzebub, the ruler of the demons" (Matt. 12:24). Jesus refuted their charge, and then made a telling point. "But if I cast out demons by the Spirit of God, surely the kingdom of God has come upon you." Luke reports a similar saying: "But if I cast out demons with the finger of God, surely the kingdom of God has come upon you."

Jesus' listeners had a decision to make, and the options were unmistakable. If Jesus' exorcisms were evidence of God's power at work in the world, the conclusion that the kingdom age had dawned was inescapable.

Matthew 16:19. Jesus has just heard Peter's confession of faith in Him as Messiah, the Son of God. Jesus then announced that "I will give you the keys of the kingdom of heaven, and whatever you bind on earth will be bound in heaven, and whatever you loose on earth will be loosed in heaven."

These enigmatic words have been taken by some to establish the claim that Peter and his supposed successors, the bishops of Rome, have a continuing authority over all Christians. Others have argued that the keys were given to the Twelve Disciples as a group. At the same time, there has been intense debate not only over the nature of the keys but also over the nature of the binding and the loosing Jesus describes.

We do know that in the Old Testament keys symbolize authority (Judg. 3:23; Isa. 22:22), and that in the New Testament one with the keys can exclude or permit entry (Rev. 9:1–6; 20:1–3). But in what sense did Peter have the keys, and in what sense did Peter bind (exclude from) or loose (welcome into) God's kingdom?

The best answer is that the reference to the keys meant that Peter would be given the privilege of being the first to proclaim the gospel message to the two first-century groups that symbolized all humankind. On the day of Pentecost it was Peter who gave the first gospel message to the Jews (Acts 2). And in the home of Cornelius it was Peter who first shared the gospel with Gentiles (Acts 10, 11). In this sense Peter has used the keys, and the gospel door now stands open to all.

But how does this bind and loose? The same gospel message that draws some to God alienates others. Those who respond are loosed, and those who reject are bound, and by their own choice.

While we can see how this verse has generated the image of Peter standing at the gates of heaven to admit some applicants and reject others, in fact Peter used the keys when he first preached the gospel. Since then the door has stood open, and all who will can enter.

Matthew 18:1–4; Mark 9:36, 37; 10:15; Luke 9:47, 48; 18:17. Each of the passages record Jesus' welcome of little children and His comment that those who would enter His kingdom must become like them. The Matthew passage provides the context as well as the quotation.

At that time the disciples came to Jesus, saying, "Who then is greatest in the kingdom of heaven?" Then Jesus called a little child to Him, set him in the midst of them, and said, "Assuredly, I say to you, unless you are converted and become as little children, you will by no means enter the kingdom of heaven. Therefore whoever humbles himself as this little child is the greatest in the kingdom of heaven."

To understand this kingdom saying we need to carefully note several details in Matthew's account. First, the issue the disciples raised was one of greatness in the kingdom, not salvation.

Second, before answering, Jesus "called a little child." The Greek word here is *paidion*, used of a child up to about age seven. Such a child was not responsible to keep God's law. Twelve was the age of responsibility when an individual was "bar mitzvahed"and became a "son of the law."

Third, Matthew tells us that Jesus "called a little child to Him" and then "set him in the midst of them." This last point is particularly important. Jesus had come, calling all Israel to Himself as messianic King and Son of God. But the nation had

Jesus presented a little child as the symbolic key to greatness in His kingdom.

not responded. While individuals did become Jesus' disciples, the religious elite who led the nation decisively rejected Jesus' claims, and the mass of the people hesitated, unwilling to go against their leaders and commit themselves to Jesus.

But when Jesus called the little child to Him, the child responded immediately and came to Him. Jesus then set the little child in the midst as an example of what true greatness would involve. Greatness could not be a matter of the Law, for little children were exempt from keeping the Law. But greatness would be a matter of a person's responsiveness to Jesus' voice. It was and always would be the person who humbly hears and responds to Jesus throughout his or her life who achieves significance in the kingdom of God.

This truly does call for a conversion, a change in the way a person thinks about and sees the world. The key to kingdom living is found in our willingness to humble ourselves and trust Christ so completely that we unhesitatingly respond whenever He speaks to you or me.

Mark 1:15; Matthew 4:17 (compare Luke 10:9, 11). Several times Jesus is reported to have spoken of the kingdom of heaven as being "at hand." Mark tells us that in preaching the kingdom of God, Jesus would say, "The time is fulfilled, and the kingdom of God is at hand. Repent, and believe in the gospel."

In this saying, the word *repent* retains its basic meaning of "change your heart, mind, and behavior." And the gospel is the good news of the kingdom of God. What is striking is Jesus' announcement that the kingdom is "at hand."

It is certain that Jesus' listeners thought at first that he meant the earthly, political kingdom the prophets described. But the announcement was not about a particular form of the kingdom but about the appearance of the King!

As we noted earlier, the biblical concept of kingdom rests on the idea of sovereignty. One's kingdom is the people or things over which he or she has authority and control. And citizenship in a kingdom rests on one's allegiance to the kingdom's ruler. The kingdom that Jesus, John (Matt. 3:2), and Jesus' disciples (Matt. 10:7) referred to as "at hand" was near simply because the King was present. And the good news of the kingdom was that one might give his or her allegiance to the Christ as king, and so enter the kingdom He proclaimed.

Mark 9:1; Matthew 16:28; Luke 9:27. Each of the three gospel writers gives a slightly different report of this incident. Mark quotes Jesus as saying, "Assuredly, I say to you that there are some standing here who will not taste death till they see the kingdom of God present with power." Matthew's account quotes Jesus saying, "Assuredly, I say to you, there are some standing here who shall not taste death till they see the Son of Man coming in His kingdom." Luke's account reads, "But I tell you truly, there are some standing here who shall not taste death till they see the kingdom of God."

Each gospel writer immediately goes on to describe what is known as Jesus' transfiguration, and specifies that this happened six days ("about eight days" in Luke) after Jesus promised that some standing there would see His glory and a visible revelation of the power of His kingdom.

Most believe that Jesus referred to His transfiguration, the account of which immediately follows in each gospel. In the trans-figuration "some standing there" saw Christ in His essential glory, as He will appear when He returns, and heard God's voice commending Him. 2 Peter 1:16-18 provides support for this view. Peter, one of the three to witness the transfiguration, later wrote that, we "were eyewitnesses of His majesty. For He received from God the Father honor and glory when such a voice came to Him from the Excellent Glory: 'This is My beloved Son, in whom I am well pleased.' And we heard this voice which came from heaven when we were with Him on the holy mountain" (compare Mark 9:1–8).

BIBLE BACKGROUND:
HARD SAYINGS OF JESUS

"Let the dead bury their own dead, but you go and preach the kingdom of God" (Luke 9:60; compare Matt. 8:22).

Jesus made this remark to an individual he had called to follow Him, but who asked first to bury his father. The saying seems almost heartless. But we need to remember that the Jews buried their dead the same day the person died. The man Jesus rebuked had actually asked to be allowed to wait until his father died. He had placed his filial obligation to his father above his commitment to the Son of God.

In the same context Jesus responded to another person who asked to bid farewell to his household, "No one, having put his hand to the plow, and looking back, is fit for the kingdom of God" (Luke 9:62). When farmers plowed, they set the course of their furrows by picking out two objects, one further away than the other. The farmer lined them up and kept one object directly behind the other. This enabled the farmer to plow a straight furrow, which set the pattern for plowing the whole field. If the farmer looked back, and took his eye off the guide, the furrow became crooked, and his working of the whole field was affected. If a person intends to follow Jesus, he or she must not look back. If he or she does, the whole pattern of the life Jesus intends for us is thrown off. The decision to follow Jesus means making him the single guiding focus of our lives.

Taken together the parables of the kingdom and Jesus' kingdom sayings do add to our understanding of the mystery form of God's kingdom that Christ initiated. It is a kingdom very unlike the earthly kingdom prophesied in the Old Testament. Yet it is a kingdom whose expression will be worked out here on earth. It is a kingdom experienced by individuals who hear and respond to Jesus' voice. And, as we will see, it is a kingdom in which citizens experience the Father's loving care as they learn to rely wholly on Him.

JESUS' PROPHECIES AND PREDICTIONS

The Sermon on the Mount and Jesus' kingdom parables help us begin to understand the kingdom theme in Jesus' public teaching. Looking at every reference Jesus made to a kingdom helps even more. When we do, we make the fascinating discovery that most of Jesus' kingdom predictions don't deal with the mystery kingdom at all!

As noted earlier, the gospels record 85 occasions on which Jesus used the phrase "kingdom of heaven" or "kingdom of God." The word "kingdom" occurs in 121 verses in the gospels. The first question we need to ask as we look at any of these references is, "Which kingdom does this verse concern?" This is an important question, for we've seen that Scripture knows at least three kingdoms of God: the universal kingdom of God, the earthly kingdom of the Messiah, and the mystery kingdom that Jesus inaugurated.

KINGDOMS REFERRED TO IN THE GOSPELS

When we run across the word "kingdom" in the gospels, it's important to distinguish the particular kingdom in view. Determining which kingdom is vital to understanding Jesus' teaching. So before looking at Jesus' predictions and prophecies, we need to note that the word "kingdom" is used with several different meanings.

KINGDOMS IN GENERAL

In some passages no specific kingdom is in mind. For instance, Jesus said "every kingdom divided against itself is brought to desolation" (Matt. 12:25). Here His statement of a general principle is true for all kingdoms.

SATAN'S KINGDOM

In the same context Jesus spoke of Satan's kingdom (12:26; compare Luke 11:18). This reality is reflected in Colossians 1:13, where Paul writes that God has "delivered us from the power of darkness and conveyed us into the kingdom of the Son of His love."

NATIONS AS KINGDOMS

A very few references are made to political kingdoms. This use is illustrated in Satan's temptation of Christ when he showed Him "all the kingdoms of the world and their glory" (Matt. 4:8; Luke 4:5).

GOD'S UNIVERSAL KINGDOM

The doctrine of God's universal kingdom is developed in the Old Testament, and there are a few references to it in our Gospels. However Jesus does imply God's universal kingdom when He taught His disciples to pray, "Your kingdom come. Your will be done on earth as it is in heaven . . . " (Matt. 6:10).

ETERNAL KINGDOM OF THE BLESSED (HEAVEN)

Jesus spoke of foreigners who would come and "sit down with Abraham . . . in the kingdom of heaven" (Matt. 8:11).

EARTHLY KINGDOM OF THE MESSIAH

There are surprisingly few of these references. Most often that kingdom is in the thoughts or questions of others rather than in Jesus' teaching. For instance, one of Jesus' stories was told "because they thought the kingdom of God would appear immediately" (Luke 19:11).

Even so, it is clear that Jesus confirmed the image of a coming messianic kingdom and envisioned a future day when He would rule and when His disciples would "sit on thrones judging the twelve tribes of Israel" (Luke 22:30). As we will see, many of Jesus' prophecies about the future are in harmony with Old Testament prophecy concerning the messianic kingdom.

MYSTERY KINGDOM

Despite the fact that "kingdom" is used in various senses, it is clear that the vast majority of Jesus' references to a kingdom focus on the mystery form of the kingdom highlighted in Jesus' Sermon on the Mount and kingdom parables.

BIBLE BACKGROUND: KINGDOMS IN THE GOSPELS

KINGDOMS IN GENERAL

Matt. 12:25; Mark 3:24; Luke 11:17; 19:12, 15; 21:10

EARTHLY KINGDOMS

Matt. 4:8; 24:7; Mark 6:23; 13:8; Luke 4:5; John 18:36

KINGDOM OF SATAN

Matt. 12:24; Luke 11:18

UNIVERSAL KINGDOM OF GOD

Matt. 6:10, 13; Luke 11:2; 23:42

ETERNAL KINGDOM OF THE BLESSED (HEAVEN)

Matt. 8:11, 12; 26:29; Mark 9:47; 14:25; Luke 13:28, 29

MESSIANIC KINGDOM OF THE PROPHETS

Matt. 13:41, 43; 20:21; 25:34; Mark 11:10; 15:43; Luke 1:33; 14:15; 17:20; 19:11; 21:31; 22:16, 18, 30; 23:42, 51

MYSTERY KINGDOM ESTABLISHED BY JESUS

Matt. 3:2; 4:17, 23; 5:3, 10, 19, 20; 6:33; 7:21; 9:35; 10:7; 11:11, 12; 12:28; 13:11, 19, 24, 31, 33, 38, 43, 44, 45, 47, 52; 16:19, 28; 18:1, 3, 4, 23;19:12, 14, 23, 24; 20:1, 21; 21:31, 43; 22:2; 23:13; 24:14; 25:1, 14; Mark 1:14, 15; 4:11, 26, 30; 9:1;10:14, 15, 23, 24, 25; 12:34; Luke 4:43; 6:20; 7:28; 8:1, 10; 9:2, 11, 27, 60, 62; 10:9, 11; 11:20;

12:31, 32; 13:18, 20; 17:21, 18:16, 17, 24, 25, 29;22:29; John 3:3, 5; 18:36

EMPHASES IN KINGDOM REFERENCES

The Gospels report Jesus' teaching about the mystery form of the kingdom of God, both in quotes and in comments made by the writers. Several recurring themes can be observed in these references.

THE KINGDOM WAS A MAJOR THEME IN JESUS' EARLY MINISTRY

The kingdom was definitely Jesus' theme when He began to preach. Like John the Baptist, Jesus called on His hearers to "repent, for the kingdom of heaven is at hand" (Matt. 4:17; compare Mark 1:15).

The call to repentance is often heard in the Old Testament. There as in Jesus' preaching repentance involves Israel's turning to God away from sin. The motivation for repentance in John's and Jesus' preaching is the imminent appearance of God's kingdom (Matt. 4:17; 10:7; Mark 1:15). The kingdom was "at hand" in the sense that the King Himself had stepped into history and was even then present among God's chosen people.

The Gospels also emphasize the fact that Jesus felt a deep obligation to teach and preach the gospel. Matthew tells us that Jesus "went about all Galilee, teaching in their synagogues, preaching the gospel of the kingdom, and healing all kinds of sickness" (4:23; see also Matt. 9:35, Mark 1:14). Luke quotes Jesus saying, "I must preach the kingdom of God to the other cities also, because for this purpose I have been sent" (4:43). When Jesus sent His disciples on preaching missions, He commissioned them to "preach the kingdom of God and heal the sick" (compare 9:60). Matthew reports Jesus' instructions: "As you go, preach, saying, 'The kingdom of heaven is at hand'" (10:7).

LIFE IN THE KINGDOM OF GOD WAS THE SUBJECT OF JESUS' EARLY KINGDOM TEACHING

In Jesus' Sermon on the Mount He called for a reorientation of life to new values and priorities. His hearers must not focus on the externals of the law, but on an in-secret relationship with God as Father. Jesus traced the impact of that relationship by showing how it frees from materialism, from anxiety, and from judgmentalism. In Jesus' kingdom what counts is an inner transformation that brings the believer into harmony with God's own character, that the believer might be more like his heavenly Father in every relationship. The kingdom lifestyle is discussed at length in chapter 3 of this book, and in a review of many of Christ's kingdom sayings in chapter 4.

Both the Sermon on the Mount and many of the kingdom sayings, such as those about little children, emphasize responding to Jesus' teachings. To live in the present and hidden kingdom of Jesus a person must have faith in Christ and be willing to put His teachings into practice.

THE NATURE OF THE KINGDOM OF GOD WAS DEVELOPED IN CHRIST'S KINGDOM PARABLES

It is Jesus' kingdom parables which help us realize that the kingdom Jesus inaugurated is very different from the earthly kingdom predicted by the Old Testament prophets. Jesus spoke of the "mystery" of His kingdom, using a technical theological term that identifies an

Jesus' miracles were divine authentication of His teachings and His claims.

element of God's eternal plan that had not been revealed in the Old Testament.

In contrast to the Messiah's kingdom, the kingdom Jesus inaugurated is a hidden kingdom. While Jesus' kingdom is also an earthly kingdom, in that it finds its expression in the here and now, the rule of God in Jesus' mystery kingdom is expressed in and through individuals who trust in Jesus as Christ and King, and who give their allegiance to Him. While the mystery kingdom is not visible to men of the world, God actively shapes the experiences and circumstances of kingdom citizens. The reality of God's active rule expressed in the lives of kingdom citizens is the reality that frees believers to give His kingdom priority in all things.

Jesus' emphasis on the nature of Jesus' mystery kingdom and on the lifestyle of its citizens raises significant questions. Jesus has defined the mystery kingdom by con-

trasting it with the kingdom of Old Testament prophecy. Does this imply that the prophets were mistaken, or indicate that the earthy images used by the prophets are to be spiritualized or allegorized?

In fact, however, when we examine the prophecies of Jesus, we discover that He Himself emphasizes an end of this age, and that He envisions future events that are in harmony with the prophets' vision of a future kingdom.

JESUS' PREDICTIONS

We need to make a distinction between Jesus' predictions and His prophecies. Jesus' predictions concern matters that would come to pass in His immediate future. Jesus' prophecies concern what is to, at, or beyond the "end of the age" (Matt. 13:39, 49; 24:3).

The mix of prediction and prophecy is characteristic of biblical prophecy. Those who spoke for God were authenticated before their contemporaries by the fulfillment of near-view predictions they made. Deuteronomy 18:21, 22 makes this very clear:

And if you say in your heart, "How shall we know the word which the LORD has not spoken?—when a prophet speaks in the name of the LORD, if the thing does not happen or come to pass, that is the thing which the LORD has not spoken; the prophet has spoken it presumptuously; you shall not be afraid of him.

Thus when Jesus said to a cripple "Get up and walk" and the cripple did so, His word and its fulfillment were immediate and clear confirmation that He was God's spokesman.

Later in His ministry Jesus began to make specific predictions about His own future, all of which came to pass. Matthew 16:21 reports that when it became clear that the general populace would not acknowledge Jesus as their Messiah, a distinct shift in the focus of Jesus' teaching took place. "From that time Jesus began to show His disciples that He must go to Jerusalem, and suffer many things from the elders and chief priests and scribes, and be killed and be raised the third day." These predictions and others are summarized below.

JESUS PREDICTED THE BRIDEGROOM WOULD BE TAKEN AWAY

When asked why His disciples did not fast as did the disciples of John, Jesus pointed out that the coming of a bridegroom was a time for partying, not for grieving. Jesus added that the time would come when He, the bridegroom, would be "taken away." That would be time enough for His disciples to mourn (Matt. 9:15; Mark 2:20; Luke 5:35).

JESUS PREDICTED THAT HE WOULD SUFFER AND BE REJECTED

The theme of suffering and rejection is found in many of Jesus predictions. His comments on His coming suffering are found in Matthew 16:21 and 17:22–23, in Mark 8:31, and in Luke 9:22 and 17:25.

JESUS PREDICTED THAT HE WOULD BE CONDEMNED BY A GENTILE COURT

Only the Roman governor of Judea had the authority to condemn a person to death. This fact underlay Jesus' prediction that the chief priests and scribes would condemn Him to death, and then "deliver Him to the Gentiles to mock and to scourge and to crucify" (Matt. 20:19; Luke 18:32).

JESUS PREDICTED HE WOULD BE KILLED

The Gospels record a number of occasions on which Jesus spoke of His coming death, stating clearly that He would be killed (Matt. 16:21; 17:23; Mark 8:31; 9:31; Luke 9:22).

JESUS PREDICTED THAT HE WOULD RISE FROM THE DEAD AFTER BEING KILLED BY HIS ENEMIES

Jesus stated on a number of occasions that He would rise again, typically whenever He spoke of being killed (Matt. 20:19; Mark 8:31; 10:34; Luke 9:22; 18:33; John 20:9).

Jesus also specified that His resurrection would take place after three days (Matt. 12:40; Mark 8:31; John 2:19–22). While Jesus spoke allegorically, calling His body "this temple," the chief priests and scribes clearly understood what He was saying. After Jesus was crucified and buried, a delegation of Jewish leaders asked that a military guard be posted at the tomb. They knew Jesus had predicted that He would rise after three days, and they said that they wanted to be sure His disciples did not come and steal the body (Matt. 27:63).

JESUS PREDICTED THE ABANDONMENT BY HIS FOLLOWERS

Both Matthew 26:31 and Mark 14:27 mention Christ's reference to Zechariah 13:7: "I will strike the Shepherd, / And the sheep of the flock will be scattered." Jesus applied this prophecy to His own situation, saying, "All of you will be made to stumble because of Me this night." Before the next day dawned each of the Twelve had fled before the mob that came to drag Jesus before the high priest and Sanhedrin.

JESUS PREDICTED PETER'S DENIAL

Peter had reacted to Jesus' prediction of abandonment with a vehement objection. Whatever the others might do, Peter was ready to die with his Lord! Each of the Gospels records the incident and Jesus' prediction that before the rooster crowed Peter would deny Jesus three times (Matt. 26:34, 70; Mark 14:30, 68; Luke 22:34, 61; John 13:38; 18:27).

OTHER PREDICTIONS JESUS MADE

The day of the Triumphal Entry, early in Easter week, Jesus told some of His disciples to go into the city. He predicted that they would find a young donkey there, and told them what to say should anyone question them when they untied it and brought it to Him (Matt. 21:2; Mark 11:2–4; Luke 19:30, 31; John 12:15).

After the resurrection, Jesus also predicted the kind of death that Peter would die (John 21:18, 19). This prediction was fulfilled around A.D. 68 when Peter was executed in Rome, tradition says, by being crucified upside down.

JESUS' SHORTER PROPHECIES

Often in the Gospel record we find brief references to the more distant future in Jesus' teaching. There are also several major passages devoted to lengthy prophecy about the future, which we will examine more closely later in this chapter. Yet a number of remarks Jesus made, to His disciples, in response to His opponents, or apparently as asides when speaking on other subjects, do contain significant prophecy. In these remarks Jesus spoke about the end of the age, about His return, about the resurrection, and about Judgment Day.

JESUS PREDICTED THE IMPACT OF ISRAEL'S REJECTION

John reminds us that "He came to His own, and His own did not receive Him" (John 1:11). The rejection of Jesus was to have a significant impact on Israel as a nation. While individual Jews would continue to be saved, the privileged position of the nation would lapse while the door was flung open to Gentiles.

Presenting Himself as the rejected cornerstone spoken of in Psalm 118:22, Jesus announced "Therefore I say to you, the kingdom of God will be taken from you and given to a nation bearing the fruits of it" (Matt. 21:43). The same thought is expressed in the story of a vineyard owner whose tenants killed his son. The owner surely would punish the guilty, "and give the vineyard to others" (Luke 20:16).

After the healing of the servant of the Roman officer, Jesus remarked on his faith. He told His fellow-countrymen,

I have not found such great faith, not even in Israel! And I say to you that many will come from east and west, and sit down with Abraham, Isaac, and Jacob in the kingdom of heaven. But the sons of the kingdom will be cast out into outer darkness (Matt. 8:10–12; compare Luke 13:29).

God had not rejected Israel; Israel had rejected God's Son. Despite Israel's historic identity as God's chosen people, soon all would have access to God's kingdom through faith in the Son. And those without faith would find themselves outside, in eternal darkness.

In fact, Jesus warned of the judgment to come upon the cities where He ministered most frequently:

Woe to you, Chorazin! Woe to you, Bethsaida! For if the mighty works which were done in you had been done in Tyre and Sidon, they would have repented long ago in sackcloth and ashes. But I say to you, it will be more tolerable for Tyre and Sidon in the day of judgment than for you (Matt. 11:21, 22; Luke 10:13, 14; compare Mark 3:8, 7:24).

Even more striking, Jesus said the same thing about Sodom and Gomorrah, cities noted for their wickedness. The miracles done in Capernaum, Jesus' headquarters for His ministry in Galilee, would have brought the people of Sodom and Gomorrah to their knees. Therefore "I say to you that it shall be more tolerable for the land of Sodom in the day of judgment than for you" (Matt. 11:24; Luke 10:12).

The repercussions of Israel's rejection of the Messiah would be great both in the future history of the world, and on judgment day.

BIBLE BACKGROUND:

HARD SAYINGS OF JESUS

"It is not good to take the children's bread and throw it to the little dogs" (Matt. 15:26; Mark 7:27).

Jesus was outside Jewish territory, in the region of Tyre and Sidon. He was approached by a Canaanite woman who begged Jesus to heal her demon-possessed daughter. Jesus refused, saying, "I was not sent except to the lost sheep of the house of Israel." When she continued to call on Him, Jesus spoke the troubling words recorded in Matthew 15:26 and Mark 7:27. A helpful solution is found in the book *Baffling Bible Questions Answered,* (Baker 1993; p. 245).

There is significant theological interplay in the dialogue between Jesus and this woman. She referred to Jesus as "Son of David" (Matt.

15:22), a title identifying the Jewish Messiah. Jesus responded by saying that he was "sent only to the lost sheep of Israel" (v. 24). As a Gentile this woman had no right to him or the benefits he brought to his own. His "bread" was for the children of Israel, not the "Gentile dogs," a common Jewish euphemism for Gentiles. The woman did not argue but agreed. She had no right to the benefits Jesus brought, and admitted that the children were to be fed first. But in saying that even the dogs eat the leftover crumbs, the woman expressed great faith. Jesus responded to her not because she had any claim on him but because the grace of God he brought was enough to meet the needs of the Jewish people, with enough left over to satisfy the Gentiles. Seeing her faith, Jesus granted her request.

The lesson here is important. No one today can claim to have a right to God's grace. But faith brings us to Jesus anyway and gives us the benefits he died to provide.

JESUS PREDICTED THAT THE SON OF MAN WOULD BE SEATED ON THE MESSIAH'S THRONE

Jesus frequently spoke of Himself as the "Son of Man," a term which emphasizes His humanity and also links Him to Daniel's prophecy of a Son of Man coming with clouds of glory to receive dominion and an everlasting kingdom (Daniel 7:13, 14).

Jesus had this prophecy in view when He predicted that the Son of Man would come "in His glory, and all the holy angels with Him, then He will sit on the throne of His glory" (Matt. 25:31). This was good news for Jesus' disciples, for Jesus had also said, "In the regeneration, when the Son of Man sits on the throne of His glory, you who have followed Me will also sit on twelve thrones, judging the twelve tribes of Israel. And everyone who has left houses or brothers or sisters or father or mother or wife or children or lands, for My name's sake, shall receive a hundredfold, and inherit eternal life" (Matt. 19:28, 29).

But Jesus' return to take up power was bad news for those who rejected Him. Jesus warned that on that occasion "all the nations will be gathered before Him" for judgment (Matt. 25:32). As Jesus stood before the Sanhedrin whose members had gathered to judge Him, Jesus warned, "I say to you, hereafter you will see the Son of Man sitting at the right hand of the Power, and coming on the clouds of heaven" (Matt. 26:64; compare Mark 14:62 and Luke 22:69).

JESUS SPOKE ABOUT HIS COMING AGAIN

As seen above, Jesus predicted that He would come again, accompanied by angels, to "sit on the throne of His glory." There is no misunderstanding such predictions. Jesus' words are in fullest harmony with the prophets' predictions of the messianic kingdom. "The Son of Man will come in the glory of His Father with His angels, and then He will reward each according to his works" (Matt. 16:27).

Jesus spoke frequently of a coming "day of judgment" (Matt. 10:15; 11:22, 24; 12:41, 42; Mark 6:11; Luke 10:14; 11:31, 32) which is associated in Jesus' kingdom parables with sending out angels at the "the end of the age" to "separate the wicked from the just, and cast them into the furnace of fire" (Matt.13:41, 49, 50).

JESUS PREDICTED THAT ELIJAH WOULD COME FIRST

Jesus emphasized the fact that no one knows when His return will take place (Matt. 24:42–50; Luke 12:39–46). At the same time, Jesus predicted that Elijah would come before He returned to assume power.

The role of Elijah is defined in the Book of Malachi, the book of the Old Testament which was written last, some 400 years before Christ. Malachi closes with a promise and a warning:

> Behold, I will send you Elijah the
> prophet
> Before the coming of the great and dread-
> ful day of the LORD.
> And he will turn
> The hearts of the fathers to the children,
> And the hearts of the children to their
> fathers,
> Lest I come and strike the earth with a
> curse (Mal. 4:5, 6).

This prediction clearly has to do with the Messiah's coming to judge, and as such relates to the Second Coming of Christ rather than the first. When asked by His disciples why the scribes and Pharisees insisted that Elijah must come first (Matt. 17:10; Mark 9:11), Jesus responded, "Indeed, Elijah is coming first" (Matt. 17:11; Mark 9:12). At the same time Jesus told them that Elijah "has also come" (Matt. 17:12; Mark 9:13).

The puzzling view that Elijah will come and has come is resolved when we note two things. One is the principle of dual or multiple fulfillment of prophecy. Many prophecies that have their primary fulfillment in the distant future may also refer to similar events prior to history's end. For instance, Moses' prediction of the coming of a prophet like Himself had its primary fulfillment in Christ. Yet this prophecy was also the basis for the ministry of the many prophets who emerged during Israel's history to serve as God's spokesman.

In the same way the prophecy of a forerunner to the Messiah could be partially fulfilled in John the Baptist, whose

Elijah-like ministry prepared the way for Jesus' first coming, and yet have its primary fulfillment in the coming of another before Jesus' return. Thus too, if God's people had responded and accepted Jesus as the Messiah, John's ministry could have constituted a complete fulfillment of the prophecy. But Israel rejected Jesus, and so the prophecy is to have to find complete fulfillment just before Jesus' return.

John the Baptist had not turned the hearts of the people to God. But in the future the coming Elijah will succeed in turning hearts to the Lord. And at that time the curse that Israel's rejection of the Messiah brought upon the nation—though not on individual Jews who respond to Jesus—will be removed.

JESUS PREDICTED RESURRECTION

Many of Christ's predictions about events to take place at His return imply resurrection. But one verse in John's Gospel gives a specific prediction. Jesus said that "the hour is coming in which all who are in the graves will hear His voice and come forth—those who have done good, to the resurrection of life, and those who have done evil, to the resurrection of condemnation" (John 5:28, 29).

In summing up, remarks made in the course of Jesus' teachings do include predictions about the future. Jesus' rejection by the Jewish people will have a terrible impact on their future. They will no longer enjoy a privileged position as a nation, and the door to the kingdom of heaven will be opened to individual Jews and Gentiles alike.

At the end of the age (of the mystery kingdom) Jesus will return in power to sit on Messiah's promised throne. At that time He will both reward and judge. And after

His return, the dead will be raised and all generations will be judged.

JESUS' MAJOR PROPHETIC DISCOURSES

Prophetic sayings of Jesus are scattered throughout the gospels. But the synoptic Gospels (Matthew, Mark, and Luke) also contain longer blocks of prophetic teaching. These are found in Matthew 24–25, Mark 13, and Luke 21. But before we look at these chapters, we need to say a word about interpreting prophecy.

INTERPRETING PROPHECY

It's common for people to study prophecy for a better understanding of things to come. If we take predictive prophecy, as we do the rest of Scripture, in its plain sense, the Old and New Testaments agree on a general description of the future. At the same time, there are problems in interpreting prophecy which make it difficult for us to speak about details of the future with confidence.

The "plain sense" may not be plain. Prophecy that has already been fulfilled has been fulfilled in the "plain sense" of its original statement. However, we may not fully understand what the prophet is saying until the predicted events come to pass. Who would have understood seven hundred years before Christ what Isaiah portrayed when he said of the Messiah, "They made His grave with the wicked— but with the rich at His death" (Is. 53:9). But after Jesus died between two thieves and was buried in the tomb of "a rich man from Arimathea, named Joseph" (Matt. 27:57), the "plain sense" of Isaiah's prophecy is clear. Thus once a prophecy has been fulfilled we can look back and see that the prophecy was fulfilled literally, not in some metaphoric or symbolic sense. This is clearly seen in

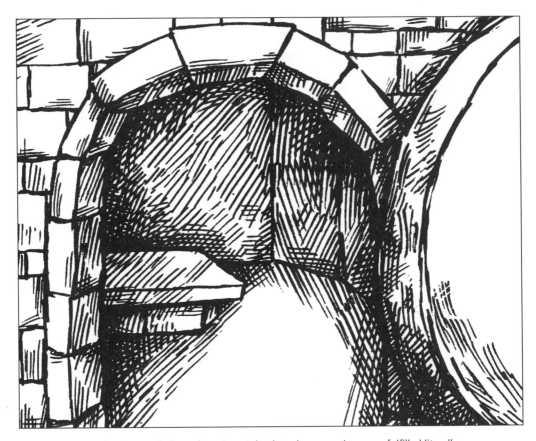

Isaiah 53's predictions about Jesus' death and resurrection were fulfilled literally.

predictions concerning the birth and death of Jesus, and the prophecies in Daniel concerning the rise and fall of world powers.

So the first problem we note concerning the interpretation of prophecy is that while we are to rely on the plain sense of the text, that plain sense may not be clear until a prophecy has been fulfilled.

The revelation may not be complete. We've confronted this problem already. The Old Testament speaks of a universal kingdom of God and also describes an earthly kingdom to be ruled by God's Messiah. The prophet's vision of a kingdom over which Christ would rule was clear. In fact that vision so shaped the expectation of the Jews that when Jesus came, despite His miracles and His teaching, they would not accept Him as the promised King.

Of course, there were many references to the Messiah's suffering, and Isaiah 53 had described His death and its purpose. Yet there was no hint in the Old Testament that God's eternal plan included the initiation of a mystery form of Messiah's kingdom. That revelation awaited the coming of Jesus, and even though Jesus carefully explained the principles on which the mystery kingdom operated, and contrasted it with the expected messianic kingdom, His revelation was rejected. Israel had a fixed idea of what the Messiah would do, but the information the Old Testament provided was incomplete.

When we approach prophecy, it's well for us to remember that God is not obligated to reveal everything He intends to do. Our interpretation of prophecy may be faulty simply because we do not have all the information we need to interpret it correctly.

Timing elements and the relationship between predicted events is normally unspecified. Peter comments on this in his first epistle when he points out that the prophets themselves puzzled over what they wrote. They studied their own writings, "searching what, or what manner of time, the Spirit of Christ who was in them was indicating when He testified beforehand the sufferings of Christ and the glories that would follow" (1 Peter 1:11).

How could the prophets' vision of a suffering Savior who was also powerful Messiah be reconciled? How did these things fit together? And what of the timing? Which came first, and what events followed what events?

The puzzlement of the prophets themselves should warn us against taking a dogmatic stand on our own understanding of future events. The big events may be clear—Jesus will return. There will be resurrection. There is a heaven to gain and a hell to avoid. But as we delve into the details we would do well to remember that God has not given us one of those charts of which prophecy teachers are so fond, showing how each revealed detail of God's plan for future fits with every other detail.

Simply put, we can't speak with authority on the timing of prophesied events, or on how events will flow together in the future.

The purpose of prophecy is to have an impact on our life today. It is also important to remember that prophecy concerning the future is relevant to life today. In writing of the rapture (1 Thess. 4), Paul does not seem concerned with explaining how Jesus' coming in the clouds for His own fits with Christ's warning of a great tribulation to come, or with an angelic separation of the wicked from the righteous when He sits on Messiah's throne. Instead Paul focuses attention on the great reunion with loved ones to take place at the rapture, and says "comfort one another with these words" (1 Thess. 4:18).

As we move into Matthew 24 and 25 we'll note the same phenomenon. Jesus will provide a graphic picture of events that will take place before His return. He will then focus our attention on the importance of being ready when He comes. What's important isn't that we understanding how each detail fits with every other detail. What's important is that that while we wait for these events to take place we concentrate on being faithful servants of our Lord.

Too often we focus so much on the construction of charts of future events that we miss the real meaning of a prophecy: the meaning that it has for our lives here and now.

As we come to our study of Jesus' prophetic teachings, then, we do so well warned. The plain sense of what Jesus says may not be enough to make clear to us all He predicts. What Jesus reveals to us may not be the whole story, and thus not enough to speak confidently about how His predictions will be fulfilled. The timing and the relationship between predicted events often remains unspecified and thus not as clear as we suppose. And, finally, we may miss the real significance of His teaching by seeking to construct charts of future events rather than looking closely for the guidance Jesus' prophecies give us for living our lives today.

THE BROAD CONTEXT FOR FUTURE EVENTS

While we remain aware of the dangers of seeking too detailed an interpretation of prophecy, Jesus' teaching does provide a broad context within which to place His more prophetic teachings.

The first thing we notice is that, like the Sermon on the Mount and the parables in Matthew 13, Jesus' predictions have a kingdom focus. Taken together, the Old and New Testaments give us a glimpse of three kingdoms of heaven, or kingdoms of God.

The first kingdom is the universal kingdom, over which God exercises sovereign control. The second kingdom is the earthly kingdom of the Messiah, the subject of so much Old Testament prophecy. The third kingdom is the mystery kingdom that Jesus inaugurated and on which so much of His public teaching focuses.

It's clear that during Christ's life on earth His disciples continued to think of "God's kingdom" in terms of its messianic expression. When James and John lobbied for positions at Jesus' right and left hands in His kingdom (Matt. 20:21–24), they were not thinking of the mystery kingdom. They were envisioning the messianic kingdom, and the power represented by being at the right and left hand of one who would rule the world! This same vision was fixed in the disciples' minds on the day Jesus ascended into heaven. Even after the resurrected Christ had spent time with His followers teaching on the kingdom, they asked Jesus, "Will You at this time restore the kingdom to Israel?" (Acts 1:6).

Jesus did not tell them that the kingdom of Old Testament prophecy was a metaphor, fulfilled in the church. Jesus told His disciples that it wasn't for them to know when, for that is something that "the Father has put in His own authority" (1:7). It was enough for the disciples to know that soon they would receive power from the Holy Spirit, and that afterward they were to devote themselves to serving as Jesus' witnesses in Jerusalem, Judea, and the entire world (Acts 1:8).

What we have then as the broad context for Jesus' prophetic teaching is simply this. First, God has always maintained sovereign control over His universe, the world, and history itself. This overarching kingdom of God exists now and forever.

Second, with Jesus' coming God was initiating a mystery form of His kingdom here on earth. It would be a kingdom that was populated by people of faith in every nation. And although the kingdom would be hidden from outsiders, those within it would relate directly to God as Father, and would experience His care of them as they lived obedient lives, forgiving and being forgiven, and extending God's kind of love to all. Citizens of the mystery kingdom would be lights in this dark world, expressing in all they say and do the transforming power of a God who is able to take sinners and make them into saints.

Third, when it comes time for the mystery expression of God's kingdom to end, Jesus will return. When He does, He will take the throne promised the Messiah, and

THE THREE KINGDOMS OF GOD

When reading the word "kingdom" in the Gospels, it's helpful to remember that any of three different expression of God's kingdom may be in view:

- His universal kingdom, which is His sovereign control over all in His universe;
- The messianic kingdom promised to Israel in the Old Testament but not initiated at Jesus' first coming; and
- Jesus' mystery, or secret kingdom (cf. Matthew 13), which is the form taken by Christ's present rule over His people, the church.

If we keep these three forms in mind, and carefully distinguish which kingdom is in view in any Gospel passage, many of Jesus' apparently puzzling teachings will become clear.

the Old Testament's prophecies of a messianic kingdom will be fulfilled—in their plain sense.

The extended passages containing Jesus' prophetic teachings deal primarily with the transition between the mystery and messianic expressions of God's kingdom here on earth. The transition is marked by the return of Jesus. Yet it is clear that events associated with the transition take place over a period of time. The first coming of Jesus was not a single event but a series of events unfolding over some thirty years of time that included three or four years of ministry. It would seem that the Second Coming also should not be viewed as a single, abrupt event but rather as a series of events also taking place over a span of time. Many apply Daniel's prophecy of the seventy weeks and suggest that the span of time involved in the transition is in fact seven years.

Yet, however long the time, the future events of which Jesus spoke do dovetail with the predictions of the Old Testament prophets. Without being dogmatic or attempting to show the relationships between each of the predicted events, it seems clear that most belong to a transition period between the mystery and messianic forms of God's kingdom here on earth.

SIGNS OF THE END OF THE AGE (MATTHEW 24—25)

It was the last week of Jesus' life on earth. As Jesus and His disciples left the temple, Christ remarked, "Do you not see all these things? Assuredly, I say to you, not one stone shall be left here upon another, that shall not be thrown down" (24:2).

The disciples mulled over this comment, and later asked Jesus three questions, recorded in Matthew 24:3. "Tell us, when will these things be? And what will be the sign of Your coming, and of the end of the age?" Jesus answered at length, dealing with the questions in reverse order.

The sign of the end of the age (Matt. 24:4–28). The first question we need to ask is whether these verses apply to the present church age of the mystery kingdom, or to the period of transition between our time and the institution of the messianic kingdom.

Turbulent times (vv. 3–14). For a number of reasons it's best to place this prophecy in the transition period. If this is correct, Jesus paints a picture of turbulent and difficult times. Counterfeit christs will appear. There will be wars and rumors of war, famines, plagues, and earthquakes. The world will turn on God's people, hating, persecuting, and killing. Under these pressures the believing community will be purified, as some are "offended" (refuse to identify with Christ). The love of others will grow cold as lawlessness abounds and temptations draw them away from the Lord.

In one sense this description has been true for Christians at various times and various places. We have lived with wars and plagues and famines, and many Christians have felt sure their suffering presages the return of Jesus. Yet Jesus' description will be especially true of the turbulent time of transition from the age of the mystery kingdom to the messianic kingdom.

BIBLE BACKGROUND:

HARD SAYINGS OF JESUS

"He who endures to the end shall be saved" (Matt. 24:13).

Here enduring to the end is the sign of the true believer. Those without a heart commitment to God are revealed by being offended (v. 10), by being deceived by false prophets (v. 11) and by surrendering to the temptations of lawlessness (v. 12). Those who endure are not saved because they endure to the end, but they endure to the end because they are saved.

Jesus reaffirmed Daniel's prophecy of a desecration of a temple in Jerusalem at history's end.

Those who remain faithful will preach "this gospel of the kingdom" in all the world. And then, Jesus says, the end will come.

It is significant that nowhere in Scripture is the good news of Christ crucified and risen called the "gospel of the kingdom." This particular gospel always is associated with the appearance of the King, and thus with Jesus' first coming or Second Coming. In this context the Second Coming must be in view.

The abomination of desolation (vv. 15–22). Jesus' reference to an event predicted in Daniel 9:27 (see also 11:31; 12:11) is especially significant. It places this prophecy of Jesus solidly in the context of the Old Testament's emphasis on a coming messianic kingdom.

Some have argued that Daniel's prophecy was fulfilled when the Seleucid ruler Antiochus III sacrificed a pig in the Jerusalem temple. But this occurred decades before Jesus uttered His prophecy. Jesus made it clear that the "abomination of desolation" still lay in the future.

That same Daniel prophecy also predicts the cutting off (death) of the Messiah, the destruction of Jerusalem, and, following this, the coming of a prince who would guarantee Israel's safety, only to break the treaty and set up an idol of himself in Jerusalem. The setting of the idol is the "abomination of desolation" of which Jesus spoke.

The abomination of desolation is the definitive sign of the end of the age, and a warning to all who live then to "flee to the mountains" (Matt. 24:16).

The reason for the flight is that "then there shall be great tribulation, such as has not been since the beginning of the world until this time, no, nor ever shall be" (v. 21).

This time of "great tribulation" is a major feature of Old Testament prophecy, and is followed there by establishment of the messianic kingdom. Many Old Testament passages speak of great suffering as the end draws near (Deut. 4:30, 31; Is. 2:12, 19; 13:6, 9; 24:1, 3, 6, 19–21; 26:20, 21; Jer. 30:7; Ezek. 13:5; 30:3; Dan. 9:27; 12:1; Joel 1:15; 2:1, 2, 11, 31; 3:14; Amos 5:18–20; Zeph. 1:14, 15; Zech.14:1).

The appearance of false Christs (Matt. 24:23–28). During this terrible time a flurry of false christs and false prophets will arise, some of whom even produce "signs and wonders" (miracles; see 2 Thess. 2:9). God's people will not be deceived. Christ's appearance will be sudden and visible to all, "as the lightning" that comes from the east and flashes to the west (v. 27).

Thus the end of the age, a transition period, is a time spoken of in the Old Testament. This period is marked by intense tribulation and the appearance of a "prince" who breaks his treaty with Israel and sets up the "abomination of desolation" in the holy city itself.

The sign of Jesus' coming (Matt. 24:29–35). Jesus does not define the "sign of the Son of Man" other than to say it appears in heaven and everyone on earth will "see the Son of Man coming on the clouds of heaven with power and great glory" (v. 30)

Jesus does say that at that time the angels will gather together His chosen ones, ostensibly to enter the messianic kingdom.

Jesus concludes by drawing an analogy with a fig tree. It puts forth young leaves and so signals the onset of summer. When the signs Jesus has described occur, the

wise person will know that He is at the door.

BIBLE BACKGROUND:

HARD SAYINGS OF JESUS

"Assuredly, I say to you, this generation will by no means pass away till all these things take place" (Matt. 24:34).

What did Jesus mean by "this generation"? If He meant the people living then, surely He was wrong! However, the word translated "generation" (genea) is used here in these sense of "race" or "people." Jesus was saying that God would preserve the Jewish people as a distinct race until His return.

A German theologian was once asked to prove to Kaiser Wilhelm that the Bible is reliable. His two word answer was, "The Jews." No other ancient people has preserved its identity through millenia of time and constant persecution as has God's ancient people.

It's significant that Jesus did not answer the first question asked by His disciples. He predicted the destruction of the temple, and the disciples asked, "When?" On this Jesus was silent, but history speaks.

In A.D. 70, the Romans under Titus razed the city of Jerusalem and destroyed the magnificent temple Herod the Great had refurbished. The Romans cut down all the nearby trees, scattering salt over the ground that nothing might grow there again. Then the Romans decreed that no Jew come within miles of what had been Israel's holy city. But just before the siege of Jerusalem, the large Christian community was warned by its prophets, and moved away from Jerusalem to a place of safety.

Jesus applies tomorrow to today (Matt. 24:36–25:46). We noted earlier that the Bible's visions of future events have an impact on the lives of the prophet's contemporaries as well as an application to our lives today. Jesus did not leave us to wonder what the application of His prophetic teaching is to be. Jesus applied it himself.

Watch and be ready (24:36–44). Christ paints a sad picture of the future. When Jesus returns, it will be "as in the days of Noah." The people of that time busied themselves with the affairs of this life, until the sudden flood swept them away.

The image of the days of Noah also suggests the moral deterioration of human society. Judgment came in Noah's time because "every intent of the thoughts of his [man's] heart was only evil continually" (Gen. 6:5). The notion that somehow our world will become better and better under the influence of the Gospel is hardly biblical. As Jesus said, in a construction that implies a "No" answer, "When the Son of Man comes, will He really find faith on the earth?" (Luke 18:8).

Christ emphasized the fact that no one knows "what hour your Lord is coming," and that we are to "be ready, for the Son of Man is coming at an hour you do not expect" (Matt. 24:42, 44).

Be faithful (vv. 45–51). There will be a lengthy time period between Jesus' ascension and His return. Some will say "my master is delaying his coming" and begin to mistreat their fellow servants (v. 48). The faithful servant will continue to serve his master and his fellow servants, knowing that Christ will appear "at an hour that he is not aware of" (v. 50).

Be prepared (25:1–13). Jesus then tells the story of the ten virgins, discussed on page 72. The time between Jesus' departure and return is time for all to prepare themselves for Jesus' coming. Again Christ said,

"Watch, therefore, for you know neither the day nor the hour in which the Son of Man is coming" (v. 13).

Use your talents (vv. 14–30). The parable of the talents has also been treated earlier (see p. 72). Here too major elements are Jesus' absence and the faithfulness of His servants in looking out for His interests while He is gone. The parable also emphasizes the fact that the traveler will return, and then his servants will be called before him to give an account.

And after Jesus has returned? (Matt. 25:31–46). The disciples had asked Jesus when the temple would be destroyed, what the sign of His coming would be, and about the end of the age. They did not ask what things would be like after Jesus returned, most likely because they felt they already knew. Surely then Jesus would establish the promised messianic kingdom and would rule.

Yet Jesus went on to talk about what He would do when He did return.

He will take the throne of His glory (v. 31). As expected, when Jesus returns He will appear in glory with angel escorts and openly take the throne. The angel Gabriel had told Mary before Jesus was conceived,

He will be great, and will be called the Son of the Highest; and the Lord God will give Him the throne of His father David. And He will reign over the house of Jacob forever, and of His kingdom there will be no end (Luke 1:32, 33).

It is this throne, the throne of the Messiah, on which Jesus will be seated when He comes again.

"All the nations will assemble before Him" (vv.32–46). The scene Jesus sketches is that of a courtroom, with Jesus serving as judge. The *Illustrated Bible Handbook* (Nelson), p. 490, sums up as follows:

In a final word Jesus speaks of judgment coming at his return. Then men's words will not be used to measure their faith. Instead faith will be measured by compassionate concern for those in need; for ministries of service performed as if for Jesus Himself. This is what will show the reality of one's relationship with the Lord. Thus Jesus turns his disciples—and us—from curiosity to commitment. We are on a mission to mankind. The future is in God's hands. The present is committed to us.

BIBLE BACKGROUND:

HARD SAYINGS OF JESUS

"Depart from Me, you cursed, into the ever-lasting fire prepared for the devil and his angels" (Matt. 25:41).

Jesus spoke more often about hell than He did of heaven. Yet here Jesus makes an important point. The pit of "everlasting fire" was not prepared for human beings. It was prepared for the devil and his angels. Yet human beings will find themselves condemned to share the fate of Satan and his demons—but only if they fail to respond to God's offer of grace and forgiveness.

TAKE HEED, WATCH AND PRAY (MARK 13:6–37)

The extended report of Jesus' prophecy found in this chapter of Mark repeats the themes found in Matthew 24 and 25.

Mark also relates Jesus' description of turbulent times marked by wars, famines, and suffering (13:6–8). During these times Jesus' followers will be persecuted and hated, as the gospel is preached to all nations (vv. 9–13). Mark reports Jesus' remarks about the "abomination of desolation" (v. 14) and His warning to flee from the great tribulation that will follow (vv.

15–20). During this transition period false prophets will arise and "show signs and wonders to deceive, if possible, even the elect" (v. 22).

Mark however gives a more graphic portrait of Christ's appearing than does Matthew. While Matthew simply spoke of signs appearing in the sky, Mark quotes Jesus as saying,

In those days, after that tribulation, the sun will be darkened, and the moon will not give its light: the stars of heaven will fall, and the powers in the heavens will be shaken. Then they will see the Son of Man coming in the clouds with great power and glory (vv. 24–26).

Mark also tells of a gathering of Christ's own by angels, and repeats the promise that "this generation will by no means pass away till all these things take place" (v. 30).

The application reported by Mark is the same as the emphasis in Matthew. No one knows the day and hour of Jesus' return (v. 32). Therefore believers are to "take heed, watch and pray, for you do not know when the time is" (v. 33).

Mark does give a slightly different image when stressing the importance of being ready. Mark tells of a doorkeeper charged to watch for his master to return. The doorkeeper's place is by the door, ready to open it to his master or to any of the friends whose voice he recognizes. Since no one knows when Jesus will return, we doorkeepers must be at our posts, ready for Jesus when He comes.

DON'T BE DECEIVED (LUKE 21:8–36)

The prophetic passage in Luke begins, as does that in Matthew, with Jesus' remarks about the destruction of the temple and with His disciples' questions. The response follows the same pattern we've seen in both Matthew and Mark, with a few special additions.

In Luke's account too Jesus begins by warning of turbulent times and persecutions (21:8–11). Luke helps us locate the warnings about persecution in the age of the secret kingdom rather than in, or as well as in the transition period (vv. 12–19). At this point Jesus adds a promise that we all would be wise to claim:

Therefore settle it in your hearts not to meditate beforehand on what you will answer; for I will give you a mouth and wisdom which all your adversaries will not be able to contradict or resist (vv. 14–15).

Luke's account also adds information not found in Matthew or Mark concerning the destruction of Jerusalem. When the city is surrounded by armies, "then know that its desolation is near" (v. 20). However it is also clear that Jesus is not speaking of the invasion by Titus in A.D. 70 but of a more distant future event. For Jesus adds that "these are the days of vengeance, that all things which are written may be fulfilled" (v. 22).

Luke's account also adds details about signs in nature that are associated with Christ's return, signs which remind us of graphic images found in Revelation 6. Jesus said,

There will be signs in the sun, in the moon, and in the stars; and on the earth distress of nations, with perplexity, the sea and the waves roaring; men's hearts failing them from fear and the expectation of those things which are coming on the earth, for the powers of the heavens will be shaken. Then they will see the Son of Man coming in a cloud with power and great glory (Luke 21:25–27).

When these signs appear, Jesus says, "know that the kingdom of God is near" (v.31).

But until that yet future kingdom comes, Jesus warns, "take heed to yourselves" for that day will come unexpectedly (v. 34). "Watch, therefore," Jesus concludes, "and pray always that you may be counted worthy to escape all these things that will come to pass, and to stand before the Son of Man" (v. 36).

The predictions and prophecies of Jesus add to our understanding of the kingdom that looms so large in His teaching. Jesus inaugurated an unexpected form of God's kingdom on earth, a mystery form. As long as this mystery kingdom remains, God will work in hidden ways in and through its citizens. But the day will come when the promised kingdom of the Messiah, the subject of so much Old Testament prophecy, will be established. This will occur when Jesus returns in power and glory. Yet Christ's prophecies make it clear that a transition period lies between the mystery and messianic kingdoms. We do not know the length of that period, but we do know some of the events that will take place in it. These events are both the subject of Old Testament prophecy and the focus of Jesus' extended prophetic discourses.

We cannot know when Jesus will return. We cannot be sure when the events that signal His return will be launched. What we can know for sure, however, is that Jesus will return.

Until He does come, we are to watch, serve, and be make ready for His coming.

OTHER STORIES AND ILLUSTRATIONS

Probably the most unusual song ever written is a piece called "Johnny One Note." It was unusual because the music so perfectly fit the title and lyrics. It was written and sung with just one note.

So far in our exploration of Jesus' teachings it must almost seem this title could be applied to Christ: "Jesus One Note." Nearly everything we've seen in Christ's public teaching seems to focus on God's kingdom and especially its new expression instituted here on earth by Jesus' coming. But many of Jesus' stories are not limited to conveying kingdom truth. Many of His stories and illustrations express spiritual truths that have general and universal application.

It's true that the kingdom of God was the central theme in Jesus' public ministry. His sermons on the mount (Matthew 5–7) and on the plain (Luke 6) were truly revolutionary, powerful statements of a new lifestyle based on a reinterpretation of Old Testament law. Many of Jesus' parables contrast the kingdom that He came to inau-

gurate with the messianic kingdom predicted by the Old Testament prophets. These same parables emphasize the fact that Jesus' kingdom is a mystery; an aspect of God's plan that was not revealed in the Old Testament, but that has now been revealed by Jesus, God's Son and ultimate spokesman. Additional aspects of Jesus' kingdom are expressed in briefer references to the kingdom of God that are scattered through the synoptic Gospels. Finally, we've seen that Jesus' prophetic teaching also has a kingdom focus. But here Jesus emphasizes the "end of the age", a transition period leading to the establishment of the kingdom of the Messiah of which the Old Testament speaks.

None of this teaching however is abstract or impersonal. Every saying in Jesus' Sermon on the Mount, every analogy in the kingdom parables, every word of warning in Jesus' prophetic teaching, has direct and powerful application to our lives today. The kingdom lifestyle is the lifestyle Christians are to live. The kingdom relationship with God is the relationship we

Those who followed Jesus surrendered even the comforts provided by God for animals.

are to nurture. The kingdom concern for others is the attitude we are to adapt.

Jesus' concern with personal commitment to Him and to His new and vital way of relating to God and others is also seen in a number of stories and illustrations that are not directly related to His kingdom teaching. It is these other stories and illustrations that were such an integral part of Jesus public teaching that we look at in this chapter.

JESUS' USE OF BRIEF ILLUSTRATIONS

Jesus frequently used brief, vivid illustrations, usually drawn from everyday life, to illuminate His teachings. Such illustrations are found in each of the synoptic Gospels, and many are as applicable to us today as they were to Jesus' listeners.

FOXES HAVE HOLES (MATTHEW 8:19, 20; LUKE 9:57, 58)

Jesus said it to a scribe who expressed his readiness to "follow You wherever You go": "Foxes have holes and birds of the air have nests, but the Son of Man has nowhere to lay His head."

This saying is a sobering one. It must have discouraged the scribe who had made such an impulsive profession, for we hear no more of him in the Gospels.

Jesus was simply saying that no one who follows Him is guaranteed a comfortable life. Even foxes and birds have a place they can call "home." But Jesus' commitment to His mission had robbed Him of a "normal" life built around home and family. Jesus' commitment to His mission had led Him into an itinerant lifestyle that He adopted in order to bring God's message to all.

What Jesus said to the scribe He says to us today. "Are you really ready to give up your comfortable way of life to follow me?"

Not every believer is called to surrender all. But anyone who commits himself or herself to follow Jesus should first consider the cost of discipleship and make that choice with a full understanding of its possible cost.

WHICH IS EASIER TO SAY? (MATTHEW 9:5–6; MARK 2:9; LUKE 5:23)

Jesus had just told a cripple, "Son . . . your sins are forgiven you." This scandalized the biblical scholars standing nearby. Why, only God could forgive sins! Jesus responded with a question. "Which is easier, to say, 'Your sins are forgiven' or to say, 'Arise and walk?'" Jesus then told the cripple to stand up, pick up the pallet on which he had lain, and go home. And the cripple did!

The answer to Jesus' question, of course, was that it's easier to say, "Your sins are forgiven." After all, these are simply words. The miracle of forgiveness takes place within, where no one can witness it. But to say to a cripple "Arise and walk" is much harder, for all can see immediately whether or not this miracle takes place.

When the cripple stood, picked up his pallet, and walked away there was no question of Jesus' right to forgive. What Jesus had done for the cripple's body was something only God could do. Who then could doubt that Jesus had also forgiven the man's sins?

There is nothing more powerful than living evidence. That is just as true today as in first-century Galilee. We claim that Jesus has forgiven our sins, and others have the right to say that these are just words. It is only when our daily lives give evidence of the transforming power of God that others will be convinced of Jesus' power to forgive.

NO NEED OF A PHYSICIAN (MATTHEW 9:12; MARK 2:17; LUKE 5:31)

Some Pharisees saw Jesus sit down to eat with "tax collectors and sinners." These were outcasts, not at all welcome in respectable circles. Worse still, they were "unclean," and the Pharisees were sure that to even converse with such people was contaminating.

When Jesus heard of their criticism, He responded with a powerful and pointed saying: "Those who are well have no need of a physician, but those who are sick." Jesus went on to challenge them. "But go and learn what this means: 'I desire mercy and not sacrifice.' For I did not come to call the righteous, but sinners, to repentance" (Matt. 9:13).

In the Old Testament, sickness is often symbolic of sin, a fact that would not have escaped the Pharisees (see Isa. 1:5–6). Christ's transition from "well versus sick" to "righteous versus sinners" was thus natural. Jesus was simply saying that as a physician ministers to the sick, so He had come to minister to sinners.

Jesus' analogy also involves an acute psychological observation. As a person who thinks he is well will not go to a physician, so an individual who thinks he is righteous will not come to Jesus. Jesus must minister to those who know they are sinners. People (like the Pharisees!) who assume they are righteous simply will not pay attention to Him.

Yet there is much more to this simple illustration. The attitude of the Pharisees toward sinners showed how far they were from understanding the heart of God.

God's focus was on mercy. The Pharisees' focus was on sacrifice. God's focus was on compassion; the Pharisees' focus was on ritual. God's focus was on the deepest of human needs; the Pharisees' focus was on outward appearances.

It was Jesus, who socialized with sinners, who reflected the heart of God, not the Pharisees who criticized Him.

What a reminder for us! How often do we forget that Christ's church is a hospital for sinners, not a club for the respectable. And how often do we feel so uncomfortable with "sinners" that we, like the Pharisees, not only keep our distance but criticize those who are willing to befriend them? How we need to be reminded that Jesus came not to comfort the righteous but to call sinners to repentance. We need to look to Him again and remember that God places His priority on mercy, not on sacrifice.

NEW WINESKINS
(MATTHEW 9:16, 17; MARK 2:22; LUKE 5:38)

Like many of Jesus' illustrations, this one is drawn from daily life. Jesus' first hearers knew exactly what He meant when He said,

No one puts a piece of unshrunk cloth on an old garment; for the patch pulls away from the garment, and the tear is made worse. Nor do they put new wine into old wineskins, or else the wineskins break, the wine is spilled, and the wineskins are ruined. But they put new wine into new wineskins, and both are preserved (Matt. 9:16, 17).

Wineskins were literally animal skins. Such skins were used to hold goat's milk and yogurt as well as wine. When used for wine the skins stiffened and lost their flexibility. If new wine was poured into an old wineskin, the fermenting process caused the skin to break and both the wineskin and the wine were lost.

Jesus' references to a patch of unshrunk cloth and new wine emphasized the fact that the truths He taught could not be patched onto first-century Judaism, or poured into the old religious framework. Jesus' teaching demanded a totally new way of thinking and living.

This illustration is as applicable today as it was in the first century. When we come to Christ, we enter a new spiritual universe. We can't fit biblical Christianity into our old categories. Christianity is not religion but relationship, where grace and forgiveness rule. That's why it is so vital to study the teachings of Jesus, and the New Testament epistles where the principles of Christian living are so beautifully taught. Those who see their faith in terms of going to church and doing their best have completely misunderstood Jesus' new wine.

LIKE CHILDREN SITTING
(MATTHEW 11:16, 17; LUKE 7:32)

The Pharisees had objected that John the Baptist was too much the fanatic. They had then criticized Jesus for being too lax. So Jesus drew an illustration from the familiar street scene of children playing at "wedding" and "funeral." The religious leaders were like street urchins, sitting on the sidelines and complaining,

"We played the flute for you,
  And you did not dance;
We mourned to you,
  And you did not lament."

The Pharisees wanted to call the tune, and when neither John nor Jesus would play their games, they sat down on the sidelines, pouting and complaining.

It's so easy to find something to criticize in every individual and in every church. And so many are willing to sit on the sidelines, criticizing others while they themselves are unwilling to become involved. But faith is not a spectator sport, and none of us are in a position to validly criticize others.

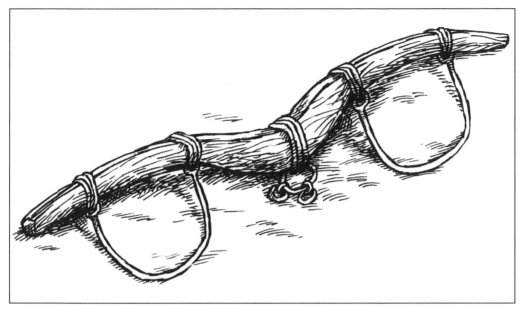

The yoke symbolized the fact that Jesus comes alongside those who accept His grace.

TAKE MY YOKE
(MATTHEW 11:28–30)

Jesus' words about taking His yoke are often quoted, and frequently misunderstood. What Jesus said was,

Come to Me, all you who labor and are heavy laden, and I will give you rest. Take My yoke upon you and learn from Me, for I am gentle and lowly in heart, and you will find rest for your souls. For My yoke is easy and My burden is light.

The yoke was a familiar object in first-century Palestine. It was a piece of wood shaped to fit over the necks of load-pulling animals. It linked them to a plow, and, when used by a pair of animals, to each other (Num. 19:2). Figuratively the yoke symbolized a heavy burden, such as slavery (Exod. 6:6; 1 Tim. 6:1). But it was also very common in the first century to speak in a positive sense of the "yoke of the law," a burden which God had in love placed on His Old Testament people.

However, the Christian community recognized that the Law was a burden "which neither our fathers or we were able to bear" (Acts 15:10).

It's likely Jesus' listeners understood Him to be referring to the yoke of the Law, which every Jewish person took up when he or she reached the age of responsibility. So here Jesus was contrasting the way of life He taught ("My yoke") with Moses' law as taught by the scribes and Pharisees. In contrast to the rigid and ever-expanding set of rules the religious leaders of Jesus' day imposed on the Jewish people, Jesus offered an easy yoke of grace, love, and forgiveness.

However, in order to exchange the yoke of the Law for Jesus' yoke, a person must learn from Him. The way of life that He taught, as reflected in the Sermon on the Mount, was dramatically different. Yet His yoke is "easy," for in coming to Him the believer gains access to the transforming power of God.

Each Jew bore the yoke of the Law alone. Each Christian experiences Christ within, bearing the load of the Christian life with and for him.

BIBLE BACKGROUND:

HARD SAYINGS OF JESUS

"I am gentle and lowly in heart" (Matt. 11:29)

What did Jesus mean when He characterized Himself as gentle and lowly in heart? Matthew often stresses Jesus' gentleness (18:1–10; 19:13–15). The emphasis reminds us that although God Himself, Jesus came as a servant. In contrast the religious leaders of the day were arrogant and proud, with no concern for others less committed than themselves.

SEVEN OTHER SPIRITS (MATTHEW 12:43–45; LUKE 11:24–26)

A major feature of Jesus ministry was the casting out of evil spirits. This stunning display of power had shaken His enemies, who desperately looked for some way to attack Him. Their solution was to suggest that Jesus must be drawing on Satan's power rather than on the power of God. In other words, they suggested that demons obeyed Jesus because Satan told them to, not because Jesus had authority over them.

In this setting Jesus provided an illustration that makes two major points.

When an unclean spirit goes out of a man, he goes through dry places, seeking rest, and finds none. Then he says: "I will return to my house from which I came." And when he comes, he finds it empty, swept, and put in order. Then he goes and takes with him seven other spirits more wicked than himself, and they enter and dwell there; and the last state of that man is worse than the first. So shall it also be with this wicked generation (Matt. 12:43-45).

The primary application of this story is to Israel itself. Jesus had appeared and was cleansing the house of Israel from demons and illness. But unless the people acknowledged Jesus as their God and Messiah, their house would remain empty. This was serious, for an empty house is vulnerable to occupation by others. The evils that Jesus had cast out would return, and more evils with them, until the situation of the Jewish people would be worse than before Jesus had come.

There is also a secondary application to our lives today. The secret of Christianity is not found in getting rid of sins, but in being filled with a dynamic holiness that infuses all of life. The cleansed house signifies reformation. Yet unless we welcome Christ into our life, mere reformation is of no help. The heart that is empty of Jesus is so vulnerable that our attempts at moral reformation will, in the end, result in even greater wickednesses entering our lives.

WEATHER (MATTHEW 16:2, 3; LUKE 12:54–56)

When some of the Pharisees demanded that He given a sign authenticating His claims and His teaching, Jesus responded with an illustration from first-century weather prediction.

When it is evening you say, "It will be fair weather, for the sky is red," and in the morning, "It will be foul weather today, for the sky is red and threatening." Hypocrites! You know how to discern the face of the sky, but you cannot discern the signs of the times.

Luke reports a similar remark, directed to the crowds that followed Christ.

Whenever you see a cloud rising out of the west, immediately you say, "A shower is coming"; and so it is. And when you see the south wind blow, you say, "There will be hot weather"; and there is. Hypocrites! You can discern the face of the sky and of the earth, but how is it you do not discern this time?

Each of the two references to weather prediction makes the same point. The evidence that authenticated Jesus and signified the inauguration of His kingdom was overwhelming. Yet those who so easily read the signs marking a change in the weather were blind to the signs that marked the changes introduced by Jesus.

This strange disjunction is deeply rooted in human nature. Human beings have shown a wonderful capacity to deal with the physical universe. We can build space ships, map the human genetic code, and create an Internet. But human beings have remained ignorant of the spiritual realm and blind to truths that seem so obvious to believers. Scientists can even look in awed wonder at the detailed works of nature and then deny the Hand that designed all things!

Only faith in the Son of God can open our eyes to the real truth, and enable us to see the signs God has graciously posted all around us.

KINGS TAKE TAXES
(MATTHEW 17:24–27)

The Old Testament called for each adult male Jew to pay an annual half-shekel tax to be used for the support of the worship center (Ex. 30:13–16). At Capernaum those responsible for collecting this "temple tax" asked Peter if Jesus paid it. Without asking Jesus, Peter blurted out, "Yes."

When Peter returned to his house, and before he could tell Jesus about the incident, Jesus asked him, "What do you think, Simon? From whom do the kings of the earth take customs or taxes, from their sons or from strangers?" When Peter answered, "From strangers," Jesus told him, "Then the sons are free."

On the surface it would seem that Jesus was simply pointing out that He, as the Son of God, did not need to pay the temple tax. But there is more to Jesus' remark than this! If indeed Israel had had a true Father-child relationship with God, the Old Testament would never have decreed such a tax! Yes, the Jews were God's covenant people. But they were not sons.

It would take the work of Jesus on Calvary to win the privilege of this most intimate of relationships for those who would trust in Him.

SETTLE ALONG THE WAY
(LUKE 12:58, 59;
MATTHEW 5:25, 26)

Jesus pictures a situation in which a man is on the way to court with an adversary. Jesus gives this advice: "make every effort along the way to settle with him."

In each passage the individual is in danger of being thrown into debtors' prison, where he will be unable to resolve the situation. In debtors' prison a person was forced to depend on friends, who might not be willing or able to help.

However, the illustration is applied in slightly different ways in the two passages. In Matthew Jesus warns against malicious anger and insists it be dealt with immediately. Anger is such an evil, and God's judgment so certain, we must do all we can to end it.

In Luke Jesus points out that in human affairs a wise person tries to resolve a critical situation as soon as possible to avoid bad consequences. How much more then should a person give urgent attention to getting right with God, where the consequences of failure are so much more serious?

A realization of Jesus' great forgiveness stimulates us to love.

DISCIPLESHIP ILLUSTRATIONS

Luke 14 contains a series of illustrations Jesus used in speaking to the crowds about discipleship.

Complete commitment (Luke 14:26). Jesus' illustration almost seems offensive. "If anyone comes to Me and does not hate his father and mother, wife and children, brothers and sisters, yes, and his own life also, he cannot be My disciple."

"Hate" is used here in a special legal sense that would have been understood by Jesus' listeners. To "hate" one person or group in favor of another that was "loved" was to decisively reject the claims of the first in favor of the second. Discipleship need not mean turning against one's own family. But it does mean giving priority to Christ in all things.

Considered commitment (vv. 28–33). Jesus' illustrated the importance of considering carefully before choosing to become one of His disciples. He spoke of a man planning to build a tower, who starts construction and then discovers he does not have enough money to finish the project. He also spoke of a king about to make war, who finds himself in the embarrassing position of having to sue for peace when he discovers his enemy's army is twice the size of his. A person thinking about discipleship needs to carefully consider the cost of following Jesus, for it will demand everything that he has!

Lifelong commitment (vv. 34, 35). Here Jesus speaks of salt loosing its flavor. A similar illustration is found in Matthew 5:13, but differently applied. Here Jesus emphasizes the fact that a disciple must maintain his or her commitment if his life is to be of value.

It is true that Jesus welcomes disciples. But volunteers must realize that a commitment to follow Jesus is to be complete, considered, and lifelong.

JESUS' STORIES TO LIVE BY

Another prominent feature of Jesus' ministry was His use of stories to instruct and to confound. Jesus wove stories into the teaching of His disciples and even into His conflicts with the religious leaders. Some of these stories were brief; some much longer and more involved. We look closely at many of these stories in other sections of this book. Here, however, there are a number of simple stories, many found only in Luke's Gospel, which communicate truths that are relevant to every person's life.

THE TWO DEBTORS
(LUKE 7:41, 42)

The story is so brief and simple it is almost an illustration. Yet it carried a powerful point.

The setting and application of the story are described in Luke 7:36–50. Jesus had been invited to eat with one of the Pharisees. As Jesus and His host and several other guests reclined at the table, a woman slipped into the house and began to anoint Jesus' feet with perfumed oil. As she did this the woman wept and wiped His feet with her hair.

The Pharisee was scandalized. The woman was a known sinner (prostitute). The Pharisee was convinced that if Jesus were truly a prophet, He would have known what kind of life the woman lived and would never have let her touch Him.

Jesus knew what the Pharisee was thinking, and told this brief story. "There was a certain creditor who had two debtors. One owed five hundred denarii, and the other fifty. And when they had nothing with which to repay, he freely forgave them both." Jesus then asked the Pharisee which of the debtors would be most grateful to the creditor. The Pharisee gave the obvious answer: "I suppose the one whom he forgave more." Jesus agreed: "You have judged rightly" (v. 43).

Jesus then went on to explain. He reminded the Pharisee that when Jesus had entered his house He was not given even the most common of courtesies, a warm greeting and water to wash the dust off His feet. But the woman had not stopped kissing His feet and anointing them with oil. Jesus then said that "her sins, which are many, are forgiven, for she loved much. But to whom little is forgiven, the same loves little" (v. 47).

As in Jesus' story, it was the forgiveness granted the woman that produced the love, not love that merited forgiveness. The Pharisee, who had not cared enough about Jesus to offer Him even the most common courtesies, had made it very clear he did not see himself in need of forgiveness. On the other hand the woman, deeply conscious of her sins, had heard and believed Jesus' message of forgiveness, and so loved Him much.

It's wrong for us to suppose that we must do terrible things to fully grasp the wonder of forgiveness, and to deeply love our Lord. But it's right for us to realize that however "good" we may seem when compared with others, we are great sinners in the eyes of God. His forgiving love is our only hope.

THE GOOD SAMARITAN
(LUKE 10:30–37)

This is a story that grew out of a conversation Jesus had with a "lawyer," another word in our text for a recognized first-century expert in biblical law. When the lawyer asked Jesus what was required for a person to gain eternal life, Jesus asked the lawyer for his opinion. This man, far more in touch with the Scriptures than the legalistic Pharisees, answered, "'You shall love the Lord your God with all your heart, with all your soul, with all your strength, and with all your mind,' and 'your neighbor as yourself.'" The answer was correct!

It would be a mistake for us to assume that all students of the Scripture in first-century Judaism were legalistic. The answer this man gave to Jesus is found in the writings of other rabbis from the era. In fact, a favorite exercise of the rabbis was to attempt to sum up the Law in the briefest possible saying. Edersheim goes so far as to suggest that the answer given by this expert in the Law sums up a conviction held by most people of his time! And as far as the command to love one's neighbor is concerned, the great first-century sage Hillel is reported to have said, "What is hateful to thee, that do not to another. This is the whole Law; the rest is only commentary."

However, after commending the lawyer's answer, Jesus said "Do this, and you shall live." And there's the rub. Humankind's problem has never been in knowing what is right. The problem is in doing what we know is right.

The lawyer seems to have been aware of this and, "wanting to justify himself" [have an excuse for his failure], asked Jesus, "And who is my neighbor?"

It was this byplay between the lawyer and Jesus that led Jesus to tell the now familiar story of the Good Samaritan.

We're all familiar with that story. A "certain man" (a Jew) was traveling from Jerusalem to Jericho. The man was attacked by brigands who took everything he had, including his clothing. The robbers then left him lying wounded alongside the road.

Shortly afterward a variety of travelers came upon the man, including a priest and a Levite. These representatives of Israel's religion hurried on by, probably afraid the brigands might be lurking nearby.

Then a Samaritan came upon the man. Even though a deep and longstanding hostility existed between Jews and Samaritans, the Samaritan stopped, bandaged the Jew's wounds, and then took him to an innkeeper. The Samaritan gave the innkeeper money and asked him to care for the wounded man, promising to pay any additional cost when he came by the next time.

Jesus then asked the lawyer, "So which of these three do you think was neighbor to him who fell among thieves?" The answer was obvious, and the lawyer responded correctly: "He who showed mercy on him."

Jesus then made one last comment: "Go and do likewise."

This story, which has captured the imagination of generations of Christians, has many levels of meaning. On one level the story reveals the bankruptcy of first-century religion, whose representatives in the story showed no mercy or compassion. On another level the story reminds us that it's never enough to know what's right—we must do it. On a third level the story challenges us to examine our attitude to others. Have we realized that our "neighbor" is not just the person next door who is like us? Have we realized that our neighbor is not defined by the social, racial, or religious group we belong to, but simply by our common humanity? And have we realized that every person we come in contact with is our neighbor, whom we are to love and to serve?

It's no wonder that we all find this simply story of Jesus' so compelling. It reaches us uniquely to remind us that to live close to the heart of God we must be men and women like that Samaritan, who was willing to risk in order to care for another human being in need.

Material wealth is no proof of favor with God.

THE FOOLISH FARMER
(LUKE 12:16–21)

A bystander had just asked Jesus to settle a dispute with his brother about an inheritance (v. 13). As one of the duties of first-century rabbis was to apply God's law to settle such disputes, the man may have viewed his request was reasonable. Indeed, he might have thought of it as a compliment!

Jesus, however, refused and commented to those around, "Take heed and beware of covetousness, for one's life does not consist in the abundance of the things he possesses" (v. 15). This interchange led Jesus to tell another of His stories.

A wealthy man's fields produced such abundant crops that the man was faced with a problem. There was so much he had no room to store everything in his barns! So the man decided to pull down his barns and build larger ones. Then he could store everything he possessed. Gleefully the man looked forward to the years ahead, confident that he had so much that he could take his ease, and "eat, drink, and be merry."

But in Jesus' story God spoke to the man and called him a fool. "This night your soul will be required of you; then whose will those things be which you have provided?" (v. 20).

BIBLE BACKGROUND:
HARD SAYINGS OF JESUS

"This night your soul will be required of you" (Luke 12:20).

The reason this is a hard saying is simply that we read into the word "soul" something that is not there. We've come to imagine that the "soul" is the invisible and immaterial part of a human being. However, in Hebrew the soul, *nephesh*, is better understood as the person himself, or the person's life. Often in Hebrew *nephesh* functions simply as a reflexive pronoun. In the Gospels the use of the Greek word for soul, *psuche*, is patterned on the use of *nephesh* in the Old. Thus when God tells the rich farmer, "this night your soul will be required of you," He is not referring to some immaterial part of the man. God was simply saying that the farmer's life was over; that night he would die.

Jesus immediately applied the story. "So [a fool] is he who lays up treasure for himself, and is not rich toward God" (v. 21).

This too is something we need to keep in mind. The materialist, who thinks that what life is all about is to see who can gather the most material possessions before he dies, is a fool. There is more to life than wealth and possessions. And, in fact, there is more to life than life!

Only those who live with eternity in view can be called wise. Those who cannot see beyond this life, or who are unwilling to live their lives for the Lord, are shortsighted indeed.

THE FRUITLESS FIG TREE
(LUKE 13:6–9)

Jesus told of a certain man who had a fig tree planted in a vineyard. When the owner came looking for fruit, he found none. Frustrated, he told the keeper of his vineyard to cut down the tree. It was just taking up space.

The keeper suggests, "Sir, let it alone this year also, until I dig around it and fer-

tilize it. And if it bears fruit, well. But if not, after that you can cut it down" (vv. 8, 9).

Fruit and fruitfulness are important themes in both testaments. This parable-story of Jesus parallels Isaiah's portrayal of Israel as a vineyard (Isa. 5). God had carefully prepared the ground for His vineyard and had planted it with the choicest vine, expecting it to produce good grapes. Instead the grapes produced were wild and bitter. Isaiah went on to explain what God would do, and why:

> "I will take away its hedge,
>   and it shall be burned;
> And break down its wall, and
>   it shall be trampled down.
> I will lay it waste;
> It shall not be pruned or dug,
> But there shall come up briers
>   and thorns.
> I will also command the clouds,
> That they rain no rain on it."
>
> For the vineyard of the LORD
>   of hosts is the house of Israel,
> And the men of Judah are His
>   pleasant plant.
> He looked for justice, but
>   behold, oppression;
> For righteousness, but behold,
>   a cry for help.
>   (Is. 5:5–7)

Isaiah's grim vision of Israel's future came to pass. God's people were torn from their homeland and scattered in many nations.

When Jesus told His story of the fig tree, some ten percent of the population of the Roman Empire were Jewish, with only a few hundred thousand living in the homeland. Even so, when Jesus came looking for fruit, he found none. For years Jesus had metaphorically dug around and fertilized His fig tree, performing His miracles and teaching everywhere. But still there was no fruit at all. It would soon be time for the fig tree to be cut down.

DINING WITH PHARISEES
(LUKE 14:7 24)

Luke reports three story-parables that Jesus told while dining at the home of a Pharisee. The first was a commentary on the behavior of several guests. The second involved advice to His host. And the third story was Jesus' commentary on His contemporaries.

Don't take the best seats (vv. 7–11). In biblical times a host carefully planned the seating at banquets. The more important persons were seated closest to the host. It was not uncommon in that time to even have a different menu and different quality of wine served to those at the head table and those of lesser rank at the tables further away.

As Jesus sat conversing with His host he noticed guests trying to take the best seats. So Christ spoke to the guests, and gave them a suggestion.

When you are invited by anyone to a wedding feast, do not sit down in the best place, lest one more honorable than you be invited by him; and he who invited you and him come and say to you, "Give place to this man," and then you begin with shame to take the lowest place. But when you are invited, go and sit down in the lowest place, so that when he who invited you comes he may say to you, "Friend, go up higher." Then you will have glory in the presence of those who sit at the table with you.

Jesus' suggestion was intended as something more than practical advice. It communicated an important spiritual principle. Our self-evaluation is bound to be faulty. Only one, God, is able to evaluate us appropriately. What's more, the attitude revealed in seeking higher positions indicates an arrogance that is certain to expose us to shame. As Jesus said, "whoever exalts

himself will be humbled, but he who humbles himself will be exalted."

In God's kingdom the way up is down.

Choose guests wisely (vv. 12–14). Jesus' next advice was given to His host. It's clear from what Jesus said that the Pharisee who hosted the dinner Jesus attended had invited only those of his own class. So Jesus suggested, "When you give a dinner or a supper, do not ask your friends, your brothers, your relatives, nor rich neighbors, lest they also invite you back, and you be repaid. But when you give a feast, invite the poor, the maimed, the lame, the blind. And you will be blessed, because they cannot repay you; for you shall be repaid at the resurrection of the just."

Jesus' comments reflect a well-known saying recorded in Proverbs 19:17: "He who has pity on the poor lends to the LORD, and He will pay back what he has given." The host hadn't been aware that his guest list revealed so much about him! But Jesus' comments were a rebuke. The Pharisee clearly was more concerned about the impression he made on his social equals than any impression he might make on God.

Accept God's invitation (vv. 16–24). Jesus then told a story that is closely linked with His earlier comments. It's the story of a man who gave a "great supper," and invited many. But when the time came to serve the supper, the invited guests began to make excuses. When the servant reported back, his master was furious. He told the servant to go out into the streets and invite the poor, the maimed, and the lame and the blind.

When there was still room, the master sent the servant even further afield. For, the master said, "none of those men who were invited shall taste my supper."

This is the main point of the story as told in Luke. While their arrogance and concern for appearances revealed much about God's people, it was their rejection of the invitation God had extended in Christ that would exclude that generation from the blessings God was about to offer to all.

BIBLE BACKGROUND:
HARD SAYINGS OF JESUS

"Go out into the highways and hedges, and compel them to come in, that my house may be filled" (Luke 14:23).

Does the word "compel" here imply that God not only chooses who will be saved but also that we have no choice in the matter? *Baffling Bible Questions Answered* (Baker, 1993) comments:

It is true that the word used here, *anankazo*, does mean to "force" or "compel." It is used only nine times in the New Testament. Each time the context determines the kind of compulsion that is involved. This is important, for this word is used of both external, physical force and of inner pressures or response to moral suasion. Here the compulsion has rightly been described as "an insistent hospitality." What is truly significant about the story is not the word *compel* but the master's command to search the street (*plateia*, a highway) and the alley (*rhyme*, the narrow lanes where the poor and ignored lived). The gospel invitation is for all, and the servants of heaven's King are to be sure that each person receives his or her invitation (p. 293).

GOD'S LOVE FOR THE LOST (LUKE 15)

Luke 15 contains two illustrations and a story. These function as a single unit to illustrate God's love for the lost.

The lost sheep (vv. 4–7). Songs have been written about "The Ninety and Nine." And one of the most famous of contemporary pictures shows Jesus as a shepherd stooping to rescue a lost lamb. The story that has stimulated such songs and art works is that of a shepherd who has a hundred sheep, but who goes after just one that is lost, searching until he finds it.

Jesus told his listeners, "When he has found it, he lays it on his shoulders, rejoicing. And when he comes home, he calls together his friends and neighbors, saying to them, 'Rejoice with me, for I have found my sheep which was lost.'" (vv. 5, 6)

What permeates this story is love for the lost sheep and the pure joy of the shepherd at its recovery. Jesus then told His listeners, "Likewise there will be more joy in heaven over one sinner who repents than over ninety-nine just persons who need no repentance."

The lost coin (vv. 8–10). Jesus went on to tell of a woman who loses one of her ten silver coins. It was common in the first century for a woman to be given a dowry of coins when she was married. A hole was often bored in the center of these coins, and they were strung on a string to be worn as a necklace. To lose one of these coins was of far more concern to a woman than is reflected in their monetary value.

No wonder then that when a woman loses one of her dowry coins she will "light a lamp, sweep the house, and search carefully until she finds it" (v. 8).

When the coin is found, she too invites friends and neighbors to rejoice with her. Jesus applied this illustration as he had before, saying "Likewise, I say to you, there is joy in the presence of the angels of God over one sinner who rejoices" (v. 10).

In each of these illustrations Jesus emphasized the value of individuals to God, vividly portrayed in heaven's joy at the one in ten or one in a hundred who repents.

The lost son (vv. 11–32). On its surface this is the heartwarming story of a father who keeps on loving his son even when the son has rejected him and adopted a sinful lifestyle. It is also the story of a son who reaches rock bottom, and only then remembers the kindness of his father and determines to return home. The story also projects a powerful image of God as the patient and loving father, who calls for a celebration when his son returns, and has not a single word of recrimination.

But Jesus introduced a third character in this story, an older brother who cannot understand his father's reaction, and who is filled with bitterness and resentment. The older brother confronts his father and challenges him. "As soon as this son of yours came, who has devoured your livelihood with harlots, you killed the fatted calf for him" (v. 30).

While the older brother acknowledges that the prodigal is a "son of yours," he simply will not accept him as brother.

Gently the father explains. "It was right that we should make merry and be glad, for your brother was dead and is alive again, and was lost and is found" (v. 32).

These three stories are triply revealing. First, they reveal the state of every human being as a lost sinner, in need of being found by God.

Second, they reveal the overwhelming grace and love of a God who is willing to put our past behind, and who calls all heaven to rejoice when a single individual is saved.

Third, the three stories reveal the hardened hearts of those religious men who claimed to represent God, yet who fiercely opposed Jesus and who condemned Him for reaching out to tax collectors and sinners. Their failure to rejoice at the repentance of those who were touched by Jesus' love made it plain how far from God they were. And how lost.

THE SHREWD STEWARD
(LUKE 16:1–8)

Of all the stories Jesus told this one seems to puzzle the most people. Jesus told this story to his disciples, although it's clear from 16:14 that He intended the Pharisees nearby to hear.

Christ's story featured a rich man and his steward. In the first century, as in our own time, it was common for the very wealthy to employ others to manage their affairs. In Jesus' story, the steward was about to be accused of mismanagement and expected to lose his position. His problem was a serious one. He couldn't work as a day laborer; he was management. But who would hire him? The thought that he might be reduced to taking charity (begging) was something he simply could not stand.

Jesus tells us how the steward solved his problem. "I have resolved what to do," the steward thought, "that when I am put out of the stewardship, they may receive me into their houses" (v. 3). The steward called in all his master's debtors and doctored his records, reducing the amount each owed some twenty to fifty percent. Afterward the steward would not even be dependent on the debtor's gratitude. All had conspired and joined him in his plot. They not only owed him; he had a hold over them!

The master commended the unjust (criminal) steward for his shrewdness. And Jesus added His own observation: "The sons of this world are more shrewd in their generation than the sons of light" (v. 8).

What has troubled so many is the notion that Jesus would commend criminal behavior. But this misses the point which Jesus went on to make, saying "make friends for yourselves by unrighteous mammon, that when you fail, they may receive you into an everlasting home" (16:9). Christ's point was simply that the worldly understand how to use money to prepare for their future here and now. In contrast, God's people seem

Jesus' story of the rich man and Lazarus has a surprise ending.

unaware that their use of money has an impact on eternity!

Jesus went on to explain further. He bases His teaching on the fact that all we possess ultimately belongs to God. What we have has been loaned to us to use on God's behalf and for His glory.

Jesus grants that money is a little thing, yet "he who is faithful in what is least is faithful also in much" (v. 10). A wise and faithful use of money is an accurate measure of our faithfulness in the greater matters of the Christian life!

Jesus also points out that our use of money is an indicator of our readiness for greater things. But, "If you have not been faithful in the unrighteous mammon, who will commit to your trust the true riches" (v. 11)?

Again Jesus reminds us that everything we have belongs to God, and "if you have not been faithful in what is another man's, who will give you what is your own" (v. 12).

In His final pronouncement Jesus reminded His listeners that, "No servant can serve two masters; for either he will hate the one and love the other, or else he will be loyal to the one and despise the other. You cannot serve God and mammon" (v. 13).

These teachings of Jesus call each of us to serious self-examination. Do we serve Jesus and use our material possessions to His glory? Or is money our Master and our use of what we have been given evidence of how little we care for Christ?

THE RICH MAN AND LAZARUS (LUKE 16:19–31)

Jesus often told stories featuring rich men and their stewards or servants. In only one of these stories does Jesus identify an individual by name. This feature has led many to the conclusion that the story of the rich man and Lazarus is not a parable, but an account of the experiences of two very real people.

Whether or not this is the case, this story is particularly fascinating, especially for its account of the experience of the lost and the saved after death.

The story. A certain rich man who enjoyed the best this world can offer is contrasted with a beggar named Lazarus. While the rich man feasted inside his palatial home, Lazarus lay outside, diseased and starving.

But when Lazarus died, he was carried to "Abraham's bosom," a common euphemism for the place God has prepared for the blessed. When the rich man died, he found himself in Hades, a first-century term for the place of punishment.

In torment the rich man looked across the gulf fixed between these two realms and recognized Lazarus close to Abraham. The rich man cried, "Father Abraham, have mercy on me, and send Lazarus that he may dip the tip of his finger in water and cool my tongue; for I am tormented in this flame" (v. 24).

Abraham refused for two reasons. First, the experiences of the two were balanced equitably. The rich man had enjoyed the best during his lifetime, and now was tormented. Lazarus had suffered great pain, and now he was comforted. There is additional symmetry. While the rich man could easily have alleviated the suffering of Lazarus without any real loss of comfort, there was nothing that Lazarus could now do for the rich man. "Besides all this, between us and you there is a great gulf fixed" (v. 26).

The rich man had one other request. "I beg you, therefore, father, that you would send him to my father's house, for I have five brothers, that he may testify to them, lest they also come to this place of torment" (vv. 27, 28).

The end of Jesus' story foreshadows His own death and resurrection (vv. 28–31). Abraham refused, saying, "They have Moses and the prophets; let them hear them." The rich man objected. "No, father Abraham; but if one goes to them from the dead, they will repent."

We can imagine Abraham shaking his head sadly. "If they do not hear Moses and the prophets, neither will they be persuaded though one rise from the dead."

Theological questions and answers. This story of Jesus raises more theological issues than any other.

What produces faith? Jesus puts to rest the notion that if only people today could witness miracles there would be a great turning to God. The miracles Jesus performed certainly did not produce any mass turning to the Lord. Even the miracle of His resurrection did not break through the unbelief of the majority in first-century Jerusalem.

Abraham answered our question when he said, "They have Moses and the prophets; let them hear him." Faith is a trusting response not to miracles but to the Word of God. As Paul says in Romans 10:17, "Faith comes by hearing, and hearing by the word of God."

What can we expect after death? Those who wonder about the individual's experience after death find much to consider in this story. Jesus describes the rich man and Abraham as self-conscious and self-aware. Each retains his own identity as it was shaped during his lifetime. In Jesus' story the rich man is able to remember, to see, to communicate, and to feel the torment of something like flames.

The notion that a person simply ceases to exist, the notion that a person falls into a sleep-like state until final judgment, the notion that the soul loses all sense of identity and blends into the deity, are all refuted by Christ's story. Even if the rich man and Lazarus are fictional characters, all of Jesus' stories reflect reality. There is no reason to suppose that His depiction of what happens after death is any less accurate than His illustrations drawn from life here on earth.

Is Jesus describing heaven and hell? The answer to that question is, "No." What Jesus describes here is the experience of those who died before Christ's own death and resurrection.

Jesus speaks of hell more often in His teaching than He does of heaven. Hell is described in Matthew 25:30 as a realm of "outer darkness" where "there will be weeping and gnashing of teeth." In Matthew 25:41 Jesus describes it as a place of "everlasting fire prepared for the devil and his angels." Revelation pictures the final judgment and tells us that after judgment "death and Hades" are cast into the lake of fire. The text adds, "This is the second death."

But what, then, is Hades?

Hades is as Jesus portrayed it, the place where the unbelieving dead await final judgment. While it is not hell, Hades too is a place of torment. We can perhaps draw an analogy between Hades and Hell, and jail and prison. A person awaiting trial is often held in jail. After trial, if found guilty, that person is sent to prison. Jail and prison are very much alike. Both are places of confinement. Both strip the prisoner of his or her freedom. In the same way, Hades and Hell are much alike, yet Hades is where the lost await judgment; hell is their eternal destiny.

What then is the relationship between Abraham's bosom and heaven? Abraham's bosom *was* the place where the blessed awaited entrance into God's presence. Before Christ died and His blood wiped their slate clean, the saved waited there. Many believe that Paul's description of Christ's triumph in His resurrection, when He "led captivity captive" (Eph. 4:8–10), refers to leading the saints from Abraham's bosom into the presence of God.

After the resurrection of Jesus, Paul tells us, "to be absent from the body" is "to be present with the Lord" (2 Cor. 5:8). Abraham's bosom has now been emptied, and Lazarus, with Abraham and a myriad of the blessed, now enjoy the very presence of God.

But even this is not "heaven." Like hell, heaven is an eternal state of being. And for us heaven awaits the return of Christ, the resurrection of our bodies, and the creation by God of a new universe where only righteousness will dwell (Rev. 21:22).

Jesus' story of the rich man and Lazarus fascinates us for it raises so many issues about which we're understandably curious. Yet we need to keep Jesus' main point in view. Jesus was warning His hearers, assuring them that heaven and hell are real. And the only way to gain the one and avoid the other is to hear God's Word about the Christ, and to respond by putting our trust in Him.

FAITH OR OBEDIENCE?
(LUKE 17:1–10)

Jesus had just warned His disciples against an unforgiving spirit, and told them that if a brother "sins against you seven times in a day, and seven times in a day returns to you, saying, 'I repent,' you shall forgive him" (17:4). This disturbed the disciples, who realized that this was a challenge indeed. Their response to Jesus was to beg Him, "Increase our faith" (v. 5).

Jesus reminded the disciples that a person with the least amount of faith ("as a mustard seed") could command a nearby mulberry tree to pull itself up by the roots and be planted in the sea, "and it would obey you" (v. 6). He then asked them to imagine a man had a servant who had spent the day plowing. At the end of the day, wouldn't the man say, "Prepare something for my supper, and gird yourself and serve me till I have eaten and drunk, and afterward you will eat and drink" (v. 8)?

Jesus went on, "Does he thank that servant because he did the things that were commanded him? I think not. So likewise you, when you have done all those things which you are commanded, say, 'We are unprofitable servants. We have done what was our duty to do'" (vv. 9, 10).

This story makes a fascinating point. Jesus, the disciples' Lord and Master, had told His followers to forgive again and again. The disciples had asked for more faith, but Jesus dismissed their request, saying in effect, "Faith is fine for moving mulberry trees." Then Jesus focused their attention on a servant, whose role was to serve and obey his owner. And Jesus concluded, "So likewise you" (v. 10).

Jesus had not *asked* His followers to be forgiving. Jesus had commanded them! Forgiveness is not a matter calling for more faith. The issue in forgiveness is one of obedience to God.

How often we make this mistake, asking God for more faith to do what He has commanded us, never realizing that the issue is not one of faith but of obedience.

BIBLE BACKGROUND:

HARD SAYINGS OF JESUS

"If you have faith as a mustard seed, you can say to this mulberry tree, 'Be pulled up by the roots and be planted in the sea,' and it would obey you" (Luke 17:6; compare Matt. 17:20).

Here as in Matthew 17, where faith is said to be able to "move mountains," the saying is proverbial. That is, Jesus was saying that with even a little faith a believer can do the impossible. But Jesus had not asked His disciples to do the impossible. He had simply asked them to keep on forgiving, and this was an issue calling for obedience, not faith.

We need to remember that what makes faith powerful is not the amount of faith we have, but the person in whom our faith is placed. In the end it is God who undertakes the impossible—and who succeeds.

THE PHARISEE AND THE TAX COLLECTOR
(LUKE 18:10–14)

The story is brief, powerful, and familiar. A Pharisee and tax collector went to the

Jesus' familiar story reminds us that God forgives those who acknowledge their sins.

temple to pray. The self-righteous Pharisee thanked God that he was "not like other men" (v. 11). In contrast the tax collector was contrite, deeply aware of his sins, and could only ask for mercy.

It was the tax collector who left a justified (forgiven) man. Jesus then applied the story: "Everyone who exalts himself will be humbled, and he who humbles himself will be exalted" (v. 14). However we may compare with others, before God we are all sinners, whose only hope lies in His mercy.

THE MURDEROUS VINEDRESSERS
(LUKE 20:9–18)

This final story in Luke's gospel is a revealing picture of God's experience with His chosen people. In the story a "certain man" planted a vineyard and leased it to a group of farmers. When the owner sent servants, the farmers beat them, treated them shamefully, and sent them away empty handed.

Finally the owner sent his own "beloved son," reasoning that "probably they will respect him when they see him" (v. 13). Instead the farmers killed the son "that the inheritance may be ours" (v. 14).

Jesus concluded his story by describing what the owner will do. "He will come and destroy those vinedressers and give the vineyard to others" (v. 16).

The meaning of the story was clear, especially in light of Isaiah 5. The owner is God. The vineyard is Israel, and the vinedressers the religious leaders. The messengers sent by the owner were the prophets, nearly all of whom were ignored and many of whom were persecuted. Jesus Himself is the dearly loved Son, whom the religious leaders would kill.

As a result, God would destroy the leaders and the people of Jesus' day, and give the vineyard, in the form of Christ's mystery kingdom here on earth, to others.

In A.D. 70 the city of Jerusalem was taken by the Romans, and the great Jerusalem temple was destroyed. Not until 1948, nearly two thousand years later, would a Jewish nation be established in the ancient homeland. And after the death and resurrection of Jesus, a universal church would emerge, a church of those "others" whom God has been pleased to call His own.

TRAINING THE TWELVE

One of the most fascinating aspects of Jesus' ministry here on earth is the time He invested in training just twelve disciples. He spoke to thousands, but the teaching that had the most lasting impact was the private instruction that Jesus gave the Twelve.

These twelve men were with Him from the earliest days of His ministry. They witnessed all He did; heard all He said. And often after a day of ministry they gathered around to ask Him questions, and to be questioned in their turn. In the end eleven of the twelve became the core of the dynamic movement Jesus founded, His Church.

MEET THE TWELVE

We all know at least several of the Twelve disciples. We surely know Peter, the foremost disciple. We also know Matthew and John, authors of two of our four Gospels. Yet many of them remain shadowy figures whose experiences after the death of Christ are mysteries to us.

WHY "DISCIPLES"?

"Discipleship" was a well-established institution in first-century Judaism. It was the one and only avenue for gaining recognition as a rabbi (teacher), often called a "lawyer" in our text.

First-century elementary education. Every Jewish boy was expected to go to school, and teachers' salaries were paid by taxes levied on all in the community. According to the Jerusalem Talmud, laws requiring the establishment of elementary schools were enacted by Simon ben-Shetach, around 75 B.C., although schools were well known before this time. Joshua ben-Gamala, high priest in the mid-60s A.D., is praised in the Talmud for his role in universalizing public education.

Boys might begin school from age five to age seven, with seven being more common. However, from age three parents were expected to help their children memorize key passages of Scripture, and some literature suggests fathers begin to bring their sons to the synagogue at this age.

The subject matter in Jewish schools was the Scripture. Children were expected to learn to read and also to memorize large blocks of Scripture. They were also taught basic arithmetic, and some learned to write. One early description of synagogue services indicated that seven members of the congregation would read from the Scriptures during the service; this is very probable, as most Jewish men were literate.

Advanced education. A few students went beyond this elementary schooling and studied the teachings of earlier rabbis. The fifth book of the *Sayings of the Fathers*, translated by C. Tayor, places the educational process in the flow of the stages of a man's life:

At five years old, Scripture; at ten years, Mishna; at thirteen, the Commandments; at fifteen, Talmud; at eighteen, marriage; at twenty, the pursuits of business; at thirty, strength; at forty, discernment; at fifty, counsel; at sixty, age; at seventy, gray old age; at eighty, power; at ninety, decrepitude; at a hundred, as though he were dead, and gone, and had ceased from the world (p. 97).

In addition to formal education in childhood the synagogue itself served the community as center for continuing education of adults. It was expected that even a workman would be a lifelong student of Scripture, an ideal which was seldom fully met but which remained an ideal. Given this commitment to religious education, those to whom Jesus spoke had a far better grounding in Scripture than do most Christians today!

Training for spiritual leadership. If one aspired to become a master of the Law and gain respect as a teacher, the one avenue open to him was that of discipleship. Such a person attached himself to a recognized rabbi, and for many years studied with his master. These studies were not the formal classes we're familiar with in our seminaries. Instead the disciple lived with his master, listening to his teachings and his discussions with others, observing him in every possible situation, asking him questions and being questioned in return. The goal of this process was not simply mastery of what one's teacher knew; the goal was to develop a character like that of the person with whom one studied. Jesus said it in Luke 6:40: "A disciple is not above his teacher, but everyone who is perfectly trained will be like his teacher."

When the New Testament identifies the Twelve as Jesus' disciples, it marks them as men who were undergoing this kind of training under Jesus. These were twelve men who abandoned their occupations to follow Jesus everywhere that they might learn from Him. Perhaps more to the point, these were twelve men whom Jesus chose for this kind of training.

As we've seen, it would be wrong to think of the twelve as ignorant men when Jesus selected them. They were men who had been taught the Scriptures from childhood, and, as we'll see, they were men who for the most part had been successful in their own demanding careers. Yet they were men, like other first-century Jews, whose old ways of thinking were about to undergo a tremendous reorientation. They, like all their contemporaries, would discover a totally new way of understanding their relationship with God and with others. Only their complete allegiance to Jesus, and the settled confidence that Jesus was the Christ, the Son of God, enabled these men to accept teachings they would not fully understand until long after Jesus' resurrection.

As we work through this chapter and those immediately following, we'll look at recruitment and early training of the Twelve. We'll look at Jesus' turning-point teachings, where the central theme of His ministry becomes the Cross and its lifestyle.

We'll look at Jesus' teachings on spiritual leadership. And we'll examine Jesus' Last Supper teachings, which have been called the seedbed of the church.

WHO WERE THE TWELVE?

The New Testament contains four lists of the twelve men Jesus chose and trained as disciples. These lists have certain similarities in common. On each list Peter is the first named. The gospel accounts make it clear that Peter was the leader of the twelve. On each list the same four disciples are grouped at the top—Peter, James, Andrew, and John—although not always in the same order. In the Gospels we read that Peter, James, and John were often called away from the others to share some special experience with Jesus (see for example Mark 5:37 and Luke 9:28). And on each list, Judas Iscariot is found last. (Note that the disciple called Thaddaeus in Matthew and Mark is called Judas, son of James in Luke and Acts.)

While some of these disciples are familiar from the four Gospels and Acts, we know little about others, and almost nothing of their post-resurrection ministries. What we do know is gained first from the biblical accounts, and second, from tradition.

Peter. After the resurrection of Jesus, Peter is prominent in the early chapters of Acts and as the author of two of our New Testament epistles. Peter's sermon on the Day of Pentecost opened the church era (Acts 2). Peter clearly played a leading role in the earliest days of the church. His healing of a man born a cripple was the occasion of a powerful sermon (Acts 3), that led to a futile attempt by the religious leaders to silence the apostles (Acts 4). Peter raised Dorcas from the dead (Acts 9), was the first to preach the gospel to Gentiles at the home of Cornelius (Acts 10) and later was freed from prison by angels (Acts 12). At the first council of the church Peter sided with the apostle Paul, arguing that Gentile Christians should not be told they must keep the Mosaic Law, although they would need to be sensitive to the convictions of their Jewish Christian brethren (Acts 15).

Later traditions suggest that Peter visited Britain and Gaul (France). A reliable tradition indicates that Peter was crucified upside down in Rome around A.D. 64–68.

Andrew. Andrew, although prominent on the lists of disciples, is seldom mentioned

Matthew	Mark	Luke	Acts
1. Simon Peter	1. Simon Peter	1. Simon Peter	1. Simon Peter
2. Andrew	2. James	2. Andrew	2. John
3. James	3. John	3. James	3. James
4. John	4. Andrew	4. John	4. Andrew
5. Phillp	5. Philip	5. Philip	5. Philip
6. Bartholomew	6. Bartholomew	6. Bartholomew	6. Thomas
7. Thomas	7. Matthew	7. Matthew	7. Bartholomew
8. Matthew	8. Thomas	8. Thomas	8. Matthew
9. James, son of Alphaeus	9. James, son of Alphaeus	9. James, son of Alphaeus	9. James, son of Alphaeus
10. Thaddaeus	10. Thaddaeus	10. Simon the Zealot	10. Simon the Zealot
11. Simon the Zealot	11. Simon the Cananite	11. Judas, son of James	11. Judas, son of James
12. Judas Iscariot	12. Judas Iscariot	12. Judas Iscariot	12. Judas Iscariot

in the Gospels. Tradition indicates that after the resurrection Andrew preached in Scythia, Asia Minor, and Greece, and that he was crucified at Petras in Achaea.

James, son of Zebedee. Acts reports that James was the first of the disciples to be martyred, executed by Herod Agrippa I around A.D. 44. The story of James' death and the subsequent judgment on Herod is told in Acts 12. (The James who appears as a leader at the Jerusalem council and who wrote the New Testament epistle of James is not James the disciple but James the brother of Jesus.)

John. John, so prominent in the gospels, was the longest lived of the disciples. John is mentioned briefly in Acts as Peter's companion at the healing of the man born a cripple (Acts 3) and as a member of the delegation sent to authenticate the unexpected conversion of Samaritans under the ministry of Philip the evangelist (Acts 8).

John ministered in Asia Minor, dying a natural death in Ephesus around A.D. 100. In the 90s John was exiled to the island of Patmos, where he recorded his vision of the future as the book of Revelation. John also wrote three epistles found in the New Testament: First, Second, and Third John.

Matthew. While Matthew wrote the Gospel that bears his name, little is known of his ministry after the resurrection. Different and conflicting traditions have him ministering in Ethiopia, Parthia, Persia, and Macedonia.

Judas Iscariot. Judas is mentioned twenty-three times in the Gospels and in Acts, more times than any of the disciples other than Peter. Judas betrayed Jesus for the paltry sum of thirty pieces of silver. Afterward, full of remorse, Judas hung himself. Apparently the rope eventually broke, tumbling his body down a cliff.

While we know nothing of the later ministries of the other disciples, there are traditions associated with each. Thomas may have ministered in India and may have founded churches there. Bartholomew is thought to have gone with Philip to Hierapolis in Asia Minor, where tradition suggests that Philip was crucified. Bartholomew was supposedly martyred after ministering in Armenia. James the son of Alphaeus is thought to have served in Syria. Traditions, less reliable, concerning the last two of Jesus' disciples place Simon the Zealot in Persia, Carthage, or Britain, while Thaddaeus has been linked to Edessa.

Whatever the eventual ministries of the twelve men Jesus chose as disciples, each was carefully trained for ministry by Jesus Himself. As Christianity spread like a flame through and beyond the Roman Empire, we can only conclude that the training was successful indeed!

RECRUITING THE TWELVE

It's easy to misunderstand the process Jesus used to recruit His disciples. Yet there are good reasons for any misunderstandings. For instance, Mark 1:16–20 contains this account of calling several of the disciples.

And as He walked by the Sea of Galilee, He saw Simon and Andrew his brother casting a net into the sea; for they were fishermen. Then Jesus said to them, "Follow Me, and I will make you become fishers of men." They immediately left their nets and followed Him.

When He had gone a little farther from there, He saw James the son of Zebedee, and John his brother, who also were in the boat mending their nets. And immediately He called them, and they left their father Zebedee in the boat with the hired servants, and went after Him.

A little later (2:14) Mark describes the call of Matthew (called Levi in the Gospels).

As He passed by, He saw Levi the son of Alphaeus sitting at the tax office. And He said to him, "Follow Me." So he arose and followed Him.

From Mark's account it almost appears as if Jesus spontaneously picked out strangers He came across, and that these strangers, with no prior acquaintance with Christ, simply dropped everything and committed themselves to a life of discipleship.

This impression, however, is a false one. What Mark describes is the call to discipleship, a call that followed a lengthy period during which Jesus and His disciples came to know each other well.

MEETING AT THE RIVER (JOHN 1:30–51)

John the Baptist had been preaching near the headwaters of the River Jordan, and many traveled to hear the fiery prophet predict the appearance of the Messiah and call for repentance. Jesus too came to hear His cousin John, and even to be baptized by him. It was while Jesus was coming up out of the waters that John saw the Holy Spirit descend as a dove on Christ, and was amazed to realize that his cousin from Nazareth, Jesus, was actually the Son of God and the Messiah (1:31–34).

The day after, John was seated with two of his adherents and pointed Jesus out to them as the Lamb of God. The two left John and trailed after Jesus. When Christ noticed them, He asked, "What do you seek?" (v. 38) and afterward invited them to spend the day with Him. One of the two was Andrew, destined to become one of the Twelve.

John tells us that Andrew later found Peter, his brother. Excitedly Andrew told Peter, "We have found the Messiah!" (v. 41). Andrew hurried Peter along to see Jesus for himself. That very day Jesus announced, "You are Simon the son of

Jonah. You shall be called Cephas" (v. 42), which translated into Greek is *petros*, Peter—a stone.

Jesus clearly knew what the future held for Simon Peter. But Peter and the others did not know, and were not yet ready to commit themselves to be His disciples.

The next day Jesus was ready to return to Galilee. But first He invited Philip, a friend of Peter and Andrew, to join Him and the others. Philip found Nathanael and excitedly tried to recruit Nathanael to join the group. Nathanael was skeptical but went with Philip to meet Jesus. As Nathanael approached, Jesus remarked, "Behold, an Israelite indeed, in whom is no deceit" (v. 47).

Nathanael, who had never met Jesus, was surprised. He blurted out, "How do You know me?" Jesus answered that He had "seen" Nathanael "before Philip called you, when you were under the fig tree" (v. 48). This remark convinced Nathanael, who knew that from where Jesus had been He could not possibly have seen Nathanael with physical eyes. "Rabbi," Nathanael said, "You are the Son of God! You are the King of Israel!" (v. 49).

THREE DAYS LATER (JOHN 2:1–11)

Jesus and those He met at the river then traveled together to Galilee. It's fascinating to speculate on what they talked about as they began to get acquainted. Clearly Jesus' companions were already more than a little in awe of Him. But just what the little company said and did as they walked along is something we will never know.

We do know, however, that "on the third day" there was a wedding in Cana of Galilee. Both Jesus and His disciples were invited, and apparently came as a group. It was there that, when the wine ran out, Jesus turned water into wine. John describes this as the "beginning of signs Jesus did." It was Jesus' first miracle, performed before His new friends rather than in public, and John says it "manifested His glory; and His disciples believed in Him" (2:11).

4. He is led by the Spirit into the wilderness to be tempted
5. He returns from this experience, moves to Capernaum, and begins His public ministry of miracle-working and teaching

BIBLE BACKGROUND:

WHERE'S THE TEMPTATION?

Mark tells us that after Jesus was baptized "immediately the Spirit drove Him into the wilderness" (Mark 1:12). Doesn't this conflict with John's account of a return to Galilee with the friends who were introduced to Jesus at the Jordan?

We need to remember, as pointed out on pages 7–9, that each Gospel writer organizes his material to support the theme of his Gospel, and that in the Gospels, time, sequence, and even the material included is subordinated to the theme. We also need to be aware that Mark uses the word "immediately" thirty-six times in a mere sixteen chapters, not so much as a temporal term, but to make a statement about Jesus and to mark transitions. In Mark, Jesus is portrayed as a man of action, and as such was appealing to the task-oriented Romans for whom Mark wrote.

In Luke's account of the temptation we clearly have room for a return to Galilee with His soon-to-be-disciples, a return which Mark simply does not mention. Luke tells us Jesus "returned from the Jordan and was led by the Spirit into the wilderness" (Luke 4:1). The phrase "returned from the Jordan" clearly supports John's statement that Jesus "wanted to go to Galilee" (John 1:43), and did so before His forty-day fast and His temptation by Satan. The sequence of events thus would be:

1. Jesus is baptized
2. He returns to Galilee with His new friends
3. He performs His first miracle at Cana, witnessed only by His future disciples

THE MOVE TO CAPERNAUM (JOHN 2:12)

Jesus now moved from Nazareth to Capernaum, the governmental center of Galilee built on the shore of Lake Galilee. Capernaum now became the headquarters to which Jesus would return from His preaching missions throughout Galilee.

Capernaum was also the home of Peter, James, and John, and it's clear that Jesus remained close to these future disciples. Mark describes a healing that Jesus performed in a synagogue at Capernaum and tells of Jesus' growing fame "throughout all the region around Galilee" (1:28). He goes on to say that coming out of the synagogue "they entered the house of Simon and Andrew, with James and John" (1:29). Peter's wife's mother was sick with a fever, and Jesus healed her. That evening "they brought to Him all who were sick and those who were demon-possessed. And the whole city was gathered together at the door (of Peter's house)" (vv. 32, 33). Jesus stayed with Peter that night, but slipped away to pray. The next morning Peter was worried when he discovered Christ was gone, and "searched for Him" (1:36).

The more we compare the accounts of Jesus' early relationship with His disciples, the more clearly we see it. Jesus did not recruit strangers. Jesus first nurtured a relationship with the men He intended to become His disciples. When His call to discipleship finally came, the disciples knew well the person to whom they were making a commitment.

THE CALL (LUKE 5:1–11)

Luke gives us a fascinating and in-depth description of the disciples' moment of decision: a moment to which other Gospel writers refer only briefly.

Jesus was preaching by the seaside, so pressed by the crowds that He asked Peter to push his boat out into the water so Jesus could speak from there. After He finished speaking, Jesus told Peter to push his boat out into the deep water and let down his nets for a catch.

Peter was reluctant. He and his partners had fished all night and had caught nothing. As a professional fisherman Peter fished only at night, and then near the shore where schools of fish came in to forage. Peter agreed reluctantly. "Master," Peter said, "we have toiled all night and caught nothing," an objection which is clearly an implied rebuke. "Nevertheless at Your word I will let down the net" (v. 5).

The Greek word translated "master" is found only in Luke. While a term of respect, it is also somewhat slang, rather like our term "boss." Peter respected Jesus. But Peter was an exceptional and successful fisherman. He had earned enough money at fishing to move from his hometown of Bethsaida (John 1:44) to the provincial capital and to build a large home on expensive land. It's likely that Peter and his partners also distributed their catch in Jerusalem itself, where Peter's partner John was well known to the high priest's servants (John 18:15). Yes, Peter respected Jesus, but Peter thought of himself as the expert when it came to fishing!

Peter was an expert. But when the nets he let down were suddenly filled with so many fish Peter had to call for his partners to bring another boat, Peter realized Jesus had performed a miracle. It apparently was one thing for Peter to see Jesus perform miracles for others, but another for Jesus to perform a miracle for him. Peter was overwhelmed. "Lord," Peter said, falling down

Jesus called weak and sinful men to be His first disciples.

❖

before Jesus, "Depart from me, for I am a sinful man" (v. 8).

Peter's whole attitude underwent a striking change. We see it in the word he now uses to address Jesus: "Lord" (kurios).

"Lord" was used in ordinary speech to express respect, much as we say "Sir." But Lord was also used of God as the object of ultimate respect. It was in this sense that Peter used it as he called Jesus Lord, begging Christ to leave him "for I am a sinful man." Suddenly and unexpectedly Peter had an overwhelming awareness of just how great the gap was between himself and Jesus. Humbled, Peter confessed that he was unworthy of associating with Jesus, the Lord.

Jesus' response must have been as comforting to Peter as it is to us. "Do not be afraid," Jesus told His friend. "From now on you will catch men" (v. 11).

There was and is no need to fear Jesus. Jesus had come, moved only by love, to save sinners. And, indeed, there was hope for Peter. For in following Jesus, Peter would be transformed. The fisher of fish would become a fisher of men, a man who would influence millions and help them come to know Jesus as their Lord as well as his.

It's the same for us. It's appropriate that we feel awe in Jesus' presence, and that we be deeply aware of our sin. But we need never fear Jesus. If we will but follow Him we, like Peter, will be transformed. We may not become fishers of men, as Peter did. But if we follow Jesus, our lives will never be the same.

CALLED AND COMMISSIONED (LUKE 6:12–16)

Jesus had spent time with the men He would call to be His disciples. He had let them come to know Him personally, not just as a public figure. We can assume that this was also the case with Levi/Matthew and the others, although we do not know the details of Jesus' association with every disciple. These men had grown to trust Jesus enough to forsake "all and follow Him" (Luke 5:11).

But the choice was a traumatic one for Jesus as well as for the Twelve. Luke 6 tells us,

Now it came to pass in those days that He went out to the mountain to pray, and continued all night in prayer to God. And when it was day, He called His disciples to Himself; and from them He chose twelve whom He also named apostles (6:12, 13).

It's helpful here to distinguish between the calling of the disciples and their com-

missioning. In a very real sense all of us are called to follow Jesus. But not everyone will be commissioned for special full time service. Jesus was now about to commission twelve, and His choices would be crucial. Even though Jesus was God the Son, the choice was so crucial that Jesus spent the night in prayer to the Father before the Twelve were officially named His apostles. These were the men who would represent Christ and herald the coming of the new day.

TRAINING THE TWELVE

Jesus' approach to training His twelve disciples was unusual only in one way. Like the rabbis of His time, Jesus took His disciples with Him everywhere. They listened and watched as He preached to the crowds and interacted with individuals. Jesus often instructed them in private, questioning and being questioned by their Master. What is unusual is that Jesus' training involved sending out the disciples to represent Him in the early stages of their training.

We can explore the training of the Twelve by looking at passages that reveal how Jesus showed, instructed, and sent His disciples.

Teaching by showing. The first and most obvious way for the disciples to learn from Jesus was simply to watch Him and listen to His teaching. Matthew 4:23–25 sums up Jesus' early ministry of teaching and healing,

And Jesus went about all Galilee, teaching in their synagogues, preaching the gospel of the kingdom, and healing all kinds of sickness and all kinds of disease among the people. Then His fame went throughout all Syria; and they brought to Him all sick people who were afflicted with various diseases and torments, and those who were demon-possessed, epileptics, and paralytics; and He healed them. Great multitudes followed Him—from Galilee, and from Decapolis, Jerusalem, Judea, and beyond the Jordan.

In Matthew's Gospel this summary statement leads directly into the Sermon on the Mount, Jesus' extended explanation of His kingdom's lifestyle (discussed in chapter 3). The miracles drew the crowds, but when they came and heard Jesus, they were amazed that He spoke with such authority.

The Gospels give us close-ups of a number of Jesus' miracles, and help us realize what the disciples learned from them.

Jesus heals a leper (Matt. 8:1–4; Mark 1:40–44). The story is related in two gospels. A leper came to Jesus and prostrated himself, saying, "Lord, if you are willing, You can make me clean." Jesus reached out and touched the leper, saying "I am willing; be cleansed." Jesus then told the leper, "See that you tell no one; but go your way, show yourself to the priest, and offer the gift that Moses commanded, as a testimony to them" (Matt. 8:4).

What did the Twelve learn by observing this healing? Both Matthew and Mark tell us that Jesus touched the leper. Mark adds that Jesus was "moved by compassion" to do so. Jesus performed most of His miracles simply by uttering a word. But Jesus was sensitive to the fact that as a leper this man was "unclean," isolated even from his family and untouchable to any Jewish person. As much as he needed physical healing, the leper needed to experience an acceptance that could only be communicated by the touch of another's hand. Jesus reached out His hand to meet this deep inner need, not because healing required His touch. And the disciples were shown that compassion is a vital element in ministering to anyone in need.

There were other lessons in this incident too. A person seeking healing must have enough confidence in Jesus to come to Him. And Jesus' instructions, that the leper should show himself to a priest and so have the healing certified (Lev. 14:1ff) as a "testimony to them," were important. Not only would this prove that healing had actually taken place, it would also show the leper's

and Christ's respect for God's Law. Jesus came as a revolutionary, but not as a radical.

BIBLE BACKGROUND:

WAS JESUS WORSHIPED BY THOSE WHO SOUGHT HIS HELP?

Our text tells us that the leper came and "worshiped" Jesus (Matt. 8:2). Similarly the ruler of a synagogue who appealed to Jesus for help is also said to have "worshiped" Him (Matt. 9:18). Does this mean that they recognized Jesus as God?

The Greek word used by Matthew is proskuneo, the most commonly used word for worship in the New Testament. However, its literal meaning is to prostrate oneself or to bow down. It is in this common sense of bowing down that we should understand "worship" in Matthew 8:2, 9:18, and other Matthew passages. Those who appealed to Jesus during His early ministry did not necessarily know that Jesus was God. But they were sure that He was the last hope for them and their loved ones. It was as supplicants rather than as worshipers that they fell at Jesus' feet.

Jesus stills the sea (Matt. 8:23–27; Mark 4:35–41; Luke 8:22–25). The story is familiar. The disciples are in a boat with Jesus, who is asleep. The Sea of Galilee has always been subject to sudden, dangerous storms. But this storm was unusually strong, a tempest. Terrified, the disciples roused Jesus, crying "Lord, save us! We are perishing!" (Matt. 8:25). Mark tells us they also cried, "Teacher, do You not care that we are perishing?"

Jesus then stilled the winds and sea, bringing a sudden and complete calm. Matthew tells us that the disciples marveled, saying "Who can this be, that even the winds and the sea obey Him?" (v. 27).

Jesus' stilling of the storm was a private miracle that deepened His disciples' trust in Him.

Each account depicts a rebuke by Jesus. Matthew tells us that He called them "little-faiths," a term Matthew also uses in 6:30, 14:31, and 16:8. Mark adds more detail. Jesus said to them, "Why are you so fearful? How is it that you have no faith?"

The incident underlined the power of Jesus but also emphasized the importance of faith in Him. It was not that with faith the Twelve could have stopped the storm by themselves. It was simply that as long as Jesus was present, they should have known there was no reason to fear.

Whatever the circumstances of our lives, faith tells us that Jesus is present and that He is in control.

Touched by a woman (Matt. 9:18–22; Mark 5:25–34; Luke 8:43–48). One day Jesus was asked to help the daughter of an important man in the local synagogue. On the way, a woman in the throng that crowded around touched Him. This woman suffered from a menstrual flow that had persisted for twelve years. She was desperate, for her husband could have no relations with her or even touch her while blood flowed. Mark tells us that she "had suffered many things from many physicians" and that she had "spent all that she had and was no better, but rather grew worse" (Mark 5:26, 27).

The woman had come to believe that if she could just touch the hem of Jesus' cloak as He passed by she would be healed. So she pressed closer and closer. She reached out and touched Him, and immediately was healed!

Jesus felt the touch as power flowed from Him, and stopped, asking, "Who touched My clothes?" (Mark 5:30).

Luke tells us that the disciples said, "Master, the multitudes throng and press You, and You say, 'Who touched Me?'" (Luke 8:45). The words seem dismissive, as if the question Jesus asked should not be taken seriously. Jesus didn't bother answering but continued to peer into the crowd. At last the woman stepped forward and told her story.

Jesus listened and then told her, "Daughter, be of good cheer; your faith has made you well. Go in peace" (Luke 8:48)

This healing too was a learning experience for the Twelve. In the theology of the day a person or thing that was ritually unclean contaminated whatever it touched. The woman with the flow of blood was unclean. Yet when she touched Jesus, rather than making Him unclean, a cleansing power flowed from Him to her.

The fact that the Gospel writers give details concerning her twelve-year struggle also show that the Twelve were learning much from Jesus about concern for persons as individuals. The Pharisees would have dismissed the woman and her complaint simply because she was a woman. Jesus took time to listen, and then commended her for her faith.

Concern for women was characteristic of Jesus, yet totally out of harmony with the religious thinking of the time. Later Jesus would encourage Mary the brother of Lazarus to join in as He taught the Twelve (Luke 10:38–41). It was unthinkable in that day for a woman to be permitted to learn from a rabbi; yet Jesus commended her for joining the Twelve rather than busy herself with "women's work." [To discover just how stunning Jesus' concern for women was, read the companion volume in this series *Every Woman in the Bible*.]

Clearly the welcome Jesus showed women was itself part of the training of the Twelve. And Jesus' example is reflected in the prominent roles many women played in the early church.

These three examples, the leper, the storm, and the healing of the woman with the issue of blood, illustrate how Jesus taught His disciples by example. The compassion Jesus showed, the faith He displayed, and the welcome He extended to all, were important components in Jesus' teaching of the Twelve.

Teaching by telling. While example was always an important element in Jesus' teaching, telling—instruction—was essential. On the one hand the Twelve listened to all of Jesus' public teaching, and tried to take it in. On the other hand they also had the benefit of private instruction. Often this private instruction followed and grew out of an event they witnessed or a public teaching that they heard.

Explaining the parables (Matt. 13:36; 15:15). This feature of Jesus' early instruction of the Twelve is illustrated in Matthew 13 and 15. Jesus had just told the crowds the parable of the sower (13:3–9). The disciples asked Jesus why He spoke to the crowds in parables (v. 10), and He explained. After Jesus told the parable of the tares (vv. 24–30) and the crowds had gone home, "His disciples came to Him, saying, 'Explain to us the parable of the tares of the field'" (v. 36). Again Jesus explained.

We see the same thing in Matthew 15. Jesus had just given a simple illustration that showed the emptiness of the Pharisee's approach to holiness (15:11). The disciples were curious. Didn't Jesus know that the Pharisees were offended by the saying (v. 12)? Jesus dismissed their concern, but then Peter said, "Explain this parable [saying] to us" (v. 15).

This interplay was a normal and essential element in Jesus' training of the Twelve. They felt free to ask Him anything, and because Jesus' teachings were so new, often questioned Him about the meaning of the things He said.

Jesus' disciples learned trust by taking neither food nor money with them on their preaching mission.

❖

Feeding the multitudes (Matt. 14:13–21; Mark 6:35–44; Luke 9:12–17; John 6:5–13). Another illustration of the interaction between Jesus and the disciples is seen in a story told in all four Gospels. Jesus had taught a great crowd of people. As it began to get late the disciples became concerned. The crowd would be getting hungry, and there was no way to feed them, for they were in wilderness area far from any town. The disciples suggested that Jesus send the crowds away.

The fact that the disciples expressed concern may be encouraging; they may have been growing in their capacity to feel for others, something consistently modeled by Jesus. But John tells us that Jesus tested His disciples. He asked Philip where they could buy the bread to feed thousands (John 6:5, 6). Matthew reports that Jesus told others, "They do not need to go away.

You give them something to eat" (Matt. 14:16).

The disciples must have been frustrated. What could they do?

In fact there was nothing. But when a boy was located who had brought a lunch, Jesus multiplied his few loaves and fishes and fed some five thousand adult men along with uncounted numbers of women and children.

Later Jesus referred back to the incident (Matt. 16:9; Mark 8:19). Clearly the disciples had not yet learned the lesson the miraculous feeding had taught. But as with every other incident and every other private time they had with the Lord during the early period of Christ's ministry, the Twelve would remember and in the end would learn.

Teaching by sending. Each of the synoptic Gospels gives considerable space to instructions Jesus gave His disciples as He sent them out two by two to teach and to heal (Mark 6:7). It is significant that the sending took place relatively early in His ministry, when the focus of Jesus' own teaching was still the good news of the kingdom of God.

The Twelve were not yet trained in the sense of being discipled. Later Jesus even sent out followers other than the Twelve on the same kind of mission (Luke 10:1-20)! But the descriptions of Jesus' "on-the-job training" of the Twelve given in Matthew 10 and Mark 6 provide many insights.

Their mission defined (Matthew 10:1–8; Mark 6:7). The Twelve were told specifically to limit their ministry to the "lost sheep of the house of Israel" (Matt. 10:6). They were not to go into Gentile or Samaritan territory. As they went, the Twelve were to preach the message that was then the central theme of Jesus' own preaching. They were to say, "The kingdom of heaven is at hand" (v. 7).

Jesus also gave the Twelve the power to perform the kinds of miracles He himself was performing. The Twelve were to "heal the sick, cleanse the lepers, raise the dead, cast out demons" (10:8). They were to do this without charging anyone for their ministry. "Freely you have received," Jesus said, "freely give." All the Twelve did was to demonstrate the grace of God, as did Jesus' own ministry.

Their dependence emphasized (Matt. 10:9, 10; Mark 6:8, 9). In His own itinerant ministry Jesus was dependent on others for support. Luke mentions several women "and many others who provided for Him from their substance" (8:3). Jesus Himself, as Teacher, was responsible to meet the needs of His twelve disciples.

The day would come, however, when the disciples would be on their own, and then they would need to depend on the Lord and on God's people to meet every need. Thus Jesus told them, "Provide neither gold nor silver nor copper in your money belts, nor bag for your journey, nor two tunics, nor sandals, nor staffs; for a worker is worthy of his food."

In the Sermon on the Mount Jesus had encouraged everyone to depend on God as Father, and "seek first the kingdom of God and His righteousness" (Matt. 6:33). Now it was time for the Twelve to discover for themselves that God is faithful.

Their approach explained (Matt. 10:11–15; Mark 6:10, 11). In Galilee and Judea hotels were unknown. Travelers depended on the hospitality of local people. The few inns (*caravanserai*) were simply way stations for business travelers with strings of animals, usually an open courtyard where the beasts of burden could rest. Thus hospitality was a prized value in the first century; individuals and communities took pride in welcoming travelers.

Jesus told His disciples that upon entering any community they should "inquire who in it is worthy" (10:11) and plan to stay with that family until they leave. The phrase "who is worthy" indicates a pious family with a good reputation.

BIBLE BACKGROUND:

HARD SAYINGS OF JESUS

"If the household is worthy, let your peace come upon it. But if it is not worthy, let your peace return to you" (Matt. 10:13).

In biblical times "peace to you" or "peace be upon you" was a blessing as well as a greeting. In essence Jesus is saying that if a household to which the pair of disciples was directed was not worthy (pious, respectable) the greeting of peace would not "stick." It was in essence, taken back.

Jesus also told the Twelve that if a household or community would not "receive or hear your words" (10:14) the disciples should "shake off the dust from your feet." This symbolic act indicated total rejection of the house or city that had rejected Jesus' message of repentance (Mark 6:12), and meant that "it will be more tolerable for the land of Sodom and Gomorrah in the day of judgment than for that city" (Matt. 10:15).

Their attitude (Matt. 10:16). Jesus then explained that in carrying out their mission the disciples would be like sheep surrounded by wolves. The image is one of constant danger. "Therefore," Jesus said, "be wise as serpents and harmless as doves." *The Bible Reader's Companion* (Chariot-Victor, p. 612) comments, "The two qualities are both vital for disciples, but must be in balance. Shrewdness without innocence is cunning, and innocence with shrewdness is ignorance. When the two are in balance Jesus' followers demonstrate both foresight and courageous trust in God."

PROPHETIC WARNINGS (MATTHEW 10:16–41).

The Matthew passage now continues with a series of prophetic warnings. In this passage the focus shifts from the immediate mission on which Jesus was sending the Twelve to the future. After opposition to Jesus had hardened, and after Christ was crucified, the disciples would face increasing dangers.

We know that this passage is prophetic for Jesus not only warns of beatings administered by the Jews (10:17) but also says that His followers will "be brought before governors and kings for My sake, as a testimony to them and to the Gentiles" (10:18). The immediate mission of the Twelve was to go to the "lost sheep of the house of Israel" (10:6), and the Twelve had been told "do not go into the way of the Gentiles" (10:5).

What then could the disciples expect in the future? It was far worse than they would experience on their upcoming mission in Galilee!

- They would be delivered up (10:19, 20). The phrase suggests being called before Jewish and Gentile courts. Jesus tells them not to worry about what to say when this happens, for "it will be given to you in that hour what you should speak" (v. 19).

- Their message will divide (10:21–25). Their message will create the most intense emotions, so powerful that family members will "deliver up" one another "to death." The gospel they would preach, far from bringing harmony and peace, would create antagonism and strife. But the hostility would be directed against Jesus, not them per se. They would be hated "for My name's sake" (10:22). It is Jesus and what He stands for that arouses hostility.

Jesus pointed out that disciples are not above their teacher. Instead disciples are expected to be like their teacher, as servants are expected to be like their masters. It follows that those who hate Jesus will hate those who are like Him.

- They are to speak boldly (10:26, 27). The disciples are not to be overawed by opposition. Instead they are to keep on boldly preaching God's word. The phrase explaining why the disciples are not to fear is fascinating. It is "for there is nothing covered that will not be revealed, and hidden that will not be known" (v. 26).

Shame was of great concern in the world of the first century. Shame is related to guilt, but very different. Guilt is awareness that one has sinned and deserves God's punishment. Shame is public exposure of the fact that what an individual has committed to is useless and empty. The Twelve had no reason to fear being ashamed. At history's end they are the ones who will be proved correct, while the foolishness of their opponents will be exposed to the whole universe.

- They are to fear God rather than men (10:26–33). Fear in this context is a healthy respect. Men could kill the disciples' bodies, but God controls both our biological and eternal destinies. It follows that we need to respect God to such an extent that we do not fear what men might do to us.

Jesus points out that ultimately mere human beings have no power over us at all. God has numbered the very number of the hairs on our heads. He knows when a sparrow dies. As we are so much more valuable to God than sparrows, we can rest secure. Nothing will happen to us apart from our Father's loving will (10:29).

The promise of God's watch care is extended to all who confess Jesus openly.

assuredly, I say to you, he shall by no means lose his reward (Matt. 10:40–42).

BIBLE BACKGROUND:

HARD SAYINGS OF JESUS

"Whoever confesses Me before men, him I will also confess before My Father who is in heaven. But whoever denies Me before men, him I will also deny before My Father who is in heaven" (Matt. 10:33, 34).

Here "confess" has its basic meaning of acknowledge. When "disown" is contrasted with confess in the New Testament it means to reject the claims of Jesus presented in the gospel. Those who reject Jesus in this life are sure to be rejected by God in the day of judgment.

They are to choose Christ over all competing allegiances (Matt. 10:34–39). If it comes to a choice between family and Jesus Christ, the choice must be for Jesus.

But the allegiance issue is not simply relational. It also involves complete commitment to the Father's will [see the discussion of taking up one's cross on page 140]. Only in that complete commitment which characterizes discipleship will a person ever become his or her true self (10:39, see page 139).

Jesus concluded His instruction of the Twelve with a word of encouragement. Their ministry will not be marked by failure, even though many will reject their teaching and many others will ignore it. Jesus promised,

He who receives you receives Me, and he who receives Me receives Him who sent Me. He who receives a prophet in the name of a prophet shall receive a prophet's reward. And he who receives a righteous man in the name of a righteous man shall receive a righteous man's reward. And whoever gives one of these little ones only a cup of cold water in the name of a disciple,

After giving the Twelve these instructions, Jesus "departed from there to teach and preach" (Matt. 11:1), and the disciples stepped out on their own.

Mark tells us that later the Twelve returned and told Jesus what they had done and what they had taught (Mark 6:30).

Another similar passage tells of a time when Jesus sent out seventy of His followers on a similar mission. They returned thrilled and excited, joyfully reporting that "even the demons are subject to us in Your name" (Luke 10:17). Christ, who had witnessed the fall of Satan from heaven (see Isa. 14:12–15), calmed them. Jesus had given them power over the enemy, but Jesus' followers were not to rejoice that evil spirits were subject to them. Rather they were to rejoice "because you names are written in heaven" (Luke 10:20).

Discipleship has its rewards. But that which is to bring us the greatest joy of all is knowing Jesus personally and being known by Him.

Jesus had recruited and begun training the twelve men who were to play such vital roles in establishing His church. Both the recruitment and training processes are instructive.

Jesus did not ask for a commitment to discipleship until each of the Twelve had a chance to come to know Him personally. Discipleship is not so much commitment to a set of beliefs as it is wholehearted allegiance to the person of Jesus Christ. People still need to have a chance to come to know Him better before being challenged to discipleship.

But once the Twelve had been called and made a decision to follow Jesus, Christ began to train them. The initial stages of this training involved spending time with Jesus, observing what He did, and listening to His teachings. As we've seen, the Twelve began to understand and to adopt Jesus' own attitude toward others, sensing His compassion and ready acceptance of all.

Being involved with Jesus also led to many opportunities to interact with Him in private. The disciples were able to question Jesus and have Him explain what He had taught and why He had acted as He had. Jesus was also able to test them, challenging and expanding their understanding.

Then, along with teaching by example and in private conversations, Jesus taught by sending out the Twelve to gain experiences that would be vital in the future. In preaching repentance and the gospel of the kingdom of heaven, the disciples had an opportunity to learn reliance on God and to see for themselves the power of the name of Jesus.

Soon Jesus' teaching would take on a new emphasis, and so would Jesus' training of the Twelve. For as it became more and more clear that Israel would not acknowledge Jesus as the promised Messiah, Jesus began to emphasize the cross rather than the crown.

TURNING-POINT TEACHINGS

Jesus and His teachings were now known to all in Galilee and Judea. Yet despite His miracles the early enthusiasm for Jesus had waned. The religious leaders openly opposed Jesus and tried to undermine His teaching. While a core of followers remained faithful, the general populace was uncertain. There was no doubt that Jesus was special. But was He the Messiah?

The turning point in Jesus ministry is recorded in Matthew 16, Mark 8, and Luke 9. Jesus asked His followers who had circulated among the crowds who men said that He was. Their report was discouraging. And from that point the focus of Christ's training of the Twelve shifted from crown to cross.

The incident is described in three of the four gospels. Jesus asked His disciples, "Who do men say that I, the Son of Man, am?" (Matt. 16:13; compare Mark 8:27; Luke 9:18). Matthew and Mark tell us the question was raised when Jesus and the Twelve were in Caesarea Philippi, a city in North Palestine on the south slope of Mount Hermon, near to headwaters of the Jordan River above the Sea of Galilee. Luke tells us

that Christ had been alone praying, and that He asked this question when His disciples joined Him.

The disciples had a ready answer. "Some say John the Baptist, some Elijah, and others Jeremiah or one of the prophets" (Matt. 16:14; compare Mark 8:28). Luke adds that one rumor held that Jesus was actually "one of the old prophets" who had risen again (Luke 9:19).

In one sense this was high praise. While the religious leaders might claim Jesus was in league with Satan (Matt. 12:24), or that He was actually a demon possessed Samaritan (John 8:48), this was not the opinion of the general populace. Whoever Jesus might be, the crowd firmly believed that He was a prophet of God. He might even be Elijah, the forerunner, whose mission was to clear the way for the promised Messiah!

While these opinions might have seemed flattering, they in fact constituted a rejection of our Lord. However highly they might regard Jesus, the crowds had rejected His claim to be the Messiah and God come in the flesh.

The fish was an early Christian symbol because its letters in Greek were the initials of the confession: Jesus Christ, Son of God, Savior.

THE TURNING POINT

Jesus then asked His disciples, "Who do you say that I am?" Peter, ever quick to speak up, answered for them all. "You are the Christ, the Son of the living God" (Matt. 16:16).

PETER'S CONFESSION

The word "Christ," *christos* in Greek, has the same meaning as Messiah in Hebrew. Both mean "the anointed." Peter and the others realized that Jesus was the one appointed by God to fulfill the promises of the Old Testament prophets.

And Peter's confession went further. Peter was convinced that Jesus was "the Son of the living God." In Jesus God had come in the flesh to keep the promises that filled the Old Testament with hope.

JESUS' RESPONSE

Jesus responded to Peter's confession with three sayings, two of which have been the subject of debate.

Flesh and blood has not revealed this to you (Matt. 16:17). By now Peter and the Twelve had spent over a year with Jesus. Yet what they had witnessed and heard had also been witnessed by thousands in Galilee and Judea. How then did Peter and the rest of the Twelve recognize Jesus for who He was while the crowds did not?

Jesus' remark reminds us that all the evidence that was available for examination by the senses was deficient. What is seen with the eyes simply is never enough to compel belief. Even the miracles which Jesus openly performed and which authenticated His claims did not create faith.

It was "My Father who is in heaven" who had revealed Jesus to Peter and the Twelve. Evidence from the natural world does not lead to belief. Only a work by God in a heart that is open to His word will bring any individual to acknowledge Jesus as the Son of God.

You are Peter, and on this rock I will build My church (Matt. 16:18). This is perhaps the most debated text in the Gospels. The

Roman Catholic Church teaches that by this saying Jesus set Peter above the other disciples, in effect making Peter the first pope. Catholic tradition notes that Peter went to Rome and died there, thus making the bishops of Rome Peter's successors. *The rock is thus not only Peter but Peter's successors.*

It would follow that the Roman Church is the true church, and all Christians are bound to submit to the authority of Christ's vicar on earth and Peter's successor, the pope.

This interpretation is rejected by Protestants, and has been since the Reformation. Indeed, many of those who are identified by the Roman Catholic church as church fathers held very different views of what Christ's words mean. Two other interpretations have strong support in church history.

Peter's confession of Christ is the rock. Those who hold this view point out that in the Greek Peter is called petra, a stone. But the rock on which the church is founded is petros, a massive rock formation. Noting this some of the church fathers argued that the rock was Peter's confession of faith in Christ. Jesus' church would be built on the shared faith of those who were convinced that He is the Christ, the Son of the Living God.

Christ Himself is the Rock. The interpretation preferred by most Protestants is that the Rock is Christ Himself, whom Peter recognized and affirmed. Jesus' church rests firmly on the fact that Jesus is the Christ, the Son of the Living God. This view is often supported by referring to 1 Corinthians 3:11, where the apostle Paul writes, "For no other foundation can anyone lay than that which is laid, which is Jesus Christ."

The gates of Hades shall not prevail against it (Matt. 16:18). *The Victor Bible Background Commentary* (Chariot-Victor, 1987, p. 62) describes two interpretations of this phrase.

The "gates of Hades" refers to death and dying. The image of gates typically suggests entering into something. The phrase "gates of . . . " is found in the Bible (Job 17:16; Ps. 9:13), in Jewish literature (Macc. 5:5), and in pagan literature as well (Iliad 9:312). If the "gates of Hades" are to be understood in this familiar literary allusion Jesus is saying that death itself cannot prevail against Him and His church.

The "gates of Hades" refers to Satan's powers. In this interpretation, "gates" are understood to represent fortifications and military power (cf. Gen. 22:17; Ps. 127:5). This imagery was used in the first-century Qumran community. If this is the allusion, Jesus is saying that all of Satan's powers cannot destroy the church which is founded on Jesus.

BIBLE BACKGROUND:

A QUMRAN HYMN

An unusual expression of Judaism is represented in the Qumran community, an ascetic sect which was established in the desert. It was members of that community who preserved what we call the "Dead Sea Scrolls." A hymn from those scrolls (Hymn 6.25-30) expresses the sense of security the believer finds in God; a security like that which Christ emphasized in His "gates of Hades" saying.

But I shall be as one who enters a fortified city, as one who seeks refuge behind a high wall until deliverance; I will [lean on] your truth, O my God, for You will set the foundation on rock and the framework by the measuring cord of justice, and the tried stones by the plumb line [of truth], to [build] a mighty [wall] which will not sway, and no man entering there shall stagger. For no enemy shall ever invade it, since the doors shall be doors of protection through which no man shall pass; and its bars shall be firm,

In Bible times keys symbolized authority and responsibility.

and no man shall break them. No rabble shall enter in with their weapons of war until all the [arrows] of the war of wickedness have come to an end. And then at the time of judgment the sword of God shall hasten, and all the sons of His truth shall awake to overthrow wickedness; all the sons of iniquity shall be no more. The hero shall bend his bow; the fortress shall open onto endless space, and the everlasting gates shall send out weapons of war.

I will give you the keys to the kingdom of heaven (Matt. 16:19). While some commentators have argued that the keys were given to the Twelve as a group, it is clear from the text that Jesus gave the keys to Peter. The question this raises is, "What are the keys?"

In biblical times keys frequently symbolized the office of a steward who was given responsibility for care of his master's household (cf. Is. 22:15, 20, 22). If this is the symbolism, Peter was given a special responsibility by Christ.

Most believe that this responsibility was to preach the gospel to Jew and non-Jew. The keys thus were used to open the door of salvation to all people. Peter used the first key when he preached the first gospel sermon on the day of Pentecost (Acts 2). Peter used a second key when he became the first to share the good news with non-Jews at the home of the Roman officer, Cornelius (Acts 10).

This understanding fits a comment Jesus made about the religious leaders in Luke 11:52. There he condemned the lawyers (experts in biblical law) "for you have taken away the key of knowledge. You did not enter in yourselves, and those who were entering in you hindered." The "key" was the "key of [the] knowledge" needed to enter the kingdom of God.

And whatever you bind on earth will be bound in heaven, and whatever you loose on earth will be loosed in heaven (Matt. 16:19). Rightly understood, this saying supports the above interpretation of the keys. Wrongly interpreted, the saying has been used to support notion that the pope or the Roman Catholic Church has the power to release souls in purgatory for entrance into heaven.

The terms "binding" and "loosing" were used in two ways in Jesus' day. But in which of these two ways did Jesus use them here?

Do binding and loosing relate to teaching? The first way these terms were used is illustrated in Rabbi Nehuya ben Hakanin's prayer that he might make only right decisions concerning application of God's law. The rabbi's prayer is recorded in *yBerakhot* 4:2,7d.

May it please You, Lord my God and God of my fathers, that I lose not my temper regarding my colleagues, and visa versa, so that we will not declare as defiled what is pure, or pure what is defiled, that we will not loosen what is bound or bind what is loosened; lest I be ashamed in this and the future world.

Here the rabbi is concerned about loosening what is bound (i. e., permitting what should be forbidden) and binding what is loosened (i. e., forbidding what should be permitted). The loosing and binding relate to the accurate interpretation of God's law by one committed to teach it.

If Jesus were using binding and loosing in this sense, His statement would be concerned with the accuracy of apostolic teaching, and Peter would be the one who made the determination of what should be permitted and what should not be permitted to believers.

Do binding and loosing relate to sharing the gospel? The Greek suggests a slight alteration of the text. A literal translation indicates that whatever things are bound or loosed by Peter on earth "have been" bound or loosed in heaven. Peter's action is not the cause of the binding or loosing. But what happens on earth will be in complete harmony with what is happening in heaven.

This phrasing makes sense if the keys given to Peter were the responsibility of being the first to preach the gospel to the two basic ethnic groups of Jew and Gentile. The message of the gospel that Peter preached does both bind and loosen those who hear. It permits those who respond with faith to enter God's kingdom, and it forbids the entrance of those without faith. And, as Jesus said, how a person responds on earth will indeed bind or loose him in heaven, now and forever more.

Peter has used the keys, and the door to salvation has been thrown open to all. With the door flung wide open there is no more use for the keys, nor any role for church leaders who futilely claim to have authority on earth to determine what happens in heaven.

THE NEW FOCUS

While Jesus would still speak of His kingdom, His teaching of the disciples took on a new focus. Jesus began to speak of His coming death and to call His followers to a life of self-denial and servanthood.

From that time (Matt. 16:21; Mark 8:31; Luke 9:21, 22). Jesus instructed the Twelve to tell no one He was the Christ, and then introduced the new theme of His coming suffering and death. Matthew marks this as a turning point with the words "from that time." Before this time, Jesus had emphasized the fact that the kingdom of heaven was at hand. But after his implicit rejection by the people,

from that time Jesus began to show to His disciples that He must go to Jerusalem, and suffer many things from the elders and chief priests and scribes, and be killed, and be raised the third day (Matt. 16:21).

Mark does not quote Jesus directly, but tells us that Jesus "*began to teach them* that the Son of Man must suffer many things, and be rejected by the elders and chief priests and scribes, and be killed, and after three days rise again" (8:31; italics mine). Luke quotes Jesus, saying essentially the same thing.

Each of the synoptic Gospel writers portrays the same new focus in Jesus' teaching of the disciples, and Matthew and Mark emphasize the fact that this was something new and directed specifically to the Twelve. It was only "from that time" that Jesus "began to teach them" about His coming crucifixion.

What Jesus now introduced had, of course, always been the central element in God's eternal plan. But it was an element in God's plan that Jesus had not taught the Twelve about before. We see this in the fact that of seven references by Jesus to His coming suffering and death, all are found at or after the turning point described in Matthew 16. Similarly, all of the five references in Mark and the seven references in Luke are also found in or after the turning-point passages of Mark 8 and Luke 9.

It's likely that by this time the Twelve, like Jesus, were aware that the tide of popular opinion was running against Him. The people respected Jesus as a prophet, but they would not acknowledge Him as the Messiah. It was time for Jesus to begin to help His disciples prepare, not only for Christ's crucifixion, but for a role the Twelve had never expected they would play.

Peter's objection (Matt. 16:22, 23; Mark 8:32, 33). For once Peter demonstrated a certain amount of sensitivity. He was terribly upset that Jesus foresaw His own death. But rather than blurt out his thoughts before the other disciples, Peter took Jesus aside.

We can almost see Peter, deeply concerned, speaking with Jesus. Despite the fact that Jesus was the Rabbi and Peter His disciple, Peter actually "began to rebuke Him" (Matt. 16:22)! Originally the word translated "rebuke" here, elencho, meant to "convince" or "refute." By the first century it had taken on the additional meaning of "to correct," often by accusing. It was hardly Peter's place to correct Jesus or to try to convince Him that He was wrong.

Jesus reacted instantly. Just moments before, Jesus had called Peter blessed. Now Jesus turned and said, "Get behind me, Satan! You are an offense to Me, for you are not mindful of the things of God, but the things of men" (Matt. 16:23).

Peter may have been expressing concern for Jesus. But it was an inappropriate concern. Peter was looking at Jesus' death through human eyes, seeing it as a tragedy and a defeat. But Christ's crucifixion was the key to God's plan of redemption. In God's eyes the cross was a triumph, marking His victory of sin, death, and Satan.

How often we are so moved by the suffering of loved ones that we fail to realize that God has a purpose in all that happens. How important to realize that our tragedies too are often God's triumphs. And how often in seeking to insulate our loved ones from pain we deprive rather than protect them.

After Jesus rebuked Peter He went on to define a principle that brings not only the cross in perspective, but our personal experiences as well.

THE GOAL OF DISCIPLESHIP

In Judaism, discipleship was the path to becoming a rabbi. And in Judaism, such teachers of the Law were highly regarded. A rabbi enjoyed the respect of all. He was looked up to. Everyone listened when he spoke. And he was honored by all for his piety and his learning. In earlier times priests and politicians were at the pinnacle of society. In the first century the rabbi enjoyed the greatest prestige, and the more prominent rabbis were held in awe by the people.

When the Twelve were recruited by Jesus, they followed Him in part because they were convinced Jesus was destined to be the greatest teacher of all, the prophet like Moses, as well as the Messiah. Surely Jesus' disciples would, when they were fully trained, be highly honored too!

But now Jesus' ministry had reached its turning point, and Christ was warning His disciples that He was destined to suffer and die and be raised again. What did this turning point imply for the Twelve and their dream of prominence? Jesus' next words must have stunned the disciples, for Christ sketched a future not one of the Twelve had expected.

Then Jesus said to His disciples, "If anyone desires to come after Me, let him deny himself, and take up his cross, and follow Me. For whoever desires to save his life will lose it, but whoever loses his life for My sake will find it. For what profit is it to a man if he grains the whole world, and loses his own soul? Or what will a man give in exchange for his soul? For the Son of Man will come in the glory of His Father with His angels, and then He will reward each according to his works (Matt. 16:24–27).

In a very real sense these words of Jesus unlock all of His turning-point teaching of the Twelve.

If anyone desires to come after Me (Matt. 16:24; Mark 8:34; Luke 9:23). The original Greek word translated "desire" emphasizes choice rather than "want to." Following Jesus into suffering and death was hardly an attractive prospect! Yet the Twelve, and millions since then, have made the words of an old hymn their personal confession:

I have decided to follow Jesus.
I have decided to follow Jesus.
I have decided to follow Jesus.
No turning back. No turning back.

No, discipleship is a choice and a commitment, not a desire. For see what the choice of discipleship involves.

Let him deny himself (Matt. 16:24; Mark 8:34; Luke 9:23). Each Gospel writer records the same formula, a formula which begins with self-denial.

Many misunderstand self-denial, assuming that we must give up anything that we enjoy or want to do if we are to be Jesus' disciples. They're wrong. To deny oneself is simply to consciously reject one's own will in favor of God's will. The disciple realizes that he or she is no longer in charge of his own life, and gives over control to the Lord.

Take up his cross (Matt. 16:24; Mark 8:34). Luke uses the same phrase, but adds the word "daily" (Luke 9:23). This saying too is often misapplied. We hear people speak of a disease or a difficult child as "my cross to bear." Yet just because an experience is painful or difficult does not make it our cross.

There are two much more appropriate ways of looking at the cross of which Jesus speaks here.

Our cross is ridicule and rejection. In the first century crucifixion was viewed as such a shameful death that it was reserved for slaves and brigands, and no Roman citizen could be crucified. On the way to the place of execution the victim carried the cross bar, which would be attached to an erected pole at the execution grounds. Along the way to execution a victim could expect the jeers and ridicule of the crowd.

What Jesus speaks of as "your cross" is not suffering and death, but rather exposure to the ridicule and rejection experienced by one carrying his cross through

In the New Testament the cross symbolizes Jesus' sacrificial death and also symbolizes God's will.

———————— ❖ ————————

life. To follow Jesus, to openly identify yourself as His disciple, is hardly the key to popularity in this world! And it was hardly the path to take if a disciple of Jesus was intent on becoming an honored and respected member of society.

"Our cross" is a symbol for God's will. It's significant that Jesus didn't say disciples are to "take up My cross." That surely would have meant suffering and death!

But Jesus said, "Take up your cross." Crucifixion was Jesus' cross to bear, for it was God's will for His Son. Jesus accepted the burden of God's will and went to meet that fate. But God has hardly called every Christian to suffering and death.

God does have a will—a plan and a purpose—for each believer's life. And, as Jesus' cross stood for God's will for Him, so our cross stands for God's will for each of us. "Your cross" is whatever God's will for you may be.

Luke's addition of "daily" is important. The decision to take up our cross and do God's will is a choice we must make daily, hourly, even moment by moment. And in choosing the will of God as our will we fulfill Jesus' call to "follow Me."

Saving and losing our lives (Matt. 16:25; Mark 8:35; Luke 9:24). Our English translation of Matthew 16:25 and 26 are confusing for a simple reason. In these two verses the translators chose to render a single Greek word by different English words. The Greek word *psyche* is translated "life" in 16:25 but "soul" in 16:26. This is unfortunate, for what these verses teach is more easily understood if we replace the English words with the one Greek term they render. Jesus therefore actually said,

For whoever desires to save his psyche will lose it, but whoever loses his psyche for my sake will find it. For what profit is it to a man if he gains the whole world, and loses his own psyche? Or what will a man give in exchange for his psyche?

The New International Encyclopedia of Bible Words (Zondervan, p. 576) points out that "the basic meaning of psyche is established by its OT counterpart, rather than by its meaning in Greek culture." While psyche might mean "soul" in Greek philosophy, its Old Testament counterpart refers to the inner person, the individual himself.

What Jesus taught is simply this. We can live our lives as we choose, following our own will. Or we can live our lives for Jesus' sake, committed to God's will. If we choose the first, we will remain the inner person we are by nature, and we will lose the transformed person God can enable us to become. So Jesus asks a question. What profit is it if a man gains the whole world, but loses the transformed self that will fit him for eternity? What indeed is valuable enough ("will a man give") to take in exchange for the person he can become by choosing God's will?

For the Son of Man will come (Matt. 16:27; compare Mark 8:38 and Luke 9:26). God's will for Jesus was suffering, death, and resurrection. But at history's end a glorified Jesus will come again! And then "He will reward each according to his works."

In this life the Twelve would never gain society's respect and honor. Neither have the millions of others who have followed them down the path of discipleship. But they would be transformed from within, and when Jesus returns they will be richly rewarded indeed.

These turning-point teachings introduced new and unexpected realities. In the immediate future Jesus would be lifted up on a cross rather than ascend Messiah's throne. Rather than be glorified, He would suffer rejection, ridicule, and death. And it would be the same for those disciples who chose to deny themselves, take up their crosses, and follow their Lord. Yet as the disciples chose Jesus' path of submission to God's will, something wonderful would happen within them. Each disciple would lose his old and selfish self and become a new self as God transformed him from within.

Two vivid lessons. Jesus' words to the Twelve recorded in Matthew 16, Mark 8, and Luke 9 laid the foundation for the next stage of the training of the Twelve. But before instruction began, the disciples would need to be reminded of Jesus' power and of their own powerlessness.

A glimpse of power (Matt. 17:1–13; Mark 9:1–13; Luke 9:28–36). When Jesus had finished telling the Twelve of His coming cross and the real import of their discipleship, He promised that some of them would "see the kingdom of God present with power" (Mark 9:1). Within a few days Jesus led Peter, James, and John to a nearby mountaintop where He was "transfigured before them." Mark tells us that "His clothes became shining, exceedingly white, like snow, such as no launderer on earth can whiten them" (9:3).

This glimpse of Jesus' glory deeply impressed the three disciples. The cross might lie ahead, and they might lose themselves in serving others as Christ served. But in the person of Jesus the kingdom was present in power even now. Surely at history's end the promised kingdom would come for all to see.

On the way down from the mountain the three asked about Elijah. Jesus explained that the coming of Elijah to restore all things did lie in the future and would presage His return (see the discussion on p. 86).

A lesson in powerlessness (Matthew 17:14–21; Mark 9:14–29; Luke 9:37–42). When Jesus and the three reached the valley, they found the other disciples surrounded by a curious crowd. A distraught father had brought his demon-possessed son to the disciples for healing, and they had been unable to cure him.

Mark's report of the incident both records a frustrated outburst by Jesus (see the Hard Sayings of Jesus on page 142) and also features Jesus' fascinating dialogue with the father. The father, uncertain after the failure of Jesus' disciples to heal his son, begged, "If You can do anything, have compassion on us and help us" (Mark 9:22).

Jesus told him, "If you can believe, all things are possible to him who believes" (9:23). Torn between hope and doubt, the father blurted out, "Lord, I believe; help my unbelief!" (9:24).

Jesus expelled the demon, and afterward the disciples asked why they could not cast it out. Jesus responded, "This kind can come out by nothing but prayer and fasting" (9:29).

BIBLE BACKGROUND:

HARD SAYINGS OF JESUS

O faithless and perverse generation, how long shall I be with you? How long shall I bear with you? Bring him here to Me (Matthew 17:17; compare Mark 9:19; Luke 9:41).

These words seem to be addressed to Jesus' disciples but also to include all onlookers. The linkage of "faithless" and "perverse" indicates willful unbelief, a refusal to accept evidence of the obvious.

Throughout the nation people had come to Jesus for healing but still refused to acknowledge Him as Messiah or the Son of God. Even the disciples failed to trust fully in Jesus' name, as their inability to cast out the demon demonstrates.

But most of all Jesus' exclamation was an anguished cry. How could the crowds fail to believe? And how could the disciples fail to sense the extent of the power He made available to them?

Earlier Jesus had given His disciples power over evil spirits, and they had used that power to heal (Matt. 10:8). So when the disciples asked why they could not cast out the demon, they were confused. Jesus' reference to fasting and prayer suggests that the disciples had assumed that the power was theirs, a permanent gift. In the future the disciples would learn the necessity of "prayer and fasting," a phrase indicating total, conscious dependence on God.

It's possible that the disciples had begun to fall into the trap of *ex opere operatum*, the idea that power resides in the formula used or the words spoken. The incident emphasized the fact that in the future they must remember that power resides in Christ and can only be accessed by complete reliance on Him. In the future the Twelve and those to whom they ministered would triumph only as they fixed their faith in Jesus, the source of all authority and power.

THE TURNING-POINT TEACHINGS

At the turning point, Jesus told the Twelve that He was to suffer, die, and be raised again. His disciples must then follow their absent Lord. They, like Jesus, must choose to do the will of God daily, even though that choice involved self-denial.

In the short span of time that now lay between the turning point and the final week of Jesus' life, Jesus engaged in intensive teaching of the Twelve. This teaching is carefully traced for us in Matthew 18–20, and involved both teaching by example and careful, detailed instruction. Matthew's account of this phase of the training of the Twelve closes with Jesus' triumphal entry into Jerusalem just one week before His crucifixion.

LITTLE-ONE-NESS: THE KEY TO GREATNESS (MATTHEW 18:1–10; COMPARE MARK 9:33–37 AND LUKE 9:46–48)

The disciples raised the issue. They came to Jesus, saying, "Who then is greatest in the kingdom of heaven" (Matt. 18:1). In essence they were asking, How do we achieve in the kingdom of heaven? What does living as a disciple involve?

This question sets the agenda for Matthew 18–20. Each teaching and each event recorded in these chapters relates to this issue in some way and was an integral part of the Twelve's training for leadership in the mystery kingdom Jesus was about to inaugurate.

Becoming as little children (18:2–4). The text tells us that in answer to the disciples' question, Jesus

called a little child to Him, set him in the midst of them, and said, "Assuredly, I say to you, unless you are converted and become as little children, you will by no means enter the kingdom of heaven. Therefore, whoever humbles himself as this little child is the greatest in the kingdom of heaven (Matt. 18: 2–4).

Looking carefully at this passage, it's clear what Jesus was saying.

Jesus called. For years now Jesus had been calling the people of Israel to Him. But rather than respond, the populace held back, undecided. Rather than respond to Jesus' words, the people debated them.

But when Jesus called the little child, he responded immediately. The text makes it clear that the child came and then "Jesus set him in the midst of them." The child was placed there as an example, for all were respond to Jesus as he had.

A little child. The Greek word used here indicates a child no older than seven. This too is significant. In Israel no person was responsible under God's Law until he reached the age of twelve or thirteen. Only then could he be held responsible before the law.

But the little child's quick response to Jesus showed that he did not need to be under the Law to please God. Jesus had said it in His Sermon on the Mount. The wise man, who built his house upon the rock, was the person who heard Jesus words and did them—just as the little child had heard and responded when Jesus had called.

Whoever humbles himself (Matt. 18:4). Again Jesus focuses attention on the example set by the child. It was not humility itself that would be the key to significance

in Jesus' kingdom. It was humbling oneself as this little child that leads to greatness.

Again, how did the child humble himself? He humbled himself by responding to Jesus' call freely, spontaneously, and immediately. Adults had heard Jesus' call, but had stopped to study and debate it. Rather than obey Jesus' words, they stood in judgment, assuming the right to decide which they would obey and which they would reject. This was hubris, an arrogance that is the opposite of the humility that the little child displayed.

It's no wonder that Jesus told His disciples, "whoever humbles himself as this little child is the greatest in the kingdom of heaven."

Preserving little-one-ness (Matt. 18:6–10; compare Mark 9:42–48). Jesus then began to speak of "these little ones who believe in Me" (v. 6). He has used a little child as an example of greatness. Now He ascribes "little-one-ness" to all true believers!

This is especially appropriate. To become a child of God one must hear God's word about Jesus and respond spontaneously, freely, and trustingly. This is the very essence of faith. And this attitude remains the key to living successfully in Jesus' kingdom.

In fact, in becoming Christians we take on little-one-ness. We no longer claim the right to stand in judgment on the gospel, we simply submit to it and to Jesus Christ. But the quality of little-one-ness that humility that enables us to respond freely to Jesus' words, unlike our salvation, is a quality that can be lost. Indeed God's people must struggle to maintain their little-one-ness, and Christian leaders must do all they can to nurture this quality in God's people.

So Jesus uttered a severe warning to any who would cause His little ones to sin—in context, rob them of their little-one-ness so that they no longer respond to Jesus' words. The strong images Jesus used in this warning are best understood as hyperbole, and the imagery has been discussed earlier (see page 69).

Jesus has made it abundantly clear. The quality of little-one-ness is necessary for our first response of faith, and it is essential that we maintain this quality in our own lives and that we nurture it in others.

Jesus summed up by saying, "Take heed that you do not despise one of these little ones, for I say to you that in heaven their angels always see the face of My Father who is in heaven" (Matt. 18:10).

THREATS TO LITTLE-ONE-NESS (MATTHEW 18:11–35)

Matthew now relates a series of stories Jesus told that illuminate threats to little-one-ness in the believing community. Each story also explains how the threat is to be met by leaders and people. This was vital instruction for the Twelve, who would soon be charged with leading Christ's church.

Going astray (Matt. 18:11–14). Jesus prefaces the first story with a statement that the Son of Man came to save that which was lost. After making this statement, Jesus then told His disciples,

If a man has a hundred sheep, and one of them goes astray, does he not leave the ninety-nine and go to the mountains to seek the one that is straying? And if he should find it, assuredly, I say to you, he rejoices more over that sheep than over the ninety-nine that did not go astray. Even so it is not the will of your Father who is in heaven that one of these little ones should perish (Matt. 18:12–14).

The first threat to God's little ones is internal. Like sheep, we human beings tend to go astray. Jesus' story of the one who went astray would surely have brought to mind Isaiah's statement, "All we like sheep have gone astray; we have turned, every one, to his own way" (Is. 53:6). The tendency to sin is not eradicated by salvation. We all are in danger of going astray, and more than one who truly are God's little ones will turn to their own rather than God's way.

What are we to do when a believer goes astray? We're to remember that Jesus came to save the lost. He Himself is the Shepherd who came to search for those who had gone astray. And when He finds lost sheep and restores it to the flock, rather than recriminate or punish, the shepherd rejoices.

Like the shepherd in Jesus' story we are to go after each individual who goes astray. When we have "found" such a person, we are to welcome him or her back with joy. It is the welcome of shepherd and community that communicates the love of God so powerfully, and expresses the truth that it is "not the will of your Father who is in heaven that one of these little ones should perish" (18:14).

Sinning against brothers (Matt. 18:15–20). Anyone who has had children knows that brothers and sisters scrap and battle. In Jesus' terms, brothers are sure to sin against one another, and hard feelings will result. In most families the daily squabbles are neither serious nor long-lived. But while most hurts are quickly forgotten, at times deep hostilities can develop which tear a family apart.

Jesus' little ones have been brought together in God's family as brothers and sisters. And as in any family, brother will sin against brother. While to be expected, this is serious indeed. Such family sins threaten the quality of little-one-ness for the individuals involved and for the community as well.

After briefly stating this problem, Jesus went on to outline a procedure for dealing with disruptive sins.

If your brother sins against you, go and tell him his fault between you and him alone. If he hears you, you have gained your brother. But if He will not hear, take with you one or two more, that "by the mouth of two or three witnesses every word may be established." And if he refuses to hear them, tell it to the church. But if he refuses even to hear the church, let him be to you like a heathen and a tax collector (Matt. 18:15–17).

There are several things to note about this prescription. First, the issue is not misunderstandings or even doctrinal differences. This problem arises when a believer sins against a brother. Brother-to-brother sins can only be resolved by the one who sinned acknowledging his fault, and by the person sinned against extending forgiveness.

Here Jesus makes the person who has been sinned against responsible to initiate the process of reconciliation, and gives these steps for the victim to follow:

1. Go speak to the brother one on one
2. Go with a few others, who can serve as witnesses
3. Bring the matter to the church for resolution

As the injured party has initiated the attempt at resolution, the burden now rests on the guilty party should he or she "refuse to hear." In fact, Jesus made it plain that a continuing refusal to address the injured party's complaint is grounds for treating that person "like a heathen and a tax collector." But what does "let him be to you like a heathen and a tax collector" mean? There are two possibilities:

BIBLE BACKGROUND:

HARD SAYINGS OF JESUS

"Therefore if you bring your gift to the altar, and there remember that your brother has

something against you, leave your gift there before the altar, and go your way. First be reconciled to your brother, and then come and offer your gift" (Matt. 5:23, 24).

Is there a conflict here? In Matthew 18 Jesus made the victim responsible to initiate reconciliation. In Matthew 5 it is the person who has done the harm that is to take the initiative. There is no conflict, because both parties are responsible to maintain harmony and little-one-ness.

What is significant here is the importance Jesus places on reconciliation. To Jesus reconciliation comes first, even before worship.

1. Jesus instructs the church to expel the brother who refuses to seek reconciliation. This interpretation fits Paul's later command to expel an unrepentant brother who persists in practicing sin after being confronted by the church (1 Cor. 5:1–5).

2. Jesus releases the victim from the obligation of settling the matter within the fellowship, and permits him to take the matter to civil courts. While Paul makes it clear in 1 Corinthians 6:1–8 that disputes between believers are to be settled within the church, there is no prohibition against seeking redress from an unbeliever through the courts. Jesus may be saying that when the sin against a brother involves damages and the person in the wrong refuses the efforts of the church to redress the situation, the injured party is free to treat his brother "like a heathen" and take him to court.

BIBLE BACKGROUND:

HARD SAYINGS OF JESUS

"Whatever you bind on earth will be bound in heaven, and whatever you loose on earth will be loosed in heaven" (Matt. 18:18)

Two uses of the terms bind and loose have already been discussed (p. 137). Here we have a judicial application: Christians have gathered as a court to deal with a sin that has disrupted the fellowship. Because the church has followed the procedure outlined by Christ, believers will be doing heaven's will and the process will be guided and confirmed by God Himself. Thus heaven and earth are agreed on the outcome, and what is bound or loosed here is bound or loosed there.

The next verses are often misapplied and taken as a prayer promise. Instead Jesus is expanding on His instructions for dealing with a situation in which a brother has sinned against a brother. The linkage is established in the first words of verse 19, "Again I say to you." Jesus said, "If two of you agree on earth concerning anything

that they ask, it will be done for them by my Father in heaven. For where two or three are gathered together in My name, I am there in the midst of them" (Matt. 18:19, 20).

This passage is explained in a companion volume in this series, *Every Promise in the Bible*, p. 172, as a continuing discussion of the process of conflict resolution.

The interpretation rests on the fact that the verb aiteisthai, which can mean asking in prayer, is used in judicial contexts with the sense of "pursuing a claim." The thought then is that when two people pursue resolving their conflict, the solution finally accepted by the two disputants will succeed in restoring harmony (Matt. 18:19).

The reason that this approach will result in resolution is given in verse 20. Wherever two or three (asked by the church to serve as judges to suggest a resolution) gather in Christ's name, Jesus is with the judges. Jesus will provide the wisdom needed to arrive at an appropriate solution.

How important it is that believers deal with interpersonal sins and conflicts of all sorts. We are never to let hurts fester, to corrupt our fellowships and rob us of our little-one-ness. How very special that our Lord has given us a procedure for dealing with such matters, including His promise to be personally involved in the process.

Finding grace to forgive (Matt. 18:21–35). The third threat to maintaining and nurturing little-one-ness is an unforgiving spirit. It's hard to welcome back a believer who has gone astray with the unalloyed joy that Jesus calls for. We are all too prone to harboring a critical rather than a forgiving spirit.

It's harder still to freely forgive someone who has sinned against us. Peter was disturbed by Jesus' teaching and asked a perceptive question. "How often shall my brother sin against me, and I forgive him? Up to seven times?" (v. 21).

The rabbis taught that a person must forgive three times. But it seemed only reasonable that, if a person continues to sin against us, the victim would need to protect himself. To do otherwise seemed too much like accepting victimization. Peter however was willing to go the distance for Jesus, and so asked if he should go beyond the understood requirement and forgive "up to" seven times.

In response Jesus told a story about an unforgiving servant. The servant had been forgiven an unpayable debt by his king, and then harshly demanded payment of a tiny debt owed him by a fellow servant (see the full discussion of this story on page 69). The point Jesus made was clear to all. Anyone whom God has forgiven the vast debt incurred by his sin should be quick to forgive others. Others may sin against us, but this cannot compare to the debt we have been forgiven by God!

Ultimately this is key to nurturing little-one-ness. To find the grace to forgive others, we need only to focus on how much God has forgiven you and me. If we fill our hearts with gratitude to God, those hearts will be tender toward those who astray and toward those who sin against us as well.

COUNTERFEIT PATHS TO GREATNESS (MATTHEW 19:1–20:16)

After Jesus finished this instruction on greatness, He led His disciples out of Galilee toward Judea and Jerusalem. On the journey a series of events occurred through which the Twelve were shown the emptiness of the pathways commonly thought to lead to spiritual superiority.

The pathway of the Law (Matt. 19:3–15). This is the path chosen by the Pharisees. These truly dedicated men were convinced

that by carefully keeping every prescription of the rabbis who taught God's Law they would please God and achieve greatness. So when some Pharisees approached Jesus to ask a question, they naturally couched it in terms of what was "lawful." Matthew tells us, "The Pharisees also came to Him, testing Him, and saying to Him, 'Is it lawful for a man to divorce his wife for just any reason?'" (v. 3).

The issue (Matt. 19:3). There were two schools of thought on divorce in first-century Judaism. The first, represented by the followers of Shammai, taught that divorce could be permitted only if a spouse was unfaithful. His was the predominant view in Jesus' day. An opposing view, held by Hillel, held that a man might divorce his wife for any reason at all, including burning his breakfast! One rabbi in this school of thought, which later became the dominant view, went so far as to add, "or if you find someone more attractive."

The question was a "test," for the Pharisees hoped to expose Jesus' expected ignorance of the finer points of an issue that was hotly debated at the time.

Jesus' initial response (Matt. 19:4–6). The first thing to note is that Jesus ignored their question of the "lawfulness" of an "any-cause" divorce. Instead Jesus returned to the creation, long before the giving of Moses' Law, and drew a simple conclusion. In the creation God had intended marriage to be a lifelong commitment between a man and a woman. In marriage the two were united in a "one-flesh" relationship, and it was as one that God intended them to live out their lives on earth.

Jesus' application of this fact has been much misunderstood. Christ said, "Therefore what God has joined together, let not man separate" (19:6).

The saying has been taken as support for the "no-divorce" position adopted by some churches. In fact, however, it is a rebuke of the Pharisees, who assumed that rabbis had a right to sit as an ecclesiastical court and judge whether or not a particular couple's divorce was "lawful." God's original intent was that marriage should be a lifelong union. What right did the Pharisees have to assume that mere men should decide when such a union ought to be broken or maintained?

The Pharisees' reply (Matt. 19:7). The Pharisees quickly objected. If God expected marriage to be a permanent relationship, "Why did Moses command to give a certificate of divorce, and to put her away?"

The reference is to Deuteronomy 24:1–4, which instructs a husband who divorces his wife to give her a certificate proving she was no longer married. With this certificate the woman could remarry. The only restriction was that should she remarry, she could not divorce her second husband and remarry the first.

From Deuteronomy, as well as early Jewish writings, it's clear that a divorced person was expected to remarry. But it is also clear from Deuteronomy 24 that no ecclesiastical court or rabbi was involved. The matter was decided between the husband and wife themselves.

Jesus' explanation (Matt. 19:8–9). Jesus explained that God permitted divorce "because of the hardness of your hearts." Because human beings are sinners, there will be times when the marriage relationship that God intended to be a blessing will be a curse. The relationship will break down, harming rather than helping and healing the partners. It was this, God's concern for sinful human beings, that led God to permit divorce!

The argument here is a stunning one, and undercut the whole approach of the Pharisees to relationship with God. The Pharisees assumed that the Law was the highest possible expression of God's will. Jesus had just shown that the Law was in fact a lower standard, an expression of God's willingness to accommodate Himself

to human weakness. In this sense the law of divorce, symbolic of all law, was a revelation of God's grace. Yet the Pharisees had turned that which was intended to display grace into a legalistic system which taught human beings to trust in their own righteousness rather than rely on God's mercy.

Jesus' next words are an even stronger expression of this truth. Jesus made it clear that divorce and remarriage, except for sexual immorality, is adultery. And even so God had stooped in grace to permit us, His flawed creatures, another chance.

BIBLE BACKGROUND:

HARD SAYINGS OF JESUS

"Except for sexual immorality" (Matt. 19:9)

This so-called "exception clause" has been much debated. Just what is sexual immorality? And did Jesus mean that divorce and remarriage are forbidden unless one partner breaks his or her marriage vows and commits adultery?

The *New International Encyclopedia of Bible Words* (Zondervan, 1985, p.24) explains *porneia*, the Greek word here. It states that "porneia is a general term for any kind of illicit sexual intercourse. In later rabbinic thought it included prostitution, forbidden marriages (such as between relatives), incest, and all kinds of unnatural intercourse. The rendering of porneia as "marital unfaithfulness" [in the NIV, for example] may suggest adultery to the English reader, but the specific word for adultery was available and not used by Jesus."

What is more important for us to note however is that Jesus is not dealing here with grounds for divorce. Like any sin, sexual immorality is grounds for repentance, forgiveness, and reconciliation. Whether or not a marriage relationship has been irretrievably broken and divorce is now the only answer remains a matter to be settled between a husband and

Husbands were responsible to provide a written statement that the marriage was over in case of divorce.

wife alone. No rabbi or contemporary pastor has the right to determine when divorce or subsequent remarriage are "lawful."

At this point Jesus' confrontation with the Pharisees was over. Their claim to spiritual superiority, based on their careful attention to every detail of the Law, had been exposed as a complete misunderstanding of the nature of law and grace.

The disciples misunderstand (Matt. 19:10–12). Jesus' disciples had been stunned by His words. They did not then understand the impact of what Jesus had said, and instead thought Christ was forbidding

divorce rather than confirming its availability. Their conclusion was that, if divorce is not an option, it's too dangerous to marry (19:10)!

Patiently Jesus told them that not everyone would be able to accept their solution. Even though while the celibate life is not for all, some have chosen it "for the kingdom of heaven's sake" (19:12).

Yet marriage, divorce, and celibacy were not the real issue in this confrontation. The real issue was the Pharisees' assumption that greatness could be achieved by a rigorous attempt to keep every detail of God's Law. And that assumption, as Jesus demonstrated, was flawed.

Let the little children come (Matt. 19:13–15). Matthew then describes an incident that summarizes Jesus' teaching. Little children were brought to Jesus to bless, but Jesus' disciples tried to shoo them away. Christ told the Twelve, "Let the little children come to Me, and do not forbid them; for of such is the kingdom of heaven" (v. 14). Again "little children" are prominent. No one in that day imagined for a moment that children under age seven were to relate to God through Moses' law. And so the significance of Jesus' words, "of such is the kingdom of heaven." It is not those who seek to establish their own righteousness via the law who enter and achieve in Jesus' kingdom. It is those who rely completely on grace and who gladly respond to Jesus' words who are the true disciples of our Lord.

The pathway of doing good (Matt. 19:16–30; Luke 18:18–23). This pathway is represented by a wealthy young man who addressed Jesus as "good teacher" and what good thing he should do "that I may have eternal life?" (Matt. 19:16).

B I B L E   B A C K G R O U N D :
HARD SAYINGS OF JESUS

"Why do you call me good? No one is good but One, that is, God" (Matt. 19:17).

It seems a strange thing for Jesus to ask. After all, He was the Son of God.

But there is a logic here that is difficult to challenge. Jesus' question was "Why do you call Me good?" Any person must either acknowledge Jesus as God, or else charge Him with being a deceiver and charlatan! It is contradictory to hold that Jesus was merely human and at the same time to consider Him good.

Good, but not good enough (Matt. 19:16–22). As the conversation developed it became clear that the young man himself was admirable by human standards. He had conscientiously kept the commandments on the second tablet of the Ten Commandments, and treated others in a loving, responsible way. But then Jesus told the young man, "If you want to be perfect, go, sell what you have and give to the poor, and you will have treasure in heaven; and come follow Me" (v. 21).

More than once in church history Christians have taken these words out of context, and supposed that Christ was calling them to poverty. Instead Jesus was confronting the young man with a choice that would reveal his sin and his need for grace.

The Ten Commandments were written on two tablets of stone. The first tablet contained commandments concerning relationship with God; the second tablet contained commandments concerning relationships with other human beings. The young man believed that he had kept the commandments Jesus specified (19:18), all of which were found on the second tablet. So Jesus, who is God, commanded the rich young man to go and sell all his possessions. And the young man refused! "He went away sorrowful, for he had great possessions!" (v. 22).

The rich young man had disobeyed a direct command of Jesus. Yet the first commandment of all was, "You shall have no other gods before Me" (Exod. 20:3).

The young man's choice revealed that despite his "goodness," he did have a god whom he placed before the Lord: his wealth.

He might have been a good person. But no one is truly good. As Jesus said, "No one is good but One, that is, God."

Pity the poor rich man (Matt. 19:23–30). Jesus' subsequent comment to His disciples confused them. "It is hard for a rich man to enter the kingdom of heaven" (v. 23; see the discussion on page 107).

Jesus' comment raised a question in Peter's mind. The rich man hadn't left everything to follow Jesus but the Twelve had! What would they receive?

The Twelve would "sit on twelve thrones, judging the twelve tribes of Israel" (Matt. 19:28). They were destined to become more prominent in Jesus' future kingdom than any had imagined! But Jesus taught that everyone who gives up something in this life "for My name's sake" will receive many times over whatever has been lost (19:29). "But," Jesus concluded, "many who are first will be last, and the last first."

Disciples are not to expect prominence in this world. Jesus' followers often seem to be the last to be admired and the first to be criticized, but when Jesus returns it is His followers who will be first.

The pathway of hard work (Matt. 20:1–16). This story also has been discussed earlier (see page 70). It is addressed to those who assume that working for God harder than others is the way to achieve greatness and reward. Yet greatness is achieved not by the one who works the hardest but by those who rely fully on the grace of God.

Not one of these pathways people take in search of greatness leads to it. The person who would be great must understand that he or she is one of Christ's little ones, and do all that's possible to protect and nurture little-one-ness in others as well.

NOT SO AMONG YOU
(MATTHEW 20:17–34)

On the road to Jerusalem Jesus again reminded the Twelve that soon He would be mocked and scourged and crucified (vv. 17–19). And then an incident occurred which showed how slow the Twelve were to learn the lesson of greatness.

A mother's request (Matt. 20:20–24). The mother of James and John approached

Hard work is no substitute for reliance on grace.

Jesus with a request. We can almost see the two brothers, hanging back and looking innocent but still close enough to overhear.

"Grant that these two sons of mine may sit, one on Your right hand and the other on the left, in Your kingdom" (v. 21). It was clear that James and John and their mother still thought Jesus was about to set up the promised Messianic kingdom on earth. When that happened, the mother wanted the two most powerful positions under Jesus to go to her sons!

It was a foolish request. The real issue was, would James and John be willing to follow Jesus' example of complete commitment to God's will, symbolically sharing Jesus' cup?

BIBLE BACKGROUND:

HARD SAYINGS OF JESUS

"Are you able to . . . be baptized with the baptism that I am baptized with" (Matt. 20:22)?

Like the cup in this verse, baptism symbolizes undergoing an experience. The original word was often used of dipping a piece of cloth in dye, until the cloth took on its hue. Jesus would be immersed in the crucible of suffering as He lived out God's will. The mother of James and John had begged Jesus that her sons might share His power. The real question was would they be ready to share His sufferings.

When the other disciples learned how James and John had tried to advance themselves, they were understandably "greatly displeased." Their anger, and the shame felt by the two humbled brothers, created a teachable moment. It was a moment Jesus used to contrast leadership in the world and leadership as it was to be in Christ's church.

The principle of servanthood (Matt. 20:25–28). These few verses sum up the concept of servant leadership more succinctly than any other Bible passage.

You know that the rulers of the Gentiles lord it over them, and those who are great exercise authority over them. Yet it shall not be so among you; but whoever desires to become great among you, let him be your servant. And whoever desires to be first among you, let him be your slave—just as the Son of Man did not come to be served, but to serve, and to give His life a ransom for many.

Chapter 18 had begun with the disciples' question about becoming great. Now Jesus signals that He is about to sum up what He has taught the Twelve with the words, "whoever desires to become great among you" (20:26).

Jesus' prescription for greatness is simple, yet profound. Don't rule: serve. Don't command: set an example. And in everything you do, give yourself for others.

A powerful example (Matt. 20:30–34). Jesus had just reminded the Twelve that betrayal, suffering, and death awaited Him in Jerusalem. Yet as they left Jericho to climb the mountain path that led to the Holy City and Jesus' destiny, two blind men heard that Jesus was passing by. Desperately they cried out, "Have mercy on us, O Lord, Son of David" (v. 30).

The crowds tried to silence the blind men but they just shouted louder. Then Jesus stood still, and called them, saying "What do you want Me to do for you?"

This is servanthood indeed. To put aside one's own burdens and needs to heed the cries of others.

This is servanthood.

And this is greatness in the kingdom of heaven.

PREVIEWS AND PROMISES

We've all heard children say it. "But why should I study this stuff?" So often the things we need to know for the future seem to have little meaning for our lives now.

Jesus' early training of the Twelve had seemed so relevant. Everything was new to them, and when Jesus sent them out to preach the good news of the kingdom and to perform authenticating miracles, they could hardly contain their enthusiasm.

Then came the turning point and Christ's teaching on servant leadership, and the disciples were puzzled and uncertain. All too quickly the end approached, and on the night before Jesus was crucified they sat down together to what we call the Last Supper.

That night Jesus introduced yet more new teaching; teaching that instructed the disciples on what life would be like for Jesus' followers when He was no longer with them.

Only one of the gospel writers invites us into that last, private supper Jesus shared with the Twelve (John 13–16).

John opens the door and welcomes us into this most intimate of settings, and the teachings that John records have been called the "seed bed of the church." Although most of what Jesus said that night must have been puzzling to His disciples, what Jesus taught then was vital. It was the key to understanding how believers would relate to Christ during the ages He would be absent.

Like so much of the curriculum children study, at the time what Jesus taught may not have made much sense to the Twelve. But as in the case of our children, it was vital truth that the twelve would have to apply all too soon.

EXAMPLES FOR ALL
(JOHN 13:1–30)

John describes two events that happened while the little company was eating together. But first he carefully set the scene. He tells us that Jesus was moved by a sense of urgency, knowing that He would soon "depart from this world to the Father" and

Jesus set the example of servanthood all Christians are to follow.

also was moved by a deep and enduring love for His own (13:1). He contrasts Jesus with Judas, who had already agreed with the high priests to betray Christ, and who was moved not by love but by greed and by Satan.

It was against this background Jesus rose to wash His disciples' feet and that Christ offered a sop to Judas and released him to do his terrible deed. It is also against this background that Jesus gave His remaining disciples his New Commandment.

THE FOOT WASHING (JOHN 13:3–17)

A task for slaves. In New Testament times it was slaves who washed the feet of those who came to a meal at the home of a wealthy person. The roads and streets even in Jerusalem were unpaved and dusty. As most people wore sandals, feet became dusty after they had walked even a little distance. If a visitor was especially prominent, a host might wash that visitor's feet himself. But foot washing was a lowly service normally performed by servants or slaves.

Thus the disciples were shocked when Jesus got up from the meal, laid his outer cloak aside, and began to wash and dry His disciples' feet. John makes it very clear that Jesus did this fully conscious of His identity: "knowing that the Father had given all things into His hands, and that He had come from God and was going to God,"

Jesus began to wash his disciples' feet anyway (13:3)!

Peter objects. The disciples seem to have sat in stunned silence until Jesus came to Peter. As usual that outspoken disciple had something to say. Peter blurted out words that we might paraphrase. "Lord, You don't really intend to wash my feet!" To Peter, and undoubtedly to the others, what Jesus was doing was totally inappropriate.

When Jesus dismissed the implied criticism, Peter took a stand. "You shall never wash my feet!" Peter simply would not permit Christ to do anything that seemed to Peter to be demeaning.

How fascinating it is. Peter rightly addressed Jesus as Lord. Yet Peter took it upon himself to tell Jesus what He should or should not do! How like you and me. We acknowledge Christ as Lord, and yet we're so likely to take it upon ourselves to judge the right or wrong of what Jesus is doing in other believers.

Jesus bluntly told Peter, "If I do not wash you, you have no part with Me." And Peter crumbled. But then Peter begged, "Not my feet only, but also my hands and my head" (v. 9). Commentators agree that Jesus' response has symbolic significance; a significance that became clear only after His death and resurrection. Jesus said, "He who is bathed needs only to wash his feet, but is completely clean; and you are clean, but not all of you" (v. 10).

Jesus used two Greek words here for washing. The first, *louo*, rightly translated "bathed" in our text, was used of washing the entire body. The second, translated "wash" (*nipto*), indicated washing a part of the body.

The metaphor reminds us that those who come to Christ in faith have been regenerated and cleansed (Titus 3:5). But as we live in this world we need continual cleansing from the corruption that clings to our feet. Peter had been bathed and was "completely clean." All Peter would need

was the cleansing from daily sins available through confession. He would not need to renew faith's cleansing bath.

Then Jesus added the phrase, "but not all." John explains. Jesus was referring to Judas, for He knew who would betray Him.

Jesus' explanation. The disciples had been shocked when Jesus washed their feet. Now Jesus explained that He had been giving the disciples an example to follow.

"You call Me Teacher and Lord" (John 13:13). In the first century a disciple would never address the rabbi with whom he studied by his name. Instead the disciple acknowledged his subordination by addressing his rabbi as "Teacher" or as "Lord." Here Jesus reminds the Twelve that they show Him this respect, and that they are right to do so.

"If I then, your Lord and Teacher" (John 13:14, 15). Jesus had washed their feet to give them an example to follow. As Jesus had taken the role of a servant, so they also should be willing to stoop to serve one another.

Jesus' example may have brought to mind words Christ had spoken just a few days before on the way to Jerusalem:

Whoever desires to become great among you, let him be your servant. And whoever desires to be first among you, let him be your slave—just as the Son of Man did not come to be served, but to serve, and to give His life a ransom for many (Matt. 20:26–28).

It had been one thing to hear Jesus speak these words. It was another to feel your face flush in embarrassment as the one you acknowledge as Lord and God knelt before you and washed your feet.

This was an experience that no disciple could possibly forget, an example of servanthood that was driven deep into their hearts.

"A servant is not greater than his master" (John 13:16–17). In the future if a disciple of Jesus was ever tempted to see

himself as better than others because of his authority, he need only remember how Jesus had stooped to take a servant's role at that Last Supper. He could hardly consider himself better than Jesus, and so he must be as willing as Christ to humble himself to serve others.

Although we were not present that night, we all need to visualize Christ washing our feet. And every leader needs to always keep in mind the fact that no one who is sent is greater than the one sending him. For, as Jesus said, "If you know these things, blessed are you if you do them."

A PIECE OF BREAD FOR JUDAS (JOHN 13:18–30)

Jesus made a comment that puzzled most of the Twelve. What Jesus said was not for all of them. "I know whom I have chosen," Jesus said, "but that the Scripture may be fulfilled, '*He who eats bread with Me has lifted up his heel against Me*'" (John 13:18). The italicized portion of this verse is a quote of Psalm 41:9, which Jesus applies to Himself. It's particularly significant that Jesus said, "I know whom I have chosen."

The choice of Judas (John 13:19). Through all the years of His public ministry Jesus knew that Judas would betray Him. Yet even as they ate that Last Supper together, the other disciples had no idea. Jesus had always treated Judas in the same way He treated the others. No change of tone in His voice, no sidelong glance, had led the rest of the Twelve to suppose that Judas was different from the rest.

Even now Jesus only mentioned the betrayal ahead of time "that when it does come to pass, you may believe that I am He" (v. 19). There would be no future doubt of Jesus omniscience, no questions such as "How could Judas have fooled Him?"

Jesus knew all along. And Judas had every opportunity to know Jesus as the others knew Him, a Man filled with compassion for people, energized by the very power of God.

BIBLE BACKGROUND:
HARD SAYINGS OF JESUS

"Most assuredly, I say to you, he who receives whomever I send receives Me; and he who receives Me receives Him who sent me" (John 13:20)

It isn't the content of this verse that makes it a hard saying. The problem is its placement in the text. These words would seem more natural following verse 16 or 17, in which Jesus speaks of "sending" His disciples.

But in fact the present placement of the verse links it with the theme of sending and with Judas. Christ had come as a servant, but God's people had rejected Him. Now it appeared that He was rejected even by one of the Twelve He Himself had chosen! Does the "servanthood" approach to spiritual leadership really work?

As an answer to the unasked question, Jesus reminds His followers that the issue is not whether the world responds to servant leaders but rather the world's underlying hostility to Him. Those who do receive the disciple's message are those who are willing to receive Jesus, and these are persons who are willing to receive God.

One last chance (John 13:21–30). When Jesus announced that one of the Twelve would betray Him, eleven of the Twelve were perplexed. John, who was reclining to Jesus' right, leaned over and asked, "Lord, who is it?" Jesus told John that "it is he to whom I shall give a piece of bread when I have dipped it" (13:26). Given the seating arrangements at a formal first-century meal, it's likely that John's question and Jesus' answer were spoken softly and were not overheard by the others.

The pain-filled announcement (v. 21). John tells us that Jesus was "troubled in spirit" when he spoke of the coming betrayal. Jesus' first words, "Most assuredly" and John's choice of the word "testify" suggest that His distress was obvious to all. Judas was determined to betray Christ, yet Christ remained deeply concerned about Judas.

And the revelation that Jesus knew what Judas planned gave that disciple one last chance to repent.

"A piece of bread when I have dipped it" (26). Most first-century Jewish meals featured main dishes from which individuals ate by dipping out the food with bread torn from a flat loaf, like pita bread. It was customary when a host wished to honor a guest for him to tear off a piece of bread, dip out a particularly succulent morsel, and hand it to the guest. Jesus, acting as host to the Twelve, dipped out such a morsel and handed it to Judas.

Even this gracious act failed to move Judas, who was now committed to the Satan-inspired act of betrayal. Christ's last words to the lost disciple were, "What you do, do quickly" (13:27).

Judas had made his decision. Since Judas was committed to being the agent who turned Christ over to His enemies, there was no more need for delay.

As in the case of foot washing, Jesus had given the disciples an example that they would understand only later. Foot washing powerfully communicated the message of servant leadership to Jesus' disciples. And Jesus' years of gracious treatment of Judas, despite His knowing that Judas would betray Him, served as a powerful lesson too. The weakest and least spiritual brother or sister

Judas' departure before Christ gave His Last Supper teachings reminds us that some truths are reserved for Jesus' own.

must be treated with the same grace and consideration as the strongest. Nothing in our attitude or our actions must drive anyone away; we must love them as we love others. As Jesus had loved Judas.

John tells us that Judas immediately went outside. "And it was night."

It was the darkest of nights for Judas, just as it is the darkest of nights for anyone who rejects our Lord. But inside the room where they were eating, Jesus began to instruct the eleven faithful disciples. And there it remained warm and bright.

FAMOUS LAST WORDS (JOHN 13)

Someone once wrote a book on the last words of famous persons. His assumption was that their last words would be particularly significant. This was hardly true in the case of the financier whose last words to his son were reputedly, "Remember, son. Buy low, and sell high."

Less meaningful words could hardly be uttered by a person about to be launched into eternity!

In contrast, Jesus' last words of instruction to His disciples are filled with the deepest significance.

INTRODUCING THE DISCOURSE (JOHN 13:31–35)

As soon as Judas had left, Jesus began to speak freely to the Eleven. There are some truths reserved only for Jesus' own. It is not that they are secrets, but rather that they are so special only members of the family will be able to understand them.

"Now the Son of Man is glorified" (John 13:31–32). The word "glorify" occurs five times in these verses. "Now the Son of Man is glorified, and God is glorified in Him. If God is glorified in Him, God will also glorify Him in Himself, and glorify Him immediately." John uses the Greek word translated "glorify" (*doxazo*) in a special way. The root typically means to exalt. But here it refers to Jesus' death. The thought is that Jesus will lift God up by obeying Him completely, even going to the cross, and that in His resurrection Jesus will be lifted up by God.

It's important to note that when Jesus speaks of His coming death He typically speaks also of His resurrection (Matt. 16:21; Mark 8:31; 9:31; Luke 9:22). Cross and resurrection are so intimately linked that they constitute a single redemptive act. Thus it is Jesus' humiliation that leads to His exaltation (Phil. 2:5–11).

"The new commandment" (John 13:34, 35). Jesus told the Eleven He would soon leave them to go where they could not follow

(13:33). Then He added, "So now I say to you. . . ."

This phrase introducing Jesus' new commandment is important. Jesus would soon be absent —"so now I say to you." These words underline the importance of what Jesus is about to say. Christ's next words will have special import for believers while Jesus is away. "A new commandment I give to you, that you love one another; as I have loved you, that you also love one another. By this all will know that you are My disciples; if you have love for one another."

A new commandment? The call to love is not an innovation introduced by Jesus. The familiar phrase, "You shall love your neighbor as yourself" is nestled among a series of commands in Leviticus (19:18), and was well known to every Jew. A number of rabbis had emphasized it, and even stated Jesus' "Golden Rule" in the negative: "What you would not that your neighbor do to you, do not to your neighbor."

Even the pagan philosopher Epictetus viewed a general love for other human beings, which required that all be treated with respect, as the one great moral obligation of humankind (see Bonforte, J., *The Philosophy of Epictetus*, New York: Philosophical Library, 1955). In what sense, then, is Jesus' command "new"?

It helps if we understand that the Greek word translated "new," *kainen*, does not mean "newly arrived" or "just appearing." Rather *kainen* indicates something that is new in the sense of both fresh and superior. And Jesus' new commandment is superior in three ways.

1. Jesus introduces a new standard. The old commandment called on God's people to love their neighbor as they love themselves. Jesus calls on His disciples to love one another as He has loved them. And Jesus loved us more than He loved Himself. No wonder Paul writes in

Philippians 2:3, "in lowliness of mind let each esteem others better than himself."

2. Jesus introduces a new relationship. The old commandment called on God's people to love their neighbor. Jesus calls on His disciples to love one another. We find the phrase "one another" is used freqently in the New Testament epistles to describe relationships between brothers and sisters in the Church, the new community Christ established that is identified as His own body. It is true that we are to love all human beings, even our enemies (Matt. 5:43–47). But the love Jesus commands here is a love that goes beyond this and is rooted in the fact that all in Christ are brothers and sisters, members of God's own forever-family.

3. Jesus also promises a new result or outcome. He told the Eleven, "by this all will know that you are My disciples, if you have love for one another." What so attracts the lost and lonely to Jesus isn't the purity of our doctrine, or even the purity of the lives we lead. It is the love that binds us close together; a love which can only be explained by and which expresses the living presence of Jesus Christ.

This is, of course, the tragedy of permitting such terrible gaps to develop between black believers and white, between rich believers and poor, between the educated and the uneducated, between charismatic and non-charismatic. Jesus commands us to love, and any person who through faith in Christ has God as his Father is our brother. And we are commanded not to debate him but to care for him.

"Where I am going you cannot come" (John 13:33). Despite Christ's continuing references to the cross and resurrection since the turning point recorded in Matthew 16 and the other Synoptics, the disciples had not really grasped what He was saying. Now Jesus said plainly that He was leaving, and that the disciples could not follow him.

This was more than Peter could endure. "Where?" Peter demanded, and "Why can I not follow you now?" Peter reminds us of a child, endlessly plaguing its parents with "Why? Why? Why?" Yet Peter's heart was in the right place. To be denied the chance to be with Jesus seemed more than Peter could stand. And so Peter blurted out a promise that events would show he could not keep: "I will lay down my life for Your sake."

Peter simply did not realize how weak he was apart from divine enablement. Soon he would learn, for Jesus' prediction of Peter's denial (v. 38) would come true before morning dawned (see John 19:25–27).

PRECIOUS PROMISES (JOHN 14)

Peter's interruptions were over now, and Jesus settled down to speak of the future. The first thing that He did was to give His followers precious promises to sustain them when He was gone. Jesus' first words tell us how badly the disciples needed to hear the promises. For Jesus begins, "Let not your heart be troubled; you believe in God, believe also in Me" (John 14:1).

The Greek construction tells us that the disciples were already troubled and upset. Jesus was saying, "Stop being troubled," an imperative we might paraphrase "Put your hearts at ease." But how can the disciples do this? The answer is, "You trust God. Trust Me."

This is the answer for each of us when we are uncertain or discouraged. Stop being troubled. Just trust Jesus.

But Jesus went on to give His disciples substantial promises that they could count on.

WELCOMED TO MY WORLD
(JOHN 14:2-3)

There are a series of promises woven into the familiar words of John 14:2, 3.

In My Father's house are many mansions; if it were not so, I would have told you. I go to prepare a place for you. And if I go and prepare a place for you, I will come again and receive you to Myself; that where I am, there you may be also.

Note the promises.

- In My Father's house are many mansions
- I go to prepare a place for you
- I will come again
- I will receive you to Myself
- Where I am, there you may be also

Many mansions (John 14:2). The word translated "mansions" is better understood as "rooms" or "resting places." The homes of the wealthy in the first century were built around an open square, and members of the family had rooms or apartments opening on this square. This was as true for married children and their families as for singles. Jesus' image is one of God the Father gathering His whole family around Him to share His heaven, not that of isolated living in many different residences, however splendid they might be.

Preparing a place (John 14:2). Jesus might be absent, but the disciples would constantly be in His thoughts. Although absent, Jesus would be at work for His own.

At the time of this writing, our daughter is leaving for college in a few weeks. She and my wife have been shopping for the apartment she'll live in. Each item is carefully considered, and the colors of sheets and towels and even kitchenware are carefully coordinated. Everything chosen has

to be just right, something that fits Sarah's personality. How fascinating to think of Jesus preparing a heavenly room for each of us, making sure that everything fits who we are—and who we will be.

I will come again (John 14:3). This promise and preparing a place are linked. Since Jesus is preparing a place for us in heaven, surely He will return and bring us there!

I will receive you to Myself (John 14:3). What makes heaven heaven isn't the room Jesus is preparing for us but Christ himself. This is something the disciples could understand, for they had abandoned everything to be close to Him. It may be fun to speculate about the rooms Jesus is readying for us, or about Revelation's portrait of streets of gold. But what draws us to heaven is Jesus.

Where I am, there you may be also (John 14:3). When Jesus returns we will be in His presence, time without end. The separation from Jesus that the Eleven would experience was temporary. The reunion would bring them together again, forever.

KNOWING THE WAY
(JOHN 14:4-6)

After making these promises Jesus added, "And where I go you know, and the way you know" (John 14:4). This statement stunned Thomas. What did Jesus mean? As far as Thomas and the others were concerned, they had no idea where Jesus was going.

Thomas spoke up. "Lord, we do not know where You are going, and how can we know the way?"

We can understand Thomas' confusion. A little earlier Jesus had told the Eleven "where I am going you cannot come" (John 13:33). When Peter objected, Jesus told him

Jesus' claim to be "the way" to God reminds us that salvation can be found in Christ alone.

that he could not follow Him now, but added "you shall follow Me afterward" (John 13:36). Now Jesus was saying that the disciples knew where Jesus was going and that they knew the way! It was just too much for Thomas. They didn't know where Jesus was going! How could anyone know the road to an unknown destination?

The answer, of course, is that Jesus had just told them that He was returning to the Father. While the Eleven might not have written directions, the disciples did know Jesus. What they still did not understand was that the way to heaven is not found by following a map or written directions. The way to heaven is a Person, a Person with whom the disciples already had a relationship. So Jesus said, "I am the way, the truth, and the life. No one comes to the Father except through Me" (John 14:6).

Many take offense at Christians who honor Jesus' statement and insist that there is only one way of salvation. They become hostile if we warn them that those who do not trust Jesus as Savior are lost. How this goes against the spirit of our age, where relativism is mistaken for truth, and tolerance exalted as the highest moral value. Yet how fascinating that those who insist Christians tolerate every foolish belief and approve of every aberrant behavior are themselves intolerant of Christians! But Jesus makes an exclusive claim here. "No one comes to the Father except through Me." There is one road to God, not many. There is one way of salvation, not dozens or even two or three. And that way is Jesus Christ.

One unknown author has written,

We should not overlook the faith involved both in the utterance and the acceptance of those words, spoken on the eve of the crucifixion. "I am the Way," said One who would shortly hang impotent on a cross. "I am the Truth," when the lies of evil men were about to enjoy a spectacular triumph. "I am the Life," when within a few hours His corpse would be placed in a tomb.

Yes, it took faith for Jesus to speak those words and faith for the disciples to accept them. And it takes faith for a person today to fix his or her hope in the crucified and risen Savior.

ONE GOD AT WORK (JOHN 14:7–14)

Jesus went on to point out that He Himself is the Way because He shares an undivided unity with the Father. Any person who knows Jesus knows the Father (John 14:7).

Christ's undivided unity with the Father (John 14:7–11). Philip still did not understand, and urged Jesus to "show us the Father." Again Jesus affirmed the truth of His unity with God the Father.

The apostle John stated this reality in the opening words of his Gospel: "In the beginning was the Word, and the Word was with God, and the Word was God. He was in the beginning with God" (John 1:1, 2). And this Word was the Person the disciples knew as Jesus, a Person they had all acknowledged as the Son of God. No wonder then that Jesus said, "He who has seen Me has seen the Father" (John 14:9). Every word that Jesus spoke, every action Jesus took, revealed God the Father. To know Jesus was to know God. The bond between them was so perfect that no seam showed: Jesus was so perfectly in the Father, and the Father so fully in Jesus that the two were one.

The next words of Jesus have puzzled many, perhaps because they have been so misunderstood. "The Father who dwells in Me does the works. Believe Me that I am in the Father and the Father in Me, or else believe Me for the sake of the works themselves." It is commonly assumed that

"works" here means miracles. It is true that *ta erga* might mean miracles, for *ergon*, especially when modified by "mighty," certainly does refer to miracles. But "work" is also a common term, indicating such things as labor, activity, achievement, and even business. More important still, John often uses *ergon* to express the idea that God is at work in everything that Jesus does (see for example John 4:34; 17:4). In this context it is far better to take *ta erga* in this ordinary sense.

Jesus has claimed to be one with God the Father. The disciples can take His word for this relationship. Or they can consider His whole life, everything He has said and done. For everything that He has said and done are *ta erga*, works that the Father has done through Him.

If the Eleven but think back over their experiences with Jesus they will be convinced that Christ and the Father are one.

The believer's divided unity with Christ (John 14:12). Jesus now introduces a great mystery. "Most assuredly, I say to you, he who believes in Me, the works that I do he will do also; and greater works than these he will do, because I go to My Father" (John 14:12). Jesus' return to the Father would be the key to His disciples' doing "the works that I do" and even "greater works than these." There are two things that help us understand what Jesus is saying.

Jesus' works were not miracles. When Jesus spoke of the "works that I do" He was speaking of that which God the Father did in Him; works that were possible because of His undivided union with the Father. As Jesus said, "The Father who dwells in Me does the works" (John 14:10).

Jesus works in the believer. Christ linked the greater works believers would do to His return to the Father. Jesus also specified that these greater works are works that "I will do."

Later in this discourse Jesus will explain to the disciples that Christ and the Father would soon take up residence in their lives. Jesus would be "in" believers then, even as Jesus Himself was in the Father and the Father in Him.

What makes the works that Jesus will do in us greater than the works that Christ Himself did is the fact that Christ enjoyed an undivided unity with the Father. From the very beginning the two had been one. But now Christ had chosen to join Himself to mere human beings, creating a divided unity. In the undivided unity those who were united were one and the same in essence. In the divided unity of which Jesus speaks those who are united are different in essence. It is this fact that makes the works that Jesus does through you and me greater and more amazing than the works God the Father did through Him.

The place of prayer (John 14:13, 14). The key to Christ's doing His greater works through us is prayer offered in Jesus' name. "And whatever you ask in My name, that I will do, that the Father may be glorified in the Son. If you ask anything in My name, I will do it." As noted earlier, the phrase "in My name" is important. It is especially significant that it is emphasized by Jesus here. Each time Jesus says "Ask," He qualifies it with "in My name."

In biblical times a name had almost mystical significance. The name was thought to share and to communicate the essence of the thing named. Thus to pray in Jesus' name was to enter into Christ Himself, to link oneself to Him and to all that He by nature is. Jesus' words "I will do it" expresses one side of the "in-Christ" relationship that we have with Him. The fact that we are to pray in His name expresses the other side.

As Christ is in us so we are to live in Him, submitting our hopes and desires, our priorities and our prayers, to His will. It is when we experience this unity with Jesus that He not only answers our prayers, He directs them.

Jesus, speaking of His unity with God the Father, said "My Father has not left Me alone, for I always do those things that please Him" (John 8:29). It is this kind of union which Jesus envisions here. Our prayers express our reliance on Him to act through us. And to pray in His name is to be in complete harmony with His will and express our eagerness to submit to His leading.

The litmus test of love (John 14:15). This is a theme to which Jesus will return. "If you love Me, keep My commandments." It fits here for a simple reason. The disciples have been invited to believe Jesus (John 14: 11). And it's vital not just to believe Jesus but to trust Him. But the only way a person can maintain that divided unity with Jesus is to keep His commandments, just as Jesus Himself did only those things which pleased the Father.

But trust alone will not move us to obedience. It is love and love alone that moves us to keep Jesus' commands.

ANOTHER HELPER (JOHN 14:16–18)

Jesus was about to leave His disciples. But He would not leave them to face the future alone. They would not be orphaned! Jesus said, "I will pray the Father and He will give you another Helper."

Christ spoke here of the Holy Spirit, and made several important points.

- The Spirit is "another" helper.
- The Spirit will abide with you forever.
- The Spirit is neither seen or known by the world.
- The Spirit is with and will be in the disciples.
- Christ will come to them through the Spirit.

Jesus taught that the Holy Spirit is God, just as He and the Father are one God in three Persons.

❖

Another Helper (John 14:16). There are two Greek words that are translated "another." One is *heteros*, and means "another of a different kind". The other word, used here, is *allos*, and it means "another of the same kind." Jesus, God the Son, the second person of the Trinity, would leave. But the Father would send God the Holy Spirit, the third person of the Trinity, to take Jesus' place.

To abide with you forever (John 14:16). Jesus was about to leave His disciples to return to the Father. But the Holy Spirit was a permanent gift; one who would never leave Jesus' own.

Neither seen nor known by the world (John 14:17). In John the "world" (*kosmos*) is the culture of the lost, driven as it is by sinful passions, selfishness, and pride. Jesus lived in this world, and although seen by men,

He remained unknown. We should not be surprised that the Spirit, who has no corporeal form that may be seen would remain unseen by the world. Jesus even tells us that the Spirit's work through believers will remain unrecognized and unacknowledged by the world.

"With" and "to be in" (John 14:17). The Holy Spirit is known from the Old Testament. No less than sixteen times does the Old Testament describe the Spirit as "coming upon" a person to enable him to perform some special task. In this same sense the Spirit had been "with" the Twelve when they preached and healed.

Yet here Jesus envisions a future time when the disciples will experience an even more intimate relationship with the Holy Spirit. In that future time the Spirit will no longer merely be "with" Jesus' people; He will be "in" Jesus' own!

Christ comes to us through the Spirit (John 14:18). Some have taken Jesus' saying "I will come to you" as a reference to the resurrection. But in this context it is better to understand the promise differently. The Holy Spirit will come from the Father to be the living link between the believer and God. And through the Spirit Jesus Himself will enter our lives, for just as the Spirit is spoken of as "in" believers, so is Jesus. As Paul says in Colossians 1:27, the great mystery of Christianity is "Christ in you, the hope of glory."

And so Jesus continues to give His disciples a preview of what the future holds for them—and what the present holds for us! Jesus, who experienced an undivided unity with the Father, will live in and work through the lives of believers who love Him and identify themselves with His name. And this is all made possible by the Holy Spirit, who by taking up residence in our lives becomes the living link between us and our Lord.

EXPERIENCING THE UNSEEABLE (JOHN 14:19–26)

Jesus went on to clarify further. Several key points are reinforced in this passage.

"I will love him and manifest Myself to him" (John 14:21). Jesus has said that the world would see Him no more, but that He would manifest Himself (make Himself visible, make Himself known) to the disciples.

This concept puzzled the disciples, and Judas (not Iscariot) asked Jesus, "How is it that You will manifest Yourself to us, and not to the world?"

The question is not, as some have taken, "Why will you take this route?" The question is, "How is this possible for You to manifest Yourself to Your disciples?"

In answer Jesus points again to indwelling. The hearts of those who love Jesus and keep His commandments (believers) become "home" for the Father and Son. God has established His real presence within believers, and believers will experience that presence and recognize it as God.

The evidence of love (John 14:21). Christ put it this way. "He who has My commandments and keeps them, it is he who loves Me." But Jesus also said, "If anyone loves me, He will keep My word" (v. 23). The link between love and obedience is two-way. Love motivates obedience. And obedience expresses love.

There are two ways to understand this extended passage. Those who "love and obey" may be all believers, and "love and obey" may be another way of saying "trust in Jesus" (see 2 Thess. 1:8; 1 Peter 4:17). In this case the joy of experiencing Christ is for all believers. As a Christian grows in the faith and is transformed, Jesus within becomes more and more real.

The other way to understand this passage is to assume that those who love and obey are a special class of believers who

have chosen the path of discipleship. In this case any believer's experience of Jesus is contingent on loving and obeying Him.

While it is true that the more responsive we are to Jesus and His Word the more real Christ becomes to us, we want to be careful here. The Holy Spirit lives in all believers, as does Jesus Christ. There are not two classes of Christians, those with and those without the Spirit (1 Cor. 12:13; Rom. 8:9). If a person is a Christian, Jesus has already settled down in his heart, and made His home there (John 14:23). And it is Jesus Himself who is the source of our joy.

He will teach you (John 14:25, 26). Jesus realizes that what He has been saying is difficult for the disciples to understand. And so Jesus promises that the Helper, the Holy Spirit, "will teach you all things, and bring to your remembrance all things that I said to you."

As we read the New Testament Epistles we realize that this promise has been kept. What Jesus said that night was unclear at first. But later the Spirit brought those teachings back to the disciples' minds and made their meaning clear. Truly this passage is the seedbed out of which the doctrines of Christianity grew, and the fruit of what Christ said that night fills the pages of Acts and the Epistles.

THE LEGACY OF PEACE (JOHN 14:27–31)

Soon Jesus and the others would leave the room where they had eaten, and Christ would continue His teaching on the walk to Gethsemane. But first Christ reviewed and summed up the significance of what He had been saying.

"My peace I give you" (John 14:27). Jesus had begun by telling His disciples not to let their hearts be troubled. He begins His

Jesus' death on Calvary was proof of His love for the Father as well as of His love for you and me.

❖

summary on this same note. "Peace I leave with you, My peace I give to you; not as the world gives do I give to you. Let not your heart be troubled, neither let it be afraid."

The promise of peace is special. The world can only provide an external peace that exists as the absence of conflict and stress. This surely cannot be the peace that Jesus gives. Indeed Christ's most stressful and agonizing hours lie immediately ahead.

To understand what Jesus means we need to understand the meaning of *shalom*, the Hebrew word which defines the meaning of the Greek term for peace used here. *The New International Encyclopedia of Bible Words* (Zondervan, 1985) notes that the Hebrew word *shalom*

is derived from a root that conveys the image of wholeness, unity, and harmony—something that is complete and sound. Although "peace" is essentially a relational concept in the OT, it also conveys the idea of prosperity, health, and fulfillment (p. 479).

Jesus' peace grew out of His relationship with and confidence in the Father. His legacy of peace is a relationship with God that nothing that happens here on earth can threaten. It is because we are secure in that relationship that we are at peace within, whatever storms may rage without.

"I have told you before it comes" (14:28–30). Jesus had spoken extensively of what was about to happen. When Jesus predictions came true, the disciples would have yet another reason to trust Him. But there was little more Jesus could add, for the end was fast approaching.

———— ❖ ————

BIBLE BACKGROUND:
HARD SAYINGS OF JESUS

"My Father is greater than I" (John 14:28)

Jesus has emphasized His oneness with the Father. Now He says, "My Father is greater than I." What can He mean?

Jesus does not refer to essence here. In essence Father and Son are one. But in the Incarnation Jesus voluntarily subordinated Himself to the Father, a subordination of which Scripture speaks frequently (see for example Phil. 2:5–8).

———— ❖ ————

The ultimate evidence of love (John 14:31). Jesus has linked love and obedience in His discourse. Now Christ looks forward to the Cross and says, "that the world may know that I love the Father, and as the Father gave Me commandment, so I do."

Jesus is about to die in obedience to the Father, and this will demonstrate to all that Christ loves the Father. And with this statement, Jesus said, "Arise, let us go from here."

THREE RELATIONSHIPS OF JESUS' DISCIPLES (JOHN 15:1–16:4)

The little company has left the upper room where they had eaten together. Walking along with His disciples, Christ continued His teaching, focusing on three relationships that the disciples would have in the future.

THE DISCIPLES' RELATIONSHIP WITH JESUS (JOHN 15:1–10)

Jesus used a familiar analogy to explore the nature of the disciples' continuing relationship with Him. In reading it, it's important to remember that Jesus is speaking here of the continuing relationship between Him and His disciples, and that the theme is fruitfulness. In fact, fruit is specifically mentioned six times.

I am the true vine, and My Father is the vinedresser. Every branch in Me that does not bear fruit He takes away; and every branch that bears fruit He prunes, that it may bear more fruit.

You are already clean because of the word which I have spoken to you. Abide in Me, and I in you. As the branch cannot bear fruit of itself, unless it abides in the vine, neither can you, unless you abide in Me.

I am the vine, you are the branches. He who abides in Me, and I in him, bears much fruit; for without Me you can do nothing.

If anyone does not abide in Me, he is cast out as a branch and is withered; and they gather them and throw them into the fire, and they are burned. If you abide in Me, and My words abide in you, you will ask what you desire, and it shall be done for you. By this My Father is glorified, that you bear much fruit; so you will be My disciples.

As the Father has loved Me, I also have loved you; abide in My love. If you keep my commandments, you will abide in My love, just as I have kept My Father's commandments and abide in His love.

These things I have spoken to you, that My joy may remain in you, and that your joy may be full.

In these verses Jesus Himself makes clear how His metaphor applies.

Metaphor elements. Jesus identifies the relevant elements in the metaphor.

The true vine (John 15:1). Jesus identifies Himself as the "true vine." In the Old Testament, Israel is presented as a vine that God planted, intending it to produce the fruit of godly character (Isa. 5:1–7). Israel failed to produce that fruit. Now Jesus says that He Himself is the true—the authentic—vine and will accomplish the transformation that ancient Israel could not.

The vinedresser (John 15:1). Jesus identifies God as the vinedresser. The Greek word is *georgos*, or farmer. God is the expert on whose skill the production of fruit depends.

The branches (John 15:5). The branches are individual believers who are united to Christ.

The fruit (John 15:2). Given the way "fruit" is consistently used in Scripture (Is. 5:7; Gal. 6:22, 23), the fruit Christ has in mind is godliness; traits which are produced by God through the transforming work of His Spirit.

Abiding in Christ (John 15:4, 7, 10). Jesus makes the obvious point that only a branch that is attached to the vine can produce fruit. Similarly believers are powerless to accomplish their own transformation. It is Jesus, the vine, who gives us the ability to bear fruit.

It follows that fruitfulness depends on maintaining our union with the Lord. Christ tells us that the union of which He speaks is maintained by keeping Jesus' commandments (John 15:10). As long as we remain in fellowship with Christ, His power will flow into our lives.

"He takes away" (John 15:2). The image of God caring for the vine has disturbed many who supposed Jesus' image was that of the Father discarding unfruitful Christians.

In reality Jesus uses two terms here which portray a gardener caring for a branch rather than discarding it. The word translated "take away" or "cut off" (*aireo*) depicts the gardener lifting up a branch and checking it for dead wood that might harbor disease, and then cutting the diseased parts away. At the same time the gardener prunes, cutting back healthy tissue to increase the vines' capacity for producing fruit.

Taken together the terms reveal a Father who is totally involved in our lives, doing everything necessary to make sure that we will be spiritually healthy and productive.

BIBLE BACKGROUND:

HARD SAYINGS OF JESUS

"If anyone does not abide in Me, he is cast out as a branch and is withered; and they gather them and throw them into the fire, and they are burned" (John 15:6).

This saying certainly would seem to threaten any believer who fails to abide in Christ with a loss of salvation.

The New International Version helps us with the point Jesus is making. A person who does not abide in Christ *"is like* a branch that is thrown away and withers; such branches are picked up, thrown into the fire and burned" (italics mine). Jesus is using a simile, not issuing a threat. His point is that a person who fails to produce fruit is like a branch that has been thrown away.

The wood of grapevines is gnarled, twisted, and stringy. It can't be used in construction. It can't even be shaped by an artist. Branches cut from a grapevine are utterly useless. Thus it was common practice for gardeners to burn discarded branches.

What Jesus is doing is reminding us that God saved us in order that we might bear fruit and glorify Him (John 15:8). If we fail to abide in Jesus, our lives become unproductive and meaningless, and we have no way of glorifying God.

That your joy may be full (John 15:11). God has saved us that we might produce fruit. But Jesus reminds us that we will find joy only in fulfilling God's purpose for us. As Jesus found joy in doing the Father's will and producing fruit that glorified Him, there we too can find joy.

THE DISCIPLES' RELATIONSHIPS WITH ONE ANOTHER (JOHN 15:12–17)

Jesus now moves on to repeat His new commandment (John 13:33, 34). "Love one another, as I have loved you."

Christ points out that this is a different kind of commandment than a master might give to a servant (John 15:15). Servants are simply given instructions. Whether they understand why their master gives an order is completely irrelevant. Now Jesus has taken the time to explain the rationale behind His commandment. "All things that I heard from My Father I have made known to you" (v. 16).

While a master might command obedience and punish any slave who fails to obey, no such relationship exists between Jesus and His friends. Christ has proven that this is the nature of His relationship with believers, for He laid down His life for His friends (v. 13). The disciples will prove their friendship by obeying Christ's commands and loving one another (v. 17).

THE DISCIPLES' RELATIONSHIP WITH THE WORLD (JOHN 15:18–16:4)

Again we remember that the "world" in John's writings points us to the motives and values that are imbedded in the outlook of lost humankind. In his first epistle John writes,

Do not love the world or the things in the world. If anyone loves the world, the love of the Father is not in him. For all that is in the world—the lust of the flesh, the lust of the eyes, and the pride of life—is not of the Father but is of the world (1 John 2:15–16).

Now in John 15 we have Christ's teaching on the disciples' relationship to the world of the lost. Several themes are emphasized.

The hatred of the world. "Hate" in verse 18 is in the perfect tense, which indicates that hatred of Jesus and His disciples is a fixed attitude.

While Jesus' own are taken from the world, they are no longer of the world (15:19). The hostility is rooted in part in the fact that Christians are "different," and human beings are always suspicious and hostile to those who are different. But the real reason for the hostility of the world is that disciples are identified with Jesus Christ. Jesus said, "Remember the word that I said to you, 'A servant is not greater than his master.' If they persecuted Me, they will also persecute you" (John 15:20).

Reasons for hating Jesus. Jesus gives His disciples two reasons for the fixed hostility of the world to Him and His own.

Christians as well as Christ can expect hostility from the world.

Ignorance of God (John 15:21). The world has no proper concept of God. This ignorance of who God is and what He is like is not so much intellectual as moral. Paul points out in Romans 1 that all human beings have an innate knowledge of God, but they "suppress the truth in unrighteousness" (Rom. 1:18). Thus human beings are willfully ignorant, a theme developed in the companion volume in this series, *Every Name of God in the Bible.*

Exposure by Jesus (John 15:22, 24). As long as the world could suppress the knowledge of God the people of the world might claim ignorance. But Jesus came into the world and by His words and works revealed the God they had struggled so hard to distance themselves from. And the light Jesus brought made it impossible for the world to hide its corruption and hypocrisy. So exposed, the world reacts angrily and violently.

As disciples follow Jesus, the same thing happens. By our lives and words we reveal the God the world has rejected, and expose the corruption and rebellion of sinful human beings.

BIBLE BACKGROUND:

HARD SAYINGS OF JESUS

"If I had not come and spoken to them, they would have no sin, but now they have no excuse for their sin" (John 15:22).

In one basic sense "sin" involves violation of a standard. A person who runs a stop sign placed at a dangerous corner is guilty of violating the law. It would be as dangerous to go through that intersection if there were no stop sign there, but it would be no violation of the law.

In the same way even the most corrupt practices of human beings are wrong whether or not they acknowledge a standard that says "No!" But those actions would not be "sin."

When Jesus came, He established a standard that cannot be ignored. Since Christ came and spoke to humankind every corrupt practice of human beings is clearly labeled for what it is. It is in this sense that "they would have no sin, but now they have no excuse for their sin."

The disciples' witness (John 15:26—16:4) Jesus tells His disciples that when the Holy Spirit comes He—and they—will continue to present Jesus to the world. As a result they too will be persecuted, for the world has "not known the Father nor Me" (John 16:3).

THREE MINISTRIES OF THE HOLY SPIRIT
(JOHN 16:5–15)

Jesus would soon finish His instruction of the Twelve. Before He did so, Jesus returned to the promise of the Holy Spirit and reiterated: "I tell you the truth. It is to your advantage that I go away; for if I do not go away, the Helper will not come to you; but if I depart, I will send Him to you" (John 16:7).

Jesus then went on to review the Spirit's ministry to the world, to the disciples, and to Jesus Himself.

THE SPIRIT'S MINISTRY TO THE WORLD
(JOHN 16:8–11)

Jesus explained that the Spirit's ministry to the world is one of "convicting." The Greek word, *elencho*, had a technical meaning when used in a legal context. To "convict" was to pronounce a verdict that established the guilt of a culprit and guaranteed his punishment. The Spirit does not merely accuse those in the world; the Spirit convinces of guilt and brings an awful awareness of doom.

Jesus told the disciples that this work of the Spirit would be focused in three areas: "When He has come, He will convict the world of sin, and of righteousness, and of judgment" (John 16:8).

"Of sin, because they do not believe in Me" (John 16:9). The ultimate sin is unbelief. This is not uncertainty or doubt, but a fixed refusal to accept God's Son. Every other sin is forgivable.

It's important for us to remember this, and in witnessing to keep the focus on Jesus. God is not interested in reforming sinners, but in transforming them. And only a personal relationship with Jesus Christ can accomplish this.

"Of righteousness, because I go to My Father" (John 16:10). Before Jesus came, righteousness had been defined by the conscience of a community (Romans 2:12–15) or by God's revealed standards. Then Jesus came and opened our eyes to the true nature of righteousness.

A few days after Jesus spoke He would be established as the standard by His resurrection. As Paul would write, Jesus was "declared to be the Son of God with power according to the Spirit of holiness, by the resurrection from the dead" (Rom. 1:4).

"Of judgment, because the ruler of this world is judged" (John 16:11). The Greek word translated "judged" is *kekritai*. In the perfect tense it indicates that the trial is over, and that Satan (the ruler of this world) has been condemned and is awaiting punishment. Paul writes in Colossians that in the cross Christ disarmed all the spiritual forces of evil, and "made a public spectacle of them, triumphing over them" (2:15). In judging sin Jesus judged Satan as well, and stripped him of his powers.

Every element of the convicting work of the Spirit is focused through our testimony to Jesus Christ. We preach Jesus, and in doing so convict of the sin of unbelief, the need for righteousness, and of the triumph of God over evil.

It is this convicting work of the Spirit that prepares human hearts to respond to the gospel.

THE SPIRIT'S MINISTRY TO BELIEVERS
(JOHN 16:12, 13)

Jesus had promised that the Spirit would teach the disciples "all things, and bring to your remembrance all things that I said to you" (John 14:26). The promise is repeated here, but with an added emphasis.

The Spirit surely would return to themes that Jesus wanted to teach the disciples but which "you cannot bear" yet. And now Jesus tells the disciples that the Spirit "will guide you into all truth."

It's important not to misunderstand. Some have assumed that "truth" is to be equated with "belief," and been troubled because Christians differ on certain teachings. Others have insisted that since the Holy Spirit has guided them into their beliefs, those who differ in any detail must be out of step with Spirit! But "truth" here is not the same as "belief."

Jesus had once told His disciples, "If you abide in My word, you are My disciples indeed. And you shall know the truth and truth shall make you free" (John 8:31, 32). The truth of which Jesus spoke could only be known by keeping Jesus' words, for God's truth is to be experienced rather than simply comprehended. Thus we come to "know" God's truth by doing His will. Unlived truth has little meaning to the believer and none at all to those in the world.

The wonderful promise Jesus gave His disciples is that the Holy Spirit will guide believers into the will of God, and that in living that truth we are set free.

This helps us understand the significance of the next phrases: the Spirit "will not speak on His own authority, but whatever He hears He will speak, and He will tell you things to come" (John 16:13). The Spirit will serve as the conduit, communicating Jesus' leading, that we might walk confidently into our future.

THE SPIRIT'S MINISTRY TO JESUS
(JOHN 16:14, 15)

As the Spirit communicates Jesus to the world and Christ's guidance to believers, Jesus is glorified. For rather than speaking on His own, the Holy Spirit "will take of what is Mine and declare it to you."

With this promise Jesus' Last Supper instruction to the Eleven is over. Christ ends it by stating again, "A little while, and you will not see Me; and again a little while, and you will see Me, because I go to the Father" (John 16:16).

The disciples then begin to talk among themselves, still questioning what this last remark of Jesus meant (John 16:17, 18). After further dialogue with Jesus, the disciples seemed satisfied and had no more questions.

Jesus knew better. Yet in the future the words Jesus had spoken during this time would comfort and instruct after Jesus had gone. Indeed, the words that Jesus had spoken would help the disciples find peace in Him. As Christ said, "In the world you will have tribulation; but be of good cheer, I have overcome the world."

JESUS' TEACHINGS ON PRAYER

Prayer was significant in Jesus' own life as well as a recurrent theme in His teaching. It's clear that despite His exhausting schedule Jesus often slipped away at night to commune with the Father, at times praying all night (Matt. 14:23; Mark 1:35; 6:46; Luke 5:16; 9:18). The Gospels also record a number of Jesus' own prayers.

Several times Jesus' personal commitment to prayer moved His disciples to ask Christ to teach them to pray, and prayer became a frequent topic of instruction. And who better to teach about prayer? For Jesus offered prayers to God the Father. And Jesus received prayers during His life on earth as God the Son. Clearly Jesus teaches us about prayer by example as well as by word.

PRAYERS ADDRESSED TO JESUS

Many books have been written about prayer. But we can rely on Jesus' teaching far more than on all the books.

JESUS RECEIVED AND ANSWERED PRAYERS

When we scan the Gospels we're impressed at the number of times ordinary people came to Jesus to ask for something only God could provide. For example, note the series of incidents recorded in Matthew 8–9.

Matthew 8:2 reports, "And behold, a leper came and worshiped Him, saying, 'Lord, if You are willing, You can make me clean.'" While it's likely that the leper used "Lord" in its ordinary sense as "Sir," no one would imagine that the leper would expect an ordinary person to heal him of his disease. Yet this is what the leper expected as he confessed his belief that if Jesus were willing, He could make him clean.

A few verses later Matthew tells of a centurion who begged Jesus to heal a servant who was wracked with pain at his home (vv. 5, 6). Then in Matthew 8:25 we hear the disciples, terrified by a violent storm at sea, cry out "Lord, save us!" Moments later we read of demons begging

Jesus answered the prayers of many desperate people.

❖

PRAYERS ADDRESSED TO JESUS IN THE SYNOPTIC GOSPELS

Matt. 8:2	Mark 5:10	Luke 4:38
Matt. 8:6	Mark 5:18	Luke 5:8
Matt. 8:25	Mark 5:23	Luke 8:24
Matt. 8:31	Mark 6:56	Luke 8:31
Matt. 9:18	Mark 7:32	Luke 8:38
Matt. 9:27	Mark 8:22	Luke 8:41
Matt. 14:30	Mark 9:24	
Matt. 14:36	Mark 10:35–37	
Matt. 15:25		
Matt. 17:15		
Matt. 20:21		
Matt. 20:30–33		

❖

Jesus to send them into a herd of swine (v. 31), of a leading citizen in Capernaum begging Jesus to restore a dying daughter (9:18), and of two blind men asking Jesus to restore their sight (9:27, 28),

In scene after scene portrayed in the synoptic Gospels we see individuals in desperate need appealing to Jesus. These people may not have grasped Jesus' true identity, but when they appealed to Him, Jesus did respond to their requests. He performed miraculous healings, again and again responding to their prayers in ways that only God could. These multiplied incidents are convincing evidence that people in Jesus' day prayed to Jesus as if He were God. And Jesus granted their requests, because He was God.

Who better can mentor us on prayer than the one who both accepts and answers the prayers of human beings?

PUZZLING RESPONSES TO PRAYER

As we look at some of the incidents listed on the chart above, we realize that most often Jesus, moved by compassion, responded quickly and positively. Yet some of Jesus' responses to prayer puzzle us. These puzzling responses are perhaps more instructive than Jesus' typical response.

Jesus answers the prayers of demons (Luke 8:27–32; Mark 5:1–13). When Jesus taught His disciples to pray, He told them to address God as "Father," indicating that it is the family relationship with God that enables us to come freely to the Lord in prayer. Yet there's one incident recorded in the Gospels that reports Jesus' answer to the prayer of demons! And demons surely have no standing with God and no right to expect a positive answer to any prayers.

The familiar story tells of Jesus coming upon a demon-possessed man who terrorized the neighborhood and who was infested by a legion of demons. When Jesus commanded the demons to leave the man, the demons begged Jesus to send them into a nearby herd of pigs. And, the Scriptures tell us, "He permitted them" (Luke 8:32).

What do we learn about prayer from this incident?

God is free to act as He chooses. God has promised to hear the prayers of His children. But this fact doesn't mean that God cannot answer the prayers of others. We see this principle throughout Scripture.

When the people of Nineveh repented at the warning of Jonah, God withheld judgment. Nineveh was the capital of Assyria, the enemy of Israel, and God was under no obligation to respond when Nineveh repented and sought forgiveness. Yet God did respond.

Naaman, the Syrian leper, came to Israel seeking healing. God was under no obligation to respond when Naaman begged the help of the prophet Elisha. But God did.

And when the "legion" of demons begged not to be sent to the abyss, where fallen angels await judgment, Christ permitted them to enter a herd of pigs. None of these had a relational basis for their appeal. Yet, in grace, God responded to each request.

We should not be surprised, then, when pagans or others who do not know Jesus tell of answers to prayer. God is compassionate and gracious, kind to all, and free to answer the prayers even of those who have no basis in personal relationship to seek His favor.

All answers to prayer are gracious. This incident reminds us that all answers to prayer are rooted in God's grace. None of us, whether God's children or not, deserve the answers to prayer that we receive. God will always hear our prayers because we have access to Him in Christ. And God will respond when we ask. Yet both our relationship to God as members of His family and His answers to our prayers are as deeply rooted in grace as any answer to

prayer He may graciously give to one who is outside.

Jesus didn't answer the healed man's prayer (Luke 8:38, 39; Mark 5:18, 19). Jesus had just cast out a legion of demons and had permitted them to enter a herd of pigs. The man who had been healed then turned to Jesus and made a request. The text tells us that he "begged Him that he might be with Him" (Luke 8:38).

The mystery of unanswered prayer. It's misleading to call any prayer "unanswered." All our prayers are answered. But in some cases the answer is "No," and in others "Not yet." Even so, it's striking to see Jesus permitting demons to do what they had asked, and not allowing the man who was freed from them to do as he asks. We sometimes wonder. Why are some requests granted, while others are not? And why are the requests of one person granted, but not the requests of another?

It's helpful in such cases to apply three tests: the test of appropriateness, the test of intent, and the test of God's purpose. Let's apply these tests to the requests of the demons and the healed man.

BIBLE BACKGROUND:

UNANSWERED PRAYER

In *Your Word Is Fire* (1977), a study of the views of Hassidic masters on contemplative prayer, Arthur Green and Barry W. Holtz give one answer to the problem of unanswered prayer that was suggested by the Jewish sages.

Why do the prayers of the righteous at times seem to go unanswered?

There is a king who has two sons.
Each of them comes to receive his gift from the royal table.

The first son appears at his father's doorway, and as soon as he is seen, his request is granted.

The father holds this son in low esteem, and is annoyed by his presence.

The king orders that the gifts be handed to his son at the door so that he will not approach the table.

Then the king's beloved son appears.

The father takes great pleasure in this son's arrival and does not want him to leave too quickly.

For this reason the king delays granting his request, hoping that the son will then draw near to him.

The son comes closer, he feels the father's love so deeply that he does not hesitate to stretch forth his own hand to the royal table (p. 24).

According to this story, the son whose prayer is not answered is privileged and most loved. Because he is not given what he asks, he comes closer and closer until he can sense the father's love.

The test of appropriateness. The demons, who were unclean spirits, begged Jesus to let them enter pigs. According to Old Testament dietary laws, swine were unclean animals. The request was appropriate.

If the demons had asked permission to enter another person, Jesus would never have permitted it. Since their request was appropriate, Jesus did allow them to do as they had asked.

The man freed of the demons begged Jesus that he "might be with Him." This was not an appropriate request. The healing took place in the land of the Gadarenes, opposite Galilee (Luke 8:26). The man who had been healed was not a Jew but a Gadarene. At this stage in His ministry Jesus was going only to the "lost sheep of the house of Israel" (Matt. 10:6).

Yet Jesus' refusal to grant the man's request did not mean that he or his service was rejected. Instead Jesus had another mission for him. Luke 8:39 tells us that Jesus sent the man away, saying, "'Return to your own house, and tell what great things God has done for you.' And he went his way and proclaimed throughout the whole city what great things Jesus had done for him."

The time would come when this man would be with Him, joining the company of the saved. But at that time Jesus had a far more significant task for him. Because of the man's witness, the whole area was prepared for the coming of the gospel message.

The test of intent. The demons asked permission to enter the pigs for two reasons. First, there was something attractive to them about inhabiting a living creature's body. There is no case in Scripture where a demon who had once invaded a person left voluntarily. Second, the demons wanted to avoid the abyss. In Scripture, as in first-century thought, the abyss is a prison where spirits are kept while awaiting judgment. The demons had strong and selfish reasons for wanting to enter the pigs.

The man from whom the demons had been expelled wanted only to be with Jesus. He was thankful and eager to commit himself to Jesus. In addition Jesus undoubtedly symbolized safety and security. If he were with Jesus, no demon would dominate him again!

While Jesus permitted the demons to enter the pigs, he did not permit the man He had healed to be with Him. From this we realize our motives for making a request are not the primary criteria God uses in deciding whether or not to grant our requests.

The test of God's purpose. The demons did enter the pigs, but these animals sensed the invasion and ran headlong into the sea, where they drowned. This incident, in spite of the healing of the demonized man, frightened the people of the district. The result was that they begged Jesus to leave!

In contrast, the demonized man was told to go home and to tell what God had done for him. His desire to serve the Lord was honored, but not in the way he asked. Christ's "No" to the man's request was a different and better way of saying, "Yes!"

While we can apply these tests to any prayer, only the third test is definitive. Is our request appropriate? We may or may not receive what we ask. Is our intent in asking to glorify God? If it is, God will honor our request, even though we may not receive what we ask. Is our request in harmony with God's purpose? This is the key! Whatever answer we receive to our prayers will be in full harmony with the purposes of God. The answers that fit God's purpose will both glorify God and will at the same time be what is best for you and me.

Peter prays, but Jesus says "No" (Luke 5:1–10). The day Peter was enlisted as a disciple Peter begged Jesus, "Depart from me, for I am a sinful man, O Lord." Peter had been overwhelmed by an awareness of his own guilt and sinfulness when Jesus performed a miracle for him, providing a great catch of fish despite the fact that it was daytime and that the fishermen had let down their nets in the deep (see the discussion of this incident on page 123).

What insights do we gain by applying the three tests to Peter's prayer?

The test of appropriateness. Peter's prayer truly was appropriate. When Peter examined his own heart and compared himself with Jesus, Peter recognized his own sinfulness and the holiness of God. This awareness moved Peter to fear, even as Adam had feared and wanted only to put distance between himself and God (Gen. 3:8, 10). In this sense the prayer of Peter was appropriate. Yet in another sense it was not. Jesus had not come to condemn but to save. A sense of sin should lead us to Jesus, not away from Him.

The test of intent. Peter's prayer represents an all too human attempt to deal with a sense of guilt. Peter tried to reduce his fear and guilt by putting distance between himself and God. Yet the only way to deal with guilt is to come to God, not run from Him.

The test of God's purpose. When we apply this test, we understand Jesus' response to Peter's prayer. The person who realizes that he or she is guilty before God is not to fear, but, recognizing Jesus' love, is to seek forgiveness in Him.

Yet there is more. Jesus came not only to forgive but also to transform. Jesus' words to Peter beautifully express God's purpose for all of us: "From now on you will catch men." The fisher of fish would be transformed into a fisher of men, just as you and I and our priorities are transformed as we come to Jesus.

A mother's request refused (Matt. 15:22–28; Mark 7:24–28). The story of the Canaanite woman who begged Jesus to heal her daughter has troubled many. Why did Jesus harshly dismiss the woman implying that she and her people were nothing but "little dogs" while the Jews were God's children? Again the three tests help us understand.

The test of appropriateness. The text tells us the woman approached Jesus twice. The first time she addressed Him as "Son of David" (Matt. 15:22). This was a messianic title, which acknowledged Jesus as the promised King of the Jews.

Jesus did not respond to her first request because the woman was a Canaanite, who had no claim to the rights and privileges of God's covenant people. Jesus' message of hope and deliverance had to be presented to the Jews first, that they might have the opportunity to accept or reject their Messiah. Thus the woman's first appeal to Jesus was not appropriate, and Christ had nothing to say to her.

Later the woman came again and worshiped Him, saying "Lord, help me!" (Matt.

15:25). This time her appeal had a different basis. She addressed Jesus simply as "Lord," and appealed for mercy.

Jesus' response to this appeal was intended to clarify the issue. His reference to "little dogs" (house pets, in contrast to the wild scavengers that roamed the streets in first-century Palestinian cities) was not intended to insult. Jesus simply pointed out that children in a household had a right to expect food to be placed on the table. House pets did not. God's covenant people had a right to expect healing miracles (Is. 35:5, 6). Pagans did not.

The woman's answer showed that she understood what Jesus was saying. She claimed no right to have her request granted. She simply pointed out that in Christ God had provided more than enough for Israel. As Lord, Jesus related to all peoples everywhere, not just to Israel. The woman's appeal for mercy showed that she believed—not that she had a right to expect aid.

Christ accepted her argument. Now her prayer was appropriate. His gift of mercy was a response to her faith in Him, foreshadowing the fact that the gospel message would soon invite all to enter the family of God through faith in Jesus.

The test of intent. The woman came to Jesus in her need, appealing for mercy for her daughter. It is never wrong to appeal to God in desperate circumstances—whoever we are.

The test of God's purpose. We can see the outworking of God's purposes on several levels.

Christ presented Himself to Israel as the Jewish Messiah. In His early ministry He carefully maintained this role. While Jesus did heal a Roman centurion's servant, the healing took place in Jewish territory with Jewish leaders interceding for the pious Roman (Luke 7:1–10; Matt. 8:5–13). The healing of the woman's daughter is the only healing of a Gentile outside Jewish

territory during the time Christ presented Himself to the Jews as their Messiah.

Christ's initial response to the woman was in harmony with God's purpose. But so was Jesus' response to the second appeal. God intended to show His own love and mercy through Jesus, and that mercy extends to all. The healing was in fullest harmony with God's commitment to save those who respond to His promises with faith.

Two disciples' request refused (Matthew 20:20–23). The mother of James and John approached Jesus to ask that her two sons might have the two most significant posts in His coming kingdom. It was clear that the two brothers were behind their mother's request, and the other ten disciples were rightly angry with them. Jesus did not grant their request, stating that God the Father had already chosen the individuals who would have these positions.

The test of appropriateness. Self-promotion may be appropriate in the world, but it is never appropriate among Jesus' own. As Jesus went on to teach the Twelve, leaders were to be servants, even as He Himself came to serve rather than be served.

The test of intent. James and John sought prominence. In earthly kingdoms the positions they sought guaranteed both wealth and power. The intent behind the request of the two disciples was seriously flawed.

The test of God's purpose. Christ's purpose was not to set up the messianic kingdom immediately, but rather to call Jew and Gentile alike to God. His first priority was a spiritual kingdom without geographic boundaries, and faith alone could provide access to this spiritual kingdom. The earthly kingdom of the Messiah would come later. Now the disciples must choose to follow Jesus because they loved Him rather than because of expected personal gain.

Seemingly unanswered prayers can be a blessing.

In time James and John found their motives turned upside down as they followed Jesus' example of service and suffering. And they did follow. It was God's purpose to purify the disciples until their motives and desires were in tune with His own.

Jesus ignores the prayer of loved ones (John 11:1–6). This is one of the most fascinating of puzzling incidents regarding prayer. When Lazarus became seriously ill, his sisters, Mary and Martha, immediately sent for Jesus. The text makes it clear that Jesus loved this family deeply. Yet when the request urging Jesus to hurry to Lazarus' aid reached Him, Jesus did not respond. He waited. It was two days later that Jesus finally told His disciples they would return to Bethany where Lazarus lived.

While the disciples didn't know it at the time, Jesus had waited until Lazarus not only had died, but had been laid in the family tomb!

The test of appropriateness. Mary and Martha were well aware of Jesus' power over sickness. For some three years He had performed His healing miracles. They also knew that they had a special place in Jesus' heart, for Jesus and His disciples stayed in their home when in Jerusalem. So when Lazarus fell ill, the first thing they thought of was to send to Jesus. They were sure that if Jesus knew Lazarus was near death, He would hurry and heal their brother.

The prayer was appropriate. It was rooted in their confidence in Jesus and their awareness of His love. But when Jesus received the message, He seemed to ignore their plight for two days!

The test of intent. The sisters' message was a cry for help. It was also an expression of complete faith in Jesus. There was no flaw in the intent of the sisters.

The test of God's purpose. During the days of waiting for Jesus to arrive, the sisters must have experienced growing anxiety.

Why hadn't Jesus come? Why hadn't He responded to their desperate appeal? Then their brother died. And the two sisters knew that if Jesus had been there, Lazarus would not have died.

The pain of their loss must have been greater for this knowledge. And they must have wondered, Why? Why hadn't Jesus come when they had cried out to Him?

Today we understand the why. As Jesus told His disciples, the sickness and death of Lazarus was intended to bring glory to God, even as the restoration of Lazarus to life intensified the joy of the two sisters.

God's purposes in seemingly ignoring our prayers are usually hidden from us. But when that purpose has worked itself out, we can expect to experience both wonder and joy at God's goodness.

Lessons in Jesus' puzzling responses to prayer. Most prayers addressed to Jesus while He lived among us were answered immediately. Jesus, moved by compassion and concern for those in need, healed the sick and exorcised demons. But, as we have seen, several times Jesus responded to prayers in a puzzling manner. Yet His responses to the prayers considered here served to remind His disciples of important truths.

- God is merciful and gracious even to those who have no standing with Him. As Jesus said, God "makes His sun rise on the evil and on the good, and sends rain on the just and on the unjust" (Matt. 5:45). At times God even answers their prayers.
- Those who have a personal relationship with God through Jesus do have standing with Him and a special privilege in prayer. We know that He hears our petitions and responds with fatherly love.
- Sometimes our petitions are appropriate and sometimes they are inappropri-

ate. While it is always appropriate to appeal to God for mercy and help, we need to test our prayers for harmony with God's revealed will.

- We also need to test our own intent. Why do we want what we are asking for? Motive is important to God and it should be to us as well.
- Finally, we need to understand that God answers our prayers in ways that fit His purposes. As story after story illustrates, God's purposes never conflict with our own highest good, and clearly glorify Him.

JESUS' FIRST PRINCIPLES OF PRAYER

While Jesus taught prayer by His own example of dependence on God and by the way He answered prayers during His life on earth, Jesus also gave explicit instruction on prayer. In the rest of this chapter we'll look at Jesus' instructions on what can be called His "first principles" of praying to God.

These are found in Jesus' Sermon on the Mount (Matt. 5:1–7:23). We've already looked at this sermon, exploring it as a statement about the nature of life in the mystery kingdom Jesus had come to inaugurate. In this section we need to focus on principles of prayer expressed in the section of that sermon that focuses on public and private piety.

BIBLE BACKGROUND:
THE SERMON ON THE MOUNT IN BRIEF

Jesus pronounced blessings on those whose values reflected those of God rather than those of sinful human society (Matt. 5:3–16).

Jesus explained that the righteousness required by the Law was far different from the righteousness of the scribes and Pharisees, who thought they had only to act correctly. Jesus gave a series of illustrations to show that God is concerned with our hearts, not just our actions. What human beings need is a changed heart, for only a transformed person can be like the Heavenly Father (5:17–48).

Jesus contrasted the public piety of the Pharisees with the private, personal relationship that believers are to nurture with God as Father (Matt. 6:1–18).

Jesus called for a commitment to God that is rooted in total trust in the Lord as a Father who knows and will meet our every need (Matt. 6:19–34).

Jesus described characteristics of the fruit that such a relationship with God will produce in those who hear and respond to His words (Matt. 7:1–27).

WHAT PRAYER IS NOT (MATTHEW 6:1–5, 7–8)

Jesus began His teaching on prayer with a warning. "Take heed that you do not do your charitable deeds before men, to be seen by them. Otherwise you have no reward from your Father in heaven" (Matt. 6:1). This warning surprised His listeners. In Jesus' time it was generally believed that giving alms to the poor—doing charitable deeds—was especially pleasing to God. Nathan Ausubel, in his *Book of Jewish Knowledge* (1984, p. 82), repeats the story of a discussion between the first-century rabbi, Akiba, and Tineius Rufus, the governor of Judea. "The Roman asked Akiba, 'If, as you say, your god loves the poor, why then does he not support them?' A reasonable question, certainly! Rabbi Akiba replied that if God left the care of the poor to the benevolence of the Jews themselves it was purposely 'so that we may be saved by its merits from the punishment of Gehenna.'"

In view of this, it's not surprising that in Jesus' day the general populace thought the wealthy were doubly blessed. They were rich and comfortable in this world, and they had the wealth needed to guarantee blessedness in the world to come!

So Jesus' words surprised His listeners. Not do charitable deeds in public? Why, many of the wealthy had servants announce their deeds of charity by blowing trumpets in the streets. The poor would flock to the sound, and the rich man would gain a reputation for piety as well as merit with God. Public deeds of charity were a benefit to all!

Jesus intended to shock. His words about giving were intended to lay a foundation for what he was about to teach concerning relationship with God, and especially what He was about to teach about prayer. So Jesus continued,

Therefore, when you do a charitable deed, do not sound a trumpet before you as the hypocrites do in the synagogues and in the streets, that they may have glory from men. Assuredly, I say to you, they have their reward. But when you do a charitable deed, do not let your left hand know what your right hand is doing, that your charitable deed may be in secret; and your Father who sees in secret will Himself reward you openly (Matt. 6:2–4).

The central point Jesus made here is that relationship with God is a uniquely personal thing. It is a one-to-one relationship between an individual and God alone. Even the poor were not to know who their benefactor was. In this way, the purity of one's intent to please God alone might be maintained.

What the wealthy of first-century Jerusalem were doing was denying the nature of personal relationship with God. They sought a public display implying a relationship rather than the reality of a private and personal relationship.

Jesus applied this illustration from charity to prayer. Just as hypocrites loved

Pagan prayers were based on false assumptions.

to do charitable deeds to be seen of men, so they loved to make public prayers (Matt. 6:5)—for the same reason, and with the same outcome! They received the reward they valued—not God's answer to their prayers, but the opinion of their contemporaries that they were especially pious.

A little later Jesus commented that prayer is not to be a matter of "vain repetitions" (Matt. 6:7, 8). The Greek phrase translated "vain repetitions" is *battalogeo*, meaning "continuous babbling." While commentators normally link this with the "many words" which Jesus suggested pagans address to their deities, neither repetition nor length of prayers is the real issue. Pagan prayers were mere babbling because they were addressed to lifeless idols.

The pagan assumption that by addressing many words to the gods one could get what he or she wanted was an empty one

indeed. Jesus told His hearers, "Do not be like them." Their assumptions about prayer were wrong.

How many believers today buy into pagan assumptions about prayer! We may have flawed ideas about the God to whom we pray, assuming that our words draw His attention to needs about which He is unaware. In saying "your Father knows the things you have need of before you ask Him" (Matt. 6:8), Jesus introduced a contrasting set of assumptions that are basic to the prayer lives of true believers.

What, again, were the false assumptions underlying pagan prayer?

- The god or goddess was a stranger, invoked because of his or her supposed ability to help.
- Prayer involved asking this god or goddess for something wanted or needed.
- Prayer required alerting the deity to something about which he or she did not know.
- The words of the prayer—its form, the gift presented to the deity—provided the basis on which the god's favor might be won.
- As we will see, neither the Jews of Jesus' time nor pagans grasped the truths about prayer our Lord was about to introduce.

JESUS' FIRST PRINCIPLE: UNDERSTAND PRAYER'S NATURE

Against the background of this warning Jesus gave what He considered a first principle of prayer.

But you, when you pray, go into your room, and when you have shut your door, pray to your Father who is in the secret place; and your Father who sees in secret will reward you openly (Matt. 6:6).

This instruction summarizes what Jesus had been saying. Prayer is first of all an expression of a personal relationship with God as Father. It is a one-to-one relationship between a believer and God. And, because it is essentially a one-to-one relationship, it is also an "in-secret" relationship.

Prayer, then, is a transaction that takes place between a person and God. As such, it is the business only of that individual and the Lord.

Jesus is not suggesting that it is wrong to pray with others. Prayer meetings have been a vital reflection of the Christian community's relationship with the Lord from the beginning (Acts 1:14; 2:42). What Jesus was saying is that we are to be careful to guard our hearts against mixed motives. We are to direct our prayers to God alone—for the purpose of communicating with Him, not to influence how others might view us.

God who knows everything will honor those who seek Him in the secret recesses of their hearts. These are the people whom God will reward openly.

JESUS' SECOND PRINCIPLE: ADDRESS GOD AS FATHER

Matthew 6:9 introduces Jesus' model prayer with these words: "In this manner therefore pray: Our Father in heaven . . . ." The one-to-one relationship Jesus had been speaking of was the relationship of a child to his or her parent!

The fatherliness of God. A number of scholars have pointed out that God is spoken of as "Father" in the Old Testament. For instance, Malachi 2:10 reads, "Have we not all one Father? Has not one God created us?" But in this context, the term *Father* is equated with Creator, and it has the meaning of "source" or "originator."

Geza Vermes, a contemporary Jewish scholar, has gone to considerable lengths to show that Jesus should be understood as a rabbi operating within first-century Judaism, rather than as the Son of God. In his efforts to humanize Christ, Vermes has searched ancient literature and pointed out that Jews addressed God as "Father" before Jesus' day.

Most frequently in Jewish prayer, however, "Father" is coupled with other terms of respect, such as "Ruler," "Lord," and "God." When Ben Sira, who wrote some 200 years before Christ, addressed God as "my Father," he explained, "for thou art the Hero of My salvation" (*Ecclus.* 51:10). He would not address God simply as Father without further explanation.

Prayer in the Jewish synagogue did at times appeal to God as "our Father." But again, God was "Father" in the sense of the source of that covenant which made Israel His people. Commenting on the pre-Christian references to God as Father, one authority has stated that the term

lacks vitality because it does not express a radical appreciation of the fatherliness of God. It seems to be confined within the very different system of a legalism which contradicts fatherly freedom. What Israel possessed in the name looks ahead to a view which goes incomparably deeper, which transcends mere formality, which is no longer tied to the idea of merit, which no longer thinks in terms of the privilege of an elite or respected teacher. The materials are there, but the spirit of true faith in the Father is still lacking (*Theological Dictionary of the New Testament,* Vol. V., 1963, pp. 981–982).

It is just this, a "radical appreciation of the fatherliness of God," which Jesus presents as the first principle of prayer.

The God to whom believers pray is not simply a Father, but is fatherly—one who "knows the things you have need of before you ask him" (Matt. 6:8). Those who appreciate this reality pray to God "in secret," assured that He knows our needs and heeds our prayers. We are heard, not because of our "many words," but because God has a fatherly concern for us.

How stunning this principle of prayer is. God knows and loves us! God has a fatherly concern for us. We relate to Him not simply as one of His creatures, or even as one of His covenant people in good standing, but as family! And because we are family, our prayers need not follow the pagan pattern of request piled upon request. In our prayers we are free to speak to God as a child speaks to his or her loving father.

An illustration of God's fatherliness (Matt. 7:7–11). A little later in the Sermon on the Mount Jesus further develops implications of the fatherliness of God.

Ask, and it will be given to you; seek, and you will find; knock, and it will be opened to you. For everyone who asks receives, and he who seeks finds, and to him who knocks it will be opened. Or what man is there among you who, if his son asks for bread, will he give him a stone? Or if he asks for a fish, will he give him a serpent? If you then, being evil, know how to give good gifts to your children, how much more will your Father who is in heaven give good things to those who ask Him! (Matt. 7:7–11; compare Luke 11:9–13).

Jesus builds on the principle of God's fatherliness in teaching about prayer. We are heard, and God responds to us when we ask, seek, and knock, but not because of our much speaking. We are heard, not because of the form of our words. We are heard, not because we have done favors for God. We are heard, not because we deserve what we request. We are heard and God responds to us because, like a human father, God is committed to give "good things" when His children ask Him.

JESUS' THIRD PRINCIPLE: KNOW HOW TO PRAY

As Jesus continued His Sermon on the Mount He gave His listeners a model prayer. We call this "the Lord's Prayer,"

even though it is a prayer Jesus taught rather than one He offered. This model prayer answers an important question. If God is our Father, and has a fatherly concern for us, how are we as His children to nurture our "in-secret" relationship with Him?

It's important to note two things before we explore this familiar prayer. First, Jesus did not say, "This is what you should pray," but "Pray in this manner" (Matt. 6:9). The Lord's Prayer establishes a pattern for our prayers; it is not a liturgy to follow. It establishes a pattern; it does not provide the words to use when praying in private or in church.

Second, Jesus' instructions in verses 5–8 emphasize "you" in contrast to the rest of humankind. Jesus' instructions on prayer are for His followers alone, as distinct from pagans as well as unbelieving Israel. The Lord's Prayer is a model for those who trust Jesus and are His followers.

How did Jesus teach us to pray? Matthew's version of the Lord's Prayer says,

> Our Father in heaven,
>   Hallowed be Your name.
> Your kingdom come,
>   Your will be done
>   On earth as it is in heaven.
> Give us this day our daily
>   bread,
> And forgive us our debts,
>   As we forgive our debtors.
> And do not lead us into
>   temptation,
>   But deliver us from the evil
>   one.
> For Yours is the kingdom and
>   the power and the glory
>   forever. Amen.
> (Matt. 6:9–13)

Jesus' model prayer is divided into two parts. The first part, and the believer's first priority, deals with God's glory. In prayer we are first of all to focus on hallowing

The "Lord's Prayer" teaches principles that are to infuse all our prayers.

God's name, extending God's kingdom, and doing God's will. The second part of the prayer concerns our needs. Luther saw three petitions here, while Calvin and those in the reformed tradition divide verse 13 and count four. But what is significant is to note the major divisions of the model prayer. Our prayers are to enhance God's glory, and express our dependence on Him for all our needs.

"Our Father in heaven" (Matt. 6:9). These opening words remind us of the kind of God to whom we pray and of our relationship with Him. God is the Father of Jesus' followers in the most intimate sense.

The words *in heaven* remind us that the one with whom we have a personal rela-

tionship is actually God the Creator and sovereign ruler of the universe. These words are a reminder of the awesome privilege we have in Christ of addressing the Creator Himself as Father. Relationally, God is Father only of those who have trusted Christ, although in the sense of "source" He is the "Father" of all.

"Hallowed be Your name" (Matt. 6:9). God's "name" captures to some extent who He actually is. To say "hallowed be Your name" is an acknowledgment of the fact that God is to be respected and treated as holy. When we come to God in prayer, we are to do so in an appropriate frame of mind. We are to come with an awareness of and respect for who He is. While God is our

Father, we are never to forget that He is God.

"Your kingdom come" (Matt. 6:10). In biblical times a "kingdom" was not primarily a geographical area, but existed wherever persons were subject to the rule of a king. It was the relationship between the ruler and subjects that constituted a kingdom.

While the earthly kingdom predicted by the prophets had not yet instituted by Jesus, God rules now in the hearts of those who acknowledge Him as King. The prayer "your kingdom come" does look ahead but has a distinctive present application as well. Until Christ returns we are to submit to God's will here and now, that through our obedience God's kingdom might find a more perfect expression in our day.

"Your will be done on earth as it is in heaven" (Matt. 6:10). The word translated "will" here is *thelema*. It expresses not what God wants but what He has willed or determined. When we pray "your will be done," we identify ourselves with God's will and commit ourselves to do it. Thus to pray "Your will be done" is both a personal commitment to moral obedience and a commitment to participate in the fulfillment of God's purposes here on earth.

Today earth is in rebellion against God. In heaven God's will is done fully, joyfully, and spontaneously. How wonderful to desire here on earth only what God wants and what He knows is best.

"Give us this day our daily bread" (Matt. 6:11). In biblical times the term *bread* included all foods. In this context it stands for all a person needs to sustain life.

While the prayer asks God to "give," this does not imply that we're relieved of the responsibility to work for what we receive. God supplied manna to the Exodus generation on a daily basis, yet each person was required to gather what God had placed on the ground.

The phrase "daily bread" looked back on the experience of the Exodus generation. But it also reflected the reality of first-century life. Workers were paid on a daily basis, and wages were just enough to sustain a family. The family of a person who was ill and could not work for a few days was in desperate straits. The prayer Jesus taught calls on us to depend on God continually, looking to Him for all good things—including our ability to work.

There is another thought here too. We are to depend on God to supply our needs, not our wants. We are to be satisfied with what God provides rather than yearn for what He has not chosen to give.

"And forgive us our debts, as we forgive our debtors" (Matt. 6:12). The word "debts" (*opheilema*) is rare in biblical Greek. It is found only two times in the New Testament, here and in Romans 4:4, where it means "obligations." But *opheilema* is used in the Septuagint to translate an Aramaic word which means "sin" or "transgression." Given this and Luke 11:4's "forgive us our sins," we can be confident that Jesus was referring to forgiveness of sins.

Some have assumed from this passage that Jesus was teaching we must earn God's forgiveness by forgiving others. But according to Greek scholar C.F.D. Moule, Jesus is referring to an attitude that makes forgiveness possible. When we sense the enormity of the sins for which God has forgiven us, we find it possible to forgive the far lesser sins others have committed against us.

"And do not lead us into temptation, but deliver us from the evil one" (Matt. 6:13). In ordinary first-century, or *koine*, Greek, the word rendered "temptation" meant "testing." New Testament usage frequently focuses attention on a specific kind of testing, such as temptation or enticement to sin. However, James 1:13 reminds us that God cannot be tempted nor does He tempt anyone to evil.

We also know from Scripture that believers are called on to face tests of many kinds, and that we are to do so with joy (1 Cor. 10:13). It would seem strange to ask God not to do what He cannot do, and just as strange to ask God not to permit what He tells us will happen.

A possible solution is suggested by the word "into." A similar verb in Hebrew would imply giving into temptation, not simply testing itself. In this case the prayer "deliver us from" would mean "preserve us during" temptation, that we might not fail the test.

Another possible solution suggests that the verb may be causative. In this case the prayer would be that God protect us from temptations devised by Satan, and "deliver us from" would then mean "spare us the experience."

A third possibility is that the prayer encourages us to maintain a humble attitude. God does not ask us to seek martyrdom or rush into a difficult situation to "prove" our faith. How much wiser to follow Paul's advice and pray for those in authority "that we may lead a quiet and peaceable life in all godliness and reverence" (1 Tim. 2:2). There is challenge enough in leading ordinary lives that glorify God.

"For yours is the kingdom and the power and the glory forever. Amen." (Matt. 6:13). The prayer ends with a doxology, praising and glorifying God.

FIRST PRINCIPLES IN THE SERMON ON THE MOUNT

We can summarize the first principles of prayer taught by Jesus in the Sermon on the Mount.

1. Authentic prayer is an expression of a believer's personal relationship with God.
2. Authentic prayer is an expression of a believer's reliance on the fatherliness of God.

3. Authentic prayer incorporates an expression of a believer's
   (a) respect for God as holy
   (b) submission to God's right to rule
   (c) commitment to moral obedience and to fulfilling God's purposes
   (d) daily dependence on God
   (e) determination to live as a forgiven and forgiving person
   (f) reliance on God for strength to meet any test successfully

THE LORD'S PRAYER IN LUKE

Another version of the Lord's Prayer is found in Luke 11. This version is essentially the same as that in Matthew 6, with minor variations. As discussed in chapter 2, such variations are to be expected in the Gospel records.

Different but the same. Variations can be accounted for first, by the fact that during His three or more years of public ministry, Jesus must have delivered the same basic sermons time and time again, with minor variations. Second, each writer of a Gospel shaped his account to appeal to a particular audience. It is not surprising then that even when describing the same event writers might select different elements to emphasize. What is much more significant is the substantial agreement that exists between Gospel accounts.

This is surely true in the case of the versions of the Lord's Prayer recorded by Matthew and Luke. In both versions, the same "first principles" of prayer are emphasized. Each version emphasizes the father liness of God. Each version instructs us to put God's concerns first when we pray. And each version calls on us to express our dependence on the Father in all things.

An added illustration (Luke 11:5–8). Luke does introduce a new illustration that Jesus

Many of Jesus' stories about prayer have been mis-understood.

provided to strengthen the disciples' confidence in God's readiness to answer prayer.

Which of you shall have a friend, and go to him at midnight and say to him, "Friend, lend me three loaves; for a friend of mine has come to me on his journey, and I have nothing to set before him"; and he will answer from within and say, "Do not trouble me; the door is now shut, and my children are with me in bed; I cannot rise and give to you"? I say to you, though he will not rise and give to him because he is his friend, yet because of his persistence he will rise and give him as many as he needs (Luke 11:5–8).

Jesus then followed with the instructions recorded in Matthew: "Ask, and it will be given; seek, and you will find; knock, and it will be opened to you" (Luke 11:9).

In telling this story, Jesus invited His disciples to consider what would happen if

a visitor arrived at their house late at night, and they happened to be low on bread. In biblical times great significance was placed on hospitality, and hospitality demanded that food and lodging be provided a visitor.

So the disciples were to picture themselves going to a friend and asking for three loaves. True, it was late. True, the friend was in bed, and he grumbled about getting up. But Jesus said despite the trouble, "because of his persistence he will rise and give him as many as he needs."

Most English versions do translate the Greek word *anaideia* as "persistence." And thus we get the impression of a person who keeps on knocking until the neighbor provides the bread just to get rid of him. But how does this fit with Jesus' warning against looking at prayer as pagans do and relying on "much speaking"?

There is another meaning of *anaideia* which better fits both first-century customs and God's character. That meaning is "avoidance of shame." In the first century, visitors were considered the responsibility not just of the host family but also of the whole village. Taking *anaideia* as "avoidance of shame," one hears Jesus teaching that the neighbor would surely get up and provide the bread because he was obliged to do so, as it was the right thing for a neighbor to do. Answering the knock on the door was his obligation as a member of the community, and to fail to meet that obligation would shame him and his village.

What Jesus is saying, then, is that God will surely respond to our prayers, simply because God will always do what is appropriate and consistent with His character. We can expect our heavenly Father to be fatherly, and to supply our needs!

God is our Father and always does what is right. When we understand these first principles of prayer, we will count on Him always, sure that He will respond to our requests and give us, His children, what is good.

MORE TEACHINGS ON PRAYER

Jesus made many references to prayer both in His public teaching and in His private instruction to the Twelve. He shared prayer promises and related prayer to such diverse issues as evangelism and faith.

The Gospels also record several prayers offered by Jesus. It's significant that Christ's recorded prayers are associated with His rejection by Israel (Matt. 11), and that three of the four recorded prayers were offered during His last hours on earth.

JESUS' PRAYER PROMISES

In the last chapter we examined Jesus' first principles of prayer. All of His teachings on this subject presuppose these first principles. Prayer is a one-to-one expression of a personal relationship with God as Father. Our confidence in prayer rests on our awareness of His fatherliness, and our willingness to fit in with His purposes.

PRAYER PROMISES IN CONTEXT

The Bible portrays human beings as sinners alienated from God. While the Old Testament focuses on the relationship of the nation Israel to God, the New Testament emphasizes the relationship of individuals to our Lord. It's not surprising that New Testament prayer promises tend to be individual. The individual who trusts Christ as Savior has a personal relationship with God as Father. Prayer promises are for such individuals. As we examine Jesus' prayer promises, it's important to keep this distinction in mind. We need to remember that prayer promises are made to people who have a personal relationship with God through faith in Christ, and who remain in fellowship with Him.

Nowhere is this principle stated more clearly than in John 15, where Jesus likened His relationship with believers to that of a vine with its branches. As Christ developed this analogy, He emphasized the need for the branches to "abide in" the vine. The Greek verb for "abide," *meno*, means to remain in—to maintain an intimate connection with—the vine. Jesus made it clear that only a believer who lives an obedient life has the intimate connection with Him that makes fruitfulness possible—and that guarantees answers to prayers. Note how these themes are developed.

Abide in Me, and I in you. As the branch cannot bear fruit of itself, unless it abides in the vine, neither can you, unless you abide in Me.

I am the vine, you are the branches. He who abides in Me, and I in him, bears much fruit, for without me you can do nothing. . . . If you abide in Me, and My words abide in you, you will ask what you desire, and it shall be done for you. . . . As the Father loved Me, I also have loved you; abide in My love. If you keep My commandments, you will abide in My love, just as I have kept My Father's commandments and abide in His love (John 15:4, 5, 7, 9, 10).

When we read any prayer promise made by Jesus, we want to keep in mind that Christ Himself defined the specific relational context here in John 15. Jesus' prayer promises assume that the person or persons have a personal relationship with God through faith in Him. These prayer promises can only be claimed by those who are living in a responsive, obedient relationship with Jesus Christ.

Only when we define the relational context of New Testament prayer promises as Jesus did can we understand what Jesus is saying to us today.

ASK, SEEK, KNOCK— AND RECEIVE

This promise is found in Matthew 7:7–11 and again in Luke 11:9–13. Matthew's version states,

Ask, and it will be given to you; seek, and you will find; knock, and it will be opened to you. For everyone who asks receives, and he who seeks finds, and to him who knocks it will be opened. Or what man is there among you who, if his son asks for bread, will give him a stone? Or if he asks for a fish, will he give him a serpent?

If you then, being evil, know how to give good gifts to your children, how much more will your Father who is in heaven give good things to those who ask Him?

In the Sermon on the Mount, of which this passage is a part, Christ first explored the attitudes to be adopted by those who would live as citizens of His kingdom (Matt. 5:3–12). He also described the righteousness which is to characterize citizens (vv. 13–48) and the personal, "in-secret" relationship with God which they are to maintain (6:1–34). The citizens Jesus describes are persons who "seek first the kingdom of God and His righteousness" (v. 33).

Clearly the prayers of such persons will not be selfish, but they will be directed toward God's purposes. It is not at all unlikely that the "good gifts" which kingdom citizens ask for, seek, and knock to obtain are the very qualities that a relationship with Jesus makes possible for them.

Luke's variation of the illustration confirms this interpretation. At another time Jesus concluded, "How much more will your heavenly Father give the Holy Spirit to those who ask Him" (Luke 11:13). How does this ending confirm our conclusion? The Holy Spirit is the one whom Christ has given to us. And His mission is to produce in us the attitudes, righteousness, and love for God and others that Jesus spoke about.

Thus the context of the promise, the Sermon on the Mount, does limit and also define the promise. The context protects us from the unwarranted assumption that God guarantees to answer every one of our prayers, whether selfish or unselfish.

This is a truly precious promise. A person may be persistent in his attempts to gain worldly wealth, yet continue to live in poverty. But any person who persistently

The promise to "two or three gathered in My name" is not a prayer promise.

seeks the kinds of gifts Jesus offers to kingdom citizens will surely receive!

THE PROMISE TO TWO OR THREE

As noted, Matthew 18:19, 20 is usually, but mistakenly, taken as a prayer promise. The verses read,

Again I say to you that if two of you agree on earth concerning anything that they ask, it will be done for them by My Father in heaven. For where two or three are gathered together in My name, I am there in the midst of them.

These verses almost certainly do not deal with prayer at all. There are two reasons to choose an alternative interpretation.

The context. These verses are found in a passage in which Jesus instructs His followers on how to deal with interpersonal conflict and disputes (vv. 15–18). The phrase "again I say to you" which introduces the "two or three" promise indicates

that verses 19 and 20 should be understood as a continuation of Jesus' instruction on conflict resolution, not as a new and unrelated topic.

The key word. The key word in the passage, translated "ask" in our English versions, is *aiteisthai.* It frequently does mean "asking in prayer." However, when used in a judicial or legal setting the word has the meaning of "pursuing a claim." This is exactly the setting in Matthew, where Jesus is urging individuals to seek resolution of a conflict, first individually and then as a last resort by bringing the church into the process. In this setting we should understand Matthew 18:19, 20 to describe what will happen if both parties pursue their claim before the church. What Jesus promises is that whenever two or three (appointed as judges to suggest a solution to the conflict) gather in Christ's name, Jesus will be present with the judges to provide the wisdom needed to reach an appropriate solution. Strikingly, this promise may well have served as a basis for Paul's parallel teaching in 1 Corinthians 6:1–6.

Although not the prayer promise most have assumed that this is, this is a precious promise indeed.

PRAY, BELIEVING

This promise, found in both Matthew 21:21–22 and Mark 11:22–24, has sometimes been transformed into a threat or warning. The passage reads,

Assuredly I say to you, if you have faith and do not doubt, you will not only do what was done to the fig tree, but also if you say to this mountain, "Be removed and be cast into the sea," it will be done. And whatever things you ask in prayer, believing, you will receive.

Many see in these verses an obstacle to answered prayer that overshadows the promise. They reason that if only believing prayers are answered, the slightest doubt must mean that a prayer will not be answered. The reasoning is flawed, for answers to prayer are not found at the end of some obstacle course we must negotiate. Prayer is an expression of our in-secret relationship with God as Father, and answers to prayer depend on God's fatherly love.

To understand these verses we need to examine the context, and to make several important distinctions.

The withered fig tree (Matt. 21:18–22). It was the last week of Jesus' life. As He and His disciples approached Jerusalem they saw a fig tree by the side of the road. Even though it had leaves, normally a sign of ripe figs, Jesus found no fruit on it and cursed the tree. "Let no fruit grow on you ever again" (Matt. 21:19).

Mark tells us that the next time Jesus and the disciples passed by, the fig tree had withered away. (The supposed conflict between Mark's and Matthew's account is removed when we realize that the word translated "immediately" in Matthew may

also be translated "soon" or "presently.") The disciples were amazed, and asked Jesus, "How did the fig tree wither away so soon?" (v. 20). It was in answer to this question that Jesus spoke the words recorded in verses 21 and 22.

BIBLE BACKGROUND:

Interpreters agree that the fig tree in Matthew 21 and Mark 11 serves as a symbol. A fig tree in full leaf would normally carry ripe figs. In a sense, the tree was a hypocrite, pretending to provide sustenance but in fact was barren and empty. In a similar way the scribes, chief priests, and Pharisees promised to show the way to God, but in fact their approach to religion left people disappointed and empty. Like the fig tree, they and their ways were about to experience judgment.

Jesus' answer explained. Jesus' response to the disciples' question is in two parts. The first part is found in verse 21, and is a commentary on faith and command. The second part is found in verse 22, and is a commentary on faith and prayer. We need to carefully separate these verses if we're to understand what Jesus said, and the prayer promise in verse 22.

Faith and command (v. 21). The disciples were amazed that the fig tree withered so quickly. Jesus told them, "If you have faith and do not doubt, you will not only do what was done to the fig tree, but also if you say to this mountain, 'Be removed and be cast into the sea,' it will be done." The definite article, "this" with "mountain" suggests that Jesus pointed to the Mount of Olives across the valley or ahead to Mount Moriah where the temple stood. Jesus was not using the image of moving mountains in the metaphorical sense of doing the impossible, but rather was making an amazing claim.

That claim is rooted in a confusion in modern thought. In our day human beings think of the material universe as somehow "real" and the spiritual universe as "unreal." In fact the material universe is a derivative of the spiritual. God spoke, and all that exists sprang into being. Hebrews 11:3 reminds us that "by faith we understand that the worlds were framed by the word of God, so that the things which are seen were not made of things which are visible."

Even more significantly, the material world is *subject* to the spiritual, as the miracles recorded in Scripture make clear. In fact, the Twelve had already exercised sovereignty over the material universe when they had been sent out by Jesus to heal (see Matthew 10:1)! It is against this background that Jesus explained, "If you say. . . ."

But Jesus preceded the phrase "If you say" with the words, "If you have faith and do not doubt." The linkage of faith and doubt is the key to understanding this particular verse.

1. *Faith.* What makes faith valid is its object. In the New Testament the usual object of faith is Jesus or, in twelve instances, God. It is trust in God as He is known in Jesus that gives us access to the spiritual universe and its powers.

2. *Doubt.* While faith is validated by its object, there is a subjective element in the exercise of faith. It is that subjective element that Jesus referred to when He added, "and do not doubt." The word translated "doubt" here is *diakrithe.* According to *The Theological Dictionary of the New Testament* (1965) this doubt is

a specifically religious phenomenon. In Mk. 11:23, Mat. 21:21 man has the promise of God and he clings to it when he speaks the word of

faith to God, or to the mountain. But he still thinks it is impossible, or at least not certain, that what he says should be done. He is at odds with himself. He believes, and yet he does not believe. . . . Jm. 1:6 gives a vivid description of the man of prayer who is a *diakrinomenos.* He does not stand firm on the promise of God but moves restlessly like a wave of the sea. He is double-minded and inconsistent in all his conduct" (Vol. 3, p. 947).

What Jesus explained, then, is that one's faith in God makes the seemingly impossible possible because the spiritual realm controls the material. But because of doubt, doing the impossible is not an everyday occurrence. Doubt, not as questioning God but as confusion about what is real, robs us of the power to which we have access. We are so accustomed to thinking of the material world as limiting that even when we are *theoretically* convinced, when we seek to put faith into practice we are at odds with ourselves. We believe, yet do not believe.

Jesus never experienced this kind of inner conflict. Jesus lived His human life in intimate relationship with the Father, knowing with utter certainty the sovereignty of the spiritual over the material. And thus when Jesus spoke, the fig tree withered away.

Faith and prayer (v. 22). Jesus then applied His explanation to prayer. Note the difference between the two verses. In verse 21 Jesus dealt with "if you say." Here Jesus says, "If you pray."

There is a vast difference between commanding mountains and appealing to God in prayer. It is one thing to believe without doubt that we can move mountains. It is another thing entirely to believe that God can move mountains. In this sense, believing prayer is an easier approach to accomplishing the impossible, not a more difficult one!

The phrase "whatever you ask . . . you will receive" challenges the faith of some. The Greek here is *panta osa,* literally "all whatever." These words are general rather than specific. Jesus was explaining that whatever kind of thing we might ask, we will receive, not guaranteeing an answer to each and every request. Jesus was telling His disciples that they have access to the One whom we *know* can do the impossible, whatever the impossible may be. There is nothing we can ask which is beyond the capabilities of our God to provide.

The New International Encyclopedia of Bible Words (1985) summarizes the significance of this prayer promise given us by Jesus.

In the Gospels, one vital fact is made clear in Jesus' words about faith: a lack of trust in the God in whom we have faith closes off life's possibilities. When we fail to believe, we do not experience the full range of God's activity (Mt 21:22). But when we trust, we open up our future to a full experience of God's power in and through us (Mt 17:20; 21:21; Luke 7:9–10). All things are possible to the one who believes (p. 117).

PRAYING IN JESUS' NAME

This promise is found in John 14:13. "And whatever you ask in My name, that I will do, that the Father may be glorified in the Son. If you ask anything in My name, I will do it."

John is the only Gospel writer who recorded the private teaching Jesus gave His disciples the night before His crucifixion (John 13–16). It's crucial to remember that Jesus was speaking to disciples who believed in Him and were committed to Him. This promise is not for those who have no personal relationship with Jesus Christ.

"Whatever you ask." This is a promise to Jesus' own. Jesus is speaking about whatever "you" ask.

"Ask in My name." This phrase helps us to define the "whatever" in this promise. In

the biblical world a "name" was thought to capture something of the essence of the thing named. To ask in Jesus' name means to bring the content and the motivation of the prayer into harmony with all that Jesus is, as well as to pray with complete confidence that the Father hears us because of the work of His Son.

"That the Father may be glorified in the Son." Here is further definition of the "whatever" covered by this promise. The prayers Jesus answers, like all of His activities, must glorify the Father.

When we look at the elements in the prayer promise we see why the "whatever you ask" must be understood in terms of Jesus' values and purposes. Nothing which reflects poorly on God, or which fails to enhance His glory, is a fit subject for Christian prayers. Yet when we do pray in Jesus' name—asking for that which is in fullest harmony with who He is and with His commitment to glorify God—we can pray with confidence. God will not only hear such a prayer; Jesus will do what we ask.

PRAYER FOR WHAT WE DESIRE

This promise is also found in Jesus' Last Supper teachings. It is recorded in John 15:7: "If you abide in Me, and My words abide in you, you will ask what you desire, and it shall be done for you." We tend to read "what you desire" as "whatever you want." But we need to be careful here. For one thing, our desires change. As a young child we may have wanted a bicycle; as an adult we may have wanted a particular job. But even more significant in understanding this promise is to realize that it is conditional. Jesus said *"If you abide in Me, and my words abide in you*, you will ask what you desire."

Jesus promises that He will act *when our desires are shaped by abiding in Him and in His word.* This is a truly wonderful promise. For it reminds us that when we abide in Jesus and His words take root in our lives, God will so work in us to conform our desires to His will. The same thought is expressed in Psalm 37:4:

> Delight yourself also in the
>   LORD,
> And He shall give you the
>   desires of your heart.

God never promised to provide everything a human being may want. But He does promise us He will give us the desires themselves. And when we want what God wants, those prayers will surely be answered.

PRAYER AND FRUITFULNESS

In another section of Jesus' Last Supper discourse Jesus linked fruitfulness and prayer.

You did not choose Me, but I chose you and appointed you that you should go and bear fruit, and that your fruit should remain, that whatever you ask the Father in My name He may give you (John 15:16).

The phrase "that whatever you ask" in this passage is specifically linked to fruit-bearing. The word translated "that" (*hina*) marks what follows as either a result or a purpose clause. Jesus has chosen and ordained His followers to bear fruit, and *in order that they might accomplish this purpose,* God will give them whatever they ask in Jesus' name.

The nature of the purpose depends on our understanding of fruit. Most often in the New Testament fruit is a transformed character (see for example Gal. 5:22, 23; 2 Cor. 3:18). Infrequently, as in Mark 4:20, converts are referred to as fruit. Thus Jesus is reminding His disciples either that prayer is a critical resource in winning others to Him,

Fruitfulness is intimately linked to prayer.

or that prayer is a significant element in seeking the good gifts the Spirit brings.

PRAYER AND POWER

Some Christians as well as non-Christians have a "magical" view of prayer. Many have taken Jesus' prayer promises in this way. If we follow the formula—believing, not doubting, using Jesus' name—God must do anything we ask. After all, Jesus did say "whatever"!

But prayer is not magic. And Jesus' prayer promises must be understood on His terms. When we grasp what Jesus taught about prayer we discover that His words are promises indeed.

Prayer gives us access to powers beyond the imagination of those who see the physical universe as the ultimate reality. Prayer gives us access to God and the spiritual realm, to which the material creation is subject. We gain this access by first placing our trust in Jesus, for He alone is the way, the truth, and the life.

Then as Christians we discover that there are other keys to prayer's spiritual adventure. We are called to abide in Christ by living close to Him and responding to His word. We are called to identify with His purposes, to share His goals, and to let those goals shape our own desires. As we grow to value what Jesus values and to want what He wants, we will pray in His name. And our prayers will be answered.

With our focus on Christ and His power, we will ask, believing. And we will find that our prayers, prayers that glorify God and which are attuned to His purposes, are answered indeed.

JESUS' PRAYER REMINDERS

The subject of prayer often came up during the years Jesus spent with His disciples. When the situation warranted, Jesus shared brief comments that served as reminders about prayer.

PRAYER AND EVANGELISM

Matthew 9 records a number of healings that Jesus performed. As the news of His miracles spread, many appealed to Jesus, and Christ threw Himself into His ministry. Matthew tells us that He "went about all the cities and villages" of Galilee teaching, preaching, and healing (4:23). And all around, Jesus saw needy people.

It was then that Christ encouraged His disciples to pray. "The harvest truly is plentiful," Christ said, "but the laborers are few.

Therefore pray the Lord of the harvest to send out laborers into His harvest" (Matt. 9:37, 38; compare Luke 10:2).

It's significant that those Jesus urged to pray for harvesters became harvesters themselves. When we pray for others, God will often use us to reach them!

PRAYER AND EXORCISM

Matthew 17:19–21, as well as Mark 9:14–27 and Luke 9:37–43, tells of a time when Jesus and three of His disciples were away on the Mount of Transfiguration. When they returned they found a distraught father upset because the other disciples had failed to heal his demon-possessed son. Jesus healed the child, and later the disciples asked why they had been unable to cast out the demon.

Jesus answered that it was because of their unbelief, and used the "moving mountains" illustration discussed on page 192 above. But then Jesus added, "However, this kind does not come out except by prayer and fasting" (Matt. 17:21).

BIBLE BACKGROUND:

PRAYER AND FASTING

"Fasting" was going without food as a spiritual discipline. Most fasts in biblical times lasted from sunrise to sunset. In Jesus' day many Pharisees showed their zeal for God by fasting each Monday and Thursday (see Luke 18:12). Four reasons for fasting are suggested in the Old Testament.

(1) Fasts were undertaken to express the depths of a person's grief or mourning (1 Sam. 31:13). (2) Fasts were undertaken as part of the nation's or an individual's most urgent prayers to God (2 Chron. 20:1–29; 2 Sam. 12:16–22). (3) Fasts were undertaken to show the sincerity of a person's repentance (1 Kings

A house of worship is to be a house of prayer.

21:27). (4) The only fast commanded in Scripture was on the Day of Atonement, and it was intended to underline the solemnity of the day (Lev. 16:29,31).

The New Testament records Jesus' own forty-day fast in the wilderness just before being tempted by Satan (Matt. 4:1, 2; Luke 4:1–3).

When we take this evidence together, we see a common thread. A person who undertook a fast set aside the time to focus entirely on the Lord. While no command to fast appears in the Epistles, fasts are mentioned as adjuncts to prayer or worship not only in the Gospels but also in Acts 13:2 and 14:23.

Jesus had spoken of "faith as a mustard seed." It was clear from this allusion that the quantity of faith was not an issue in the disciples' failure. The mustard seed was the smallest of the seeds used in Jewish herb gardens, and faith that small was sufficient to move mountains. What seems to have been the problem was a flawed faith. Because of the disciples' past successes, they may have begun to believe that they could cast out demons themselves! They needed to be reminded that they must count on God to act through them.

Only after making this point did Jesus mention prayer, and say, "This kind does not go out except by prayer and fasting." Dealing with "this kind" of demon—one as powerful as the demon who had seized the child—called for prayer and fasting.

The role of prayer and fasting is to restore a flawed faith by concentrating on the Lord, so that we will be able to exercise the authority He has granted to us. Prayer and fasting as a means of purifying faith can make any Christian more effective in carrying out ministries for which he or she is gifted. The closer we are to the Lord, the more we rely on Him, the more effective any service we offer Him will be.

PRAYER AND WORSHIP

When Jesus cast the money changers out of the temple He challenged them, saying "Is it not written, 'My house shall be called a house of prayer for all nations'? But you have made it a 'den of thieves'" (Mark 11:17; compare Matt. 21:13; Luke 19:46; John 2:16).

The greed and lack of concern for others that characterized the merchants in the temple and priests who authorized—and profited from!—their business, left no place for worship. Neither of these should have any place in our lives. Jesus died that our hearts might become His temple—a house of prayer dedicated to Him.

PRAYER AND PRETENSE

We've already seen that Jesus condemned the Pharisees for their public piety, a show performed not out of concern for their relationship with God but because they want their fellow citizens to admire them. A similar thought is expressed in Matthew 23, where Jesus pronounces a series of woes on the Pharisees.

Woe to you, scribes and Pharisees, hypocrites! For you devour widows' houses, and for a pretense make long prayers. Therefore you will receive greater condemnation (Matt. 23:14; compare Mark 12:40).

While in private the religious elite were busy foreclosing on the homes of widows, in public they stood on street corners "and for a pretense" made long prayers.

The story of the Pharisee and the publican who went to the temple to pray (Luke 18:10–14) gives us added insight into this condemnation. Jesus' description of the Pharisee's prayer, in which the Pharisee thanked God he was not like "other men," portrays a person who was insensitive not only to the nature of prayer but also to his own hypocrisy.

—————————— ——————————

BIBLE BACKGROUND:

A PHARISEE'S PRAYER

Some have wondered if the prayer of the Pharisee recorded in Luke 18 accurately reflects the attitude of these very religious men. A prayer found in the Talmud (b. Ber. 28b) suggests that it does. The prayer reads,

I thank thee, O Lord, my God, that thou hast given me my lot with those who sit in the seat of learning, and not with those who sit at the street-corners; for I am early to work, and they are early to work; I am early to work on the words of the Torah, and they are early to work on things of no moment. I weary myself, and they weary themselves; I weary myself and profit thereby, while they weary themselves to no profit. I run and they run; I run toward the life of the Age to Come, and they run toward the pit of destruction.

This prayer as well as the prayer of the Pharisee in Jesus' parable expresses thanks to God for the benefits of dedication to Him. From Jesus' viewpoint, however, both prayers display a self-righteous attitude and a contempt for others that is out of harmony with God's love for human beings.

—————————— ——————————

Both Jesus' condemnation of the Pharisees and the story of the Pharisee at the temple remind us that there is a moral dimension to prayer. It is not just that the motives of the Pharisees were flawed. In private they foreclosed on "widow's houses"! Rather than show compassion for the needy, many of these religious men exploited them.

If we love others we will neither exploit them nor oppress them. Our private morality will be shaped by a love of mercy, not a love of money or reputation. We will have no need for pretending, to ourselves or before others, for our love for God will overflow in love for others.

This is what happened in the early church. And when love for God and others filled the fellowship, God's people were powerful in prayer (see Acts 4:31–35).

PRAYER AND HISTORY'S END

When Jesus shared His predictions about the future in answer to His disciples' questions (Matt. 24; Mark 13; Luke 21), he twice mentioned prayer. "And pray that your flight may not be in winter or on the Sabbath" (Matt. 24:20; compare Mark 13:18). "Take heed, watch and pray; for you do not know when the time is" (Mark 13:33; compare Luke 21:36 and Matt. 24:36–44).

The first of these instructions is directly linked to a future fall of Jerusalem. The second is a general statement of how believers should live their lives while waiting for Jesus to return.

Why do Mark and Luke both include prayer when reporting Jesus' encouragement to watch? The answer is that it is all too easy for us to be distracted from our service to God by other concerns. We are to keep our focus on God and His kingdom (Matt. 6:33), and daily communion with God in prayer will keep us fixed on Him.

PRAYER AND WEAKNESS

The night that Jesus prayed in Gethsemane He urged three of His disciples to watch and to pray with Him. Yet they were tired, and while waiting for Jesus they fell asleep. When Jesus found them sleeping He encouraged them with these words: "Watch and pray, lest you enter into temptation. The spirit indeed is willing, but the flesh is weak" (Matt. 26:41; compare Mark 14:38; Luke 22:40, 46).

In biblical times the normal position for prayer was standing. In times of extreme distress a person might fall on his face to pray, but normally one stood (see Luke 18:11, 13), often with upraised hands (1 Tim. 2:8). If the disciples had obeyed Jesus' command, they would have remained standing rather than sit on the ground.

We know that the disciples were concerned about Jesus and wanted to be supportive. But instead of remaining standing to pray, they sat on the ground and fell asleep. Their motives were good. But their flesh (here a reference to human limitations) was weak. Jesus knew it, and we need to recognize it too. We are limited, imperfect, and weak, and there is so much we want to be and do that we simply can't bring ourselves to accomplish.

It is fascinating that Jesus did not ask the disciples to pray for Him. They were to pray for *themselves*, "that you do not enter into temptation." The greatest challenge facing the disciples was their own weakness and their need for God's help.

Jesus' command to watch and pray reminds us first of all that obedience is vital if we are to overcome our human weaknesses. If the three disciples had obeyed Jesus and remained standing in prayer, they would not have fallen asleep. If they had prayed as Jesus told them, they might have responded differently to the events that followed. We must obey Jesus if we are not to fall victim to our own weaknesses.

Prayer was a vital element in Jesus' relationship with the Father.

And we must pray "lest you enter temptation."

In prayer we turn our eyes away from ourselves and our situation to focus on the Lord. We acknowledge our dependence on Him, and we draw on His strength.

A familiar Old Testament passage contains a promise that combines awareness of the weakness of the flesh and states the promise implied in the words, "watch and pray."

> He gives power to the weak,
> And to those who have no might He
>   increases strength.
> Even the youths shall faint and be weary,
> And the young men shall utterly fall,
> But those who wait on the LORD

> Shall renew their strength;
> They shall mount up with wings like
>   eagles,
> They shall run and not be weary,
> They shall walk and not faint
>   (Is. 40:29–31).

Today too we need to watch and pray. As we rely on the Lord, He will provide the strength we need to run and not be weary, to walk and not faint.

RECORDED PRAYERS OF JESUS

The Gospels frequently refer to the fact that Jesus slipped away for a time of private prayer. Luke's Gospel alone mentions Jesus' habit of prayer six times (Luke

3:21–22; 5:15–16; 6:12–13; 9:18; 9:28–29; 11:1). Even without knowing the specific content of Christ's prayers, the Gospels make it clear that prayer was vital to Him. Prayer, as well as at time for fellowship with the Father, was an expression of Christ's dependence of the Father as well as His need for guidance and support.

While we do not know the content of most of Christ's prayers, we do have several recorded in the Gospels, and we can learn much from each of them.

A PRAYER WHEN DISAPPOINTED

Jesus had been teaching and healing in Galilee for over a year. The crowds flocked to hear Him, but failed to welcome Him as the Messiah. Instead the same people who found fault with John for being too stern and distant found fault with Jesus for being accessible to sinners (Matt. 11:16–19).

On one occasion Jesus rebuked the cities where He had concentrated His ministry and warned them of the consequences of their failure to acknowledge Him (Matt. 11:20–27). The failure of that district to acknowledge Jesus as the promised Messiah had doomed its cities and towns. The nation would not welcome Jesus, but Christ made it clear that individuals who came to Him were welcome. The weary and the heavy-laden could find rest by trusting in Jesus, the Son of God (Matt. 11:28–30).

This is the context for the first recorded prayer of Jesus.

I thank You, Father, Lord of heaven and earth, that You have hidden these things from the wise and prudent and have revealed them to babes. Even so, Father, for so it seemed good in Your sight (Matthew 11:25, 26).

Jesus went on, addressing those who heard rather than speaking to God. "All things have been delivered to Me by My Father, and no one knows the Son except the Father. Nor does anyone know the Father except the Son, and the one to whom the Son wills to reveal Him" (Matt. 11:27).

The content of the prayer. The wording of this prayer is significant.

"I thank You, Father, Lord of heaven and earth." The word translated "thank" here and "praise" in other English versions is *exhomologoumai*. In Matthew 3:6 this word is rendered "confess" or "acknowledge." Used in reference to God it is best understood as an acknowledgement of who God is. We might render it, "I honor You, Father, Lord of heaven and earth."

Christ began His prayer by acknowledging the sovereignty of God the Father. The rejection of His own people hurt Jesus deeply, but Christ affirmed that His rejection was in accord with the purposes of God. Thus the experience called for praise rather than recrimination.

What an example for us to follow when we find ourselves disappointed by others about whom we care!

"You have hidden these things from the wise and prudent and have revealed them unto babes." The phrase "wise and prudent" is ironic. The generation that rejected Jesus considered itself wise, yet the people did not recognize the significance of the miracles Jesus performed. In contrast the "babes," who were looked down on by the "mature," were eager to learn from Jesus.

Jesus seemed to ascribe these reactions to God's activity of concealing and revealing. Could the people then be blamed for failure to recognize Jesus? To answer this question we need to note the reactions to John described in the context. John had warned his hearers that unless they repented there would be judgment. While some had responded to this warning and been baptized, most people did not. God's activity in concealing "these things" from the wise and understanding was an act of judgment on those who had *already rejected* the divine message delivered by John. Indeed, God's activity in revealing "these things" to babes was a gracious gift to those whose hearts were open to Him.

God may still conceal and reveal, but not to show favoritism. God has done what is right, and what "seemed good in Your sight."

Jesus' invitation. Jesus went on to affirm His own unique claims. "No one knows the Son except the Father." Only Jesus had the knowledge of God and the relationship with God that the wise imagined was possessed by all descendants of Abraham. "Nor does anyone know the Father except the Son, and the one to whom the Son wills to reveal Him." No person has access to God except through Jesus, who is history's sole revealer of the Father.

Yet Jesus followed this statement with an open invitation for people to come to Him and find rest. The invitation to the weary and burdened is open to us today. Whoever chooses to come to Jesus will find that he has also been chosen by Christ.

JESUS' PRAYER AT LAZARUS' TOMB

When word came that Jesus' friend Lazarus was ill, Christ waited two days before setting off to Bethany where Lazarus lived. When Christ arrived, Lazarus had been dead and had lain in his tomb for three days.

Jesus had been met by Lazarus' sisters, Mary and Martha. Jesus had reassured each, announcing that He Himself was the resurrection and the life. Yet the sisters never expected that Jesus was about to restore their brother to life.

Jesus went with the sisters to the tomb, and ordered the stone that closed its entrance removed. Then Jesus "lifted up His eyes" and offered this prayer:

Father, I thank You that You have heard Me. And I know that You always hear Me, but because of the people who are standing by I said this, that they may believe that You sent Me
(John 11:41, 42).

Having offered this prayer, Jesus cried out, "Lazarus, come forth!" and the dead man was restored to life.

The content of the prayer. This prayer, like the miracle that followed, was intended to call those who witnessed the event to faith in Him.

"I thank You that You have heard Me." Jesus had already communed with the Father concerning Lazarus, and His prayer that Lazarus might be raised had already been answered.

"I know that You always hear Me." R. H. Fuller, in *Interpreting the Miracles*, commented on this passage:

Jesus lives in constant prayer and communication with His Father. When He engages in vocal prayer He is not entering, as we do, from a state of non-praying into prayer. He is only giving overt expression to what is the ground and base of His life all along (p. 107).

God always hears Jesus, and this demonstrates Jesus' union with the Father and their shared identity as God.

"Because of the people who are standing by I said this." Jesus did not need to put His union with the Father to the test. His words were not uttered because of any need for confirmation of their relationship. Rather He spoke them so that the people standing by would grasp the significance of what they were about to witness. The prayer verbalized a relationship with God that was about to be confirmed by indisputable proof.

The significance of the prayer. While the content of the prayer explains the reason why Jesus verbalized it, one of Christ's sentences expresses a basic truth about

Christ's prayer life. For Jesus, prayer was not infrequent or sporadic. Christ lived His life in the presence of God the Father, fully aware of the Father every moment.

Any person who lives constantly in God's presence will naturally be immersed in prayer.

JESUS' PRAYER AT GETHSEMANE

The night before His crucifixion Jesus prayed at the garden of Gethsemane. Immediately after uttering this prayer Christ was taken by force, to be tried, beaten, and crucified. Each of the synoptic Gospels gives us a report of what happened there.

Then Jesus came with them to a place called Gethsemane, and said to the disciples, "Sit here while I go and pray over there." And He took with him Peter and the two sons of Zebedee, and He began to be sorrowful and deeply distressed. Then He said to them, "My soul is exceedingly sorrowful, even to death. Stay here and watch with Me."

He went a little farther and fell on His face and prayed, saying, "O My Father, if it is possible, let this cup pass from Me; nevertheless, not as I will, but as You will."

Then He came to the disciples and found them sleeping, and said to Peter, "What! Could you not watch with Me one hour? Watch and pray, lest you enter into temptation. The spirit indeed is willing, but the flesh is weak."

Again, a second time, He went away and prayed, saying, "O My Father, if this cup cannot pass away from Me unless I drink it, Your will be done." And He came and found them asleep again, for their eyes were heavy.

So He left them, went away again, and prayed the third time, saying the same words. Then He came to His disciples and said to them, "Are you still sleeping and resting? Behold, the hour is at hand, and the Son of Man is being betrayed into the hands of sinners. Rise, let us be going. See, My betrayer is at hand." (Matt. 26:36–46; compare Mark 14:32–42; Luke 22:39–46).

It's important to remember that Jesus' death was unique. Christ knew that He would soon face a moment when He would be entirely alone. Jesus was to be the true sacrificial lamb, and in that moment when He bore our sins Jesus would be forsaken even by the Father (Matt. 27:46). It's no wonder that Luke tells us that as Jesus prayed, "His sweat became like great drops of blood falling down to the ground" (Luke 22:44).

What then was the content of this anguished prayer?

The content of the prayer. Two things in this prayer merit our earnest attention.

"Let this cup pass from Me" (Matt. 26:39). Only a superficial reading of the Bible would lead a person to suggest that the "cup" Jesus longed to avoid was physical death. The imagery of a cup is often used in the Old Testament as a symbol of suffering and death and also as a symbol of God's wrath (see Ps. 11:6; Jer. 25:15, 16). But most importantly, a "cup" can indicate any experience a person might undergo.

Many suggest that what Jesus begged for was an alternative—any alternative—to the means of carrying out His mission of redemption. Yet Hebrews refers back to this incident and tells us that "He was heard because of His godly fear" (Heb. 5:7). This suggests that Jesus' prayer was answered in the affirmative. In this case the "cup" was neither death nor the bearing of our sins on the cross, but continuing to bear our sins endlessly. And what was the Father's answer? Resurrection!

"Nevertheless, not as I will, but as You will." Throughout His time on earth Jesus had gladly done the Father's will. Now Jesus faced the ultimate challenge. The almost unbearable pressure He felt is reflected in the anguish He displayed. Yet Jesus said, "Not my will, but Yours." In the ultimate act of submission Jesus purged our sin, providing all who believe with eternal salvation.

The significance of the prayer. It is fascinating that each of the Gospels reports that Christ offered essentially the same prayer three times. Why three prayers?

Submission to God's will is something we need to renew moment by moment. In Gethsemane Jesus provided an example of moment-by-moment obedience. He reminded us that our commitment to the Lord must be constantly renewed. Like Jesus, we need to affirm in every prayer, "Nevertheless, not my will, but Yours."

JESUS' HIGH PRIESTLY PRAYER

The longest of Jesus' recorded prayers is found in John 17, at the end of the Last Supper discourse. It is often called Christ's High Priestly prayer, for in it Jesus prayed for His disciples and for believers of every succeeding generation. Because of the length of this prayer, we need to look at it section by section.

Prayer for glorification (John 17:1–3). Jesus began His prayer with these words.

Father, the hour has come. Glorify Your Son, that Your Son also may glorify You, as You have given Him authority over all flesh, that He should give eternal life to as many as You have given Him. And this is eternal life, that they may know You, the only true God, and Jesus Christ whom You have sent. I have glorified You on the earth. I have finished the work which You gave Me to do. And now, O Father, glorify Me together with Yourself, with the glory which I had with You before the world was.

The hour has come (v. 1). The moment toward which Christ's mission on earth focused was at hand. The ultimate revelation of God's love and justice was about to be given.

That He should give eternal life (v. 2). God is glorified by the provision of eternal life. Only God could find a solution to the problem of human sinfulness that was both loving and just.

I have glorified you on the earth (v. 4). Jesus looks back on His incarnation and sums up His accomplishment. Every word and deed of Jesus revealed more of the Father and His glory.

With the glory which I had with You before the world was (v. 5). The Incarnation called for Christ's self-emptying. On His return to heaven Jesus would again fully manifest the glory that was His from eternity past.

Prayer for Jesus' disciples (John 17:6–19). In this lengthy section of the prayer, three themes are developed: (1) Jesus' reasons for praying for the disciples, verses 6–11. (2) Prayer that the disciples might be kept, verses 11–16. And (3), prayer that they might be sanctified with Jesus, verses 17–19. While this section of the prayer was specifically for those who shared the Last Supper with Jesus, the prayer has application to us as well.

Jesus' reasons for praying for the disciples (John 17:6–11). Throughout this section Jesus referred to "the world." The particular word Jesus used, *kosmos*, has a distinctive theological cast. In John's writings particularly, the "world" refers to human society as shaped by humankind's sinful nature. The "world" is that system of beliefs and values which grows out of and is driven by sin. In saving us, Jesus delivers us from the world, transferring us to His own kingdom, where we are to be motivated by desires that grow out of our relationship with the Lord.

I have manifested Your name to the men whom You have given Me out of the world. They were Yours, You gave them to Me, and they have kept Your word. Now they have known that all things which You have given Me are from You. For I have given to them the words which You have given Me; and they have received them, and have known surely that I came forth from You, and they have believed that You sent Me.

I pray for them. I do not pray for the world but for those whom you have given Me, for they are Yours. And all Mine are Yours, and Yours are Mine, and I am glorified in them. Now I am no longer in the world, but these are in the world, and I come to You (John 17:6–11).

Several things in this prayer clarify what makes the disciples—and all believers—so special.

- They are God's gifts to Jesus (v. 6).
- Jesus has revealed to them God's name, including His nature and character (v. 6).
- They have welcomed and responded to the Word Christ brought them (v. 8).
- They have acknowledged that Jesus was sent by God (v. 8).

Jesus prayed here only "for those whom You have given Me" and not for the world. Yet Jesus left the disciples in the world that they might minister, as He had, and deliver many others from Satan's grasp.

Prayer that the disciples might be kept (John 17:11–16). The world that was hostile to Jesus will be hostile to Jesus' disciples. So Christ prayed that the Father would keep them from the evil one when Jesus returned to heaven.

Holy Father, keep through Your name those whom You have given Me, that they may be one as We are. While I was with them in the world, I kept them in Your name. Those whom You gave Me I have kept; and none of them is lost except the son of perdition, that the Scripture might be fulfilled. But now I come to You, and these things I speak in the world, that they may have My joy fulfilled in themselves. I have given them Your word; and the world has hated them because they are not of the world, just as I am not of the world. I do not pray that You should take them out of the world, but that You should keep them from the evil one. They are not of the world, just as I am not of the world (John 17:11–16).

Several phrases in this passage fascinate us.

1. "That they may be one as we are." Jesus is not praying for an institutional unity, or even oneness between Christians. The oneness Jesus is speaking of here is that oneness with the Father that Jesus knew so well. It is an experiential oneness that is known when we live our life in fellowship with God and in submission to His will.

2. "None was lost except the son of perdition." Judas was lost not because of any failure by Christ but because he followed his own warped and twisted nature, as the Scripture had predicted. Judas took sides with Satan against the Lord.

3. "The world has hated them." Jesus gives us two reasons for the world's hostility. Jesus gave them God's word, and the identity of the disciples is now rooted in heaven, even as Christ's is. The hatred of the world is instinctive, a deep hostility directed toward those who are different and whose difference exposes and threatens the world's way of life.

Prayer that the disciples might be sanctified (John 17:17–19). The key word in these verses is the word translated "sanctify." The word means "to set aside from ordinary use and consecrate for God's use."

Sanctify them by Your truth. Your word is truth. As You sent Me into the world, I also have sent them into the world. And for their sakes I sanctify Myself, that they also may be sanctified by the truth.

Christ's disciples were no longer to live by the world's passions, but were to live in the realm of God's truth, guided by His Word.

Prayer that all believers might be one (John 17:20–23). This is undoubtedly the most misunderstood element in Jesus' prayer.

Many people have viewed it as a call to organizational unity. Many sermons have been preached and many well-intentioned movements have been launched based on a misinterpretation of these verses.

I do not pray for these alone, but also for those who will believe in Me through their word; that they all may be one, as You, Father, are in Me, and I in you; that they also may be one in Us, that the world may believe that You sent Me. And the glory which You gave Me I have given them, that they may be one just as We are one: I in them, and You in Me; that they may be made perfect in one, and that the world may know that You have sent Me; and have loved them as You have loved Me.

Jesus asked that the disciples might be one "as You, Father, are in Me, and I in You" (v. 21). The unity of which Jesus spoke is organic. It is a unity which believers can have with the Lord, not with one another. This oneness is clearly defined in the text.

- "As You, Father, are in Me, and I in You" (v. 21).
- "That they also may be one in Us" (v. 21)
- "I in them, and You in Me" (v. 23).

What Christ described here is a mutual indwelling, patterned on the relationship with God that Jesus experienced during His life on earth.

The outcome of a life lived in such intimate relationship with God is that Jesus will be seen in us, a witness to the world that God truly has sent Jesus. It's not enough for oth-

ers to hear about Jesus. They need to see Jesus in us. As we live in union with our Lord, God's glory will be on display.

Prayer that believers might be with Him (John 17:24-26). The end of Jesus' prayer echoes its beginning.

Father, I desire that they also whom You gave Me may be with Me where I am, that they may behold My glory which You have given Me; for You loved Me before the foundation of the world. O righteous Father! The world has not known You, but I have known You; and these have known that You sent Me. And I have declared to them Your name, and will declare it, that the love with which You loved Me may be in them, and I in them.

The wonder of the Lord's high priestly prayer is that it has been answered. The Holy Spirit unites us to Jesus Christ. No less than eighty-seven times in eighty different verses, the New Testament speaks of believers being "in Christ." Through this mystical union we have with Jesus, we are kept, empowered, and enabled to live for Him in this world.

Prayer is one of the major themes in the teaching of Christ. Jesus gave His disciples many precious prayer promises. He instructed them how to pray, and answered our most pressing questions about prayer. And through His own prayers recorded in the Gospels, Jesus invites us to enter into His most holy relationship with the Father, and sense the deepest meaning of prayer.

THE SABBATH CONTROVERSIES

Three groups of people appear in the Gospel accounts of Jesus' life on earth. One of these groups is composed of ordinary people, the masses who came to wonder at Jesus' miracles and to ponder His teachings. A second group is made up of just twelve men, whom Jesus chose to train for leadership. Most of Christ's time was spent in ministry to these two groups.

But there's another group that we meet again and again in the Gospels. This is the religious elite, the spiritual authorities. They are called by various names: Pharisees, Sadducees, chief priests, scribes, and lawyers (teachers of the law), the first two sects representing different points of view within Judaism, and the others representing priests and professional students of Scripture. But they were united in one thing. They were suspicious of Jesus. The more popular Jesus became, the more hostile the religious elite became to Him. And many of Jesus' most powerful teachings grew out of confrontations with these men

who ultimately demanded that Jesus be put to death.

In a way, the conflict between Jesus and the elite was bound to happen. The elite enjoyed influence and moral authority and, in the case of the Sadducees, wealth as well. The elite also controlled access to influence in their society. Many of the power positions were passed down from father to son. And anyone who sought to become a teacher of the Law had to be trained by one of the elite before he would be acknowledged as a teacher himself. When Jesus appeared and was acclaimed a prophet, He was perceived by the elite as a possible threat to their power and position. The more popular Jesus became, the more worried and antagonistic the elite became. And as it became clear that Jesus' actions and His teaching challenged the very approach to Scripture on which their power over ordinary people rested, antagonism became hostility and eventually hardened to become a firm resolve to see Jesus dead.

Many Pharisees were easily identifiable from their dress.

❖

MEET THE ELITE

First-century Judaism was marked by the existence of several sects, even as Christianity is marked by the existence of various denominations.

THE SECTS OF FIRST-CENTURY JUDAISM

The sects whose members were part of the elite in first-century Judaism were the Pharisees and the Sadducees. Josephus adds a third sect that we know about today through the Dead Sea Scrolls, but which is not mentioned in the Gospels. This third sect, the Essenes, was a monastic group whose members had withdrawn from society to await the Messiah. Having rejected worldly power, they were not actively involved in the conflict with Jesus.

A Jewish general, Josephus, who went over to the Romans, describes the sects in a book on the Jewish–Roman war that led to the destruction of the temple in A.D. 70.

At this time there were three sects among the Jews, who had different opinions concerning Jewish actions. The one was called the sect of the Pharisees, another the sect of the Sadducees, and the other the sect of the Essenes. Now for the Pharisees, they say that some actions, but not all, are the work of Fate [e. g., divine providence], and some of them are in our own power, and that they are liable to fate, but are not caused by fate. But the sect of the Essenes affirm that fate governs all things, and that nothing befalls men but what is according to determination. And for the Sadducees, they take away all fate, and say there is no such thing, and that the events of human affairs are not at its disposal, but they suppose that all our actions are in our own power. (*War,* 13:5)

While Josephus focuses on one theological issue, there were many other ways in which the first-century sects differed.

THE PHARISEES

The Pharisees had the greatest influence with the ordinary people in the Jewish homeland. It has been estimated that there were only about 6,000 members of this group in Christ's day. Yet they were held in such regard that they were able to force the Sadducees, who controlled the temple worship, to adjust temple rituals to the Pharisees' interpretations.

The Pharisees' influence derived from their reputation for piety. Most members of this sect were not rabbis or teachers of the law, but rather relatively well-to-do businessmen, who dedicated themselves to the practice of their religion. Josephus describes them this way in his *Antiquities:*

The Pharisees simplify their standard of living, making no concession to luxury. They follow the guidance of that which their doctrine has selected and transmitted as good, attaching the chief importance to the observance of those commandments which it has seen fit to dictate to them. They show respect and deference to their elders, nor do they rashly presume to contradict their proposals.

Though they postulate that everything is brought about by fate, still they do not deprive the human will of the pursuit of what is in man's power, since it was God's pleasure that there should be a fusion and that the will of man with his virtue and vice should be admitted to the council-chamber of fate. They believe that souls have power to survive death and there are rewards and punishments under the earth for those who have led lives of virtue or vice; eternal imprisonment is the lot of evil souls, while the good souls receive an easy passage to a new life.

Because of these views they are, as a matter of fact, extremely influential among the townsfolk; and all prayers and sacred rites of divine worship are performed according to their exposition. This is the great tribute that the inhabitants of the cities, by practicing the highest ideals both in their way of living and in their doctrine, have paid to the excellence of the Pharisees (*Antiquities* 18:12–15).

In another place Josephus comments on the Pharisees' influence: "The Sadducees have the confidence of the wealthy alone but no following among the populace, while the Pharisees have the support of the masses" (*Antiquities* 13:298).

BIBLE BACKGROUND:

NOT ALL PHARISEES WERE PHARISEES!

The Gospels tend to portray the Pharisees in the worst possible light. And surely many if not most members of that sect were offended by Jesus, and felt threatened by Him. Yet even in Jesus' day people made a distinction between Pharisees, identifying seven types.

- The Shoulder Pharisee wore good deeds on his shoulders so all could see and admire him.
- The Wait-a-Little Pharisee put off good deeds until tomorrow.

- The Bruised Pharisee covered his eyes to keep from seeing any woman he might meet on the street—and ran into walls!
- The Hump-Backed Pharisee walked bent over in a show of false humility.
- The Ever-Reckoning Pharisee kept on adding up his good deeds to make sure they exceeded his bad deeds.
- The Fearing Pharisee was terrified of God's anger and moved to do right out of fear.
- The God-Loving Pharisee lived to please God and to serve others.

The existence of these categories reminds us how difficult it is to fool everyone all of the time. Yet the fact that the Pharisees were so influential suggests that most were sincere in their commitment to what they believed.

THE SADDUCEES

As noted by Josephus, the Sadducees had influence with the wealthy, but not with the masses. The power base of the Sadducees was the temple, and the chief priests and other temple functionaries were Sadducees. As members of the wealthy upper class the Sadducees were the most comfortable with Roman rule and with the Hellenization of Palestine.

While Rome ruled its empire, the culture of the empire was Greek rather than Roman. Greek was the common language of the Roman world, and the values expressed in Greek culture dominated. Even in Jerusalem itself there were *gymnasia* where physical training and athletics were practiced in the nude, and a *hypodrome* where races and circuses were held. A significant number of upper class and wealthy Jews were eager to Hellenize their children, a choice which further undermined the influence of the Sadducees with the masses. In fact, in later writings the

Sadducces were charged with attempting to corrupt Jewish life by introducing Greek ways. Still, in the time of Christ and afterward, the Sadducees retained a large block of members in the Sanhedrin, the ruling body of the Jews (see Acts 23:6–11).

Unfortunately, the only writings that survive from the first century express the views of the Pharisees and early Christians. We do know, however, that the Sadducees favored cooperation with the Romans and some assimilation of Hellenism. Doctrinally, the Sadducees denied the existence of angels and bodily resurrection. They believed that God is utterly transcendent and above all human concerns. Because God has no interest in human actions He neither rewards nor punishes. The Sadducees accepted the five books of Moses as authoritative, but did not accept the other books of the Old Testament. And while the Pharisees held that interpretations of the rabbis of biblical texts constituted an oral Torah that had the same authority as Scripture itself, the Sadducees rejected the oral Torah of the Pharisees entirely.

It is fascinating that these two very different sects, whose members were constantly at odds with each other, were united in their determination to rid their land and their religion of Jesus, the Messiah.

THE CHIEF PRIESTS

In the first century the priesthood was divided into "ordinary priests" and temple officials. The ordinary priests lived and worked in their own villages, coming to Jerusalem to serve in the temple only two weeks each year.

The chief priests lived in Jerusalem the entire year and administered temple affairs. These chief priests organized and supervised the Levites who worked in the temple, administered temple funds, saw to the temple's distribution of tithes to the ordinary priests and to the poor, licensed the merchants who bought and sold in the temple courts, and controlled all temple activities. The chief priests were Sadducees, and control of the temple provided their power base. It also provided much of their wealth. Jewish writings from this period describe the family of the high priest of Jesus' day as consumed by avarice, and condemn the family for defrauding the poor who came to the temple to worship.

THE SCRIBES

After the return of the Jews from exile in Bablyon in the sixth century B.C., a class of professional students of God's Law developed. These were the scribes, also called "teachers of the law" in the Gospels. Another term, *rabbi*, also means "teacher," but in the Gospels is only used when addressing Jesus.

As teachers of the Law, scribes trained apprentices, their disciples, who were expected to master what was taught and to transmit it in exact form to the next generation. By New Testament times this training was open to members of every social class, from priest and merchant to day laborer.

Scribes also served on the Sanhedrin, which was the supreme religious and secular court in Judea and to whose rulings Jews throughout the Roman empire were subject. Josephus indicates that most scribes sided with the Pharisees, although the phrase "scribes of the Pharisees" (Acts 23:9) indicates that some scribes were associated with other parties.

While the scribes had made a major contribution by carefully transmitting the biblical text, their interpretations of that text came to be considered by the Pharisees as an "oral Torah," to be given as much and at times even more weight than the Scriptures themselves.

BIBLE BACKGROUND:

IN PRAISE OF THE SCRIBES

By the first century, scribes were viewed with the utmost respect in Judaism. The book of Ecclesiasticus, from around 200 B.C., praises the scribe and gives us some insight into his role in Judaism.

If the great Lord is willing,
  he will be filled with the spirit of
  understanding;
he will pour forth words of wisdom,
  and give thanks to the Lord in prayer.
He will direct his counsel and knowledge
  aright,
  and meditate on his secrets.
He will reveal instruction in his teaching,
  and will glory in the law of the
    Lord's covenant.
Many will praise his understanding,
  and it will never be blotted out;
His memory will not disappear,
  and his name will live through all
  generations.
Nations will declare his wisdom,
  and the congregation will proclaim his
  praise;
If he lives long, he will leave a name
  greater than a thousand,
And if he goes to rest, it is enough for him.
                    Ecclesiasticus 39:6–11

We can readily understand how those who had achieved the position of scribes, and who expected to be remembered for generations, would react when Jesus challenged, as He certainly did, the oral traditions they had transmitted and the interpretations on which their hope of lasting fame depended!

With this brief background into first-century sects and thinking about religion, we can better understand the controversies which developed as Pharisee and Sadducee, scribes and teachers of the Law, were driven to confront Jesus Christ.

CONFLICTS AND CONTROVERSY

The conflicts between Jesus and the religious elite focused on an apparently simple issue. Jesus did not acknowledge the traditions that had been established by "the elders"—those scribes whose legal interpretations and applications of Scripture had come to assume the force of divine law itself. In a series of events recorded in the Gospels we see how important this issue was to the religious elite, and how distorted their understanding of their ancient faith had become.

Eight incidents of conflict with the scribes and Pharisees are associated with Jesus' ministry prior to the turning point, when Jesus began to speak of His coming death and to focus on instruction of His disciples. Each incident is recorded in at least two of the synoptic Gospels, and frequently reported in the same order. As we look at these incidents we can better understand the reason for the hostility of the Pharisee party in particular.

JESUS ESTABLISHES HIS AUTHORITY

This incident is reported in Mark 2:1–12, Matthew 9:2–8, and Luke 5:17–26. These accounts parallel each other so closely that it's clear that they refer to a single incident. Matthew's account reads as follows.

Then behold, they brought to Him a paralytic lying on a bed. When Jesus saw their faith, He said to the paralytic, "Son, be of good cheer; your sins are forgiven you."

At once some of the scribes said within themselves, "This Man blasphemes!"

But Jesus, knowing their thoughts, said, "Why do you think evil in your hearts? For which is easier, to say, 'Your sins are forgiven you,' or to

Jesus' healing of the paralytic established His authority to forgive sins.

❖

say, 'Arise and walk'? But that you may know that the Son of Man has power on earth to forgive sins,"—then He said to the paralytic, "Arise, take up your bed, and go to your house." And he arose and departed to his house.

Now when the multitudes saw it, they marveled and glorified God, who had given such power to men.

Luke adds "and Pharisees" to the scribes who, Jesus said, were thinking evil in their hearts.

The choice. This first recorded incident of confrontation with the scribes and Pharisees served to establish Jesus' identity and His claim of authority.

The silent objection raised by the scribes and Pharisees was well taken. Who *can* forgive sins but God only? At the same time, the thought itself was "evil." Each of the Gospels reports a number of miracles

that Jesus had performed before the incident with the paralyzed man. Jesus had cast out evil spirits (Mark 1:23–28) and had "healed many who were sick with various diseases" (vv. 33–34). He had in fact been preaching in synagogues "throughout all Galilee, and casting out demons" (v. 39), and was so well known by the time Jesus healed the paralyzed man that Jesus "could no longer openly enter the city," yet even then "they came to Him from every direction."

It was clear from the miracles and exorcisms that Jesus had already performed that He acted with an authority that could only have been given to Him by God. Even Nicodemus, a member of the Sanhedrin who came to Jesus by night, admitted that "we know that You are a teacher come from God; for no one can do these signs that You do unless God is with him" (John 3:2). The thought of the scribes and Pharisees, that Jesus spoke blasphemy, was "evil" in that it contradicted what they already must have known: that whether or not they understood what Christ said, He was God's messenger and as such they were obligated to hear Him and accept His word.

Knowing their thoughts, Jesus then posed a simple question. Would it be easier for a person to say "Your sins are forgiven," or to say "Arise and walk"? The answer of course is that it is easier to say "Your sins are forgiven." Jesus could *claim* that the sins of the paralytic were forgiven, but there was no objective proof that such a transaction had taken place. But if Jesus said, "Arise and walk," there could be no mistaking His authority. If the man did not arise, Jesus could be dismissed as a charlatan. If the man did arise and walk, there was proof that Christ spoke with God's own authority, and they would know that "the Son of Man has power [literally, 'authority'] on earth to forgive sins."

The paralytic did arise, pick up the pallet on which his friends had carried him to Jesus, and walked home. And while the onlookers praised God, subsequent events would show that the scribes and Pharisees were unmoved and unconvinced.

What is your authority? The issue of authority is critical in understanding the conflict between Jesus and the scribes and Pharisees. Christ came and demonstrated His authority by word and by deed. Yet the scribes and Pharisees refused to accept the authority of Jesus. The reason for this is that these religious men were convinced that Scripture, as interpreted and applied by the scribes who had gone before them, was to be their sole authority. And they would allow nothing to shake this conviction.

We've already mentioned one reason why the scribes and Pharisees were so invested in this position. The Pharisees had pinned their hope of heaven and their reputation as pious individuals on the fact that they were rigorous in keeping the Law, as it was traditionally applied. The scribes' position in society and their hope of lasting fame was based on the value future generations would place in their interpretations. Both groups simply had too much to lose to even consider any other authority than the one on which they had quite literally built their lives!

This unshakable conviction that the Scripture as interpreted by previous rabbis was the sole authority is expressed in a fascinating tractate recounting a debate that supposedly took place late in the first century A.D. The rabbis at Jamnia were arguing whether or not an oven constructed in sections was a utensil and thus subject to the laws of household purity. The debate recorded in *bBaba Mezia 59b* hinges on the fact that they refused to consider any authority other than the written and oral law! The text describes the debate.

On that day, Rabbi Eliezer replied with every legal argument in the world, but the rabbis would not accept them. Thereupon, he said to them, "If the halachah is on my side, let that carob tree show it!" The carob suddenly uprooted itself and flew through the air one hundred cubits—some say four hundred cubits. They said to him, "No bringing of proof from a carob tree!" He said to them, "If the halachah is on my side, then may that stream of water show it." The stream of water turned around, and flowed backward. They said to him, "No bringing proof from streams of water!" He turned and said to them, "If the halachah is on my side, may the walls of the House of Study we are in show it!" The walls of the House of Study leaned inward, as if about to fall. Rabbi Yehosua rebuked the walls, saying to them, "If the sages battle each other over halachah, why do you interfere?" They did not fall out of honor for Rabbi Yehosua, nor did they straighten up out of honor for Rabbi Eliezer; they continue crookedly standing to this day. Again Eliezer said to them, "If the halachah is on my side, let Heaven show it!" A Voice from Heaven cried out, "What do the rest of you have against Rabbi Eliezer? The halachah is on his side in everything!" Rabbi Yehosua leaped to his feet and quoted (Deut. 30:12), "It is not in Heaven."

What did Yehosua mean by saying, "It is not in Heaven"? Rabbi Yeremiah explained, "Since the Torah has already been given from Mount Sinai, we do not pay heed any longer to a Heavenly Voice."

No wonder when commitment to the written and oral Torah was so complete that Jesus' restoration of the paralytic left the scribes and Pharisees unmoved.

JESUS EATS WITH TAX COLLECTORS AND SINNERS

The second incident mentioned in the Gospel accounts of conflict with the scribes and Pharisees is recorded in Mark 2:15–18, Matthew 9:11–13, and Luke 5:27–32. Luke describes the occasion.

After these things He went out and saw a tax collector named Levi, sitting at the tax office. And He said to Him, "Follow Me." So he left all, rose up, and followed Him.

Then Levi gave Him a great feast in his own house. And there were a great number of tax collectors and others who sat down with them. And the scribes and the Pharisees complained against His disciples, saying, "Why do you eat and drink with tax collectors and sinners?"

Jesus answered and said to them, "Those who are well have no need of a physician, but those who are sick. I have not come to call the righteous, but sinners, to repentance."

In Matthew's account he makes it clear that the scribes and Pharisees challenged the disciples to explain why their Master ate with such people. It was undoubtedly safer to challenge the disciples than it was to challenge Jesus!

Clean versus unclean. One of the major features of Old Testament law is the distinction it makes between what is ritually unclean and what is ritually clean. The book of Leviticus particularly identifies clean and unclean foods as well as practices that make a person unclean. For instance, an issue of menstrual blood made a woman unclean for the duration of her period, as an issue of semen rendered a male unclean. A person who touched a dead body became unclean, as did a person with an infectious skin disease. In fact, uncleanness was transmitted by touch, so that anyone who touched an unclean person or thing became unclean himself.

Generally uncleanness was removed with the passage of time and cleansing with water, although some kinds of uncleanness called for removal by a blood sacrifice.

Like other Old Testament rules, those governing ritual cleanness and uncleanness were intended to impress on the Israelites that they were God's own people, called to be different from the peoples surrounding them. These reminders were underlined by the fact that a person in an unclean state was not allowed to participate in public worship.

By the first century the scribes and Pharisees had extended the concept to include certain types of persons. In Jesus'

day persons with certain occupations, such as shepherds or tanners, were considered unclean. Tax collectors, who collaborated with the Roman government, were unclean. Prostitutes, Samaritans, and all Gentiles were unclean. The pious Pharisee would not enter the home of a person thought to be unclean, for fear of contamination; and some sought to avoid even stepping in the shadow of anyone deemed unclean.

We can understand then the complaint of the scribes and Pharisees who accused Jesus' disciples of sitting down in Levi's house to eat with "tax collectors and sinners."

A conflict of values. It's clear from Jesus' reply that there was a vast difference between His values and those of the scribes and Pharisees. The scribes and Pharisees viewed tax collectors and sinners as unclean, and thus to be condemned and avoided. Jesus viewed tax collectors and sinners as spiritually sick and in need of a physician. Jesus sought out sinners; the scribes and Pharisees tried to avoid them.

Matthew adds an important phrase to the reply that Jesus gave when challenged by the scribes and Pharisees. "But go and learn what this means: 'I desire mercy and not sacrifice.' For I did not come to call the righteous, but sinners, to repentance" (9:13).

That phrase, "I desire mercy and not sacrifice," is taken from Hosea 6:6, and is part of God's lament over Israel. God's people have failed Him, their faithfulness is as insubstantial as a morning fog or like the "early dew it goes away" (6:4).

Jesus' quote from Hosea must have called to mind a parallel passage in Micah 6 that deals with this same issue. There the prophet Micah writes,

With what shall I come before the LORD,
And bow myself before the High God?
Shall I come before Him with burnt
    offerings,

Why did the Scriptures say, "I desire mercy and not sacrifice"?

With calves a year old?
Will the LORD be pleased with thousands
    of rams,
Ten thousand rivers of oil?
Shall I give my firstborn for my
    transgression,
The fruit of my body for the sin of my
    soul?
He has shown you, O man, what is good;
And what does the LORD require of you
But to do justly,
To love mercy,
And to walk humbly with your God?
                Micah 6:6–8

What has happened to God's people?
Certainly during and after the return from
captivity the Jews placed a renewed emphasis on the role of the Scriptures in the life of
God's covenant people. How then have
they strayed so far from the mercy and concern for others the Scripture calls for and
which Jesus demonstrated in eating with
tax collectors and sinners?

God gave the answer to this question
through the prophet Isaiah. He had spoken
to Israel a word that could cause the weary
to rest, and announced that "this is the
refreshing." But God's people would not
hear. So the Lord announces that,

The word of the LORD was to them,
"Precept upon precept, precept upon
    precept,
Line upon line, line upon line,
Here a little, there a little,"

That they might go and fall backward,
  and be broken
And snared and caught.
                    Isaiah 28:13

This was exactly what the word of the Lord had become to the scribes and Pharisees of Jesus' day, who argued violently over whether or not an oven made in separate pieces was a utensil and who condemned rather than cared for the lost and hurting.

What a contrast in values! And what a warning for us! Like Jesus we are to be physicians in our society, ever seeking to help and to heal sinners, rather than those who stand off and condemn, fearful that in our supposed holiness we might be condemned.

Jesus, and the scribes and Pharisees, represent two very different approaches to religion and to faith. It's no wonder that the religious elite of Christ's day felt threatened by Him. They were! For everything Jesus said and did exposed the fallacies on which their lives and reputations had been constructed.

DARING TO BE DIFFERENT

One of the practices that the Pharisees assumed established their spiritual superiority was that of fasting. In New Testament times, as in Muslim lands today, fasting meant refraining from food (and sometimes drink) from dawn to sunset. In the first century, the Pharisees tended to fast on Mondays and Thursdays, and apparently John's disciples also practiced fasting as a spiritual discipline. Each of the three synoptic Gospels tells of an occasion when Jesus was asked why He did not have His disciples follow this practice (Matt. 9:14–17; Mark 2:18–22; Luke 5:33–39). Mark's account reads as follows.

The disciples of John and of the Pharisees were fasting. Then they came and said to Him, "Why do the disciples of John and of the Pharisees fast, but Your disciples do not fast?"

And Jesus said to them, "Can the friends of the bridegroom fast while the bridegroom is with them? As long as they have the bridegroom with them they cannot fast. But the days will come when the bridegroom will be taken away from them, and then they will fast in those days.

"No one sews a piece of unshrunk cloth on an old garment; or else the new piece pulls away from the old, and the tear is made worse. And no one puts new wine into old wineskins; or else the new wine bursts the wineskins, the wine is spilled, and the wineskins are ruined. But new wine must be put into new wineskins."

Christ's response was twofold. First, fasting was inappropriate for His disciples. Jesus was present with them, and fasting—a sign of grief or mourning—would be as out of place for them as it would be at a wedding feast! Jesus' disciples would know grief when Christ was taken away, an allusion to those days between His crucifixion and resurrection. But now it was time for them to rejoice.

Jesus offered another reason as well. Fasting was a carryover from Old Covenant times, a symbol of that covenant's failure to produce the fruit of a righteous life (see Zech. 7). Jesus had not come to patch up the old but, as His Sermon on the Mount established, to introduce something entirely new! The forms of the old religion, like worn out garments or stiff and cracked wineskins, would not be patched but replaced by the Son of God.

BIBLE BACKGROUND:
HARD SAYINGS OF JESUS

"And no one, having drunk old wine, immediately desires new, for he says, 'The old is better.'" (Luke 5:39).

Luke reports that Jesus added this observation to His comment on the new wineskins. People will naturally prefer "old wine," which has had a chance to age, to new wine (grape juice). But as time passes, the new wine matures, and the old wine turns to vinegar. As time passes, all would see the superiority of God's new revelation in Christ which both fulfilled and superceded the old.

FOCUS ON THE SABBATH

As He continued to teach and heal, criticism of Jesus began to focus on His failure to observe the rules that governed Sabbath observance. Again all three of the synoptic Gospels report the incident (Matt. 12:1–8; Mark 2:23–28; Luke 6:1–5).

Now it happened that He went through the grainfields on the Sabbath; and as they went His disciples began to pluck the heads of grain. And the Pharisees said to Him, "Look, why do they do what is not lawful on the Sabbath?" (Mark 2:23, 24; compare Matt. 12:1, 2 and Luke 6:1, 2).

What is lawful on the Sabbath? To understand this and other Sabbath controversies we need to know something about the relationship between the Old Testament command to "remember the Sabbath day and keep it holy" (Ex. 20:8) and the rules that governed first-century Sabbath observance. The command continues,

Six days you shall labor and do all your work, but the seventh day is the Sabbath of the LORD your God. In it you shall do no work, you, nor your son, nor your daughter, nor your male servant, nor your female servant, nor your cattle, nor your stranger who is within your gates. For in six days the LORD made the heavens and the earth, the sea, and all that is in them, and rested the seventh day. Therefore the LORD blessed the Sabbath day and hallowed it (Exod 20:9–11).

The commandment made it clear that the seventh day was to be a day of rest, on which no one was to work. But what concerned the rabbis was, What does it mean to "work"? And so the scholars of Judaism set out to define "work," and from that definition to determine what could and what could not be done on the Sabbath.

The rabbis' goal was to "build a hedge around the law." That is, their approach to the 660-some positive and negative commandments they found in the Old Testament was to carefully define every *implied* violation, so that a pious Jew would not break one of the commandments inadvertently. From the simple command to refrain from work on the Sabbath the rabbis derived such rules as

- the maximum weight to be carried on the Sabbath was about the weight of a teaspoon
- it was work to tie a knot on the Sabbath
- a tailor sinned if he carried a needle in his robe on the Sabbath

Later rabbis argued over whether a person who wore false teeth or wore a wooden leg broke the Sabbath!

Writing in *The Jewish People in the First Century* (Fortress Press, 1976) S. Safri, an Israeli scholar, observes that "so many of these [Sabbath] restrictions had no real basis in the Torah that an early mishnaic text could say: 'The rules for the Sabbath are like mountains hanging by a hair, for Scripture is scanty and the rules are many'" (vol. 2, p. 804).

Yet it was rules created from such scanty Scripture that the Pharisees referred to when they accused Jesus' disciples of doing what was not "lawful" to do on the Sabbath. They were not violating Scripture; they violated rules invented by men!

Jesus rejected the traditional interpretation of Sabbath law.

BIBLE BACKGROUND:

THE MISHNAH ON SABBATH

The Mishnah is an important six-point code of rules intended to govern the daily life and worship of the Jewish people. It is in the form of sayings of rabbis from the late first and second centuries A.D., and reflects the approach taken by teachers of the law in the time of Jesus. The following quote is taken from the Mishnah's extensive discussions of Sabbath-keeping.

A. The generative categories of acts of labor [prohibited on the Sabbath] are forty less one:

B. (1) He who sews, (2) ploughs, (3) reaps, (4) binds sheaves, (5) threshes, (6) win-nows, (7) selects [fit from unfit produce], (8) grinds, (9) sifts, (10) bakes;

C. (12) he who shears wool, (13) washes it, (14) beats it, (15) washes it;

D. (16) spins, (17) weaves;

E. (18) makes two loops, (19) weaves two threads, (20) separates two threads;

F. (21) ties, (22) unties;

G. (23) sews two stitches, (24) tears in order to sew two stitches;

H. (25) he who traps a deer, (26) slaughters it, (27) flays it, (28) salts it, (29) cures its hide, (30) scrapes it, and (31) cuts it up; (32) he who writes two letters, (33) erases two letters in order to write two letters;

J. (34) he who builds, (35) tears down;

K. (36) he who puts out a fire, (37) kindles a fire;

L. (38) he who hits with a hammer; (39) he who transports an object from one domain to another —

M. lo, these are the forty generative acts of labor less one.

Jesus' response. First we should note that Moses' law specifically permitted a traveler to pluck and eat grain that grew alongside a path (Deut. 23:25). This was part of the Old Testament's provision for the poor and needy. So the disciples had not violated any Scripture, nor were they "stealing" from the owners of the fields. But in plucking grain to eat they were violating the scribes and Pharisees' ruling against harvesting (see B.3 in "The Mishnah on the Sabbath").

Jesus answered the critics in a most surprising way. He said,

Have you never read what David did when he was in need and hungry, he and those with him; how he went into the house of God in the days of Abiathar the high priest, and ate the showbread, which is not lawful to eat except for the priests, and also gave some to those who were with him (Mark 2:25, 26)?

Matthew 12 adds another illustration:

Or have you not read in the law that on the Sabbath the priests in the temple profane the Sabbath, and are blameless?

Yet I say to you that in this place there is One greater than the temple. But if you had known what this means, "I desire mercy and not sacrifice," you would not have condemned the guiltless. For the Son of Man is Lord even of the Sabbath (Matt. 12:5–8).

Mark 2:27 provides one additional remark: "The Sabbath was made for man, and not man for the Sabbath."

Robert C. Girard, in volume 1 of his *Life of Christ* (Starburst Publishers, 2000, p. 178), notes that Jesus gave six reasons for disagreeing with the Pharisees.

First, Jesus pointed out that David had violated a law actually inscribed in the Pentateuch and was not punished for it. Fleeing from King Saul, David had taken consecrated bread that was to be eaten only by priests. He was excused because of his hunger and his greatness.

Second, priests worked every Sabbath, making temple sacrifices and carrying the vessels used in worship. The Law declared them exempt from the Sabbath law of work on the basis that service at the temple is more important than the Sabbath regulation.

Third, Jesus Himself was greater than the temple. God had promised to be invisibly present in the temple; in Jesus God was visibly present among His people! It followed that those who served Him (the disciples) were exempt from some Sabbath rules because of the One they serve.

Fourth, Jesus pointed out that the Sabbath had been set aside by God as a day of spiritual and physical refreshment. People were not created to be enslaved by burdensome Sabbath regulations; rather the Sabbath was created for their benefit.

Fifth, God's purpose in forbidding work was to benefit His people. It was never meant to stifle concern for human

beings. The leaders' condemnation of the disciples for eating showed that they had never grasped the meaning of the "mercy-not-sacrifice" principle woven throughout the Old Testament.

Finally, Christ was Lord of the Sabbath. He was the One who ultimately had the right to explain its meaning and purposes. And Christ now ruled against the Pharisees and their legalism.

These teachings of Jesus are compelling reminders to us today. When we are so bound by our customs or lists of dos and don'ts that we cannot show mercy to those in need, or give priority to people, we have wandered far from the spirit of Jesus Christ.

HEALING ON THE SABBATH

The next incident depicting Jesus' conflict with the scribes and Pharisees follows immediately in the Synoptics. Shortly after Jesus' rejection of the Pharisees' Sabbath regulations, He entered a synagogue where there was a man with a withered hand. The story is told in Mark 3:1–6, Matthew 12:9–14, and Luke 6:6–11. Matthew tells the story this way.

Now when He had departed from there, He went into their synagogue. And behold, there was a man who had a withered hand. And they asked Him, saying, "Is it lawful to heal on the Sabbath?—that they might accuse Him. Then He said to them, "What man is there among you who has one sheep, and if it falls into a pit on the Sabbath, will not lay hold of it and lift it out? Of how much more value then is a man than a sheep? Therefore it is lawful to do good on the Sabbath." Then He said to the man, "Stretch out your hand." And he stretched it out, and it was restored as whole as the other. Then the Pharisees went out and plotted against Him, how they might destroy Him.

Luke adds one more detail. After the man stood up, Jesus directly challenged His challengers. "I will ask you one thing: 'Is it lawful on the Sabbath to do good or to do evil, to save life or to destroy?'"

So saying Jesus called on the man to stretch out his hand, and it was healed.

Exceptions to every rule. It's fascinating that the rabbis who were so eager to define every "don't" even tangentially implied by an Old Testament Law were just as concerned with determining conditions under which a rule might be lawfully violated. It was one of these exceptions that Christ referred to when confronting his critics in the synagogue. Saving the life of an animal that had fallen into a pit on the Sabbath was one of those recognized exceptions to the Sabbath work rules. We'll see other exceptions developed by the rabbis, and hear Jesus' comments about them, later in this chapter.

Jesus restates a principle. It is interesting that Jesus raised the dual question, "Is it lawful on the Sabbath to do good or to do evil, to save life or destroy?" There seems to be no doubt that healing would be doing good. But why "to save life or destroy"? Surely the man with the withered hand was in no danger of dying, and to put off healing would hardly "destroy" him. But Jesus was making an important point concerning the radical heart of Old Testament commandments. God's commandments were intended to bring life and health to all who obeyed them. Thus anything that impairs the quality of human life as God intended it to be does destroy life. And any failure to set right what is destructive of well-being is like killing.

Jesus' teaching here is in total harmony with His teaching in the Sermon on the Mount. There also Jesus contrasted the Jews' understanding of God's Law with the divine intent. And both there and here, the view of the scribes and Pharisees is shown to be inadequate and flawed.

The reaction of the Pharisees. Each Gospel tells us that the Pharisees were "filled with rage" and that they discussed what they might do to be rid of Jesus. There was good reason for their anger. The basis for the Pharisees' influence with the masses was their reputation for piety. Jesus' courageous and compassionate action had revealed the fatal flaw in Pharisaism. That piety on which they prided themselves was empty hypocrisy. Underneath their appearance of righteousness were hard, unloving hearts that were far from the heart of the Lord their God.

RUMORS FLY

After Jesus healed the man with the crippled hand in the synagogue, the Gospels tell us that the Pharisees began to discuss how they might destroy Jesus. While this may be a reference to a dawning intent to do away with Christ, it seems more likely at this stage of Jesus' ministry that the Pharisees discussed ways to destroy His reputation and His influence on the masses. Their effort to show Jesus up as a Sabbath-breaker had backfired on them. Instead of providing a basis on which they might have accused Christ, His words had exposed their own hypocrisy. Jesus had shown that they wished to appear pious without truly being pious.

Planting the rumor. The Pharisees and scribes now launched a different kind of attack by which they hoped to undermine Jesus. That approach is described in Mark 3:22–30 and Matthew 12:22–32. Luke's more extensive report of a later incident in chapter 11:14–26 indicates that this strategy was used continuously to attack Jesus and undermine His credibility.

Mark describes the launching of the new strategy. "And the scribes who came down from Jerusalem said, 'He has Beelzebub,' and 'By the ruler of the demons

He casts out demons'" (Mark 3:22). The uniqueness of Jesus and His failure to fit in with the religious elite would be explained by demon possession! And as far as Christ's exorcisms were concerned, it was all a plot of Satan to get people to pay attention to Jesus. The demons left because the prince of demons, Satan (called Beelzebub here), told them to!

Jesus' response. Jesus responded by ridiculing their suggestion, and then by delivering a warning that even now makes people uneasy.

1. *The negative argument*: Satan wouldn't be so foolish (vv. 23–26). Jesus pointed to a fallacy in his enemies' argument. Satan can't be casting out Satan. That would be a spiritual civil war, and no kingdom can survive civil war. Abraham Lincoln used this same argument in calling for a restoration of the Union. "A house divided against itself cannot stand." Jesus concluded, "If Satan has risen up against himself, and is divided, he cannot stand, but has an end" (v.26).

2. *The positive argument:* the exorcisms show that Jesus is stronger than Satan (v. 27). Jesus observed that "no one can enter a strong man's house and plunder his goods, unless he first binds the strong man. And then he will plunder his house." The exorcisms that Jesus continued to perform showed that He had overpowered Satan, and that Satan was powerless against Him. This alternative interpretation of the exorcisms makes far more sense than the rumor started by the scribes and Pharisees.

3. *The warning*: this sin is unforgivable (vv. 28, 29). In attributing the exorcisms that Jesus performed in the power of the Holy Spirit to Satan, the scribes and Pharisees committed an unforgivable sin. They showed that their hearts were so hard-

ened against God and His truth that there was no possibility of repentance and faith.

BIBLE BACKGROUND:

HARD SAYINGS OF JESUS

"He who blasphemes against the Holy Spirit never has forgiveness, but is subject to eternal condemnation" (Mark 3:29; compare Matt. 12:31).

The context defines the nature of "blasphemy against the Holy Spirit." The Pharisees and scribes had credited Satan with the exorcisms and miracles that Jesus performed through the power of the Holy Spirit. It was this sin that Jesus said will not be forgiven.

The reference to this unforgivable sin has troubled many unnecessarily. Those who are most concerned show a very different attitude than that which characterized the scribes and Pharisees, who refused to accept even the most compelling evidence that Jesus was the Son of God. Only a person who rejects the Spirit's evidence of Jesus' authority will not be forgiven. Anyone who seeks Jesus' forgiveness surely has not committed this unforgivable sin.

Matthew provides additional details about how Jesus responded to the accusation.

And if I cast out demons by Beelzebub, by whom do your sons cast them out? Therefore they shall be your judges. But if I cast out demons by the Spirit of God, surely the kingdom of God has come upon you (Matt. 12:27, 28).

In the first century, Jews were viewed throughout the Roman world as the most powerful of exorcists. This was because pagans viewed exorcism as being in the realm of magic. And first-century magic involved calling on supernatural powers to aid the exorcist. It was generally held that only Jews knew the correct pronunciation of the secret name of their God, and thus had an advantage over other magicians and exorcists.

Christ's question, however, argued a different point. If the scribes and Pharisees wished to assert that demons were exorcised in the name of Satan, wouldn't they have to conclude that Jewish exorcists ("your sons") were in league with Satan too? This surely was someplace that the scribes and Pharisees did not wish to go!

On the other hand, if Jesus were casting out Satan by the power of God, then "surely the kingdom of God has come upon you." This, too, was someplace that the scribes and Pharisees did not wish to go!

In raising the charge in the first place, the Pharisees had placed themselves in an utterly untenable position. They must draw one conclusion or the other, but neither conclusion was acceptable to Christ's accusers.

TRADITIONS OF MEN

As the time drew nearer and nearer to the turning point, when it was clear that neither the leaders nor the masses would affirm Jesus as their Messiah, Jesus' confrontations with the scribes and Pharisees became more and more intense. Matthew 15:1–20 and Mark 7:1–23 tell of a time when a group of scribes and Pharisees from Jerusalem again challenged Jesus.

We need to understand that in first-century Judaism religious questions launched a war of words, and the person who provided the best argument was considered to have won. These wars of words were vitally important to the scribes and Pharisees, who were constantly trying to find some way to show Jesus up. Matthew

and Mark describe a question which may seem innocent enough to us, but which was clearly intended to launch a debate in which the scribes hoped to defeat Christ.

Then the scribes and Pharisees who were from Jerusalem came to Jesus, saying, "Why do Your disciples transgress the tradition of the elders? For they do not wash their hands when they eat bread" (Matt. 15:1, 2; compare Mark 7:1–5).

The issue joined was not a matter of hygiene, but of ritual purity. Previous scholars had prescribed that before eating, a person should give his or her hands a ritual cleansing. This involved dipping one's hands in water, and lifting the hands up so that the water ran down the forearms and off the elbows.

We need to remember that the authority to which the scribes and Pharisees constantly appealed were just such rules of behavior which had been established by preceding generations. These traditions were viewed by the Pharisees as oral law, and the oral law was held to have the same authority as the written Torah. In fact, the Pharisees held that the oral law, like the written law had been delivered complete to Moses on Mount Sinai! So what the scribes and Pharisees sought to stimulate was a debate about religious authority—a debate on which they felt they were on firm ground.

Rather than answer the question, Jesus immediately moved to the issue of authority and raised a devastating challenge.

Jesus' challenge to tradition (Matt. 15:3–6). Jesus first attacked the notion that the traditional interpretations were authoritative at all.

He answered and said to them, "Why do you also transgress the commandment of God because of your tradition? For God commanded, saying, 'Honor your father and your mother'; and, 'He who curses father or mother, let him be put to death.' But you say, 'Whoever says to his father or mother, "Whatever profit you might have received from me is a gift to God"—then he need not honor his father or mother.' Thus you have made the commandment of God of no effect by your tradition."

What Jesus referred to was the practice of "corban." The rabbis all agreed that providing for parents financially was implied in the command to honor them. But then they searched for an lawful exception for those who did not wish to support their parents. What the scribes decided was that if a son dedicated that portion of his estate to God that would have been used to support his parents, he was freed from his obligation to them. Of course, during the son's lifetime he would enjoy the income from what had been dedicated to God, for that would only be transferred to the temple after his death!

This legal fiction was patently and obviously a hypocritical attempt to avoid a moral and financial obligation. Yet it was part of the "tradition." Far from honoring the traditions that Pharisees put such stock in, Jesus condemned tradition as a means of avoiding a clear command of God! Tradition was worthy only of contempt!

Jesus' condemnation of the scribes and Pharisees (Matt. 15:7–9). Angrily and scornfully Jesus condemned the scribes and Pharisees as hypocrites, quoting a pointed passage from Isaiah 29:

> These people draw near to
>   Me with their mouth,
> And honor me with their lips,
> But their heart is far from Me.
> And in vain they worship Me,
> Teaching as doctrines the
>   commandments of men.

Jesus points out the Pharisees' fallacy (Matt. 15:10, 11). The Pharisees had again paid attention to externals and ignored spiritual realities. Evil did not reside in what a person ate. It was "not what goes into the mouth [that] defiles a man; but what comes out of the mouth, this defiles a man."

Later Jesus explained further to His disciples. What defiles a person is the evil in his or her heart: things like "evil thoughts, murders, adulteries, fornications, thefts, false witness, blasphemies. These are the things that defile a man, but to eat with unwashed hands does not defile a man" (Matt. 15:19, 20).

There is no record of any attempt by the Pharisees to defend themselves. There was really nothing they could say. The text does tell us, however, that Jesus' disciples reported that the Pharisees "were offended when they heard this saying."

Jesus dismissed the Pharisees and their sensibilities. They were plants which the Father had not planted, and would be uprooted (Matt. 15:13). They were "blind leaders of the blind," and they and all who followed them would fall into a ditch (v. 14).

How utterly vital that believers today avoid the pitfalls that trapped the scribes and Pharisees. For Jesus reminds us that we must read God's Word to learn more about the heart of God, and to discover the principles of life and love that glow on its pages. We must remember always the example of Jesus, and emphasize God's compassion, love, and grace in all that we do.

NO MORE SIGNS FROM HEAVEN

The scribes and Pharisees had made one last effort. We're told about it in Matthew 16 and Mark 8:11, 12. Mark tells us,

Then the Pharisees came out and began to dispute with Him, seeking from Him a sign from heaven, testing Him. But He sighed deeply in His spirit, and said, "Why does this generation seek a sign? Assuredly, I say to you, no sign shall be given to this generation."

A similar demand is reported in both Matthew 12:38–42 and 16:1–4. In each context Jesus gives one exception. There would be no more public miracles for the religious elite or the masses who had ignored the many miracles Jesus had already performed. There would be no more public miracles "except the sign of the prophet Jonah. For as Jonah was three days and three nights in the belly of the great fish, so will the Son of Man be three days and three nights in the heart of the earth" (Matt. 12:39, 40).

When that miracle came, all that Jesus had taught would be confirmed. And all that the scribes and Pharisees had built on their "doctrines of men" would be exposed as empty and useless. Only Jesus' authoritative interpretation of God's word would stand, as would the secret kingdom of heaven He came to initiate here on earth. For by the Resurrection Jesus would be declared to be the Son of God with power (Rom. 1:4), and all humankind would be called to listen only to Him.

OPEN WARFARE

The conflict between Jesus and the scribes and Pharisees was impossible to miss. Undoubtedly the hostility of the Pharisees toward Jesus was one of the major reasons why the masses hesitated to commit to Him. After all, the Pharisees were the most respected of the religious establishment in first-century Judaism.

John's Gospel best portrays the Pharisees' strategy of constant harassment of Christ's response. Yet Christ's most open condemnation of the scribes and Pharisees and of the priests who ran temple worship took place during the last week of His life, and is reported in each of the synoptic Gospels. It is there that we read Jesus' devastating critique and repudiation of the religious elite.

From the time Jesus emerged as a prophet and healer in Galilee, the religious establishment was concerned and hostile. Over the years the Jewish homeland had been one of the most troublesome of the provinces of the Roman Empire. Although the emperors had granted the Jews of the empire many political and religious concessions, the Jews of the homeland remained difficult to govern. When Jesus appeared and began to preach, an uneasy truce was in place, and none of the leaders welcomed a movement that might change the status quo. The politically-oriented Sadducees, supportive of the emperor and the Herods, wanted to maintain their privileged position. And the Pharisees were jealous of the influence their supposed piety gave them over the masses and in the Sanhedrin.

Jesus was an unknown factor. But as great crowds gathered to listen to Him and seek miraculous healings, all factions of the religious elite were troubled. What did this Jesus from Nazareth want? How did He fit in the already complex and delicately-balanced religious politics of the Jewish homeland?

It soon became clear that, although Jesus made no move to proclaim Himself the Messiah and raise an army to throw the Romans out of Palestine, Jesus presented Himself as the prophet like Moses come to reveal and implement very different faith than that supported by the elite. It also

In John's Gospel the phrase "the Jews" indicates the leaders who were hostile to Jesus.

became clear that Jesus intended to establish what He called the "kingdom of heaven." And even though Jesus' description of His kingdom differed significantly from the earthly kingdom predicted by the prophets, Jesus seemed to be presenting Himself as the promised Messiah, and even to indicate that He was the Son of God!

This was too much for the scribes and Pharisees particularly. The authority that Jesus claimed undermined their own. And very quickly the Pharisees stepped up to challenge Jesus and to harass Him.

THE CONFLICT IN JOHN'S GOSPEL

John's Gospel differs in several respects from those of Matthew, Mark, and Luke.

One of the most significant differences is that while the other three Gospels are organized chronologically, John's Gospel is not. John organizes His report of Jesus' life around seven miracles, and the discourses [teachings] that developed from them.

In this sense the Synoptics give us a longitudinal study of Jesus' life, describing His life from birth to the cross with special emphasis on His years of public ministry. John gives us a cross-sectional study, selecting out incidents and reporting each in depth. While we cannot be sure just when most of the incidents John describes took place, John's picture of the constant harassment that Jesus experienced from the religious elite is sharper than that found in the other Gospels.

As we look at three incidents which John describes we'll notice that John speaks often of "the Jews." It's important to remember that in John's Gospel the phrase "the Jews" is his way of referring to the scribes and Pharisees and the chief priests of the Sadduceean party. John generally does not mean the masses of ordinary Jewish men and women when using this term.

A FESTIVAL HEALING
(JOHN 5:1–23)

There were three religious festivals which able-bodied Jewish men were expected to celebrate in Jerusalem. The festival mentioned in John 5 is not identified but was one of the three.

The healing (John 5:1–15). John tells us that during this festival Jesus saw a man who had been a paralytic for thirty-eight years, lying near the pool of Bethesda. The pool was famed as a place of miraculous healings, and many infirm people were crowded around it. Jesus stopped beside the man and asked a pointed question: "Do you want to be made well?"

After thirty-eight years of dependence on others, the thought of becoming responsible for himself might have made the man hesitate. Instead he explained that he had simply been unable to reach the pool when the waters were stirred, a sign the healing power was operating. Jesus then told the man, "Rise, take up your bed and walk." The man was healed immediately, strength was restored to his withered legs, and he did as Jesus commanded.

John tells us that "that day was the Sabbath." The Jews (the scribes and Pharisees) confronted the man when he was seen carrying the pallet on which he'd lain. "It is the Sabbath; it is not lawful for you to carry your bed."

The man's answer was simple and straightforward: "He who made me well

said to me, 'Take up your bed and walk.'" The man didn't know that his benefactor was Jesus, which may suggest the healing took place early in Christ's ministry. But clearly a man who had authority to command such a devastating illness was someone to be heeded!

Later Jesus found the man and identified himself, saying, "See, you have been made well. Sin no more, lest a worse thing come upon you."

BIBLE BACKGROUND:

HARD SAYINGS OF JESUS
"Sin no more, lest a worse thing come upon you" (John 5:14)

Jesus' words seem to imply that the man by the pool had been crippled for thirty-eight years because of some sin. Does the Bible teach that sickness is God's punishment for sin?

In Deuteronomy 28 God promised the people of Israel that if the nation obeyed God's laws He would bless them, and that if they disobeyed He would punish them. Sicknesses are among the punishments described in this passage, and health is one of the blessings. The apostle Paul also notes that some in Corinth were sick and others had even died because they misused the Lord's Supper (1 Cor. 11:29–32). Certainly God may use illness to correct and discipline.

But it would be wrong to view all sickness as a sign of divine displeasure. When the disciples later asked Jesus what sin had caused a certain man to be born blind, Jesus assured them that the blindness was not caused by sin (John 9:1–3). God had a different purpose in permitting the man they asked about to be born blind, even as God had a different purpose in permitting Paul to suffer from his "thorn in the flesh" (2 Cor. 12:7–10).

Ultimately all sickness can be traced back to Adam's fall and the entrance of sin into our world. But whether God permits us to experience sickness or actively causes our sickness as a punishment, we can be confident that when we are close to Him He will be with us, and will bring good out of our most painful experiences.

The Jews' reaction (John 5:16–18). If the other Gospels fail to fully portray the intensity of the anger Jesus' Sabbath healings aroused, John's certainly makes it clear. John tells us that "for this reason the Jews persecuted Jesus, and sought to kill Him, because He had done these things on the Sabbath." In a sense, the Sabbath regulations, that mountain of rulings hanging from a mere thread of Torah, was the centerpiece of rabbinic Judaism's approach to the religion and relationship with God. Challenge the validity of the Sabbath laws, and the whole edifice erected by the scribes and Pharisees would crumble. Sabbath law was sacrosanct, and not even an implicit challenge to it could be permitted.

Jesus responded to the Jews' hostility by saying, "My Father has been working until now, and I have been working" (5:18). John tells us that these words engendered even greater anger. "Therefore the Jews sought all the more to kill Him, because He not only broke the Sabbath, but also said that God was His Father, making Himself equal with God" (v. 19).

BIBLE BACKGROUND:

HARD SAYINGS OF JESUS

"My Father has been working until now, and I have been working" (John 5:17).

What did Jesus mean by this saying? Christ justified His own works of healing on the Sabbath by pointing out that God continued to be active. The scribes had noted that the Genesis description of creation spoke of a morning and evening to the first six days, but only a morning of the seventh. They concluded that it was still the Sabbath for God, and that He was at rest. Jesus pointed out that even during this Sabbath rest, God the Father continued to work. That is, natural law still operated, broken bones continued to mend, and cuts continued to heal. Thus Jesus compared His work of healing the paralyzed man with God's work.

By identifying His works with the works of God, Jesus claimed to be on a par with God, which the scribes and Pharisees clearly understood as claiming to be God. It was "for this reason" that the leaders tried all the harder to kill Jesus.

Jesus' response. Jesus reinforced His claim by His next words.

> Most assuredly, I say to you, the Son can do nothing of Himself, but what He sees the Father do; for whatever He does, the Son also does in like manner. For the Father loves the Son, and shows Him all things that He Himself does; and He will show Him greater works than these, that you may marvel (John 5:19–20).

The significance of these words is something of a mystery to us in the twenty-first century, yet the implication was immediately grasped by Jesus' listeners.

In the first century, craftsmen, from silversmiths to pottery makers, had their own trade secrets. These were family businesses, although some craftsmen might employ additional workers or utilize slaves. While the master craftsman would teach his workers their trade, every master craftsman maintained some secrets that made his work unique, lest an employee set up a

The leaders were so hostile to Jesus that ordinary people were afraid to talk openly about Him.

competing shop. These trade secrets were however passed from father to son. Only the son was allowed to see everything the father did, so that "whatever He does, the Son also does in like manner." It is only a son that a father loves "and shows Him all things that He Himself does."

Jesus' point was this. The fact that Jesus was doing what everyone realized only God could do was proof of His claim of equality with the Father. The Father would only share such secrets with His Son.

Jesus then specified two things greater than the healing which the Father had "shown" the Son and equipped Him to do. Jesus, like the Father, would raise the dead and give them life (v. 21). And Jesus had already been charged with the task of judgment, which the Father had put into His hands (v. 22).

It was clear, then, that all should honor the Son as they honored the Father, and that anyone who refused to honor the Son could not be honoring the Father who sent Him (v. 23).

The scribes and Pharisees who hated Jesus so intensely were not acting in ignorance. There was no doubt about who He claimed to be. And in performing His miracles, those unique works displayed the trademark of God the Father. Jesus had clearly established Himself as God the Son, whether or not the religious establishment would acknowledge Him.

SWIRLING CONTROVERSY
(JOHN 7:11–53)

There is no clearer picture of the running dispute of scribes and Pharisees with Jesus than is found in John 7. The setting is again a religious festival in Jerusalem, this time later in Jesus' ministry. Jesus did not appear for the first days of this eight-day celebration, although it's clear His name was on everyone's lips. John describes a series of incidents that reveal the controversy that continually swirled around Him.

Everyone's whispering Jesus' name (John 7:11–13). Jesus' name was on everyone's lips, but opinions were exchanged in hushed whispers. The reason was simple. The scribes and Pharisees were determinedly hostile to Jesus, and no one wanted to risk offending such powerful individuals. John tells us,

The Jews sought Him at the feast, and said, "Where is He?" And there was much complaining among the people concerning Him. Some said, "He is good"; others said, "No, on the contrary, He deceives the people." However, no one spoke openly of Him for fear of the Jews.

The hostility of the religious elite was so great that it was dangerous for anyone even to mention Jesus' name!

Jesus preaches publicly (John 7:14–18). In the middle of the feast Jesus appeared in Jerusalem and began to preach. The phrase "up into the temple" indicates that He preached in the great inner courtyard where only Jews could gather, not that Jesus or any of the crowds He spoke to entered the temple buildings. His teaching was so powerful that "the Jews marveled, saying, 'How does this Man know letters, having never studied?'"

The reference, of course, was to the fact that Jesus had not gone through the process of studying with an established rabbi, discussed on pages 117–118. Jesus responded by stating the basis of His authority, and by indicating how others could test the truth of His teachings.

The basis of Jesus' authority (John 7:16). As we have noted, in first-century rabbinic Judaism the practice of quoting earlier scholars as authority for one's teaching was firmly established. What a particular scribe taught could be trusted, because he was passing on the interpretation rabbi so-and-so, the son of so-and-so, had expressed generations earlier. The more ancient the tradition, the more confidence contemporary scribes and Pharisees had in it.

Jesus, however, claimed "My doctrine is not Mine, but His who sent Me." That is, Jesus claimed that He was not "inventing new doctrine," but that the source of His teaching was the most ancient of all, God the Father Himself!

Self-authenticating truth (John 7:17). Jesus then stated how any individual could tell if His teaching were true. "If anyone wills to do His will, he shall know concerning the doctrine [teaching], whether it is from God or whether I speak on my own authority."

What Jesus was saying was that anyone who committed himself to doing God's will, no matter what, would recognize the truth of Jesus' words. In context this meant then, and now, a willingness to put aside all preconceived ideas about God and His will, and a commitment to submit to God's will, whatever that will might prove to be. Jesus did not ask the scribes or Pharisees to reject their heritage, but He did call on them to be willing to abandon their most cherished beliefs if this was God's will. This the religious elite were not willing to do!

Christ made it clear that if anyone approached faith with this attitude, "he shall know concerning the doctrine" [of Jesus], whether it is from God or an invention.

Theologians speak of the "self-authenticating" nature of God's Word, and this is what Jesus spoke of here. Our conviction that God has spoken to us in the very words of the Bible does not rest on logic or argument, even though there are logical arguments to support this view. Our conviction that God has spoken rests on the simple fact that we recognize His voice in the words of Scripture.

This is what Jesus claimed for His teachings. They are self-authenticating. They resonate as truth within our hearts. And even those who do not yet recognize the authoritative nature of Scripture will recognize it—if only they will to do God's will. If anyone determines to do God's will before knowing what that will is, God will reveal it to them, and they will know.

Seeking God's glory (John 7:18). The person who invents teachings is seeking glory for himself. But all that Jesus taught was for the glory of the Father. Christ's clear desire to glorify God set Him apart from those who hungered not to bring praise to God, but to win public recognition and a reputation as pious men for themselves.

Jesus justifies the Sabbath healing (John 7:19–24). Amid the swirling controversy Jesus did not hesitate to challenge His opponents. "Did not Moses give you the law, yet none of you keeps the law? Why do you seek to kill me?"

False prophets were to be killed, but the prophet like Moses was to be followed. The Jews had been treating Jesus like a false prophet because He healed a man on the Sabbath. Jesus pointed out that this was utterly unreasonable. The Jews circumcised infants on the eighth day even when that day fell on the Sabbath. How then could the authorities be angry with Jesus for healing on the Sabbath? If it was acceptable to wound on the Sabbath, why wasn't it more acceptable to make a man "completely well?"

The Pharisees panic (John 7:25–51). Jesus' healing miracle and His teaching stirred the public debate over who He might be. Those who were ready to listen to Jesus made a number of compelling points. Jesus was preaching openly, and the religious authorities were doing nothing to stop Him. Did the leaders know that Jesus was the Christ (7:26)? They argued, "When the Christ comes, will He do more signs than these which this Man has done?" (v. 31).

Others argued that "we know where this Man is from." Jesus seemed to be just an ordinary person, while tradition suggested that the Messiah would appear suddenly and unexpectedly (v. 27). Jesus answered that the people did know where He was from: He had made it clear that He had been sent by God (vv. 28, 29)!

There was enough support for Jesus that the Pharisees and chief priests were panicked and ordered the temple police to arrest Jesus (v. 32). Later, however, the temple police return without Jesus, saying "No man ever spoke like this Man!" (v. 46). The Pharisees were furious, pointing out that none of "the rulers or the Pharisees" had believed in Jesus. The arrogant Pharisees dismissed the rest, saying, "This crowd that does not know the law is accursed" (v. 49).

BIBLE BACKGROUND:

HARD SAYINGS OF JESUS

"He who believes in Me, as the Scripture has said, out of his heart will flow rivers of living water" (John 7:38).

Jesus made this announcement during a special service that was the culmination of the Tabernacles festival and featured pouring water on the altar of sacrifice. Alfred Edersheim, in his *Life and Times of Jesus the Messiah*, describes the scene:

The welcome given to Jesus on Palm Sunday led His enemies to move against Him.

We can have little difficulty in determining at what part of the services of "the last, the Great Day of the Feast," Jesus stood and cried, "If anyone thirst, let him come unto Me and drink!" It must have been with special reference to the ceremony of the outpouring of the water, which, as we have seen, was considered the central part of the service. Moreover, all would understand that His words must refer to the Holy Spirit, since the rite was universally regarded as symbolic of His outpouring. The forthpouring of the water was immediately followed by the chanting of the *Hallel* [praises]. But after that there must have been a short pause to prepare for the festive sacrifices [the *Musaph*). It was then, immediately after the symbolic rite of water-pouring, immediately after the the people had responded by repeating those lines from Psalm 117—given thanks, and prayed that Jehovah would send salvation and prosperity, and had shaken their *Lulabh* [bundled branches that were supposed to fulfill Lev. 23:40] toward the altar, thus praising "with heart and mouth, and hands," and then silence had fallen upon them—that there rose, so loud as to be heard throughout the Temple, the Voice of Jesus. He interrupted not the services, for they had for the moment ceased. He interpreted, and fulfilled them.

In Hebrew idiom "living water" was water that flowed in contrast to the quiet waters of a pool. Jesus promised that the Holy Spirit would constantly bubble up within the hearts of those who responded to Jesus' invitation, and that the Spirit would be the source within the believer's life of continuing salvation from sin's power.

As the festival reached its conclusion, the support for Jesus seemed to have grown. By the last day of the feast "many from the crowd" were convinced that Jesus was either "the Prophet" or "the Christ." Others, assuming that Jesus was born in Nazareth, pointed out that the Christ was to be born in Bethlehem. That issue could have easily been resolved, as the Jews maintained careful genealogical records. Apparently no one bothered to check until the events surrounding Jesus' birth were published by Matthew and Luke.

It is important to note in John 7 that the masses feared the religious leaders who had power to deny them access to the synagogue and temple (see for example John 9:19–23). At the same time the leaders were terrified that the masses might commit to Him. Frustrated in their attempts to discredit Jesus, the hostility of the leaders to Jesus would become even more obvious during the last week of Christ's life on earth.

FINAL CONFRONTATIONS

The course Jesus had set now reached its culminating moments. His crucifixion was just a week away when Jesus entered Jerusalem, riding on a donkey, to the acclamation of crowds shouting,

Hosanna to the Son of David!
"Blessed is He who comes in the
  Name of the Lord!"
Hosanna in the highest!
(Matt. 21:9)

These words both terrified and enraged the chief priests and scribes. The use of the title "Son of David" and the quote from the messianic Psalm 118 indicated that the masses might be about to commit themselves to Jesus! Certainly Christ's decision to enter the city riding on a donkey was understood by the scribes as a tacit claim to the Messiah's mantle, for the prophet Zechariah had written,

Tell the daughter of Zion,
"Behold, your King is coming to you,
Lowly, and sitting on a donkey,
A colt, the foal of a donkey"
(Matt. 21:5; Zech. 9:9)

This deeply upset the chief priests and the scribes. And from this point in Matthew's Gospel the two major factions in Judaism, the Pharisees and the Sadducees, were united in their determination to be rid of Jesus. The chapters in each Gospel that describe the final week of Christ's life show a concerted effort by the religious establishment to solve the "Jesus problem" once and for all.

As the final week of conflict intensified, the religious leaders challenged Jesus again and again. Christ responded with a series of stories and with open denunciations which made it unmistakably clear that there was no way to reconcile the differences between Jesus and the religious elite.

What makes the last-week conflict so fascinating is not that Jesus had been unwilling to confront the religious leaders earlier. What makes these last-week conflicts so significant is that they were public. Jesus had previously offered the same devastating critique of the scribes and Pharisees that he offers during the last week, but he had reproached the Pharisees and Scribes in private, when He was alone with members of their party.

THE PRIVATE WARNINGS OF JESUS
(LUKE 11:39–54)

Luke gives us a fascinating portrait of one such private critique of the religion of the Pharisees and scribes. He tells us what happened on an occasion when Jesus was invited to eat at the home of a Pharisee. When they sat down to eat, Jesus failed to perform the ritual hand washing practiced by the Pharisees. His host noticed the omission with surprise. Jesus then volunteered a critique of the Pharisees' approach to religion. A lawyer (scribe) who was also at the dinner complained that "in saying these things You reproach us also" (Luke 11:45). Jesus agreed, and continued His discourse on the flaws in first-century rabbinic Judaism.

Misplaced emphasis (Luke 11:39–41). The Pharisees' focus was on the outside rather than on their "inward part." This approach was foolish, for inside and outside are parts of a single whole. It's useless to concentrate on externals and ignore the greed and wickedness within.

BIBLE BACKGROUND:
HARD SAYINGS OF JESUS

"Give alms of such things as you have; then indeed all things are clean to you" (Luke 11:41; compare Matt. 23:26).

Some have noted that the word translated "give alms" ("to do a charitable deed") is similar to the Aramaic word for "cleanse." They suggest that Luke adopts one nuance while Matthew ("cleanse the inside") adopts another.

It's better, however, to note the relationship between "greed" and "give alms." The first indicates a corrupt heart; the second indicates a cleansed heart. If the Pharisees would only look within and pay attention to the motives that drive their actions, they would realize how foolish it was for them to focus on externals while they were desperately in need of spiritual renewal.

Woes (Luke 11:42–52). Each "woe" identifies something for which the Pharisees will be judged.

Tithing herbs while ignoring justice and love (11:42). The rigorous Pharisee would carefully count each leaf from an herb garden to make sure God received His tenth, but cared little for justice and the example of love God had set before them. It was not wrong to be careful about the tithe. But the concern the Pharisees showed for such details while ignoring the primary obligations of justice and love condemned them.

Loving the best seats (v. 43). The best seats at a meal were reserved for those who were most important. In the same way, being greeted "in the marketplace" by others was a sign of respect. The Pharisees were self-important, and consumed with selfish desires.

Corrupting the innocent (v. 44). Jewish law required that graves be clearly marked, usually by the application of whitewash. The reason was that contact with the dead made a Jew ritually unclean. In comparing the scribes and Pharisees with "graves which are not seen," Jesus implied both that the religious leaders were spiritually dead and that they corrupted those who came in contact with them.

Burdening others (v. 46). In interpreting biblical law the lawyers (scribes) had made up hard-to-keep rules that they insisted others bear; "and you yourselves do not touch the burdens with one of your fingers." Jesus was not saying that the religious elite failed to keep their own rules; most did. But the one who interpreted

Scripture aright made the believer's burden *easier to bear*, not harder. The religious elite burdened others rather than helping them with their burdens (in contrast, see Matthew 11:30: "My burden is light").

Rejecting God's prophets (vv. 47–51). Jesus pointed out that "you build the tombs of the prophets, and your fathers killed them." The saying parallels our proverb, "like father, like son." It also reflects the practice in first-century Judaism of building monuments to ancient prophets and righteous men. In effect the tombs and monuments acknowledged the authority of the prophets, to which neither the fathers who killed them nor the sons who honored them responded. In fact, the sons would soon act as their fathers had and kill yet another Prophet sent to them by God, Jesus Himself. And the consequences of that act would be terrible, for the cumulated blood-guilt of all would "be required of this generation."

Taking away the key of knowledge (v. 52). The scribes claimed that only they understood the Scriptures. In fact they had kept Scripture's good news locked up by their legalistic treatment of God's Word. They themselves failed to enter the kingdom of God, and their teachings hindered others who were eager to do so.

BIBLE BACKGROUND:

SIX CALAMITIES OF HYPOCRISY

In his excellent new book *The Life of Christ* (Starburst, 2000), Pastor Robert Girard highlights six calamities of hypocrisy seen in Luke 11.

1. Slavishly doing the impersonal, formal, institutional aspects of religion while ignoring personal aspects of fair treatment of others and love for God (Luke 11:43).

2. Seeking honor and recognition from people instead of leaving the rewards of spirituality to God (v. 43).

3. Hiding your own spiritual deadness, while infecting others with it (v. 44).

4. Expecting others to live by moral and spiritual standards you are not willing or able to live by, and judging rather than helping them when they fail (v. 46).

5. Honoring dead saints, while inwardly rebelling against the things they stood for (vv. 47–51).

6. Hindering others from discovering the truth by substituting religious rules and rituals for real knowledge of and relationship with God (v. 52).

In speaking to the scribes and Pharisees in private, Jesus gave them a unique opportunity to reevaluate and to repent. Luke however tells us that the religious leaders reacted with increased hostility. "The scribes and Pharisees began to assail Him vehemently, and to cross-examine Him about many things, lying in wait for Him, and seeking to catch Him in something He might say, that they might accuse Him" (Luke 11:53, 54).

The next time Jesus made such charges He would do so openly and in public.

THE PUBLIC CLEANSING OF THE TEMPLE (MATTHEW 21:12–17; MARK 11:15–18; LUKE 19:45–47)

Both Matthew and Mark carefully trace the sequence of events during Jesus' last week, and feature His public confrontations with the religious authorities. Here again Jesus taught by example as well as by word. And immediately on entering the city, His first act was significant indeed.

"Jesus went into the temple of God and drove out all those who bought and sold in the temple" (Matt. 21:12). John's Gospel describes a cleansing of the temple that may have taken place at the beginning of

Christ's ministry (John 2:13–22). From first to last, Jesus' concern was for the glory of God and true expressions of faith in Him. That which God intended to be a house of prayer and a place of rejoicing had been transformed into a "den of thieves."

History tells us that the chief priests had decreed that the only valid money that could be used at the temple was a certain coin, a Tyran silver drachma or tetradrachma. Money changers charged 8 percent to change ordinary money into "temple money," and often cheated their customers by charging even more. And the chief priests demanded a share of each transaction! By this and other similar practices God's temple had literally become a "den of thieves."

The next verse is significant. Matthew tells us, "Then the blind and the lame came to Him in the temple, and He healed them" (Matt. 21:14). God's power now flowed in the cleansed temple.

It's the same with us. We who are the temple of God in our day are also to be channels of God's love, and this can only be if we too remain cleansed and pure.

BY WHAT AUTHORITY?
(MATTHEW 21:23–27; MARK
11:27–33; LUKE 20:1–8)

A critical issue in the conflict between Jesus and the religious leaders was over authority. The scribes and Pharisees claimed to have authority based on their supposed position as the only valid interpreters of Scripture. Jesus claimed that His authority was granted by His Father and that His miracles were evidence that His claim was valid.

The issue was raised again by the scribes and Pharisees when Jesus was teaching in the temple. They asked Him, "By what authority are You doing these things? And who gave You this authority" (Matt. 21:23). Rather than answer, Jesus issued a challenge. If the chief priests and Pharisees would openly state whether John's baptism was from heaven or from men, Jesus would answer their question.

This riddle, for so it was, placed the religious leaders on the horns of a dilemma. They couldn't say "from heaven," because they had not responded to John's message. And if they declared that John had spoken as a mere man, how would the crowds, who considered John a prophet, react? So the leaders admitted, "We do not know."

This admission was itself a defeat. It was the responsibility of the chief priests and elders to make just such determinations and so guide the people. These "leaders" claimed to have authority, but were unwilling to accept responsibility! Their claim to authority was empty!

Jesus then announced that since the leaders had not passed His test, He was not responsible to answer their question. "Neither will I tell you by what authority I do these things" (Matt. 21:27).

THE PARABLE OF THE TWO
SONS
(MATTHEW 21:28–32)

Matthew reports three stories that Jesus then told which were direct, public attacks on the chief priests and Pharisees. Each of these stories is discussed in another chapter of this book as well. Matthew also describes the response of the so-called religious authorities to what Jesus said. "They perceived that He was speaking of them. But when they sought to lay hands on Him, they feared the multitudes, because they took Him for a prophet" (Matt. 21:45, 46).

The first of the stories attacking the chief priests and Pharisees is found only in Matthew's Gospel. Jesus told of two sons, each of whom was told to go to work in the father's vineyard. One son said "I will not," but later regretted what he'd said and went. The other said "I go, sir," but never went. When asked which did the will of the father, Jesus' opponents said "the first." Christ then turned the story against them.

"Assuredly I say to you that tax collectors and harlots enter the kingdom of God before you. For John came to you in the way of righteousness, and you did not believe him; but tax collectors and harlots believed him; and when you saw it, you did not afterward relent and believe him" (vv. 31, 32). The chief priests and Pharisees gave lip service to obeying God, but when put to the test they rejected His messenger and thus rejected Him!

THE PARABLE OF THE VINEDRESSERS (MATTHEW 21:33–41; MARK 12:1–12; LUKE 20:9–19)

This familiar story exposed the motivation of the religious leaders.

The story and its meaning (Matt. 21:33–41). The owner of a vineyard leased it out to professional vinedressers. But every messenger the owner sent to claim payment was mistreated or even killed. Finally the owner sent his son. When the vinedressers saw the son they plotted to kill him "and seize his inheritance" (Matt. 21:38). When asked what the owner would do to those who killed his son, the Jewish leaders unknowingly pronounced their own judgment! "He will destroy those wicked men miserably, and lease his vineyard to other vinedressers who will render to him the fruits in their seasons" (v. 41).

Those who were supposed to be Israel's spiritual leaders were motivated by greed and arrogance. They refused to submit to God because they wanted the honor and power that rightly belonged to Him for

Jesus' story of two sons was directed against the religious elite.

themselves. And so when the Son of God came to receive what was His, rather than submit, the chief priests and Sadducees would choose to kill Him!

Jesus' application (Matt. 21:42–44). The response of the chief priests and Pharisees had been predicted in the Old Testament. The "chief cornerstone," the key to the entire structure, was Jesus Himself. He had been rejected by the "builders." Without Jesus the religion of the Old Testament was incomplete and useless.

As for those builders who rejected the chief cornerstone, "the kingdom of God will be taken from you and given to a nation bearing the fruits of it" (Matt. 21:43). The leaders had rejected Jesus; God would reject them and hand the care of His kingdom over to another "nation," here as elsewhere a new people, the Gentiles.

BIBLE BACKGROUND:

HARD SAYINGS OF JESUS

"And whoever falls on this stone will be broken; but on whomever it falls, it will grind him to powder" (Matthew 21:44).

The servant in the *Man from La Mancha* speaks of his wife as a stone and himself as a pot. He laments that whether the stone hits the pot or the pot hits the stone, it's the pot that suffers. A later rabbi warned, "If a pot falls on a rock, woe to the pot; if a rock falls on the pot, woe to the pot—either way, woe to the pot."

Jesus' saying captures some of this imagery, but in fact alludes to passages in the Old Testament in which "stone" is a key word. Falling on the cornerstone refers to Isaiah 8:14-15, which speaks of the Messiah as a rock over which many "shall stumble; they shall fall and be broken." The cornerstone falling on a person is a reference to Daniel 2:33, 34, which portrays the coming of God's kingdom as crushing to powder every competing power. Both references are messianic, and warnings that rejecting Him has terrible consequences, now and in the future.

But the chief priests and Pharisees were no more open to Jesus' public warnings than they had been to His private warnings.

THE PARABLE OF THE WEDDING FEAST (MATTHEW 22:1-14)

This story like that in Matthew 21:28–32 is found only in Matthew's Gospel. Again it is told to expose the chief priests and Pharisees. This story has been treated on page 109. It combines elements found in other stories told by Jesus, unifying them into a single powerful condemnation of the religious elite.

The invitation refused (Matt. 22:1–6). Failure to attend a wedding when invited by a king was a serious social offense. As noted earlier, it was typical to send two invitations to such an occasion, one long before the event so guests would have a chance to clear their calendars, and then another when the feast was ready and it was time for the guests to appear. When the second invitation was extended, the king's invited guests "made light of it" and ignored him. Some even "seized his servants, treated them spitefully, and killed them."

The insult avenged (Matt. 22:7). The king then "sent out his armies, destroyed those murderers, and burned up their city."

This saying clearly is prophetic. God's response to the rejection of His Son would doom the murderers and the city of Jerusalem. In A.D. 70 the Roman armies under Titus did raze the city, killing thousands. Note that there is historic precedent for calling the Roman forces "his [God's] armies." In the Old Testament the forces of Assyria were sent by God to punish the northern kingdom of Israel for its sins (Isa. 7:17).

Others fill the places reserved for the invited guests (Matt. 22:8–10). Since those who had been invited refused the invitation, the king's servants went afield to invite others. Again Jesus' words were prophetic, as the message of salvation went far beyond the confines of Judea to include Gentile and Jew alike.

The man without a wedding garment (Matt. 22:12–13). It was not unusual at very special occasions for a host to provide special clothing for his guests. Here again Jesus builds on well-known social customs to make His point. Only those who have been clothed by the king in wedding garments are true guests.

This imagery has its roots in the Old Testament and its fulfillment in the New. The prophet had made it clear that all our righteousnesses are as filthy rags in God's sight (Isaiah 64:6). Only when God would clothe believers in the righteousness of Christ could anyone stand in His presence. Those without this wedding garment would be cast "into outer darkness; there will be weeping and gnashing of teeth."

While the images blended together in this story would be fully understood only after Jesus' death and resurrection, it was clear that the parable Jesus told was an attack on the religious leaders. And at this point, the leaders determined to counterattack.

BIBLE BACKGROUND:

HARD SAYINGS OF JESUS

"Many are called but few are chosen" (Matthew 22:14).

Some see the doctrine of election in these words which conclude Jesus' parable of the wedding feast. However this doctrine can't really be supported from this particular text. Rather, the saying sums up the point Christ has just made. Despite the king's willingness to extend his invitation to all, many will not be at the celebration. In Jesus' parable it was only those who "made light of" the king's invitation and those who tried to crash the party without a wedding garment who were excluded.

PAYING TAXES TO CAESAR (MATTHEW 22:15–23; MARK 12:13–17; LUKE 20:20–26)

Luke describes the strategy devised by the chief priests and scribes.

So they watched Him, and sent spies who pretended to be righteous, that they might seize on His words, in order to deliver Him to the power and the authority of the governor (20:20).

We saw earlier that most first-century theological battles were wars of words, battlefields on which reputation and influence would be won or lost. But here we have something different. The goal of the religious leaders was to "entangle Him in His talk" (Matt. 22:15) and trick Jesus into saying something for which He might be charged in a Roman court.

Matthew tells us the story, and we can clearly sense the hypocrisy of Christ's questioners.

And they sent to Him their [the Pharisees'] disciples with the Herodians, saying, "Teacher, we know that You are true, and teach the way of God in truth; nor do You care about anyone, for You do not regard the person of men. Tell us, therefore, what do You think? Is it lawful to pay taxes to Caesar, or not?" (22:16, 17)

BIBLE BACKGROUND:

WHO WERE "THE HERODIANS" (MATTHEW 22:16)?

The *Revell Bible Dictionary* suggests that the Herodians were a political group and that the term "most likely designates those who were political supporters of Herod Antipas. Their concern was probably to maintain the political status quo, which Jesus appeared to threaten, rather than with the religious issues that alienated the Pharisees from Jesus" (p. 483).

Jesus avoided a trap set by the Herodians, and established a principle we are to live by today.

This trap was carefully thought out and seemed certain to entangle Jesus. If he supported the tax structure that truly was oppressive, he would alienate the masses, especially since many viewed paying taxes to Rome as a repudiation of the Jews' ancient status as a people of God. They reasoned that since the only allegiance they owed was to God, payment of the taxes Rome required was tantamount to being unfaithful.

On the other hand, if Jesus spoke out against payment of taxes, He could be accused of fomenting rebellion, something the Romans traditionally dealt with most harshly. It seemed a fool-proof trap. Yet Jesus easily evaded it.

We know what Jesus answered, telling His listeners to render unto Caesar the things which are Caesar's, and to God the things which are God's (Matt. 22:21). We live in the world, although we are not of the world. We are responsible to both secular and spiritual authorities. In the case of taxes, as in most cases, there is little or no conflict in obeying both. While Paul explores this question more fully in Romans 13, it was enough for Jesus to state the principle. Defeated, "they left Him and went their way" (v. 22).

MARRIAGE AND THE RESURRECTION (MATTHEW 22:23–33; MARK 12:18–27; LUKE 20:27–40)

The Pharisees had been put to flight, and now the Sadducees mounted their attack. Matthew notes in introducing this event that members of the Sadducean party "say there is no resurrection" (Matt. 22:23). Some of the theological differences between the Sadducees, who included the chief priests and the Herodians, and the Pharisees, with whom most of the scribes (lawyers) were identified, have been noted earlier. On the facing page is a more complete summary of the beliefs of these two major first-century parties, found in the NIV *Study Bible*.

The Sadducees' challenge (Matt. 22:23–28). The puzzle with which the Sadduccees now hoped to humble Jesus was one that they had long used to ridicule the Pharisees' belief in resurrection. Old Testament law provided for something called Levirite marriage. If a man died childless, his brother could marry the widow, and the first son produced would be considered the child of the dead husband (see Deut. 25:5, 6). In this way the dead husband's name would be preserved and "not blotted out of Israel."

The question the Sadducees posed was intended to reduce the belief of the Pharisees in resurrection to an absurdity. They presented a hypothetical case of seven brothers, the first of whom died and left his widow to the next. Then, one after the other, each

Pharisees	Sadducees
1. Along with the Torah, they accepted as equally inspired and authoritative all that was contained within the oral tradition.	1. They denied that the oral law was authoritative and binding.
2. On free will and determinism they held a mediating view that made it impossible for either free will or the sovereignty of God to cancel out the other.	2. They interpreted Mosaic law more literally than did the Pharisees.
3. They accepted a rather developed hierarchy of angels and demons.	3. They were exacting in Levitical purity.
4. They taught that there was a future for the dead.	4. They attributed everything to free will.
5. They believed in the immortality of the soul and in reward and retribution after death.	5. They argued there is neither resurrection of the dead nor a future life.
6. They were champions of of human equality.	6. They rejected a belief in angels and demons.
7. The emphasis of their teaching was ethical rather than theological.	7. They rejected the idea of a spiritual world.
	8. Only the books of Moses were canonical Scriptures.

brother died. The question was, in the resurrection, which of the seven brothers, all of whom she had married, would have her as a wife in the resurrection?

Jesus' surprising response (Matt. 22:29–32). Jesus' answer was devastating. The Sadducees were "mistaken, not knowing the Scriptures nor the power of God" (Matt. 22:29). In fact they had made two major errors.

The afterlife is not like this life (v. 30). It's fascinating how human beings assume that the afterlife must be essentially the same as the life we know. How many cul-

tures have placed food and drink, carvings of boats and animals, or even the bodies of servants and soldiers in tombs on the assumption that the person buried there will need these things after death? The same unquestioned assumption, that the afterlife must be like life on earth, is implicit in the Sadducees' question, "Whose wife of the seven will she be?"

Jesus not only challenged the assumption, he stated that "in the resurrection they neither marry nor are given in marriage, but are like angels of God in heaven." This verse has sometimes been taken to imply that the faithful *become* angels. But

Jesus simply stated that as far as marriage is concerned, those raised from the dead, like angels, live without marriage.

This teaching of Jesus should not disturb us or cause any grief. Those we love here on earth will be precious to us in heaven, and we can expect to experience far greater intimacy with them after resurrection than we know now. Whatever it will be like in the resurrection, we can be sure that God has planned something far better than the best we know now.

The Scriptures do teach resurrection (Matt. 22:31–32). Jesus then went on to demonstrate that the Sadducees were wrong to doubt resurrection. Exodus, one of those books of Moses that the Sadducees accepted as authoritative, records God's statement "I am the God of Abraham" (3:6, 15). Jesus pointed out that God did not say "I *was* the God of Abraham." Moses' use of the present tense long after Abraham had died constituted proof that Abraham was living, not dead.

The argument brought an admiring reaction from one of the scribes: "Teacher, you have spoken well" (Luke 20:39). Jesus' exposition of the Scriptures was clear and powerful. The Sadducees were wrong!

Jesus' reasoning highlights His conviction concerning the absolute reliability of Scripture, and supports belief in verbal, plenary inspiration. This theological proof that rests on the tense of a single Hebrew word makes it absolutely clear. The Scriptures are God's Word, utterly reliable and trustworthy in all things.

THE FIRST AND GREAT COMMANDMENT (MATTHEW 22:34–40; MARK 12:28–34)

Mark tells us that one of the scribes who had been impressed with Jesus' response to the Sadducees now asked Jesus his own question. Unlike the trick questions posed by the Herodians and the Sadducees, this question seems to have been an honest one. The question: "Which is the first commandment of all?"

As noted in an earlier chapter, first-century rabbis enjoyed the mental exercise of seeking to reduce the biblical commandments to the fewest that would incorporate all. This was what Jesus now did: total love for God and a commitment to love one's neighbor as himself were the greatest of the commandments, for they imply all the rest. The scribe commended Jesus, agreeing fully with Him. Mark notes that "when Jesus saw that he answered wisely, He said to him, 'You are not far from the kingdom of God'" (Mark 12:34).

These words are important for us to remember as we move closer to the Crucifixion. Not every scribe and Pharisee was a hypocrite. There were godly men among the religious leaders, some of whom, like Nicodemus, became believers after Jesus' resurrection. Yet as a class the leaders were threatened by Jesus and closed to all He taught and did.

"WHOSE SON IS HE?" (MATTHEW 22:41–45; MARK 12:35–38; LUKE 20:41–44)

Jesus had met every challenge raised by His enemies. Now Jesus silenced them once and for all. The text tells us that while the Pharisees were gathered together, Jesus challenged them.

"What do you think about the Christ? Whose Son is He?" (Matt. 22:42). The Old Testament clearly taught that the promised Messiah would be a descendant of King David, and so the Pharisees gave the expected, and correct, answer: "The Son of David."

Jesus then quoted an acknowledged messianic psalm, and raised a question which could be answered in only one way.

How then does David in the Spirit call
Him "Lord," saying:
"The LORD said to my Lord,
'Sit at My right hand,
Till I make Your enemies Your foot-
stool?'"
If David then calls Him "Lord," how then
is He his Son?" (vv. 43–45).

The question hinges on the fact that in
Hebrew thought a father is always greater
than his son; the ancestor greater than the
descendant. But in this one case David
acknowledges that his descendant, the
Messiah, is greater than he. In fact, David
goes so far as to call the Messiah Lord,
acknowledging His superiority.

There was only one way that the
Christ, the Messiah, could be greater than
His ancestor. The Messiah must actually be
David's Lord, God Himself come in human
flesh, just as Jesus had claimed all along
to be.

The Pharisees did not even try to
answer. Matthew tells us, "and no one was
able to answer Him a word, nor from that
day on did anyone dare question Him any-
more" (v. 46).

THE DENUNCIATION

The war of words is over now, and
while Jesus has defeated His opponents
they continue to reject the Truth He represents. Jesus now turns to the multitudes
and to His disciples, and gives a final, devastating and public critique of the scribes
and Pharisees.

AUTHORITY OR EXAMPLE?
(MATTHEW 23:2–3)

Jesus began by commenting on the
claim of the scribes and Pharisees to "sit in
Moses' seat" (Matt. 23:2). Moses was the
recognized authority on faith and morals,
an authority that these interpreters of

Moses claimed for themselves. The pair-
ing of "whatever they tell you to observe,
that observe" with "but do not do according to their works" marks this opening
remark of Jesus as bitter irony. Moses
taught—and was honored—because he
lived the word he communicated. The
scribes and Pharisees "say, and do not do"
(v. 3). Their claim of spiritual authority is
an empty one. They may be in a position to
coerce the obedience of the masses. But
Jesus' listeners are to reject everything that
these so-called spiritual leaders represent.

THE WAY OF THE PHARISEE
(MATTHEW 23:4–7)

In a few brief statements Jesus exposes
the hollowness that lies at the heart of
Phariseeism. The Pharisees are uncon-
cerned with the burdens of others, and
unwilling to move a finger to provide any
relief (v. 4). Everything they do is calcu-
lated for the effect it will have on others (v.
5). What they really care about is the best
places at feasts, the best seats in synagogues, and to have men call them "Rabbi."
They are the self-centered men, the hollow
men, to whom outward appearance is
everything.

THE WAY OF JESUS'
FOLLOWERS
(MATTHEW 23:8–12)

Just as Jesus' description of the way of
the Pharisees made a single point, so does
His description of the way His followers are
to adopt.

But you, do not be called "Rabbi"; for One is
your Teacher, the Christ, and you are all
brethren. Do not call anyone on earth your
father; for One is your Father, He who is in
heaven. And do not be called teachers; for One
is your Teacher, the Christ. But he who is greatest among you shall be your servant. And whoever exalts himself will be humbled, and he who

humbles himself will be exalted (Matthew 23:8–12).

The Pharisees saw the community of faith as a hierarchy, and scrambled desperately to reach the top. But Jesus' community of faith is a family, of which God alone is Father and every believer a brother. Rather than seek authority over others, the follower of Jesus is to seek to serve others, cheerfully subordinating himself or herself to others' needs.

Jesus' community of faith is the religious world of the Pharisees turned upside down. The Pharisees, who spent their energy exalting themselves, would be humbled. In contrast the follower of Jesus who humbles himself to serve others will be exalted by God.

WOE TO YOU, SCRIBES, PHARISEES, HYPOCRITES (MATTHEW 23:13–33)

Jesus then pronounced a series of woes on the scribes and Pharisees, calling them hypocrites. Here the repeated word "woe" is an exclamation of grief and also denunciation. Jesus was rendering a judicial verdict of "guilt" against the Pharisees, but He did so with a heavy heart.

The repeated phrase "scribes, Pharisees, hypocrites!" focuses attention on the central flaw of the religious leaders. The word "hypocrite" was originally used to describe an actor in a Greek play, who held a mask in front of his face to represent himself as the character he was playing. The word came to mean anyone who behaved insincerely, or who presented himself as something he was not. Jesus' harshest denunciation of the Pharisees was for pretending piety when their true motives were selfish and self-serving.

What were the Pharisees guilty of? Jesus lists a number of charges and specifications.

They barred the way to the kingdom of heaven (Matt. 23:13). By corrupting true religion the scribes and Pharisees "shut up the kingdom of heaven against men." They refused to enter themselves, and all they did made it harder for others to find God's way.

They pretended public piety while practicing private wickedness (Matt. 23:14). The Old Testament called on the faith community to show special concern for widows and orphans. God stated, "You shall not afflict any widow or fatherless child. If you afflict them in any way, and they cry at all to Me, I will surely hear their cry; and My wrath will become hot" (Ex. 22:22–24). The very fact that these "religious" men could show no concern for the powerless while "for a pretense" making long prayers, made them deserving of "greater condemnation."

They sought converts but then corrupted them (Matt. 23:15). Evangelism was not a Christian invention. Many scribes and Pharisees actively sought to convert pagans to Judaism. In the first century, synagogues outside of Palestine often attracted Gentiles who were captured by God and the high moral vision of the Old Testament. Those who continued to attend without conversion were called "God-fearers." The Pharisees took pride in seeing one of these Gentiles become a Jew in a conversion ceremony which featured circumcision and a ritual bath. The trouble was that these converts then became the Pharisees' kind of Jew, not God's! And so Jesus condemned them because "when he is won, you make him twice as much a son of hell as yourselves."

They were blind guides and fools (Matt. 23:16–22). Here Jesus gives an illustration of the kind of foolish (corrupt) rulings that revealed the spiritual blindness of the scribes and Pharisees.

The Pharisees tended to major on the minors of faith.

One debate in Judaism was over the issue of vows, and the question was, "What vows are binding, and what vows can be broken?" Yet God had stated in Deuteronomy 23:23, "That which has gone from your lips you shall keep and perform, for you voluntarily vowed to the LORD your God what you have promised with your mouth."

The scribes and Pharisees weren't satisfied with this clear and unequivocal word from God. They had to establish complicated rules to determine when a vow had to be kept and when it might be broken. And the rules they were so proud of were foolish rules! If one swears "by the temple," the vow can be broken, but not if one swears "by the gold in the temple." Jesus ridiculed such reasoning. "Fools and blind! For which is greater, the gold or the temple which sanctifies the gold?"

It was wrong to even consider breaking any vow. But to do so and then make up such idiotic rules showed the scribes and Pharisees to be fools as well as blind!

Majoring on the minor (Matthew 23:23, 24). Jesus had brought up this issue earlier in His private conversations with the Pharisees (see Luke 11:42). The Pharisees were careful to tithe the tiny leaves gathered from their herb gardens while neglecting "the weightier matters of the law: justice and mercy and faith" (Matt. 23:23).

The next saying, "Blind guides, who strain out a gnat and swallow a camel" (v. 24), makes this same point. Gnats were unclean and so the Pharisee was careful to strain his drink lest a gnat be in it. But camels too are unclean, and far bigger than gnats! Yet the Pharisees figuratively were adept at swallowing camels!

Polishing the outside while ignoring what is within (Matt. 23:25–28). The image of a cup being cleaned on the outside while its inner surface is ignored picks up on a hotly-debated issue in first-century Judaism. The debate was whether the outside of a cup or the inside should be cleansed first. The answer of the rabbis was, the outside. This debate had symbolic implications, which Jesus picked up on. And Jesus answered very differently than did the Pharisees.

The first concern of a human being should be to deal with the "extortion and self-indulgence" in the human heart. It is the heart that is the measure of a man, and a man whose heart is clean will be clean outwardly as well. Again Jesus condemns the Pharisees as "blind."

This same point is made in Jesus' reference to "whitewashed tombs." However beautiful such tombs might appear, inside they contain dead men's bones, contact with which made a person ritually unclean. Similarly the Pharisees "appear righteous to men" but inside they are "full of hypocrisy and lawlessness." They corrupt all with whom they have to deal.

Participating in their father's sins (Matt. 23:29–33). The scribes and Pharisees built monuments to the prophets that their ancestors had killed, claiming that "if we had lived in the days of our fathers, we would not have been partakers with them in the blood of the prophets" (Matt. 23:30). Jesus' condemnation is based on a rabbinic principle of interpretation later applied by the writer of Hebrews to establish the superiority of the Melchizedekian priesthood to the Aaronic priesthood (see Heb. 7:4, 5). That principle is that descendants actually participate in the acts of their ancestors as germinally present in them. Simply by identifying themselves as the sons of those who murdered the prophets, the scribes and Pharisees implicated themselves!

There is of course another point. The scribes and Pharisees acknowledged the authority of the prophets who spoke of Jesus, but they rejected Jesus Himself and were about to kill Him. In this they would "fill up" the "measure of your fathers' guilt."

THE VERDICT
(MATTHEW 23:33)

Jesus has presented His charges against the scribes and Pharisees. Jesus' next words express His verdict: "Serpents, brood of vipers! How can you escape the condemnation of hell?"

THE IMMEDIATE
CONSEQUENCES
(MATTHEW 23:34–36)

Ultimately the verdict expressed in Matthew 23:33 will be carried out. But there is a more immediate doom that the generation that rejected Jesus is to experience. After Christ has been crucified and raised He will send even more messengers, which the Jews will reject and persecute (v. 34). As a result, their generation will experience the consequences of blood-guilt that God has decreed. In a sense the horrors to be experienced by their generation when the Romans take Jerusalem will serve as a demonstration of God's righteous judgment of all throughout history who have slain the righteous.

JESUS' LAMENT OVER
JERUSALEM
(MATTHEW 23:37–39)

Jesus has tried, convicted, and condemned the scribes and Pharisees who would soon engineer His death. But despite the anger that burns in Christ's words, it hurt our Lord to consider the consequences these men and those who followed them were about to experience. We sense Jesus' grief as He laments, "How often I wanted to gather your [Jerusalem's] children together, as a hen gathers her chicks under her wings, but you were not willing."

The nation which rejected Jesus would see Him no more, until a time to come when they will recognize Jesus as the Messiah, and say, "Blessed is He who comes in the name of the LORD" (Ps. 118:26).

THE CROSS AND BEYOND

During the early days of Jesus' ministry His emphasis was on teaching the crowds. After the turning point, when it had become clear that the masses would not respond to Jesus' presentation of Himself as the Messiah, Jesus' emphasis shifted to teaching His disciples. And during the last week of His life Jesus taught through a series of confrontations with the chief priests, scribes, and Pharisees.

We have now come to the last day of Christ's life on earth. Jesus' teaching ministry ends—for a time. He will teach again after His resurrection. But even so, the words Jesus spoke during His last hours on earth are instructive.

After praying in the Garden of Gethsemane Jesus was taken by a mob. The mob was led by Judas and by temple officials. Jesus was taken first to the home of Annas, the father-in-law of the high priest, Caiaphas. Christ underwent a series of trials that night and the next day as He was successively examined at the homes of Annas and Caiaphas, then the Sanhedrin,

by the Roman governor, Pilate, by Herod, and finally by Pilate once again. In the end Pilate condemned Jesus and sentenced Him to be crucified. Jesus was nailed to a cross in midmorning, and seven of Christ's cries from the cross are recorded for us in the Gospels.

The Gospels also report Christ's resurrection. They also give us insights into Christ's post-resurrection teaching of the disciples. In this chapter we look at what Jesus said during His trials, from the Cross, and after He was raised from the dead.

JESUS ON TRIAL

The mob took Jesus and roughly dragged Him to the home of Annas, a former high priest and the father-in-law of the current high priest, Caiaphas. Annas was still the most influential member of the priestly party. The following chart traces the events that rapidly unfolded the rest of that night and the next day.

❖

Events	Matthew	Mark	Luke	John
Jesus is arrested in Gethsemane	26:47–56	14:43–52	22:47–53	18:2–12
Jesus is tried before Annas				18:12–23
Jesus is tried before Caiaphas	26:57–68	14:53–65	22:54–65	18:24
Peter denies Jesus	26:69–75	14:66–72	22:54–62	18:15–27
Jesus is condemned by the council	27:1	15:1	22:66–71	
Judas commits suicide	27:3–10			
Jesus is tried by Pilate	27:11–14	15:2–5	23:1–5	18:28–38
Jesus is tried by Herod			23:6–12	
Jesus is condemned by Pilate	27:15–26	15:6–15	23:13–25	18:39–19:16
Jesus is mocked and scourged	27:27–30	15:16–19		19:2, 3
Jesus is led to Calvary	27:31–34	15:20–23	23:26–33	19:16, 17

❖

We do not have a record of the words Jesus spoke in each setting. Yet those we do have are truly instructive.

JESUS IS ARRESTED IN GETHSEMANE
(MATTHEW 26:47–56; MARK 14:43–52; LUKE 22:47–53; JOHN 18:2–12)

Taken together, the Gospels provide a clear picture of what Jesus said and did during His arrest.

Jesus' words to Judas (Matthew 26:50; Luke 22:48). Judas had left the other disciples during their last supper with Jesus. Earlier Judas had agreed to lead Jesus' enemies to a place where they could seize Him privately, away from the crowds who believed that Christ was a prophet. Now Judas, with a mob behind him, approached the isolated hillside where Jesus had paused to pray. On the way Judas told the leaders of the mob that he would identify Jesus with a kiss.

In that age a kiss was a sign of special affection between family members or close friends, and also of a disciple's relationship with his teacher. To betray with a kiss was a contemptible act, a violation of one of the most significant values in ancient society. Even knowing what Judas intended, Jesus called Judas "friend" as he approached.

"Friend, why have you come?" The word translated "friend" here is not an intimate word, but it is an open-hearted one. All the rancor and betrayal were on the side of Judas; Jesus had done nothing to alienate His betrayer. The question "Why have you come?" is idiomatic, and might be rendered, "Do what you've come to do."

"Are you betraying the Son of Man with a kiss?" (Luke 22:48). Before Judas reached Jesus, Christ let Judas know that He was aware of the plot. The realization must have chilled Judas, for it was yet another evidence of the deity of the one he had pledged to turn over to His enemies. But Judas was committed to his course. Neither

Jesus was taken by night, and led away to undergo an illegal trial.

a reminder of past friendship or evidence of Christ's deity would prevent Judas from fulfilling the bargain he had struck with the chief priests.

Jesus' words to the mob (Matt. 26:55–56; Mark 14:48, 49; Luke 22:52–53; John 18:4–9). Each Gospel account records words that Jesus spoke to the mob. The Synoptics record words of contempt, but John gives us a unique vision of Jesus' innate power.

The question Jesus asked the mob focused on the cowardliness of Jesus' enemies. "Have you come out, as against a robber, with swords and clubs to take Me? I sat daily with you, teaching in the temple, and you did not seize Me" (Matt. 26:55). Each of the synoptic writers reports these words, with added phrases.

"But all this was done that the Scriptures of the prophets might be ful-

filled" (Matt. 22:56; Mark 14:49). And, "But this is your hour, and the power of darkness" (Luke 22:53).

Jesus' assertion of His identity (John 18:4–9). John reports the following dialogue in which Jesus used the phrase, "I am He." In Greek the phrase is *ego eimi;* in Hebrew or Aramaic the equivalent would simply affirm "I AM." And "I AM" is the Old Testament's personal name of God, Yahweh (Ex. 3:13, 14)!

When Jesus said these words, Judas and the crowd were driven backward and fell to the ground.

The mob had swords and clubs, yet all were felled by a word spoken by Jesus Christ. The only way that Christ could be taken by such persons was if He permitted it. Thus these words of Jesus not only affirmed His essential deity, but remind and reassure us. Humanly speaking the

Cross was both a tragedy and a miscarriage of justice. Yet at the same time it was a voluntary act by the Son of God, who could have refused to undergo the humiliation and pain, but who chose to go to Calvary for our sakes.

Jesus words to the disciples (Matt. 26:52–54; Luke 22:49–51; John 18:10, 11). The disciples were shaken by the appearance of the mob. But Peter drew a weapon. Striking out at the servant of the high priest, one Malchus, he cut off his ear! Jesus restored the ear and told Peter,

Put your sword in its place, for all who take the sword will perish by the sword. Or do you think that I cannot now pray to My Father, and He will provide Me with more than twelve legions of angels? How then could the Scriptures be fulfilled, that it must happen thus?" (Matt. 26:52–54)

John adds, "Put your sword into the sheath. Shall I not drink the cup which My Father has given me" (18:11)?

We might wonder why Peter was carrying a sword. It's likely that what Peter used was his fisherman's knife, for the Greek word used here can mean either "sword" or "knife." In either case it was used as a weapon, with the intent of protecting Jesus from a destiny He himself had chosen! While Peter's urge to defend Christ in the face of overwhelming numbers was magnificent, it was also misguided. And Peter's courage would dissolve when he realized that Jesus was intent on going with His captors.

BIBLE BACKGROUND:

HARD SAYINGS OF JESUS

"All who take the sword will perish by the sword" (Matthew 26:52).

This verse is often quoted in support of pacifism. However, in context it conveys a dif-

ferent message. Those who rely on worldly weapons in support of Jesus are doomed to failure. As the apostle Paul wrote, "the weapons of our warfare are not carnal but mighty in God for pulling down strongholds" (2 Cor. 10:4).

Those who adopt the weapons of the world will suffer defeat. Reliance on spiritual resources is the key to victory.

JESUS IS TRIED BEFORE ANNAS (JOHN 18:12–23)

John is the only writer who reports what happened when Jesus was taken to the house of Annas, where he was interrogated "about His disciples and His doctrine." Rather than respond, Jesus reminded His questioners that He had always spoken "openly to the world." There were plenty of witnesses who had heard what Jesus had said.

This answer angered the onlookers, although it was true. Undoubtedly every one of His accusers also knew exactly what Jesus had taught and said, for they were there too!

JESUS IS TRIED BEFORE CAIAPHAS (MATTHEW 26:57–68; MARK 14:53–65; LUKE 22:54–65; JOHN 18:24)

Jesus was then taken to the house of Caiaphas, where the members of the Sanhedrin had gathered. This was an "unofficial" trial, for the council was not legally able to sit as a court except during daytime. Nevertheless the high priest called in men willing to serve as false witnesses, seeking grounds on which Jesus might be put to death. Frustrated by the failure of their witnesses to lay a legal foundation and by Jesus' silence, the high priest demanded, "I put you under oath by the living God: Tell us if You are the Christ, the Son of God!"

Both Matthew and Mark report Jesus' reply.

> It is as you said. Nevertheless, I say to you, hereafter you will see the Son of Man sitting at the right hand of the Power, and coming on the clouds of heaven (Matt. 26:64).

And,

> I am. And you will see the Son of Man sitting at the right hand of the Power, and coming with the clouds of heaven (Mark 14:62).

The only difference between the two is that Mark translates Matthew's idiomatic expression, "It is as you said," for his Gentile readers, writing instead "I am."

There was no further need of witnesses. To the council Jesus' answer constituted blasphemy. Mark tells us that "they all condemned Him to be deserving of death." "Then some began to spit on Him, and to blindfold Him, and to beat Him, and to say to Him, 'Prophesy!' And the officers struck Him with the palms of their hands" (Mark 14:65).

JESUS IS CONDEMNED BY THE SANHEDRIN
(MATTHEW 27:1; MARK 15:1; LUKE 22:66–71)

Luke tells us that "as soon as it was day" Jesus was led to the council chamber. The unofficial trial had served its purpose. The prosecutors knew just what approach to take in order to condemn Jesus. This is clear as we read Luke's account. There is no attempt to locate witnesses. Jesus had

shown Himself willing to "admit" to being God!

> "If You are the Christ, tell us."
> But He said to them, "If I tell you, you will by no means believe. And if I also ask you, you will by no means answer Me or let Me go. Hereafter the Son of man will sit on the right hand of the power of God."
> Then they all said, "Are You then the Son of God?"
> So He said to them, "You rightly say that I am."
> And they said, "What further testimony do we need? For we have heard it ourselves from His own mouth."

It is fascinating that the members of the Sanhedrin were so elated at the opportunity to condemn Jesus to death for blasphemy that they gave not a moment's thought to what it would mean if He were telling the truth. Nor did they stop to think that if Jesus were not firmly convinced of His deity, He would hardly profess it when He knew such a profession guaranteed His execution! Truly the chief priests and scribes were blinded by hatred and by the prospect of being rid of Jesus once and for all.

JESUS IS TRIED BY PILATE
(MATTHEW 27:11–14; MARK 15:2–5; LUKE 23:1–5; JOHN 18:28–38)

While the Sanhedrin was the ruling body of the Jews, even when sitting as a court it had no authority to put anyone to death. That power was reserved by the Romans and vested in the district governor, Pilate. But in going to Pilate, the Jewish leaders had a problem. Old Testament law decreed death for blasphemy, but there was no such penalty in Roman law. And so the Jewish leaders brought an entirely different charge against Jesus than the one for which they had convicted Him!

The charge the Jews brought was that Christ had claimed that He Himself was King of the Jews. Such charge was thus one of rebellion, and for this the Romans were quick to execute! They also added other charges, claiming that Jesus was "perverting the nation, and forbidding to pay taxes to Caesar" (Luke 23:2). These added charges were false, but when Pilate asked Jesus, "Are You the King of the Jews?" Jesus replied, "It is as you say" (v. 3).

John gives us more information about Jesus' first appearance before Pilate. When Pilate raised the charge that Jesus claimed to be king of the Jews, Jesus asked, "Are you speaking for yourself about this, or did others tell you this concerning me?" Pilate had no independent knowledge of the charge against Jesus.

Jesus then made several startling statements which puzzled Pilate and made him, a man noted for his cruelty and lack of concern for others, pause. "My kingdom is not of this world. If My kingdom were of this world, My servants would fight, so that I should not be delivered to the Jews; but now My kingdom is not from here" (John 19:36).

This statement serves us well as a reminder and a corrective. Too often Christians have confused secular power and spiritual authority. The reformers in the sixteenth century dreamed of establishing a Christian state, and too often resorted to killing to do so. In our day too many call for Christian churches to become involved in party politics as a way to purify society morally. But Jesus' kingdom is not of this world, and we are not to adopt worldly means to achieve spiritual ends.

Yet Jesus was careful to say, "*Now* My kingdom is not from here." The day will come when Jesus returns to establish God's rule on earth. And then the spiritual and earthly kingdoms of God will be one, and Jesus will be King indeed.

Pilate did not understand Jesus' answer, and so asked, "Are you a king then?" Jesus replied,

You say rightly that I am a king. For this cause I was born, and for this cause I have come into the world, that I should bear witness to the truth. Everyone who is of the truth hears my voice (John 18:37).

Pilate no more understood Jesus' talk of "truth" than he grasped how Jesus could be king of a kingdom that was "not of this world." But Pilate was impressed with Jesus, and realized that the Jewish leaders had an ulterior motive in bringing Jesus before him. So Pilate went out and told Jesus' accusers, "I find no fault in Him at all" (John 19:38).

It's clear that Pilate did make an honest effort to free Jesus. He even suggested that he release this "King of the Jews" in honor of Passover. The Jews were incensed, and insisted that Pilate release a robber called Barabbas instead of Jesus. The choice was a striking one, for the word translated "robber" indicates a brigand, who takes away other's goods by violence. The symbolism is striking. The religious leaders preferred a man of violence to the Prince of peace. And the consequences of that choice doomed their society to a violent end.

JESUS IS TRIED BY HEROD (LUKE 23:6–12)

Only Luke tells us that after Jesus' first appearance before Pilate, the Roman governor sent him to Herod. This was Herod Antipas, who was given the courtesy title "King" but who really had a minor role in governance. This was a subtle attempt by Pilate to avoid taking any position on Jesus. Herod was titular ruler of Galilee, and Jesus was a Galilean, so technically Jesus fell in Herod's jurisdiction!

Pilate, although the Roman governor, was not free to release Jesus as he wished.

Pilate's plan failed. While Herod had long wanted to see Jesus, and perhaps watch Him perform a miracle, Jesus remained silent before the king. In the end, pressured by the chief priests and scribes, Herod sent Jesus back to Pilate.

JESUS IS CONDEMNED BY PILATE
(MATTHEW 27:15–26; MARK 15:6–15; LUKE 23:13–25; JOHN 18:39–19:16)

Matthew reports no sayings of Jesus during this second appearance before Pilate. Neither does Mark or Luke. John however goes into details concerning what happened, and includes one strange and difficult saying of Christ's.

John also gives us additional insight into Pilate's motivation, and the reason

why Pilate gave in to the demand of the religious leaders. We know from history that Pilate was a man who cared little for the opinion of others, and who indeed seemed to take a perverse delight in irritating those he ruled. Why then did Pilate, who was now convinced of Jesus' innocence and more than a little in awe of Him, allow himself to be pressured into ordering Christ's crucifixion?

The answer comes to us from history. Some time before, the emperor Tiberius had retired to a private island where he indulged himself in a variety of perverted practices. He left the commander of his Praetorian Guard, Sejanus, in charge in Rome. Sejanus was emperor in all but name. But then Sejanus asked to marry into the royal family. Tiberius viewed this as a threat to his life, for such a connection to the royal family might give legitimacy to a claim by Sejanus to the throne. Tiberius returned to Rome, and once there ordered the execution of Sejanus, and many of those who had obtained offices through his influence. The purge frightened all who had been protegés of Sejanus—including Pilate, procurator of Judea!

So when Pilate seemed about to release Jesus, the Jewish leaders told Pilate, "If you let this Man go, you are not Caesar's friend. Whoever makes himself a king speaks against Caesar" (John 19:12). These words were a threat. If Pilate did not crucify Jesus, the Jews would accuse him to the already paranoid Tiberius. Such an accusation would surely doom Pilate, who had been appointed by Sejanus.

For Pilate the choice was obvious. It was Jesus' life or his! And Pilate's life was too precious for him to sacrifice for a strange young Jew who claimed to be king.

It was during this second appearance, before Pilate had given in to the Jewish threats, that the frustrated Roman demanded of Jesus, "Do You not know that I have power to crucify You, and power to release You?" (John 19:10). It was then that Jesus gave this puzzling reply: "You could have no power at all against Me unless it had been given you from above. Therefore the one who delivered Me to you has the greater sin" (John 19:11).

Most commentators understand Jesus to be saying here that Pilate is simply an instrument that God has chosen to use to accomplish His purposes. Pilate's action was sin, but a sin that flowed from weakness rather than malice. Caiaphas, however, and the others who brought Jesus to Pilate demanding His execution, acted from malice and in spite of proof that Jesus was who He claimed to be. Their sin was greater by far.

JESUS IS LED TO CALVARY (MATTHEW 27:31–34; MARK 15:20–23; LUKE 23:26–33; JOHN 19:16, 17)

Each Gospel gives us a brief portrait of Jesus as He is led to Calvary, weakened by loss of blood from His beatings and struggling under the weight of the cross bar to which He was to be nailed. But only Luke records words that Jesus spoke on that last, pain-filled journey.

Luke tells us that a number of women who "mourned and lamented Him" followed. Turning to them, Jesus said,

Daughters of Jerusalem, do not weep for Me, but weep for yourselves and for your children. For indeed the days are coming in which they will say, "Blessed are the barren, wombs that never bore, and breasts which never nursed!" Then they will begin "to say to the mountains, 'Fall on us!' and to the hills, 'Cover us.'" For if they do these things in the green wood, what will be done in the dry?

Jewish women viewed children as a blessing. But the day was coming when women without children would consider themselves blessed, for they would be spared seeing the horrors that even young boys and girls would experience. Christ then quoted Hosea 10:8, which in that prophet is a plea for protection from disaster. The same image is used in Revelation 6:16, 17 to describe the reaction of earth's inhabitants as divine judgments batter our planet.

The reference to green and dry wood is an allusion to the fact that fire races through a dry forest much more rapidly than through a wet one. What the leaders have done to Jesus will be followed by even worse treatment for the daughters (inhabitants) of Jerusalem.

These words of Jesus were uttered in sorrow rather than judgment. Yet within a generation Jesus' prophecy of suffering for the Holy City came true. During the Roman siege of the city, parents would see their children starve. Some would even be killed and eaten by neighbors, as mobs roamed the neighborhoods desperate for anything to eat. In that day truly the daughters of Jerusalem would mourn.

JESUS' WORDS FROM THE CROSS

The Gospels record seven utterances Jesus made while on the cross. Nelson's *Illustrated Bible Handbook* (p. 537) gives us the sequence of Crucifixion events.

Event	Scripture
Jesus offered drugged drink to lessen suffering	Matt. 27:34
Jesus crucified	Matt. 27:35
Jesus cries, "Father, forgive them"	Luke 23:34
Soldiers gamble for Jesus' clothing	Matt. 27:35
Jesus mocked by onlookers	Matt. 27:39–44; Mark 15:29
Jesus ridiculed by the two thieves	Matt. 27:44
One of the thieves believes	Luke 23:39–42
Jesus promises, "Today you will be in paradise"	Luke 23:43
Jesus speaks to Mary, "Behold your son"	John 19:26, 27
Darkness falls on the scene	Matt. 27:45; Mark 15:33; Luke 23:44

Jesus cries, "My God, My God"	Matt. 27:46, 47;
	Mark 15:34–36
Jesus cries, "I thirst"	John 19:28
Jesus cries, "It is finished"	John 19:30
Jesus cries, "Father, into Your hands"	Luke 23:46
Jesus releases His spirit	Matt. 27:50; Mark 15:37

Each of Jesus' seven utterances from the cross teaches lessons we need to learn.

"FATHER, FORGIVE THEM" (LUKE 23:34)

Jesus had reached the killing ground, a site set aside on a hill beyond Jerusalem's walls called Golgotha. There the soldiers went about preparing for the executions. They nailed Jesus' hands to the crossbar He had been forced to carry. Lifting Him up they attached the crossbar to the fixed pole that was a permanent fixture on the hilltop. Then they drove a spike through His heels into the fixed pole. They did the same to two thieves who had been scheduled to die the same day. It was then that Jesus said, "Father, forgive them, for they do not know what they do." And the text continues, "And they [the soldiers] divided His garments and cast lots."

The Romans often placed a *titulus* above a sufferer naming his crime. Scourging before crucifixion hastened death, as did breaking a victim's legs.

Thousands were crucified by the Romans. In 71 B.C. some 60,000 of the followers of Spartacus died at one time! But the death of Jesus was different. That death came about according to the "determined purpose and foreknowledge of God" (Acts 2:23).

The Epistles concentrate our attention on God's purpose. "Christ died for sins," Peter explains, "to bring you to God" (1 Pet. 3:18, NIV). "We have redemption through His blood," Paul says (Col. 1:14; Eph. 1:7). The writer of Hebrews looks back on the Old Testament sacrifices and realizes that all of them merely point us to the one final sacrifice by Jesus of Himself on Calvary's cross. He says, "by one sacrifice He has made perfect forever those who are being made holy" (Heb. 10:14, NIV).

The message of the gospel, then, is the offer to all of a salvation won for us by Jesus' death on the Cross. Through simple faith in Him, and confidence in the forgiveness earned by His blood, we are brought to eternal life, beyond every taint of sin, in the presence of God and the resurrected Jesus.

BIBLE BACKGROUND: CRUCIFIXION

Crucifixion was practiced as a method of torture and execution by the Persians before it was adopted by the Romans. Roman law allowed only slaves and criminals to be crucified. Roman citizens were not crucified. The victim's arms are stretched out above him, fastened to a cross bar fixed near the top of the stake slightly taller than a man. Suspended in this way, blood is forced to the lower body. The pulse rate increases, and after days of agony the victim dies from lack of blood circulating to the brain and heart.

In this context it is clear that Jesus' prayer was for the soldiers who did the work of execution. Truly they did not "know what they do." They were simply soldiers, carrying out a lawful order with no understanding of the issues involved.

It would be wrong to assume that this prayer of Jesus extended beyond that hilltop to include the chief priests and scribes and Pharisees, or even to include Pilate. These men had knowingly chosen to plot against Jesus, and vindictively conspired in the judicial murder of an innocent Man. In condemning Jesus they had condemned themselves.

Centuries before, God had spoken to Jeremiah three times about the rebellious generation of his time, saying "do not pray for this people, nor lift up a cry or prayer for them, nor make intercession to Me; for I will not hear you" (Jer. 7:16; 11:14; 14:11). Surely the leaders who had plotted to murder the Son of God had passed that same point. As Jesus said in the parable of the vinedressers who killed the owner's son, "He will come and destroy those vinedressers and give the vineyard to others" (Luke 20:16).

But for the Roman soldiers who carried out the execution, unaware of who Jesus was, there was both prayer and forgiveness.

"TODAY YOU WILL BE WITH ME IN PARADISE" (LUKE 23:43)

Two "thieves" were crucified with Jesus. The Greek word here is used by Josephus with the sense of "revolutionaries." These were not men who simply stole others' possessions, but brigands who had probably murdered as well as looted. It is likely that they were members of the band of Barabbas, who had been scheduled for execution but had been released by Pilate in Jesus' place (Luke 23:16–19).

At first both ridiculed Jesus. But then one underwent a complete change. He rebuked his partner, saying, "Do you not even fear God, seeing you are under the same condemnation? And we indeed justly, for we receive the due reward of our deeds; but this Man has done nothing wrong" (Luke 23:40–41).

The repentant revolutionary then turned to Jesus and said, "Lord, remember me when You come into Your kingdom" (Luke 23:42). This request was a clear affirmation of faith in Jesus, and this at a moment when He seemed stripped of all power, a victim rather than a conqueror! It was then that Jesus spoke the second of His seven utterances from the cross. "Assuredly, I say to you, today you will be with Me in Paradise."

In the first century, "Paradise" was a term used of the abode of the blessed dead. This helps us correct an impression some have as they recite the Apostles' Creed and say, "He descended into Hades." Jesus went to the place reserved for the saved, not to the place reserved for the lost. And the repentant thief went with Him.

This event is often pointed to by evangelists as a reminder that it is never too late to put one's trust in Christ. This is so. Yet it is also never too early. The thief on the cross went to heaven regretting his past choices. How much better to trust Jesus early, to follow Him faithfully, and to glorify Him all our days!

"WOMAN, BEHOLD YOUR SON" (JOHN 19:26, 27)

The crowd around the cross was a mixed group. Jesus' enemies were there, ridiculing and reviling Him. The curious were there, indifferent but wondering if He might yet perform some miracle. And those who loved Jesus were there too. Among them were Jesus' mother, several other women, and the apostle John, identified here as "the disciple whom He loved" (John 19:26).

In first-century Galilee and Judea a widow did not inherit property. This went to the son or sons who were obligated to care for their mother until they died. As Mary's eldest it was Jesus' responsibility to provide for His mother. This was an obligation that Jesus fulfilled while hanging on the cross. He commended John to His mother Mary, saying, "Woman, behold your son," and he committed His mother's care to John, saying, "Behold your mother."

The text says "and from that hour that disciple took her into his own home."

"My God, My God! Why have You forsaken Me?"

"MY GOD, MY GOD" (MATTHEW 27:46, 47; MARK 15:34)

Sometime after Jesus was nailed to the cross a supernatural darkness fell on Palestine, shrouding the events at Golgotha. This darkness lasted from the sixth through ninth hours (12 noon to 3 P.M.). It was near the end of this period that Jesus cried out in anguish His fourth utterance from the cross.

Matthew describes the scene: "And about the ninth hour Jesus cried out with a loud voice, saying, 'Eli, Eli, lama sabachthani?' that is 'My God, My God, why have You forsaken Me?'"

Jesus' cry is a quote of the first verse of Psalm 22, a psalm of David that is unmistakably messianic. Many verses in this psalm vividly portraying the scene at the Cross.

All those who see Me ridicule Me,
They shoot out the lip, they shake the
    head, saying,
"He trusted in the LORD, let Him rescue
    Him;
Let Him deliver Him, since He delights in
    Him!"
            Psalm 22:7, 8

They pierced My hands and My feet;
I can count all My bones.
They look and stare at Me.
They divide My garments among them,
And for My clothing they cast lots.
            Psalm 22:16–18

These and other details make it clear that the psalm that Jesus quoted captures the events and the emotions of the Messiah as He hangs on the Cross.

This fourth cry from the Cross, "My God, My God, why have you forsaken Me," is more an exclamation than a question. It is an exclamation of unimagined anguish, for it expresses the greatest mystery of all.

From eternity past, long before the creation of the universe, Father, Son, and Spirit existed in unbroken harmony as a perfect unity; Three who were in every essential One. Throughout Jesus' life on earth He and the Father had maintained that perfect unity. But on Calvary something both awful and wonderful happened. As Jesus hung on the cross all the sins of humankind were laid on Him. And in that moment when Jesus became sin for us (2 Cor. 5:21), the very fabric of the Godhead was torn apart and Jesus experienced a separation from God which is the essence of hell.

Jesus' cry of anguish captured the moment the Son was forsaken by the Father; the moment when Jesus paid for our sins, experiencing spiritual death in our place and as our substitute.

"I THIRST"
(JOHN 19:28)

John tells us that Jesus, "knowing that all things were now accomplished, that the Scripture might be fulfilled, said, 'I thirst.'"

These words remind us of the humanity of Jesus, and of its importance. To be able to die for humankind's sin God the Son had to become a human being. The writer of Hebrews states this clearly: "Inasmuch then as the children have partaken of flesh and blood, He Himself likewise shared in the same, that through death He might destroy him who had the power of death, that is, the devil, and release those who through fear of death

were all their lifetime subject to bondage" (Heb. 2:14, 15).

We are not to underestimate the significance of the bodily death of Christ, or of the cry "I thirst" which reminds us of the fact that Jesus was a true human being. Yet we need to remember that Jesus' true anguish on the Cross was not due to physical suffering but to the tearing of the very fabric of the Godhead as expressed in the cry, "My God, My God, why have You forsaken Me?"

"IT IS FINISHED"
(JOHN 19:30)

This sixth word from the Cross and the seventh seem to have been uttered together. Luke tells us that after Jesus gave this cry, "He breathed His last," while John tells us after uttering "It is finished," Jesus "gave up His spirit."

The words "it is finished" are self-explanatory. Christ had earlier announced that He had come into the world to seek and save that which was lost (Matt. 18:11; Luke 19:10). Now His work was done. On the Cross Jesus accomplished what He had come to do, saving us by the sacrifice of Himself. He had borne our sins and experienced all that hell has to offer in that endless moment in time that will echo throughout eternity; that moment when God the Father forsook His Son.

Jesus' work was done; it was time for His body to die.

"FATHER, 'INTO YOUR HANDS
I COMMIT MY SPIRIT'"
(LUKE 23:46)

Jesus' words were another quote from the Old Testament, this time Psalm 31. The Psalm is a both a plea for deliverance and a beautiful expression of trust. Whatever sufferings Christ has endured, and whatever anguish He has suffered at the hands of sinful men, His trust in God cannot be shaken.

The Psalm continues,

> But as for me, I trust in You, O Lord;
> I say, "You are my God."
> My times are in Your hand;
> Deliver me from the hand of my enemies,
> And from those who persecute me.
>
> Psalm 31:14, 15

Christ's times were in God's hand. After three days in a borrowed tomb, Christ arose. The darkness was past, and a new day dawned for Jesus, and for the world.

THE POST-RESURRECTION TEACHINGS

The death and resurrection of Jesus launched a new day. The Old Covenant with Israel was superceded by the New Covenant predicted long before by the prophet Jeremiah. And the secret kingdom marked by personal relationship with God as Father, unrevealed in previous ages, was initiated.

The teachings Jesus had given the crowds and His disciples were poured into the new wineskins created by Jesus' resurrection, and took on fresh meaning for all. But Jesus had not finished teaching His disciples yet. After the resurrection Jesus appeared to His followers a number of times before ascending into heaven. It is these post-resurrection teachings we look at in this chapter.

The New Testament records a number of post-resurrection appearances of Jesus. Each of the Gospels record words Jesus spoke to His followers. Nelson's *Illustrated Bible Handbook*, p. 538, gives the sequence of resurrection day events and lists additional post-resurrection appearances of Jesus (see

following page). While frequently these appearances are simply described in the Gospels or Epistles, a number of post-resurrection appearances do record words that Jesus spoke.

JESUS' APPEARANCES AT THE GARDEN TOMB (JOHN 20:11–18; MATTHEW. 28:9–10)

The first persons to speak to Jesus after His resurrection were women, and the first of all was Mary Magdalene. Several women had come to the tomb early Easter morning, intending to add spices to the grave clothes in which Jesus' body had been wrapped. They found the stone that had sealed His tomb rolled away. And there were angels there, who urged the women to tell the disciples to go to Galilee where Christ would join them. On the way Jesus met the women, saying, "Rejoice," and "Do not be afraid. Go and tell My brethren to go

RESURRECTION DAY EVENTS

ADDITIONAL APPEARANCES OF JESUS

to Galilee, and there they will see Me" (Matt. 28:9, 10).

It's a little noted but fascinating fact that these women were the first Christian missionaries, commissioned by Jesus to tell his male disciples that He had risen.

When the disciples heard their report, Peter and John rushed to the tomb and discovered it empty. They also saw that the strips of cloth in which Jesus had been wrapped were on the shelf inside the tomb where His body had been laid, still shaped as if He were there, but empty. After the disciples left, Mary Magdalene, who had returned to the grave, stood outside weeping. She was distraught because she assumed that someone had stolen Jesus' body. It was there that Mary saw Jesus, who asked her why she was weeping. "Supposing Him to be the gardener," Mary begged the figure she saw only dimly through her tears to tell her where Jesus' body had been hidden. Then Jesus uttered her name, "Mary," and she realized it was the Lord.

Falling at His feet she clutched His legs, and was told, "Do not cling to Me, for I have not yet ascended to My Father;

but go to My brethren and say to them, 'I am ascending to My Father and your Father, and to My God and your God" (John 20:17).

The New King James Version rightly translates the phrase "Do not cling to Me." Mary was not to detain Jesus, who had not yet returned to the Father. Some believe that Jesus was referring here to an event described in Hebrews 9:11–12. There Christ is referred to as our High Priest who entered the "more perfect tabernacle not made with hands, that is, not of this creation. Not with the blood of goats and calves, but with His own blood He entered the Most Holy Place once and for all, having obtained eternal redemption."

Whether this is a correct interpretation or not, there was no need for Mary to cling to Jesus. Jesus would be with His Father, who now was the Father of Mary and the disciples in the most intimate and personal sense of that relationship. Jesus would be, and is, available to all!

JESUS' APPEARANCE ON THE ROAD TO EMMAUS (LUKE 24:13–25)

Later the same day Jesus appeared to two of His followers who were walking back to Emmaus, a village about seven miles from Jerusalem. The two were Cleophas and, most believe, his wife. As they walked Jesus joined them, unrecognized. He questioned them about recent events and they shared their despair at the death of Jesus. Yet as Cleophas told what had happened he even included the report of the women who had found the tomb empty and stated that Jesus was alive! "But," Cleophas added, "Him they did not see."

Jesus then rebuked them, calling them foolish ones and slow to believe "in all that the prophets have spoken." Jesus' closest followers had, like the leaders who rejected Jesus and the masses who remained uncer-

tain, focused on those predictions which cast the Messiah in His role as conqueror and ruler. They simply had not believed "all" that the prophets had spoken. They had ignored the fact that the Old Testament prophecy portrayed a suffering as well as victorious Savior. So Jesus asked, "Ought not the Christ to have suffered these things and to enter into His glory?" Christ then proceeded to explain the Scriptures about Himself, beginning at Moses and working through the prophets (Luke 24:26, 27).

When the travelers reached Cleophas' home they invited Jesus to share a meal. It was then, as He blessed the bread and broke it, that they realized their companion had been Jesus Himself. And at that moment Jesus "vanished from their sight" (Luke 24:30).

The two hurried back to Jerusalem and found the disciples. There they added their testimony to that of the women, and discovered that Jesus had also appeared to Peter (Luke 24:34). Yet despite the fact that testimony to Jesus' resurrection was multiplying, the little group of disciples was not yet ready to believe.

JESUS APPEARS TO THE DISCIPLES, WITHOUT THOMAS (JOHN 20:19–24; LUKE 24:36–49)

John's account of the appearance. That resurrection day Jesus appeared to ten of the disciples, who were hiding inside a locked room "for fear of the Jews" (John 20:19). Despite the reports of Jesus' resurrection and despite the evidence of the empty tomb, the disciples were still disoriented and fearful. When Jesus appeared among them He displayed His hands and side, and the ten were convinced. John says in understatement, "then the disciples were glad when they saw the Lord" (John 20:20).

John records four significant sayings of Jesus on this occasion.

Peace be with you (John 20:19, 21). In His Last Supper discourse Jesus had promised the disciples His peace, a peace unlike anything that the world could give (John 14:27;16:33). This was an inner peace, a calm and confident assurance that grows out of a trust in God as heavenly Father. The resurrection of Jesus had resolved every question about who was in control of this universe and sovereign in every situation. Knowing God as All Powerful, and trusting Him as Father, peace was the disciples' legacy, as it is ours.

"As the Father has sent Me, I also send you" (John 20:21). Jesus had been sent into the world with a mission. That mission was to seek and to save, to restore lost human beings to a personal relationship with God. Jesus was now sending His followers on the same mission. The world would not be home to Jesus' followers; it would be a field in which they did Jesus' work.

Receive the Holy Spirit (John 20:22). This saying has puzzled many, as later Jesus told His disciples to wait in Jerusalem until the Holy Spirit came upon them (Acts 1:4). Calvin saw in this verse the description of a partial gift of the Spirit, who was given fully on the Day of Pentecost. He spoke of the disciples' being "only sprinkled with his grace and not saturated with full power." Others suggest that John, whose Gospel is not organized chronologically, took this opportunity to sum up the meaning of Christ's death and resurrection. A third suggestion is that the Spirit was given to the disciples at that time to empower them, but that His baptizing work (1 Cor. 12:13), by which they were united to Christ and one another as His church, took place at Pentecost.

"If you forgive the sins of any, they are forgiven them; if you retain the sins of any, they are retained" (John 20:23). This is a more difficult saying, but the solution lies in the unusual construction in the Greek.

The Greek reads, "Those whose sins you forgive have already been forgiven; those whose sins you do not forgive have not been forgiven (see the comment on Matthew 16:19, p. 137). The *Zondervan NIV Bible Commentary, New Testament,* explains.

God does not forgive people's sins because we decide to do so, nor does he withhold forgiveness because we will not grant it. We announce it; we do not create it. That is the essence of salvation. And all who proclaim the Gospel are in effect forgiving or not forgiving sins, depending on whether the hearer accepts or rejects the Lord Jesus as the Sin-Bearer (p. 370).

Luke's account of the appearance. Luke also gives an account of the resurrection day appearance of Jesus to the disciples. While Luke does not mention Thomas' absence, he does add details not recorded by John.

"Peace to you" (Luke 24:36). The greeting of peace (*shalom*) was a common one. But Luke's account makes it clear that Christ's greeting was a blessing, with far more meaning than the ordinary greeting.

"Handle Me and see" (Luke 24:38–40). Jesus could sense the doubt that gripped the disciples despite the fact that He was there with them. There was always the possibility it was a ghost! So Jesus said to them, "Why are you troubled? And why do doubts arise in your hearts? Behold My hands and My feet, that it is I Myself. Handle Me and see, for a spirit does not have flesh and bones as you see I have."

There may well have been reason for the disciples to fear that Jesus might be a spirit. John tells us that they were in a locked room, when Jesus simply appeared among them. He had not knocked at the door. He had not climbed in any window. He simply appeared! This was not something that a human being was capable of. So Jesus showed them that His body was real.

It is significant that Jesus did not say, "A spirit does not have flesh and blood," but rather said, "A spirit does not have flesh and bone." Leviticus 17:11 states that "the life of the flesh is in the blood." While the emphasis there is on the fact that the blood represents the life of a sacrifice, there may be more involved. Flesh and blood speak of mortality; of a biological life that can and will end. Jesus was no longer flesh and blood. Jesus had been raised from the dead bodily, but the resurrection body was different from the body that had died. Jesus' was no longer limited by the rule governing the material universe; He had transcended its limits in appearing to the disciples. Jesus in His resurrection was no longer flesh and blood; His body spoke of a new order of being infused with a spiritual life that could never end and had powers unimagined by the disciples, or by us.

Jesus opened their understanding (Luke 24:41–49). Luke definitely expands on what John related of the teaching given in that first post-resurrection appearance to the disciples as a group.

Jesus explained the prophecies found in the Old Testament that concerned Him. Christ's death and resurrection were placed in perspective alongside the predictions that spoke of the establishment of an earthly messianic kingdom (Luke 24:44, 46).

Jesus outlined the next stage in God's plan. The Father intended "that repentance and remission of sins should be preached in His name to all nations, beginning at Jerusalem." This verse helps us put the reference in John to the forgiveness and retention of sins in perspective. The mission of the disciples was to preach remission of sins, and to do so "in His name." The disciples would open wide the door of salvation, and how each individual responded would determine whether his or her sins were forgiven or retained.

Jesus defined the role of the disciples in carrying out God's plan. Jesus told the disciples, "and you are witnesses of these things." The disciples, like Christians today, were simply to present what they had seen and experienced concerning Jesus. God Himself would do the work in the listeners' hearts.

The disciples would be empowered for their mission by the Holy Spirit, who would come in the near future. It is not clear whether we should adopt Calvin's interpretation of John 20:22, or take Jesus' words there as a simple reference to the future which was understood as such in the context of the conversation. But Luke does make it clear the Holy Spirit Jesus "gave" them on this occasion was to empower them in the future. Not then.

To be "endued with power from on high" the disciples must wait in the city of Jerusalem.

JESUS APPEARS TO ALL ELEVEN IN JERUSALEM (MARK 16:14–18; JOHN 20:24–29)

Two passages in the Gospels describe appearances of Jesus to all eleven disciples before the Eleven went home to Galilee.

Mark's description of one appearance (Mark 14:18). This description comes at the end of Mark's Gospel. Ancient manuscripts of Mark's Gospel agree up to verse 8 of chapter 16. Several different endings adding to these eight verses have been found in Greek manuscripts. While verses 9 through 20 in our English version is one of the oldest of these endings, the most reliable Greek manuscripts do not include it. Most New Testament scholars doubt that these verses were written by Mark.

At the same time there is nothing here which does not harmonize with teachings of Jesus found in other sources or with the experience of the early church.

Preach the gospel (Mark 16:15). Mark's version of the Great Commission is less complete, but there is no doubt that Jesus

Thomas saw, and believed!

commissioned His disciples to "Go into all the world and preach the gospel to every creature."

He who believes and is baptized (Mark 16:16). The early church practiced believer's baptism, and those who believed were baptized in water as a matter of course. Those who do not believe "will be condemned."

This verse does not suggest that baptism is a condition for salvation. It does suggest that the New Testament church baptized those who were saved.

These signs will follow those who believe (Mark 16:17–18). The debate over these verses focuses on *how long* the signs mentioned would follow believers. There is clear

evidence in Acts that during the early years of the church the apostles did cast out demons, speak with new tongues, and heal. Acts also relates an experience of the Apostle Paul in which he was bitten by a poisonous snake and was unharmed (Acts 28:1-6).

Some Christians believe that such signs are or should be marks of believers today, while others argue that these signs were intended to authenticate the early gospel messengers only until the canon of Scripture was complete. Certainly these signs did operate during the apostolic age, and there are no valid theological grounds on which to question the authenticity of this report of Jesus' words.

John's description of an appearance of Jesus (John 20:24–29). John tells us of an appearance of Jesus to all eleven disciples some eight days after the resurrection.

Not unbelieving, but believing (John 20:27). Jesus had joined the disciples that first day, but at the time Thomas had been absent. Despite the fact that all ten told Thomas that they had seen the Lord, Thomas could not bring himself to believe. He told them, "Unless I see in His hands the print of the nails, and put my finger into the print of the nails, and put my hand into His side, I will not believe" (John 20:25). Thus the Apostle became the first "doubting Thomas."

When Jesus appeared among the disciples again, Thomas was with them. Jesus spoke directly to Thomas, inviting him to perform the tests Thomas said he required, and "Do not be unbelieving, but believing" (John 20:27). The call was not simply for Thomas to believe Jesus lived, but for a change of attitude. Rather than being closed to faith as a basic approach to life, Jesus called Thomas to be "believing." Thomas, like you and me, needed to open himself to the miraculous working of God in our world and in our lives.

Thomas never did reach out to claim the proofs he had said were necessary. Instead Thomas fell down before Jesus and confessed, "My Lord and my God!"

"Blessed are those who have not seen and yet have believed" (John 20:29). It took a personal appearance by Jesus to convince Thomas. Since then, untold billions of men, women, and children have trusted Christ based on the testimony of Scripture and of others who have known Jesus as personal Savior. In the words of the apostle Peter, Jesus is one "whom having not seen you love. Though now you do not see Him, yet believing, you rejoice with joy inexpressible and full of glory" (1 Peter 1:8).

APPEARANCES OF JESUS IN GALILEE
(JOHN 21:1–23; MATTHEW 28:16–20)

The women who went to the tomb where Jesus had been laid that first Easter morning were told by angels and later by Jesus to "go and tell My brethren to go to Galilee, and there they will see Me" (Matthew 28:10; Mark 16:7). It's clear from the Gospels that the eleven remaining disciples spent some of the forty days between Jesus' resurrection and ascension in Jerusalem and some in Galilee. John and Matthew related two different appearances of Jesus to His disciples while they were in Galilee.

Jesus appears by the seaside (John 21:1–25). John tells us that seven of the disciples (21:2) were together in Galilee when Peter, apparently frustrated waiting for Christ to show Himself, announced that he was going fishing. This decision was more significant than it may seem. Peter was not a sport fisherman: fishing had been his occupation before he became a disciple of Jesus. Apparently the six who went with him had been fishermen too. Was Peter

simply bored, or was he considering going back to his old life? Or was Peter destitute and in need of food (see v. 5)?

Whatever Peter's motivation, while the men were fishing that night Jesus appeared unrecognized on the shore. He shouted out, telling the men to "cast the net on the right side of the boat," promising that they would find fish (vv. 5, 6). When the nets filled, John realized that "It is the Lord." Peter then plunged into the sea and swam to Jesus, while the boat followed him dragging the net full of fish. On land they found Jesus tending a fire on which He was already cooking several fish for them to eat.

The scene as sketched by John seems amazingly ordinary: a group of men gathered around a fire on the lakeshore, fish cooking on the coals; Jesus checking the fish and then saying, "Come and eat breakfast" (v. 12). Yet there was a definite tension, for this was just the third time Jesus had shown Himself to disciples after His resurrection (v. 14). Peter was even more tense than the others, for the issue of Peter's denial of Jesus had not yet been resolved, and Peter hung back, uncertain.

John then goes on to describe the restoration of Peter, a prediction which Jesus made concerning Peter, and the answer that Jesus gave when a curious Peter asked a most inappropriate question.

Jesus restores and commissions Peter (John 21:15–17). To understand what is happening we need to note three repeated themes in John's description.

1. John tells us that Jesus asked Peter three questions.

- "Do you love Me more than these?" (John 21:15). The phrase "more than these" seems ambiguous. In view of Peter's earlier boast that whatever the other disciples did he would never desert Jesus, what Jesus probably meant was "Do you love Me more than these other men do?"

- "Do you love Me?" (John 21:16).
- "Do you love Me?" (John 21:17).

It is obvious that the three questions parallel Peter's three denials of Jesus the night of the Crucifixion. Yet the repetition seems even more significant when we note that in the Greek two different words for love are used. In asking the first two questions Jesus used *agapao*, the word used in the New Testament to describe God's love for us as expressed in John 3:16. In asking the last question Jesus used *phileo*, a weaker term denoting fondness or friendship rather than total commitment.

2. Peter answered each question, "Yes, Lord; You know that I love you" (John 21:15–17). Significantly, in answering each question Peter used the word *phileo* rather than the much stronger *agapao*. The significance of this choice has been much debated by commentators. Yet two things seem to stand out.

First, Peter is no longer the over-confident man who was so sure that he would never fail his Lord. Peter *had* failed Him, and the experience had shattered Peter's self-assurance. Peter now simply could not claim to be able to love Jesus in the total, selfless and committed way that *agapao* requires. Peter did love Christ and professed that love, but he used the weaker word.

Second, when Jesus asked Peter the third time, "Do you love Me?", Christ shifted to Peter's term, *phileo*. Jesus accepted what Peter was able to offer at that moment in time, just as Jesus accepts what we are able to give. Later Peter's life showed that he did love Jesus in the total, selfless sense of *agapao*. Just as our lives will show an increasing commitment to Christ as we grow in Him.

3. After asking each of the three "Do you love Me?" questions and hearing Peter's answer, Jesus charged Peter with a mission. Peter was to "Feed my lambs" (v. 15), "Tend My sheep" (v. 16), and "Feed my sheep" (v. 17).

Peter's failure had not disqualified him from leadership. Despite Peter's failure, Jesus had enough confidence in Peter to trust young believers to his care.

This is an encouraging thing for us to remember, for like Peter we also too often fail our Lord. Such failures reflect our human frailty. Yet if we love Jesus, God will work in our lives and make us fruitful in His service.

Jesus predicts Peter's end (vv. 18, 19). Jesus told Peter,

Most assuredly I say to you, when you were younger, you girded yourself and walked where you wished; but when you are old, you will stretch out your hands and another will gird you and carry you where you do not wish (v. 18).

John then explained that Jesus was "signifying by what death" Peter would glorify God. Having said this, Jesus told Peter, "Follow Me" (v. 19).

A strong and early tradition tells us that Peter indeed did follow Jesus and stretch out his arms. In his old age, around A.D. 65, Peter was crucified in Rome. This same tradition tells us that Peter asked to be crucified upside down, feeling unworthy to die the same death as His dearly loved Lord.

Peter's inappropriate question (John 21:20–25). Peter had been humbled but not changed. He was still the impulsive and direct person he had always been. And when Peter observed John listening to the conversation, Peter blurted out, "But Lord, what about this man?" Peter had learned something about his own calling and his future. Now he wanted to know what Jesus planned for John!

Jesus' response was a rebuke. "If I will that he remain till I come, what is that to you? You follow me." These words of Jesus are words that every believer must take to heart. Jesus is Lord. We are to respond to Him as *our* Lord, and seek earnestly to follow Him. We are to search for and discern Christ's will for us. But God's will for others is their business, not ours! We are to encourage others to follow Jesus by seeking His will for them. But we are not to play God in another's life, or seek to make them responsible to us rather than to the Lord.

Jesus commissions His disciples (Matt. 28:16–20). Matthew reports a meeting of Jesus with the Eleven in Galilee (v. 16), at which Jesus gave His followers what we now call "the Great Commission."

All authority has been given to Me in heaven and on earth. Go therefore and make disciples of all the nations, baptizing them in the name of the Father and of the Son and of the Holy Spirit, teaching them to observe all things that I have commanded you; and lo, I am with you always, even to the end of the age (vv. 18–20).

Each phrase in this commission is significant.

"All authority." In the Greek the word "all" is a consistent emphasis. Jesus speaks of *all* authority, *all* nations, *all* things, and *all* times. The universal authority of Jesus exists and is to be established everywhere, over everything, and always.

This statement is both a challenge and an encouragement. The challenge is to bring everything in our lives as well as in our world into submission to Jesus. The encouragement is in the fact that Jesus is all-powerful, fully able to work within and through us to accomplish His purposes.

"In heaven and on earth." There is no secular nor spiritual force that can thwart the accomplishment of Jesus' purposes. We

step out confident that in Christ we are already victors.

"Go therefore." We "go" to carry out Jesus' mission in recognition of His authority over us and over all. Jesus has launched His kingdom of the heart, and it is our mission to establish His rule in the hearts of those who will respond to the gospel in "all nations." The confidence we have in Jesus energizes and inspires us, impelling us to "go" as He commands.

"Make disciples of all nations." Jesus does not send His followers out to make converts but to make disciples. There is a significant difference. A convert believes in Christ. A disciple is transformed from within to become like Christ. Conversion is the first step in disciple-making, but it can never be the last. Like the disciples of the first century a disciple today is a follower of Jesus, who spends time with Him, who responds to His Word, and who lets Christ set the course of his or her daily life. A convert is convinced; a disciple is committed. And in the end, as Jesus said, "a disciple . . . who is perfectly trained will be like his teacher" (Luke 6:40).

The phrase "all nations" reminds us that our vision is never to be limited to our neighborhood or to our acquaintances. Our vision is to extend to every nation, every ethnic and socioeconomic group, to all people without distinction.

"Baptizing them in the name of the Father and of the Son and of the Holy Spirit". The imperative in verse 19 is "make disciples." "Baptizing" here is a participle, indicating that those who become disciples will make a public and open profession of faith.

The "Trinitarian formula" linking the Father, Son, and Holy Spirit is common in the New Testament, and convincing evidence of the fact that God exists in three Persons who are distinct, yet One (see also 1 Cor. 12:4–6; 2 Cor. 13:14; Eph. 4:4–6; 2 Thess. 2:13–14; 1 Pet. 1:2; Rev. 1:4–6).

BIBLE BACKGROUND:

BAPTISM

The Old Testament introduced a washing with water to cleanse from ritual uncleanness. In later Judaism, self-baptism was part of the service of conversion to Judaism. But when John the Baptist appeared preaching his message of repentance he introduced something totally new: water baptism became a profession of a commitment to change.

The gospel preaching in early Acts also stresses repentance. Repentance does not mean mere sorrow for sin, but a change of heart and mind. Those who heard of the resurrected Jesus in Jerusalem were to reverse their opinion of Him—and to acknowledge Him now as the Son of God. It was appropriate in view of the meaning of the symbol introduced by John the Baptist to continue the practice as an open confession of faith: a public testimony to the fact that the individual has changed his or her mind about Jesus and now acknowledges Him as the Christ, God's Savior from sin.

But when John introduced baptism, he also announced that when Jesus came He would "baptize with the Holy Spirit" (Matt. 3:11; Acts 1:5). This promise was kept at Pentecost, fifty days after Jesus' resurrection. From that time on believers have been united to Jesus and one another by the baptizing ministry of the Holy Spirit when they believe (1 Cor. 12:13). Paul teaches in Romans 6 that Christians are united with Jesus in His death, so that Jesus' death is considered ours. Likewise, we are united with Jesus in His resurrection, so that His new life is ours too!

The baptism practiced by the early church, which was most likely baptism by immersion (Mark 1:10), pictured graphically the burial of one's old life with Christ and the raising of the believer to a new life, to be lived in Jesus' power.

There is no New Testament passage that instructs us on mode of baptism. Church history shows that at various times believers have been baptized by sprinkling and pouring as well as by immersion. What is important is to recognize that beyond the symbolism of the rite there lies a great spiritual truth which water baptism is intended to picture. We have died with Christ. We have been raised with Him to a new life.

When we accept water baptism we make a public commitment. We will turn our backs on all that is evil, to live holy lives that reflect the goodness and love of our Lord. (Adapted from the *Illustrated Bible Handbook*, pages 580–581.)

"Teaching them to obey all things that I have commanded you." "Teaching" is also a participle, indicating that it, like baptism, is an element in disciple-making. But the teaching that Jesus emphasizes is not "teaching to *know*," but "teaching to *obey*." This does not mean that instruction in basic Bible doctrine is not important. It does mean that instruction in doctrine is not an end in itself, and that understanding the faith without practicing it is a distortion of true Christianity.

Paul puts this in sharp perspective for us in Philippians 4:9, where he writes, "the things which you learned and received and heard and saw in me, these do, and the God of peace will be with you." We need to learn and receive instruction in God's Word. We need to hear and see God's Word lived out by others. Yet it is only when we "do" that we live close to our Lord and that we experience the God of Peace with us.

"All things that I have commanded you." As we've seen in earlier chapters in this book, Jesus came and exposed the deepest and truest meaning of the Old Testament. He set faith on a new and exciting course, a course marked by personal relationship

Christian baptism differs from the baptism Jesus Himself underwent.

with God as Father and by a commitment to love and serve one another as well as to spread the gospel's good news. It is this new course, which captures the truest meaning of the Old as well as the New Testaments, which is defined by Jesus' commandments.

"I am with you always, even to the end of the age." Jesus who gives us this Great Commission is with us as we carry it out. He is with us and will be with us until this phase of human history comes to its end, and we are caught up to join Him in the air, where we will be with Him forever more (1 Thess. 4:16, 17).

JESUS' FAREWELL
(ACTS 1:1–8)

The last reported words of Jesus before His ascension are recorded in the first chapter of Acts. Luke tells us that Jesus spent additional time with the Eleven during the forty days between His resurrection and being taken up into heaven. Luke also tells us that, in addition to the post-resurrection teachings that we have in the four Gospels, Jesus spoke to them extensively "pertaining to the kingdom of God."

By that fortieth day the disciples had returned from Galilee to Judea and were again near Jerusalem. The Eleven and a number of others had been gathered together to witness Jesus' ascension into heaven. Just before Jesus rose up into the air and disappeared from sight, He gave the Eleven final instructions, which Luke records in Acts 1:4–8.

And being assembled together with them, He commanded them not to depart from Jerusalem, but to wait for the Promise of the Father, "which," He said, "you have heard from Me; for

John truly baptized with water, but you shall be baptized with the Holy Spirit not many days from now." Therefore, when they had come together, they asked Him, saying, "Lord, will You at this time restore the kingdom to Israel?" And He said to them, "It is not for you to know times or seasons which the Father has put in His own authority. But you shall receive power when the Holy Spirit has come upon you; and you shall be witnesses to Me in Jerusalem, and in all Judea and Samaria, and to the end of the earth" (Acts 1:4–8).

This passage also contains much significant teaching.

"The promise of the Father" (Acts 1:4, 5). Jesus had spoken frequently during His last week with the disciples of the Holy Spirit, that "other Helper" God would send the disciples when Jesus left.

It's clear from what Jesus said here that the Holy Spirit had not yet been given to the disciples. Jesus had not yet gone away, and so the Spirit could not have been given yet (John 16:7). But, Jesus promised, the Holy Spirit would come "not many days from now."

The Spirit did come to baptize and to fill the disciples just ten days after the ascension, on the Day of Pentecost. And at His coming the disciples were bonded forever to Jesus as members of His body, and bonded to each other as well. As Paul writes in 1 Corinthians 12:12, this baptizing work of the Holy Spirit now takes place whenever a person believes, for "by one Spirit we were all baptized into one body—whether Jews or Greeks, whether slaves or free—and have all been made to drink into one Spirit."

"It is not for you to know the times" (Acts 1:6, 7). The eager disciples asked Jesus if He would "restore the kingdom to Israel" at this time. The phrase "the kingdom to Israel" makes it unmistakably clear that the disciples were thinking of the glorious messianic kingdom described by the

prophets. Jesus had died and been raised again. He had fulfilled the prophet's predictions of a suffering and dying Messiah who surrendered His life to win forgiveness for those who believed in Him. So, the disciples wondered, is Jesus' fulfillment of the kingly prophesies next on God's agenda?

While Jesus rebuked the disciples, saying that times and seasons were not for them to know, His answer makes it clear that one day God will fulfill the predictions of a glorious messianic rule on earth. There was no correcting of the disciples' impression; no hint that the prophecies of an earthly kingdom might have a merely "spiritual" fulfillment or were done away with entirely. Instead Jesus simply observed that the time for the restoration was in the Father's authority. God would bring it to pass when it was time. In the meantime, "when" was not something with which Jesus' followers needed to be concerned!

"But you shall receive power when the Holy Spirit has come upon you and you shall be witnesses to Me" (Acts 1:8). God did however have an agenda for the immediate future, and they were to be part of it.

You shall receive power. The first item on God's agenda was to imbue Jesus' disciples with power. God had a mission for Jesus' followers that they would never be able to accomplish without supernatural aid. And the disciples were to wait in Jerusalem until they received that promised power.

You shall be baptized with the Holy Spirit. The Holy Spirit would be source of the power that Jesus' followers required. Only when the Spirit had come to serve as the living link between the believer and Christ would the disciples be equipped to fulfill their mission.

There is considerable confusion among some Christians between the "baptism" of the Spirit and "filling" with the Spirit. As we've noted, the baptism of the Spirit is that work of the Spirit by which He unites the believer to Jesus and forges an organic link between the individual and other believers. This work of the Spirit is, according to 1 Corinthians 12:13, performed for all. And until the Spirit came on Pentecost and initiated this work, the disciples were to wait. Only when a living link with the resurrected Jesus had been established would the power they needed to do God's work flow to and through them.

In contrast, the "filling" of the Spirit is directly linked with empowerment and equipping. When we are in right relationship with God, He fills us and enables us not only to grow but also to serve Him effectively. Thus Acts 2 tells us that the day on which the Spirit came, He not only baptized but also filled the disciples (Acts 2:4; see also Acts 4:8, 31; 9:17; 13:9).

You shall be witnesses to Me. The disciples did not yet imagine what the course next decades would hold for them and for other believers in Jesus. But now they did know the part they would play in God's plan, or how His agenda would work itself out in history. All they did know was that the Eleven were to be witnesses to Jesus. *The New International Encyclopedia of Bible Words* (Zondervan) explains.

The root *martyreo* forms the basis for the Greek words in the NT that are translated by various forms of "witness," "testify" and "testimony." All of the basic forms and several compounds constructed on them have the same emphatic sense. The witness, who gives testimony, offers evidence of actual events, evidence based on his direct personal knowledge.

This emphasis is maintained throughout the NT. When the disciples met to choose a replacement for Judas, they said, "It is necessary to choose one of the men who have been with us the whole time the Lord Jesus went in and out among us, beginning from John's baptism to the time when Jesus was taken up from us. For one of these must become a witness with us to his resurrection" (Ac 1:21–22). This same strong sense of objective evidence given by an eyewitness is seen in 1 John. John reports, "That which we have heard, which we have seen with our eyes, which we have looked at and

our hands have touched—this we proclaim concerning the Word of life. The life appeared; we have seen it and testify to it . . . . . We proclaim to you what we have seen and heard" (1 John 1:1–3).

The emphasis in Greek culture and in the Bible on one's personal experience of objective reality as a basis for one's witness or testimony, makes an important statement about Christian faith. Our faith is based on historic events. The resurrection of Jesus was not some subjective experience but an objective event that took place in the real world (p. 595).

The mission of those first disciples, as our mission today, was to testify to others out of their personal knowledge of Jesus Christ and so point them to Him. As we witness, the Holy Spirit speaks to others through us, and it is His power that makes our witness effective.

"In Jerusalem, and in all Judea and Samaria, and to the end of the earth" (Acts 1:8). This final phrase reflects a phrase in the Great Commission. We are to proclaim Jesus "to all nations" (Matt. 28:19). Acts 1:8 however gives us a strategy. We begin sharing Christ in our Jerusalem, the place where we live, to the people we know well. We then move out into our neighborhoods, our Judea, filled with people like us, and our Samaria, populated by people who are different. Ultimately our vision expands and we witness "to the end of the earth."

These concentric circles of influence are historically and psychologically significant. This is how the early church grew in the first century, establishing a base in Jerusalem, spilling over into Judea and Samaria, and ultimately exploding out into the wider Roman Empire. Many use these circles of influence to outline the Book of Acts.

At the same time these circles reflect the growth of an individual or a church. We reach out first to family and friends. As we grow, we reach out to others with whom we come in contact. Ultimately our concern extends to the whole world, and we become involved through prayer or giving or going to missions worldwide.

Yet for the disciples the initial impact of Jesus' words was simple and clear. The Eleven now had a mission in life. That mission was to witness to Jesus, in life and in word, wherever they might be.

And this should be the impact of Jesus' words on believers today as well. We too have a mission in life. We are to represent Jesus, and through our warmth and love Jesus is to shine, even as our words point others to Him.

TEACHINGS OF THE GLORIFIED CHRIST

With the coming of the Holy Spirit to help the disciples recall and interpret Jesus' teachings, all that Jesus had told them during His time on earth fell into place. The disciples, now called apostles, began the work of building the church. They evangelized and taught, nurtured and led. Gradually a body of doctrine emerged, rooted in Jesus' initial teachings and developed under the guidance of the Holy Spirit.

But in two cases Christ Himself was directly involved in teaching. It was Jesus who enlisted the thirteenth apostle, Paul of Tarsus, and who personally spoke to Paul several times during Paul's years of service. And near the end of the first century, the glorified Jesus appeared and spoke to the apostle John on the Isle of Patmos.

JESUS SPEAKS TO PAUL OF TARSUS

Paul without doubt was the most significant single Christian leader of the first century. His role in penetrating the Gentile world with the gospel cannot be overestimated. His thirteen epistles, written to young churches and to individuals, dominate our New Testament, as Paul more than any other worked out the theological and practical implications of the New Covenant that Jesus established in His death and resurrection.

PAUL, THE MAN

Paul was raised in Tarsus, and although trained as a Pharisee, was familiar with Greek thought and philosophy. Like other Pharisees, Paul was totally dedicated to the law and tradition, and zealous about keeping its every detail. It isn't surprising that Paul's reaction to the Christian movement was as hostile as the reaction of the elders of Israel had been to Jesus. Paul was so committed to stamping out a movement he thought heretical that he obtained a commission from the Sanhedrin to arrest Jewish Christians in Damascus and bring them back to Jerusalem for trial.

Saul of Tarsus was the first to be confronted by the glorified Jesus.

The story of Paul's conversion on the road to Damascus is one of the most familiar stories in the New Testament. While traveling along the highway, Paul was blinded by a burst of light and fell to the ground. There he heard the voice of Jesus and spoke with Him.

After that experience Paul, who had been known by his Hebrew name Saul, became as zealous a promoter of Christ has he had been a persecutor of Christians. While before his conversion Saul had been harsh and judgmental, God worked an inner transformation. Without any loss of zeal Paul became a loving and nurturing person (see 1 Thess. 2:4–12).

Paul's missionary journeys, reported in Acts, describe the adventures and challenges faced by Paul and the committed team of Christians that accompanied him as he planted churches throughout Asia Minor and in Mediterranean Europe as well. Paul was not the only apostle to evangelize and plant churches in pagan lands. But Luke's report of his ministry in the book of Acts gives us insight into how the gospel spread so rapidly in the first century and beyond.

PAUL'S CONVERSION

Three accounts of this event are found in the book of Acts. In Acts 9, Luke describes what happened. Acts also records Paul's own words on two occasions where he gave his personal testimony.

Paul told his story when defending himself before the people of Jerusalem (Acts 22). And Paul also told his story while a prisoner, witnessing to the Roman governor and a local ruler, Agrippa (Acts 26).

The Vision (Acts 9:3–6; 22:7–10; 26:14–18). After a burst of light stunned Paul, he fell to the ground. There he heard a voice speaking to him in Hebrew. The speaker identified Himself as "Jesus, whom you are persecuting." This revelation must have been as stunning as the light had been, for suddenly everything that Paul had believed so intensely was shown to be in error. But unlike the scribes and Pharisees who had rejected every evidence that Jesus was the Son of God, Paul immediately acknowledged Jesus and His authority, saying, "Lord, what do You want me to do?"

BIBLE BACKGROUND:

HARD SAYINGS OF JESUS

"It is hard for you to kick against the goads" (Acts 9:5; 26:14).

Kicking against the goads was a Greek proverb referring to fighting against a god. It may have come from the classical Greek playwright Euripides. The apostle, trained in Greek thought and philosophy as well as in the Old Testament, would have understood the allusion. In persecuting the church Paul had been fighting against God! A difficult task indeed.

Paul was instructed to go into the city of Damascus and wait.

Paul is commissioned (Acts 9:10–15; 26:18). Acts 9 introduces a believer named Ananias whom the Lord sent to heal the blinded Paul. In Paul's testimony before the Roman governor and Agrippa, Ananias is left out, and the story is told as if Paul were commissioned there on the road to Damascus. For simplicity's sake Paul simply left Ananias out and reported what God told Paul as if it were one event rather than two.

Ananias' role (Acts 9:10–15). Jesus spoke to Ananias and sent him to the house where Paul was staying, "for behold he is praying." Ananias was also told that Paul had been given a vision in which Ananias came and laid hands on Paul, restoring his sight.

Ananias was less than enthusiastic. He knew Paul's reputation as a persecutor of Christians. But "the Lord said to him, 'Go, for he is a chosen vessel of Mine to bear My name before Gentiles, kings, and the children of Israel. For I will show him how many things he must suffer for My name's sake'" (Acts 9:15, 16).

Paul had been

- chosen by God
- to carry the name of Jesus
- to Gentiles, kings, and the Jewish people

Yet the mission for which Paul had been chosen would bring him much personal pain and suffering (see 2 Cor. 11:23-31).

Paul's summary (Acts 26:14–18). When Paul tells the story of his commissioning, he expands slightly on the explanation given to Ananias. It's likely that Paul here is quoting Jesus' words as reported to him by Ananias (Acts 22:10). Or the message may have been given to Paul directly by the Lord on the Damascus road. In either case Acts gives us the words of Jesus to Paul at the time of Paul's conversion. How strange these words must have seemed to Paul, but what a clear grasp he would have had of his commission.

Rise and stand on your feet; for I have appeared to you for this purpose, to make you a minister and a witness both of the things which you have seen and of the things which I will yet reveal to you. I will deliver you from the Jewish people, as well as from the Gentiles, to whom I now send you, to open their eyes, in order to turn them from darkness to light, and from the power of Satan to God, that they may receive forgiveness of sins and an inheritance among those who are sanctified by faith in Me (Acts 26:16–18).

Paul was commissioned. He was given a preview of the work to which he was called. And most significantly Paul was informed that God intended the Gentiles to "receive . . . an inheritance among those who are sanctified by faith in Me." This last revelation must have stunned Paul the Pharisee. Like others of his class Paul had seen Gentiles as subordinate to Jews rather than as partners in the grace of God. It seems likely that this revelation from Jesus was the critical one which sent Paul back to the Old Testament to work out, under the guidance of the Holy Spirit, the implications of God's opening up of the New Covenant promises to all.

ADDITIONAL REVELATIONS

Acts mentions other occasions on which Jesus spoke directly to Paul. (The voice from heaven that Peter heard [Acts 10, 11] was likely that of Jesus as well, although the text does not specifically say so.) It is significant that on none of these occasions does Jesus teach. Instead He appears to provide guidance or encouragement.

The Lord speaks to Paul in a vision (Acts 18:9–10). Paul was ministering in Corinth when Jesus spoke to him, saying "Do not be afraid, but speak, and do not keep silent; for I am with you, and no one will attack you to hurt you; for I have many people in this city."

The Lord warns Paul to leave Jerusalem (Acts 22:18, 21). In his defense before the people of Jerusalem Paul told of an earlier appearance of Jesus not long after his conversion. Paul had spoken so boldly in Damascus that he was forced to leave the city. Back in Jerusalem the Lord spoke to Paul when he was praying in the temple. "Make haste and get out of Jerusalem quickly, for they will not receive your testimony concerning Me. . . . Depart, for I will send you far from here to the Gentiles."

The Lord encourages Paul (Acts 23:11). Paul had been saved from a mob in Jerusalem, but was confined in a Roman army barracks. There "the Lord stood by him and said, 'Be of good cheer, Paul; for as you have testified for Me in Jerusalem, so you must also bear witness at Rome.'"

These three incidents cover a span of some thirty years, so we should avoid the conclusion that Christ often spoke directly to the apostle Paul. We should also note that all of the appearances to Paul were to provide personal guidance and encouragement, not to reveal some new truth. Christ's teachings are preserved for us in the Gospels and their implications are worked out in the Epistles. With the closing of the canon of Scripture, revelation was complete. Even in the first century Jesus appeared to Paul not to teach or to reveal new truth, but to guide and encourage.

JESUS SPEAKS TO JOHN ON PATMOS

Jesus' words to John are preserved for us in the Book of Revelation. It is fascinating to note that what Jesus says in this setting is also intended to guide rather than to teach. That is, Jesus is not providing new teachings, as for instance in the Sermon on the Mount or in the Last Supper discourse. Instead Jesus is intent on encouraging and guiding those to whom His words are addressed.

For many years John had lived in Asia Minor and guided the churches there. Then around A.D. 90 the churches there experienced a flurry of government persecution, and John was exiled to the Isle of Patmos. While John was praying one Sunday, Christ appeared to John. After identifying Himself, Jesus directed John to record Christ's message to churches in the seven major cities of Asia Minor. The account of the appearance of Jesus, and His words to the seven churches, are recorded in the first three chapters of Revelation.

Jesus does not directly address the readers of Revelation again until the last chapter of the book, and then again His words are exhortation and encouragement rather than instruction.

While we cannot treat Jesus' words in Revelation as "teachings," they are instructive and have valid application to our lives as well as to the lives of those to whom they were addressed originally.

JOHN SEES THE GLORIFIED JESUS (REVELATION 1:8–11)

The Jesus who appeared to John looked very different than the Jesus the apostle had known. This time John saw Jesus glorified, in His essential splendor and majesty. John had to struggle for words to describe the bright and brilliant vision of Christ fully unveiled as God the Son. The best that John could do was to note that the figure seemed human, with white head and hair that glow, eyes "like a flame of fire," and a face "like the sun shining in its strength." Even the feet of the figure glowed like brass being refined in a furnace.

John was stunned at the sight, and "fell at His feet as dead." There was no way that John, who had had the closest relationship of any to Jesus during His time on earth, could bear to gaze on the Son of God revealed in all His glory.

Jesus identified Himself, and told John to record what he saw and to send his writings to the seven Asia Minor churches.

Jesus' reveals His true identity (Rev. 1:8). John had known Jesus during His incarnation. Now the figure that John sees announces His true identity. The one whose glory was both revealed and concealed during His time on earth now announces: "'I am the Alpha and the Omega, the Beginning and the End,' says the Lord, 'who is and who was and who is to come, the Almighty.'"

These titles leave nothing to the imagination. Now and from eternity to eternity, the glorified Jesus is God, the Almighty. (For a study of the names and titles of God, see the companion book in this series *Every Name of God in the Bible*.)

Jesus commissions John (Rev. 1:11; 17–20). Jesus tells John to write what he sees to "the seven churches which are in Asia" (1:11). The announcement of Christ's identity and the commission to write are repeated (v. 18). The next two verses are significant for interpreting Revelation, but less so for our purposes here.

The structure of the book (v. 19). Jesus tells John to "write the things which you have seen, and the things which are, and the things which will take place after this." Many commentators see this verse as the key to understand Revelation. The "things which you have seen" are in 1:1–17. The "things which are" are the subject of Revelation 2 and 3. And the rest of the book, Revelation 4–22, concern "the things which will take place after this." If this is correct we must treat the Book of

John's description of the glorified Jesus draws on Old Testament symbols.

Revelation as prophecy rather than as mere apocalyptic literature.

The symbols explained (Revelation 1:20). When Jesus appeared to John He was standing in the midst of seven golden lampstands holding seven stars. Jesus explained,

The mystery of the seven stars which you saw in My right hand, and the seven golden lampstands: The seven stars are the angels of the seven churches, and the seven lampstands which you saw are the seven churches.

The seven churches have already been named. They are the Asia Minor churches in the cities of Ephesus, Smyrna, Pergamos, Thyatira, Sardis, Philadephia, and Laodicea. There is some question about the "angels" of the seven churches. While some take these

as literal guardian angels watching over the churches, it is more likely that the word should be translated "messenger." The basic meaning of both *mal'ak* in Hebrew and *angelos* in Greek is "messenger," with angels being "heavenly messengers." If the text should read "messenger" rather than "angel," Jesus would be referring to the person in each church responsible to read aloud Jesus' message to the congregation.

JESUS DICTATES LETTERS TO THE SEVEN CHURCHES (REVELATION 2:1—3:22)

The seven letters are contained in two chapters of Revelation. Each letter shares a common structure with the others. The church is designated and described, and an aspect of Jesus' description is provided along with the statement of a desired response to Jesus as He has just revealed himself. A chart in Nelson's *Illustrated Bible Handbook* (pp. 825, 826) sums up each of these elements. (See facing page.)

Some have taken these churches of Asia Minor as symbols marking the course of church history. Such an interpretation is forced, however. We know that these seven churches did exist in the first century, and there is reason to believe that each is characterized accurately in the seven letters. At the same time, we can find points of comparison with churches today. Certainly the words of Jesus to the seven churches of Asia contain many insights which we can and are to apply to ourselves today.

TO THE CHURCH AT EPHESUS (REVELATION 2:17)

Ephesus was one of the churches founded by the apostle Paul. Politically, Ephesus was the seat of the provincial Roman governor and bore the title of the "Supreme Metropolis of Asia." Ephesus

❖

Church	Characteristic	Description of Jesus	Desired response
Ephesus, the steadfast (2:1–7)	works hard, perseveres, rejects wicked, endures, left first love	walks among the seven lamps (in heaven)	return to first love
Smyrna, the persecuted (2:8–11)	undergoing suffering, poverty, persecution	the one who died but is alive again	remain faithful
Pergamum, the compromising (2:12–17)	remains true, faithful to death, tolerates immorality	holds sharp, two-edged sword (Word of God)	repent of evil ways
Thyatira, the doctrinally compromising (2:18–29)	doing more than at first, tolerates immorality, false teaching	eyes of fire, feet of bronze (The Judge)	hold to the truth
Sardis, the counterfeit (3:1–6)	has reputation as alive, but is dead; deeds incomplete	holds the Spirit, angels in His hand	wake up, obey what has been heard
Philadelphia, the obedient (3:7–13)	has little strength, yet kept the word; patiently endures	holds the key of David (royal authority)	hold on to what you have
Laodicea, the materialistic (3:14–22)	neither cold nor hot, wealthy but poor spiritually	ruler of creation	be earnest, repent under discipline

❖

was also the center of the cult of the goddess Artemis (Diana). Pilgrims from all over the Mediterranean world ventured there to see the magnificent temple, which served as a bank and often financed the projects of kings. Under Paul's ministry, multitudes of citizens turned to the Lord (Acts 19). The Christians publicly burned occult books, and the revival was so great that it threatened the income of those who made their living selling religious idols. A strong and vigorous church had been established, and from the Revelation letter to Ephesus it is clear that the church remained strong and vital. For thirty to forty years the Christians in Ephesus had persevered and remained patient, laboring for the sake of Jesus' name and had not become weary (Rev. 2:3).

These things says He who holds the seven stars in His right hand, who walks in the midst of the seven golden lampstands: "I know your works, your labor, your patience, and that you cannot bear those who are evil. And you have tested those who say they are apostles and are not, and have found them liars; and you have persevered and have patience, and have labored for My name's sake and have not become weary. Nevertheless I have this against you, that you have lost your first love. Remember therefore where you have fallen; repent and do the first works, or else I will come to you quickly and remove your lampstand from its place—unless you repent. But this you have that you hate the deeds of the Nicolaitans, which I also hate.

"He who has an ear, let him hear what the Spirit says to the churches. To him who overcomes I will give to eat from the tree of life which is in the midst of the Paradise of God."

He who holds the seven stars in His right hand (Rev. 2:1). In this letter Jesus presents Himself as sovereign over the seven churches (stars). Jesus is Lord over the church, a theme Paul developed in his epistle to the Ephesians. Christ as Head of the church not only directs and guides, but He also protects and empowers. His authority is something that this church and every church must acknowledge, and to which it must submit.

"I know your works" (Rev. 2:2, 3). The church has remained faithful and active since its founding. Jesus notes especially that the believers "cannot bear those who are evil" and that they have "tested those who say they are apostles and are not." Most believe that "those who are evil" are the false apostles mentioned immediately afterward.

It is unlikely that the evil men claimed to be apostles in the sense that the Twelve or Paul were apostles. The New Testament also applies the title "apostle" to itinerant teachers and missionaries who traveled from church to church (Rom. 16:7), and it is this sense in which those who troubled the Ephesians presented themselves as apostles. But Ephesians were not deceived and remained doctrinally pure.

Interestingly, some fifteen years after John's death, the church father Ignatius wrote to the church at Ephesus and commended them for refusing to provide a "home" to heresy!

You have left your first love (Rev. 2:4, 5). While an outstanding church in many ways Jesus had "this against" the church at Ephesus. Commentators differ on what that first love was, whether love for the brethren within the community (Eph. 1:15; 3:17, 18) or love for the Lord. Either may be correct, or both may be in view. The solution the problem of lost love, however, is clearly stated in three imperatives: remember, repent, go.

This pattern is helpful for us to use in self-examination. Do we remember what it was like when we first came to know Christ? Do we recall the excitement and glow of discovery? And does our heart beat with the same passion now?

Repent is a simple word, like the military command "about face." It doesn't mean be sorry for past sins or for our present spiritual state. It does mean change! Reverse course. Then we will do our former works—and our present works—motivated by pure love (1 Cor. 13:1–3).

The threat to remove the Ephesian lampstand is a serious one. Without love, a church is doomed to fall into dead orthodoxy or purposeless activity. No such church will long endure.

"This you have, that you hate the deeds of the Nicolaitans" (Rev. 2:6). The identity, beliefs, and practices of the Nicolaitans remains a mystery. Eusebius in his *Ecclesiastical History* indicates that this group existed for only a short time.

"What the Spirit says to the churches" (Rev. 2:7). The promise made to "him who overcomes" is for all the churches, not just the Ephesians. This and the promises to the other churches are eschatological, having to do with the eternal state as described in Revelation 21 and 22. Thus eating from "the tree of life which is in the Paradise of God" is parallels to eating from "the tree of life" in Revelation 22:2.

There is a future for the people of God. And that future is not limited to this tiny planet or by an individual's brief span of years here. That future is unlimited, to be lived and enjoyed in the Paradise of God.

TO THE CHURCH IN SMYRNA (REVELATION 2:8–11)

The city of Smyrna, about forty miles north of Ephesus, was noted as the birthplace of the epic poet Homer. It was also a center of emperor worship, and had been given the privilege by the Roman Senate of building the first temple to honor the Emperor Tiberius. Under the Emperor Domitian (A.D. 81–96), who exiled John to Patmos, emperor worship became compulsory. Once each year a citizen had to appear before representatives of the emperor and burn incense on the altar to the god Caesar, after which the citizen received a certificate. Some sixty years after Revelation was written, the church father Polycarp was burned alive for refusing to make this offering. Eusebius quotes the martyr as saying, "Eighty-six years have I served Christ, and he has never done me wrong. How can I blaspheme my King who saved me?"

The active persecution of Christians in this city of some 200,000 is reflected in Jesus' words to the angel of the church of Sardis. This is the one church about which Christ has no criticism.

These things says the First and the Last, who was dead, and came to life: "I know your works, tribulation, and poverty (but you are rich); and I know the blasphemy of those who say they are Jews and are not, but are a synagogue of Satan. Do not fear any of those things which you are about to suffer. Indeed, the devil is about to throw some of you into prison, that you may be tested, and you will have tribulation ten days. Be faithful until death, and I will give you the crown of life.

"He who has an ear, let him hear what the Spirit says to the churches. He who overcomes shall not be hurt by the second death."

"The First and the Last, who was dead, and came to life" (Rev. 2:8). Death was the penalty for those who refused to worship the emperor. But Christ was dead and came to life. He conquered death, and has a word for those who are in danger of dying for His sake.

Those who say they are Jews (Rev. 2:9). Apparently the Jewish population of Smyrna enthusiastically betrayed to the authorities Christians who did not have their certificates. The Jews had many privileges in the Roman Empire, and one of those would have been exemption from offering sacrifices to the emperor. But the Jewish faith was a licit (recognized) religion, and Christianity was classified as an illicit faith. There were no exemptions for Christians.

The Jewish hostility toward Christians follows a pattern seen frequently in Acts. Those Jews who did not welcome the gospel message became increasingly hostile to Christians and initiated persecutions (see for example Acts 13:45, 50 and 14:19). In writing that the Jews in Smyrna "say they are Jews and are not," Christ reminds us that those who were the biological seed of Abraham were not necessarily his spiritual descendants (Rom. 2:28; 9:6). Rather than following in the path of Abraham they follow in the footsteps of Satan, who was behind the persecution in Smyrna (John 8:44).

"Be faithful unto death" (Rev. 2:10, 11). Jesus warns the church at Smyrna of coming persecution. The reference to "ten days" seems best understood as an Aramaic expression indicating an unspecified but relatively short period of time. During this burst of persecution some Christians were to be imprisoned and others would suffer. But Christ holds out a hope on which they can depend. Although death may claim some of the faithful, Christ will give them "the crown of life."

While believers are subject to biological death, they "shall not be hurt by the second death," a phrase used in Revelation to indicate an eternity of separation from God in hell (Rev. 20:14; 21:8).

TO THE ANGEL OF THE CHURCH IN PERGAMOS (REVELATION 2:12–17)

Pergamos was a prominent city in the first century, a rival to Ephesus and Smyrna. It boasted a library of some 200,000 volumes and a number of famous temples. One of its major religions was the worship of Asclepius, the god of healing, and many came to that city in hopes of being restored to health.

These things says He who has the sharp two-edged sword: "I know your works, and where you dwell, where Satan's throne is. And you hold fast to My name, and did not deny My faith even in the days in which Antipas was My faithful martyr, who was killed among you, where Satan dwells. But I have a few things against you, because you have there those who hold the doctrine of Balaam, who taught Balak to put a stumbling block before the children of Israel, to eat things sacrificed to idols, and to commit sexual immorality. Thus you also have those who hold the doctrine of the Nicolaitans, which thing I hate. Repent, or else I will come to you quickly and will fight against them with the sword of My mouth.

"He who has an ear, let him hear what the Spirit says to the churches. To him who overcomes I will give some of the hidden manna to eat. And I will give him a white stone, and on the stone a new name written which no one knows except him who receives it."

He who has the sharp two-edged sword (Rev. 2:12). The title here goes back to a messianic passage in Isaiah, specifically 49:2. There and here the sword is the Word of God (Eph. 6:17). There is another interesting historical note here. Pergamos possessed a rare power, seldom granted to cities: the power of capital punishment, which was symbolized by the sword. How much greater the power of the Word of God and Him who utters it, for His sword is doubled-edged, able to create as well as to destroy!

Where you dwell; where Satan's throne is (Rev. 2:13). As a center for pagan worship and a stronghold of Satan, Pergamos was a difficult place for Christians to live. Yet the believers had been faithful "even in the days in which Antipas was My faithful martyr." We know nothing of Antipas beyond this reference. But how good to know that God knows our name even when we have been forgotten by others.

"I have a few things against you" (Rev. 2:14, 15). Jesus specifically mentions the "doctrine of Balaam" and also the "doctrine of the Nicolaitans." While the Christians in Pergamos had stood up against external pressures, their doctrine was being corrupted from within. Interestingly, the name *Balaam* can mean "conquer the people," as does the title *Nicolaitans*.

The seer Balaam had been hired by King Balak to curse the Israelites during the Exodus period. When he failed and learned of God's intention to bless them, Balaam advised the pagan king to set a "honey trap." Young women should set up tents outside the Israelite camp, to seduce Israelite men and then lead them into idolatry. The plot succeeded, and God punished His people with a plague, but did not destroy them as Balak had hoped. As many first-century pagan rites involved immorality as well as the worship of idols, the allusion undoubtedly fit the situation in Pergamos. It's likely that some of the Christians in Pergamos were deeply involved in pagan worship and sexual immorality.

"Repent, or else I will come to you quickly" (Rev. 2:16). Jesus called for a radical change in the permissive attitude that the church seems to have adopted toward the sinning Christians. Thus the whole church

is called on to repent. If the believers there fail to purify the church, Jesus "will fight against them [those sinning] with the sword of My mouth."

Discipline of brothers and sisters who sin openly and habitually is the responsibility of the local congregation. If the church fails to discipline, Christ will intervene, and the result will be much more painful (see Rev. 2:21, 22).

"To him who overcomes I will give some of the hidden manna to eat" (Rev. 2:17). Jesus mentions two gifts that are to be given to those who remain faithful to Him.

The hidden manna. The festival foods provided at feasts held to honor pagan gods were tempting. Their presentation and their aroma, as well as their taste, appealed to the senses. But the spiritual food on which believers are to feast is hidden; it cannot be seen or savored by the senses. Yet that manna sustains us spiritually.

The white stone. The significance of the white stone is uncertain. Different colored stones sometimes served as tickets to events, and in the criminal trials white stones were often cast as "innocent" votes, while black stones were votes of "guilty." Whatever the allusion, the white stone here was an indication of innocence and an invitation to enter God's presence.

A new name. Commentators suggest that the new name written on the white stone is a name of Christ. In the ancient world the names of demons or deities were thought to give the person who knew them occult power. If the gift Jesus offers the overcomers of Pergamos is a name of His "which no one knows except him who receives it," the white stone not only symbolizes access to God but also a promise by Christ to be available to those who are faithful. Through His power they can overcome every challenge.

TO THE ANGEL OF THE CHURCH IN THYATIRA (REVELATION 2:18–24)

Thyatira was a working city, specializing in trade in wool, linen, clothing, leatherwork, and bronzes. As was typical in the first century, each occupation had its guild (labor union), which honored its own patron deity. The guilds sponsored feasts and festivals, paid for the burial of members, and in general served as the center of a member's social life as well as a source of political influence. The letter to the Christians at Thyatira is the longest of the seven letters to churches.

These things says the Son of God, who has eyes like a flame of fire, and His feet like fine brass: "I know your works, love, service, faith, and your patience; and as for your works, the last are more than the first. Nevertheless I have a few things against you, because you allow that woman Jezebel, who calls herself a prophetess, to teach and seduce My servants to commit sexual immorality and eat things sacrificed to idols. And I gave her time to repent of her sexual immorality, and she did not repent. Indeed, I will cast her into a sickbed, and those who commit adultery with her into great tribulation, unless they repent of their deeds. I will kill her children with death, and all the churches shall know that I am He who searched the minds and hearts. And I will give to each one of you according to your works.

"Now to you I say, and to the rest in Thyatira, as many as do not have this doctrine, who have not known the depths of Satan, as they say, I will put on you no other burden. But hold fast to what you have till I come. And he who overcomes, and keeps My works until the end, to him I will give power over the nations—

"He shall rule them with a rod of iron, They shall be dashed to pieces like the potter's vessels"—
as I also have received from My Father; and I will give him the morning star.

"He who has an ear, let him hear what the Spirit says to the churches."

"The Son of God" (Rev. 2:18). The image presented here of eyes like blazing fire and feet like burnished bronze emphasize judgment, which is a dominant theme in this fourth letter.

"I know your works" (Rev. 2:19). The commendation section in this letter is very brief. It's clear that the Christians have grown in loving service and patience. But there are serious problems at Thyatira.

"Nevertheless I have a few things against you" (Rev. 2:20–23). The problems in the church grow from the influence of a false prophetess symbolically identified as "Jezebel."

The Old Testament Jezebel was the pagan wife of King Ahab of Israel. She was committed to stamping out the worship of Yahweh and supplanting Israel's ancient faith with the worship of her own deity. Like her namesake, the Jezebel of Revelation promoted false teaching and a wicked lifestyle, and had gained great local influence. Commentators disagree whether this Jezebel is a literal woman or if she stands for a clique of false prophets in the church. Her "children" are her followers.

Jezebel's characteristic sins (v. 20). Like the Nicolaitans whose influence was felt in other churches, Jezebel's teaching involved both sexual immorality and participation in feasts dedicated to idols.

Her refusal to repent (v. 21). Christ had patiently given Jezebel time to repent of her sexual immorality, but His grace was rejected. This suggests that Jezebel may have been a believer who had willfully gone her own way and influenced others to follow her. The refusal to repent and change is as serious an offense now as it was then, and is sure to be followed by severe discipline.

I will cast her into a sickbed (v. 23). This language suggests that Jezebel actually is an individual rather than a group. Christ also says that he will bring great tribulation

on those who "commit adultery with her" (follow her ways and teaching).

The phrase "unless they repent" again suggests those who have turned aside after Jezebel are believers who have either foolishly or willfully lost their bearings. However, a failure to repent now will lead to swift and severe judgment.

I will kill her children with death (v. 23). The judgment that will strike members of the Jezebel party will be so startling that "all the churches shall know that I am He who searches the minds and hearts."

What happened after the letter to Thyatira was delivered? Did the followers of Jezebel repent? Or did some devastating judgment sweep away those who followed her, filling the other churches in Asia with awe? Church history does not record the answer. But the image of Christ with penetrating, burning eyes and glowing bronze feet reminds us that when God rebukes us, it is not only right to repent. It is safer.

"Now to you . . . who do not have this doctrine" (Rev. 2:24). Christ's sole command in this letter is directed to those who have not been led astray by Jezebel. The only command Jesus gives them is to "hold fast what you have till I come."

There are times when it takes all our energy simply to hold fast to what we have. This is true for individuals as well as for the little group of faithful Christians at Thyatira. When this happens, looking forward to Christ's return provides hope and strength.

"I will give him power over the nations" (Rev. 2:26, 27). There is a fascinating contrast here between the present weakened condition of Christians who have only enough strength to "hold on" and the reward of power over the nations.

This promise is to be fulfilled after Jesus returns, as indicated by the quote from Psalm 2, where the Messiah is portrayed as ruling earth with a rod of iron.

One day the persecuted will rule, and the persecutors will be humbled. What an encouragement for those who suffer unjustly now!

"I will give him the morning star" (Rev. 2:28, 29). Jesus identifies a second reward for the overcomers in Thyatira. The nature of this promise is also debated. Some see it as symbolic of resurrection. Others link it with Peter's analogy of Christ's return to the rising of the morning star (2 Peter 1:19). In any case, the return of Christ marks the beginning of blessings for the faithful who have been so hard pressed.

TO THE ANGEL OF THE CHURCH IN SARDIS (REVELATION 3:1–6)

Sardis was a prosperous commercial center and a military stronghold. It had often been attacked, but only twice in recorded history had its walls been breached. Sardis was also famous for its great "thousand hills" cemetery marked by hundreds of burial mounds. Although Sardis no longer was of political significance it remained wealthy for two hundred years into the Christian era.

These things says He who has the seven Spirits of God and the seven stars: "I know your works, that you have a name that you are alive, but you are dead. Be watchful, and strengthen the things which remain, that are ready to die, for I have not found your works perfect before God.

Remember therefore how you have received and heard; hold fast and repent. Therefore if you will not watch, I will come upon you as a thief, and you will not know what hour I will come upon you.

You have a few names even in Sardis who have not defiled their garments; and they shall walk with Me in white, for they are worthy. He who overcomes shall be clothed in white garments, and I will not blot out his name from the Book of Life; but I will confess his name before My Father and before His angels.

"He who has an ear, let him hear what the Spirit says to the churches."

He who holds the seven Spirits of God (Rev. 3:1). The reference here is to the Holy Spirit who gives life and strengthens believers. While there is a small minority in the church who are vitalized by the Spirit, most are spiritually dead. There is a functioning organization there called a Christian church—a "name that you are alive"—but in fact the majority are not believers at all!

How often today also there are groups who assemble in "churches," but who have never known the Spirit's vitalizing touch and whose members have never trusted Christ for salvation. These are dead churches, corpses propped up on Main Street.

Strengthen the things which remain, that are ready to die (Rev. 3:2). The first Greek word in this verse is not "be watchful" but "Wake up!" The congregation is dying and the believers there do not even realize what has happened. There is no room for complacency; the true believers must act quickly to salvage what remains. The phrase "I have not found your works perfect" indicates failure to come close to meeting Christ's expectations. Praise found in letters to other churches for such works as love, faithfulness, and perseverance are utterly absent here.

Hold fast and repent (Rev. 3:3). Repentance and a return to the teaching of the apostles is the only hope for Sardis. If the people fail to repent, Jesus will act to judge them when they least expect it.

"A few names even in Sardis" (Rev. 3:4, 5). The emphasis on a few makes it all too clear that the majority had departed from the faith. The contrast between "defiled garments" and "white garments" marks a distinction between those who depend on their own righteousness for acceptance by God and those who by faith have been clothed in the righteousness of Christ. Only those who wear the white garments are secure, for their names will never be blotted out of the Book

of Life. Christ will acknowledge them before God, and their acceptance in heaven is assured.

TO THE ANGEL OF THE CHURCH IN PHILADELPHIA (REVELATION 3:7–13)

A main highway and imperial post road ran through Philadelphia, an important commercial and fortress city that had played a role in disseminating Greek culture and language in what is now Turkey. Significantly a Christian presence persisted in Philadelphia up until A.D. 1392.

These things says He who is holy, He who is true, "He who has the key of David, He who opens and no one shuts, and shuts and no one opens": "I know your works. See, I have set before you an open door, and no one can shut it; for you have a little strength, have kept My word, and have not denied My name. Indeed I will make those of the synagogue of Satan, who say they are Jews and are not, but lie—indeed I will make them come and worship before your feet, and to know that I have loved you.

"Because you have kept My command to persevere, I also will keep you from the hour of trial which shall come upon the whole world, to test those who dwell on the earth.

"Behold, I am coming quickly! Hold fast what you have, that no one may take your crown.

"He who overcomes, I will make him a pillar in the temple of My God, and he shall go out no more. I will write on him the name of My God and the name of the city of My God, the New Jerusalem, which comes down out of heaven from My God. And I will write on him My new name.

"He who has an ear, let him hear what the Spirit says to the churches."

He who is holy, He who is true (Rev. 3:7). Christ presents Himself as the Messiah, who holds the key to the kingdom promised in Old and New Testaments alike. The reference to the "synagogue of Satan" suggests that the Jews in Philadelphia claimed to be the authentic heirs of the Old Testament promises. But the Christ who Christians worship is the holy and true one who "has the key of David," and who alone can open or shut the door to heaven.

"I know your works" (Rev. 3:8, 9). The Christians of Philadelphia had been faithful to the gospel and had never denied Christ's name. The door that Christ set before them would remain open, and they are assured of a place in His kingdom. As for their Jewish opponents the day will come when they will be forced to acknowledge that those they had persecuted were right. As Isaiah predicted, "The sons of those who afflicted you shall come bowing to you, and all those who despised you shall fall prostrate at the soles of your feet" (Is. 60:14).

"I will keep you from the hour of trial" (Rev. 3:10). This special promise to the church at Philadelphia, like other distinctive promises to individual churches, is generally taken as a promise to all believers. Christ had commanded the Philadelphians to persevere, and they had done so. The phrase the "hour of trial which shall come upon the whole world" recalls the Old Testament prophets' vision of a Great Tribulation, about which Christ Himself taught (Matt. 24:15–22). While this eschatological interpretation is rejected by some writers, it seems least strained to interpret it in the context of Christ's own and Old Testament prophecy. This makes it a reference to the terrifying judgments God will bring on the earth at history's end.

Those who believe the Bible teaches Christians will be raptured (caught up to be with Christ, 1 Thess. 4) see support for their belief in the reference to being "kept from the hour of trial." Whether this is correct or not, the promise is a wonderful one. Whatever comes, Christ Himself will protect those who have been faithful.

Hold fast (Rev. 3:11). Jesus encourages contemporary as well as first-century Christians by promising that "I am coming quickly."

God's plan is racing toward His intended conclusion. Although the pace may seem slow to us, everything is on schedule, hurtling toward history's culmination. We are to hold fast to this hope, lest we be robbed of our crown.

Here as elsewhere the "crown" symbolizes the reward God graciously intends to give to those who have been enabled by grace to serve Him well.

"I will make him a pillar in the temple of My God" (Rev. 3:12). Two additional promises are given to overcomers.

A pillar in the temple. The district around Philadelphia was subject to earthquakes. When a quake struck, often only the pillars of one of the pagan temples in the area would be left standing. In Christ we are not just building blocks in God's temple, but pillars who stand firm and secure.

I will write on him the name of My God. This promise seems to reflect a first-century custom of honoring an individual by having a special pillar added to a local temple that is inscribed with his name. Yet Christ may be speaking of an even more special inscription, one with His own name, indicating that the believer is identified with God and God's own special possession.

TO THE ANGEL OF THE CHURCH OF THE LAODICEANS (REVELATION 3:14–22)

Laodicea lay in the fertile Lycus valley, and a major Roman road ran through the city. As well as being a commercial and communications center, Laodicea was known for its black wool and banking facilities. It also boasted a medical school famous for ointments that were used to treat eyes and ears. Despite its wealth the water supply was poor, drawn from hot or cold springs that became lukewarm as it flowed through a six-mile long aqueduct.

These things say the Amen, the Faithful and True Witness, the Beginning of the creation of God: "I know your works, that you are neither cold nor hot. I could wish you were cold or hot. So then, because you are lukewarm, and neither cold nor hot, I will vomit you out of My mouth. Because you say, 'I am rich, have become wealthy, and have need of thing'—and do not know that you are wretched, miserable, poor, blind and naked—I counsel you to buy from Me gold refined in fire, that you may be rich; and white garments, that you may be clothed, that the shame of your nakedness may not be revealed; and anoint your eyes with eye salve, that you may see. As many as I love, I rebuke and chasten. Therefore be zealous and repent. Behold, I stand at the door and knock. If anyone hear my voice and opens the door; I will come in to him and dine with him, and he with Me. To him who overcomes I will grant to sit with Me on My throne, as I also overcame and sat down with My Father on His throne.

"He who has an ear, let him hear what the Spirit says to the churches."

"The Amen, the Faithful and True Witness," (Rev. 3:14). Christ is the one who established the pattern; He is the faithful and true witness who never in any way failed to reveal and glorify God. In this identification Christ stands in stark contrast to the Laodicean church, which has failed God in every way.

"You are neither cold nor hot" (Rev. 3:15–16). Like the water from the aqueduct, the church in Laodicea was lukewarm, indifferent to God. This is revolting to the Lord, who will "vomit you out of My mouth."

You do not know that you are wretched, miserable, poor, blind, and naked (Rev. 3:17). In terms of material possessions this was a wealthy church. In terms of spiritual assets, the church was stripped of every true blessing. It is always tragic when a believer is deceived into assuming that earthly riches are symbols of God's blessing, when the true blessings are not material at all. When evaluated by eternity's values, the Laodiceans were wretched and pitiful, for they were spiritually poor, blind, and naked.

What a contrast with the church at Smyrna, which was outwardly poor, but inwardly rich (Rev. 2:9)!

"I counsel you" (Rev. 3:18). God's solution is to turn from all those things in which the Laodiceans took such pride and focus on that which is true and faithful.

"Buy from Me gold refined in the fire." Peter explains the image when he speaks of the testing of faith by various trials as "more precious than gold that perishes." When faith is tested by fire it will be "found to praise, honor, and glory at the revelation of Jesus Christ" (1 Peter 1:7).

The lukewarm Laodiceans were so complacent and ready to compromise that they offended no one, and challenged no cultural sin. They got along, and were satisfied to do so. Yet while Christ does not tell us to seek trials or persecution, we are to stand for something. If we stand for something, we are sure to spark the very trials which will purify our faith.

"Buy from Me . . . white garments, that you may be clothed." White garments represent righteousness, here not an imputed righteousness but an experiential righteousness. The Laodicean Christians were settled into their culture so comfortably that they saw nothing wrong with its sins, and had adopted the loose ways of their fellow-citizens. In fact their behavior was shameful, a compromise with the world.

"Anoint your eyes with eye salve, that you may see." The remedy for eye problems that the city produced was useless in curing spiritual blindness. And it was spiritual blindness that was the problem in Laodicea.

All three images point to the dire need of the members of this church, many for salvation, others for renewal.

"As many as I love, I rebuke and chasten" (Rev. 3:19). The harsh words spoken to the Laodicean church were evidence of Christ's love for them. He spoke harshly to awaken them from their spiritual slumber, and says to them, "Therefore be zealous and repent."

"I stand at the door and knock" (Rev. 3:20). The image presented in this verse is a familiar one. A visitor stands outside and knocks at mealtime. The porter or the owner of the house listens carefully to see if he recognizes the voice. Because the cord that is attached to the latch has been pulled inside, the door can only be opened from within. Yet the visitor is eager to come in and dine, symbolizing in the first century intimate fellowship.

Christ, who stands at the door, will not force His way in. The door must be opened from within. But once the door is opened and the invitation extended, Jesus will enter the life of any individual, for God is eager for an intimate relationship with men.

This particular image suggests that most in the church in Laodicea were professing Christians without an authentic relationship with Jesus Christ. And the image is one that speaks to the unsaved to this day. Christ is eager to enter every life, and He waits, just outside, for us to open our hearts to Him.

"I will grant to sit with Me on My throne" (Rev. 3:21). Christ saves, raises, and rewards believers. Now we learn that we are also to share His own exalted position. Paul says it in his second letter to Timothy:

> This is a faithful saying:
> For if we died with Him,
>   We shall also live with Him.
> If we endure,
>   We shall also reign with Him (2:11, 12).

And Revelation 20:6 portrays the fulfillment of the promise: "Blessed and holy is he who has part in the first resurrection. Over such the second death has no power, but they shall be priests of God and of Christ, and shall reign with Him a thousand years."

Common themes that run throughout these letters challenge Christians today. We are called to be overcomers: people who struggle with the world, the flesh, and the devil, and through the Spirit's power remain committed to Jesus Christ.

That commitment shows itself in the qualities commended in these letters, qualities of service, faith, patience, and perseverance, all motivated by love. While these qualities arouse the hostility of the world and lead to tribulations here, they will bring untold blessings to us when Jesus comes. And until He comes, we must reject corrupt teaching and immorality, and guard against complacency and compromise with the values of this world.

CONCLUDING PROMISES (REVELATION 22)

The last chapter of the Book of Revelation features a promise of Jesus that is repeated three times.

Behold, I am coming quickly! Blessed is he who keeps the words of the prophecy of this book (Rev. 22:7).

And behold, I am coming quickly, and My reward is with Me, to give to every one according to his work. I am the Alpha and the Omega, the Beginning and the End, the First and the Last (Rev. 22:12, 13).

Surely I am coming quickly (Rev. 22:20).

I well remember my mother telling me when I was a child, over sixty years ago, that she expected Jesus to come during her lifetime. Today I have the same expectation and hope that thrilled her and kept her gaze fixed beyond the horizon of this world. Generations of Christians have heard these promises of Jesus, and looked eagerly for His appearance.

Does it matter that nearly 2,000 years have passed since these promises were given? Not at all! Christ is coming! He is on the way. And that, not when, makes all the difference.

As the apostle Peter wrote so long ago,

The Lord is not slack concerning His promise, as some count slackness, but is longsuffering toward us, not willing that any should perish but that all should come to repentance. But the day of the Lord will come as a thief in the night, in which the heavens will pass away with a great noise, and the elements will melt with fervent heat; both the earth and the works that are in it will be burned up.

Therefore since all these things will be dissolved, what manner of persons ought you to be in holy conduct and godliness, looking for and hastening the coming of the day of God, because of which the heavens will be dissolved, being on fire, and the elements will melt with fervent heat? Nevertheless we, according to His promise, look for new heavens and a new earth in which righteousness dwells.

Therefore, beloved, looking forward to these things, be diligent to be found by Him in peace, without spot and blameless (2 Peter 3:9–13).

THE TEACHINGS OF JESUS FOR TODAY

Despite the efforts of some to cast Jesus' teachings within the framework of first-century rabbinic Judaism, Christ had a revolutionary message. It was not simply His miracles that amazed those who heard Him. It was the content of His teaching, and the fact that He spoke as one having authority.

Today for many Christians the teachings of Jesus seem commonplace and familiar. But tragically this is because many believers have been as slow to understand what Jesus taught as were His early disciples. We read or hear the familiar words, and their very familiarity seems to strip them of the sharp edge of a meaning that is as exciting in the twenty-first century as in the first.

In this chapter we review major themes in Jesus' teaching. As a review and overview, we touch on themes that have been developed in detail in previous chapters. Our goal is to highlight truths Jesus taught that truly can revolutionize our lives today.

When Jesus began His prophetic and teaching ministry in Galilee, those to whom He spoke were a people of the Book. They revered the Old Testament and acknowledged its teachings as authoritative in faith and morals. However, over the centuries the scribes who interpreted the Scriptures had added layer upon layer of traditional applications. In the process the true message of the Scriptures was less and less understood. The towering commandments of the Old Testament were whittled down into dozens of irrelevant rules and rituals. The Scripture's foundational message of faith, grace, and mercy was ignored, replaced by pride in Israel's selection as God's own and by a spirit of self-righteousness.

The Jewish sages had also failed to grasp the significance of a promise made by God, that one day a Prophet like Moses would appear. That Prophet would both explain the true meaning of the older revelation and would set sacred history on a new course. The sages had also failed to grasp the significance of Jeremiah's promise of a New Covenant that would supercede the Old Covenant given by Moses. The Law under which Israel had lived for some 1400 years was not to be a permanent fixture!

But, entrenched in legalism and blind to the clues in the Old Testament that God intended to set their way of life aside for something better, neither the religious leaders nor the masses were prepared to welcome Jesus and His truly revolutionary words.

To some extent a similar process has taken place in Christianity. Too many professing Christians seem to view the gospel message simply as a call to "believe in God and do good." Jesus' words about relationship with God, about discipleship and about power, are too often glossed over as familiar platitudes rather than experienced as the revolutionary truths they are.

We need to attend as closely to the teachings of Jesus today as ever before. And we need to take them to heart. When we do, Jesus' teachings will transform us as they transformed not only His disciples but the first-century world as well.

THE AUTHORITY OF JESUS

As we begin our brief review of the teachings of Jesus we need to remember who Jesus is. His words are not the insights of a great philosopher or the imperatives of a moral giant. Jesus' words are the very words of God.

There is no question that Jesus made this clear to His first listeners. The Gospels report His frequent claims to be the Son of God. Those claims incensed Jesus' opponents among the scribes and Pharisees, who charged Him with blasphemy. Their reaction was unreasonable in the extreme. Jesus had performed multiplied authenticating miracles, including those which the prophet Isaiah indicated would be performed only by the promised Messiah! Even the Sanhedrin, the supreme religious

court of the Jews, had agreed; so Nicodemus told Jesus that He was "a teacher come from God; for no one can do these signs that You do unless God is with Him" (John 3:2).

Ultimately the religious leaders rejected Jesus not because they were uncertain about who He was, but because they did not want to submit to Him and surrender their privileges and position.

But Jesus was and is God the Son. His teachings, however revolutionary, are teachings that you and I are to study. And to follow.

JESUS' MYSTERY KINGDOM

Much of Jesus' early teaching ministry focused on a unique expression of the kingdom of God that He would to initiate.

The Old Testament portrayed God as sovereign over the whole world and over the flow of history, and thus both the spiritual and material universes as well as time itself constituted His kingdom. The Old Testament also looked forward to an earthly kingdom to be established by a promised deliverer called the Messiah. The prophets predicted that He would sit on David's throne in Jerusalem and rule the world. This vision of an earthly kingdom in which the Jewish people were preeminent was especially attractive to first-century Jews, who had for five hundred years been oppressed and governed by Gentiles. At first the masses expected Jesus to establish this earthly kingdom. But instead Jesus spoke of a very different kind of kingdom of God to be established here on earth.

While the kingdom Jesus had come to initiate was not a subject of Old Testament prophecy, the fact that the promised Messiah would appear to heal, to suffer, and ultimately to die and be resurrected is a theme woven throughout the Old Testament. But the prophecies of suffering and spiritual deliverance were largely ignored, for the image of a worldwide kingdom ruled by the

Messiah captured the imagination of all. Thus when Jesus taught about the kingdom He was about to initiate, His words created doubt rather than faith. Ultimately Jesus resorted to parables to describe a kingdom that would exist in secret. Jesus' kingdom would be established in the hearts of human beings who would be scattered among the political kingdoms of humankind.

This secret kingdom would not replace the messianic kingdom envisioned by the prophets. But the secret kingdom was the one that Jesus would establish here on earth at His first coming. The kingdom of power and glory would be established only when Jesus returned from heaven.

The fact that God would establish two kingdoms here on earth, one a secret kingdom and the other a visible and glorious kingdom, had not been revealed in the Old Testament. This was in fact a mystery kingdom, a hidden aspect of God's eternal plan that was unveiled by Jesus as He began to teach. In fact, Jesus' early ministry focused on teaching about this secret or mystery kingdom. This is something that we need to understand, for today we too live as citizens of a secret or hidden kingdom of Jesus here on earth.

The key to our life as citizens of Jesus' mystery kingdom is the personal relationship with God as Father which Christ's death and resurrection enables us to have. The men and women of Jesus' day focused on externals. They cast relationship with God in the framework of ritual observance and public displays of piety. In contrast Jesus rejected their approach to religion and stressed a focus on our inner spiritual life.

This theme is developed several ways in Christ's Sermon on the Mount. In the Beatitudes Jesus gives us a picture of the values that are to characterize citizens of the mystery kingdom. Jesus then goes on to point out that the righteousness claimed by the scribes and Pharisees was a works righteousness, rooted in a misun-

derstanding of God's Law. Yes, the Law lists right and wrong acts. But God's intent was not to encourage human beings to try to live up to its standards. God's intent was that human beings would use the Law as a mirror, and look within to see in their corrupt motives and desires the need of an inner transformation!

That inner transformation can come only through a personal relationship with God as Father, marked by an inner desire to please Him and by such a complete trust in His loving care that we are freed to give priority to His kingdom and to seeking His righteousness.

Today, as in the first century, too many Christians have lost sight of the fact that the very heartbeat of life in Jesus' kingdom is our in-secret, personal relationship with God. It is only in focusing on loving and trusting Him that we experience that inner transformation that citizenship in Jesus' kingdom requires. Those who practice their faith simply by going to church and seeking to live moral lives are as far from experiencing life in Jesus' kingdom as were the scribes and Pharisees of Jesus' day.

JESUS' DISCIPLESHIP TEACHINGS

When it became clear that the masses were not about to acknowledge Jesus as the promised Messiah, the focus of Jesus' teaching ministry changed. He no longer emphasized public teaching about the kingdom, although this theme was not abandoned. Instead Jesus began to speak to His disciples about His coming death and resurrection, and to prepare them for leadership.

Jesus had always taken time to instruct His disciples in private. But after the turning point described in Matthew 16 and the other synoptic Gospels, Jesus devoted much more time to His disciples, and the topics on which He gave instruction were fresh and new.

First, Jesus spoke of His coming cross, and challenged His disciples to take up their crosses and follow Him. Jesus had committed Himself to do the will of His Father, despite the terrible cost. A person who follows Jesus must be willing to deny himself, and thus set aside his own plans and purposes in favor of whatever the will of God for him might be. God's will, represented as our cross, may not call for us to suffer as Jesus did. But it will involve self-denial and the choice of God's will as we know it in every situation.

In this same pivotal passage Jesus spelled out the consequences of our choice. Those who choose to lose their selves for Jesus' sake will find themselves. And those who choose to hold on to their selves will lose themselves. The choice of discipleship is a critical one for Christians. If we abandon our wills for God's will, He will transform us and we will become the persons we can be in Him. However, if we insist on holding on to our wills, the person we have the potential to become will be lost. And Jesus said, "and what will a man give in exchange for his soul [himself]?"

In another extended passage in Matthew's Gospel Jesus pointed the way to greatness in His kingdom. The person who would become great as a Christian must become like a little child, ever responsive to Christ's voice. The person who would become great must be willing, as Jesus was, to give of himself or herself to serve others. Leadership in Christ's church, as in Jesus' secret kingdom, is a matter of adopting Christ's own willingness to give of Himself for the sake of others, whatever the cost.

Discipleship is another theme that is too often misunderstood in our time. We think of spiritual leadership in terms of seminary training, ability to speak, and titles such as "pastor" and "elder." Too often we fail to realize that spiritual leadership is simply an ability to encourage others to have a closer walk with Jesus, and that those who are most effective in doing so are the quiet men and women who see their calling as caring for and serving others.

Christ first, others next, and self last, remains a prescription that true disciples of Jesus apply consistently in daily life.

JESUS' TEACHINGS ON POWER

A third recurring theme in the teachings of Jesus is that of power. Jesus often spoke of prayer and invited us to ask in His name, promising that "I will do it." And in John's report of Christ's Last Supper teachings Christ emphasized the importance to us of His own return to heaven. Christ would leave the disciples, but He would send the Holy Spirit, the Helper like Himself, to be within them.

Each of these themes, of prayer and of the indwelling Holy Spirit, reminds us that we have available to us God's own unlimited power. As disciples who are citizens of Jesus' secret kingdom, we have access to the ultimate power in the universe! We are not powerless, but power-full.

The key to accessing the very power of God is described in John 15. There Jesus uses the image of a vine and its branches. Jesus is the vine, the source of vitality and power. When we abide in Jesus, as branches are intimately connected to the vine, His vitality and power flow through us.

The same passage helps us understand how we maintain this connection. Jesus said, "If you keep My commandments, you will abide in My love, just as I have kept my Father's commandments and abide in His love" (John 15:10). It is our responsiveness to Jesus' word, both His word given in Scripture and His word whispered to us by the Holy Spirit within, that is key to maintaining a close, abiding relationship with Jesus Christ.

As we remain close to Him, listening to and responding to His voice, Jesus guides and empowers us. As we remain close we pray in His name, identified with who He is and with

His purposes. And Jesus acts in our lives, in our circumstances, and in the lives of others.

And this is power indeed.

When we read the Gospels that record Jesus' teachings, we find these three themes recurring often.

We are citizens of the secret kingdom of God, and our in-secret relationship is, through Jesus Christ, with God as a Father who loves us and whom we both trust and seek to please.

We are called to be disciples of Jesus, choosing to follow Him and to do the will of God in service to others.

And we are a people who have access to the very power of God. Through the Holy Spirit God has given us and through the privilege of prayer, Jesus Christ's limitless power is ours. We live not as a defeated people helplessly awaiting Jesus' return, but as victors here and now through His name!

How important then that we do study the teachings of Jesus. How important that we come to know who we are as citizens of His kingdom and Jesus' disciples. And how important that we exercise the power that is ours in Him.

EXPOSITORY INDEX

An expository index organizes information by topic and guides the reader to Bible verses and book pages which are critical to understanding the subject. It does not list every verse referred to in the book, but seeks to identify key verses. It does not list every mention of a topic in the book, but directs the reader to pages where a topic is discussed in some depth. Thus an expository index helps the reader avoid the frustration of looking up verses in the Bible or the book, only to discover that they contribute in only a small way to one's understanding of the subject.

This expository index organizes references to the teachings of Jesus by topic. Topics and sub-topics are identified in the left-hand column. Key Bible verses and passages are listed in the center column under "Scriptures." The far right column identifies pages in this book where the topic is covered.

In most instances, several of the key verses in the "Scriptures" column will be discussed on the book pages referred to. Very often additional verses will be referred to on the pages where the topic is covered. Our goal is to help you keep in focus the critical Bible verses and passages. Similarly, the book pages referred to are only those which make a significant contribution to understanding a topic, not every page on which a topic may be mentioned.

Please note that material under sub-topics is sometimes organized chronologically by the sequence of appearance in Scripture, and sometimes alphabetically, depending upon which organization will be most helpful in understanding and locating information.

SCRIPTURE INDEX

(Bible references are in boldface type, followed by the pages on which they appear in this book.)

MARK